LIBRARY OF NEW TESTAMENT STUDIES

652

Formerly Journal for the Study of the New Testament Supplement Series

Editor
Chris Keith

Editorial Board
Dale C. Allison, Lynn H. Cohick, R. Alan Culpepper, Craig A. Evans,
Jennifer Eyl, Robert Fowler, Simon J. Gathercole, Juan Hernández Jr., John S.
Kloppenborg, Michael Labahn, Matthew V. Novenson, Love L. Sechrest, Robert
Wall, Catrin H. Williams, Brittany E. Wilson

PAUL AND THE CORINTHIANS

Leadership, Ordeals, and the Politics of Displacement

Jonathan B. Ensor

t&tclark

LONDON • NEW YORK • OXFORD • NEW DELHI • SYDNEY

T&T CLARK
Bloomsbury Publishing Plc
50 Bedford Square, London, WC1B 3DP, UK
1385 Broadway, New York, NY 10018, USA
29 Earlsfort Terrace, Dublin 2, Ireland

BLOOMSBURY, T&T CLARK and the T&T Clark logo
are trademarks of Bloomsbury Publishing Plc

First published in Great Britain 2022
Paperback edition published 2023

Copyright © Jonathan B. Ensor, 2022

Jonathan B. Ensor has asserted his right under the Copyright, Designs and Patents Act, 1988, to be identified as Author of this work.

For legal purposes the Acknowledgments on p. ix constitute an extension of this copyright page.

All rights reserved. No part of this publication may be reproduced or transmitted in any form or by any means, electronic or mechanical, including photocopying, recording, or any information storage or retrieval system, without prior permission in writing from the publishers.

Bloomsbury Publishing Plc does not have any control over, or responsibility for, any third-party websites referred to or in this book. All internet addresses given in this book were correct at the time of going to press. The author and publisher regret any inconvenience caused if addresses have changed or sites have ceased to exist, but can accept no responsibility for any such changes.

A catalogue record for this book is available from the British Library.
Names: Ensor, Jonathan B., author. Title: Paul and the Corinthians : leadership, ordeals, and the politics of displacement / by Jonathan B. Ensor.
Description: London ; New York : T&T Clark, 2022. | Series: The library of New Testament studies, 2513-8790 ; 652 | Includes bibliographical references and index. | Summary: "Jonathan B. Ensor revisits the scholarly consensus concerning Paul's intermediate visit to Corinth, re-evaluating the textual evidence and interpreting the event through a socio-historical lens"-- Provided by publisher.
Identifiers: LCCN 2021043591 (print) | LCCN 2021043592 (ebook) | ISBN 9780567700797 (hb) | ISBN 9780567700834 (pbk) | ISBN 9780567700803 (pdf) | ISBN 9780567700827 (epub)
Subjects: LCSH: Bible. Corinthians, 2nd--Criticism, interpretation, etc. | Paul, the Apostle, Saint.
Classification: LCC BS2675.52 .E57 2022 (print) | LCC BS2675.52 (ebook) | DDC 227/.206--dc23
LC record available at https://lccn.loc.gov/2021043591
LC ebook record available at https://lccn.loc.gov/2021043592

ISBN: HB: 978-0-5677-0079-7
PB: 978-0-5677-0083-4
ePDF: 978-0-5677-0080-3
ePUB: 978-0-5677-0082-7

Series: Library of New Testament Studies, volume 652
ISSN 2513-8790

Typeset by: Forthcoming Publications Ltd

To find out more about our authors and books visit www.bloomsbury.com and sign up for our newsletters.

For Savannah, the delight of my life

Contents

Acknowledgments ix
Abbreviations xi

Chapter 1
INTRODUCTION 1
  1.1. Second Corinthians: Review of Relational Dynamics 2
  1.2. Second Corinthians: Review of Socio-Spatial Dynamics 10
  1.3. Sources of Conflict: Insights from the Social World 19
  1.4. The Problem 25
  1.5. Methodology: Relevance-theoretic Considerations 27
  1.6. Plan of Study 30

Part I
Paul and Political Displacement in Corinth

Chapter 2
POLITICAL DISPLACEMENT IN GRAECO-ROMAN ANTIQUITY 35
  2.1. The End of Exile: Reconciliation and Return 36
  2.2. Socio-cultural Institutions and Conventions:
      Enmity, Ordeals, and Absences 39
  2.3. Political Theory: Displacement within Political Communities 50
  2.4. Penology: Enforced Absences 59
  2.5. Absence as Judgment among Non-Elite,
      Graeco-Roman Political Communities 65
  2.6. Second Temple Political Communities 73
  2.7. Conflict, Absence, and Judgment in Paul's Corinthian Ἐκκλησία 76
  2.8. Summary and Conclusions 85

Chapter 3
THE INTERMEDIATE ORDEAL 87
  3.1. Four Roadblocks 88
  3.2. The Intermediate Visit 90
  3.3. The Character of the Intermediate Visit and Subsequent Absence 102
  3.4. Evaluating the Evidence 130
  3.5. Conclusions 132

Chapter 4
Testing the Hypothesis:
Embezzlement, Levity, and Deviant Character — 134
- 4.1. Πλεονεκτέω in 2 Corinthians — 135
- 4.2. Embezzlement and Paul's Failure to Discipline — 146
- 4.3. Paul's Inconsistent Travel (2 Corinthians 1:15-17) — 153
- 4.4. Communal and Political Consequences in Corinth — 158
- 4.5. Conclusions — 163
- Conclusion to Part I — 164

Part II
Discourses of Displacement in 2 Corinthians

Chapter 5
Paul's Art of the Ordeal:
Apostolic Impotence and Divine Aid in Other Places — 171
- 5.1. Ordeal Narrations, Exemplarity, and Communal Formation — 172
- 5.2. The God Who Raises the Dead (2 Corinthians 1:3-11) — 174
- 5.3. The God Who Comforts the Abased (2 Corinthians 2:12-13; 7:5-16) — 184
- 5.4. The God Who Delivers the Weak (2 Corinthians 11:30-33) — 191
- 5.5. Summary and Conclusions — 200

Chapter 6
Paul's Return to Corinth (2 Corinthians 13:1-10) — 202
- 6.1. Paul's Impending Test in Corinth (2 Corinthians 13:1-4) — 202
- 6.2. The Corinthian Test (2 Corinthians 13:5-10) — 216
- 6.3. Conclusions — 226
- Summary of Findings — 227

Appendix I
Campaigning for Reconciliation and Return — 235

Appendix II
The ὁ ἀδικήσας Conflict — 238

Bibliography — 246
Index of References — 263
Index of Authors — 278

ACKNOWLEDGMENTS

Completing a monograph can be as paradoxical as Paul's gospel to the Corinthians. The countless hours adrift in a sea of research may feel profoundly lonely. Yet in truth, research is always a communal affair. Such is the case with the present work. I owe an immeasurable debt of gratitude to a number of communities and individuals who embodied the love and life of Christ throughout this project. As an alumnus and former instructor, I am thoroughly grateful to my longtime employer, Wright Christian Academy, for their long-suffering support throughout this process. Thanks are especially owed to Wright's principal, Jeffrey L. Brown, who supplied time for research and most importantly, the gift of lifelong friendship. I also thank my colleagues and students for their encouragement and inspiration. Our church community, Asbury United Methodist Church, deserves special mention for their most generous support throughout my doctoral program. At a time of great uncertainty, Tom Harrison, Janet Day, and Guy Ames of Asbury UMC as well as Jason Jackson of New Life Church came to my aid and encouraged me to complete my doctoral thesis, which is presented below in revised form. Many thanks are owed to my supervisor, Fredrick J. Long, who challenges his students to present their research to God as an act of worship. That is my intention in the present work. Throughout this project, Fred has practiced what he preaches, kindly standing by my side through my personal difficulties, when other projects likely appeared more promising. His penetrating observations and challenging questions coupled with his generosity of spirit allowed me to follow a line of inquiry otherwise impossible. Any ability I have as a scholar is owed to him. The shortcomings in this work are mine alone. Thanks are due as well to Jamie Davies for his critical insights, which have improved the present work and for his encouragement to pursue publication. Many thanks to the team at T&T Clark, especially for the reassuring guidance of Sarah Blake and Duncan Burns' sharp, editorial eye.

I offer my thanks to my mother- and father-in-law, Melody and Stephen Smith, for their encouragement and support. They have stood in our corner since the beginning. To my parents, Brent and Kathryn Ensor, who first introduced me to the Scriptures, I give the most heartfelt thanks. To my boys, Graeme and Ansen, thank you for keeping life fun and always wanting to play even when dad arrived home late. I love you both dearly. To our newest child, Estienne, your arrival now brings a season of toil and challenge to such an unexpected and joyful conclusion. To my wife and the delight of my life, Savannah, words fall short of expressing my love for you. You are the most faithful friend a person could hope to find. It is the love of Christ that I know in you that has compelled me to finish this work.

All translations of classical works are from the Loeb Classical Library unless otherwise attributed. All translations of scripture are my own unless otherwise attributed.

ABBREVIATIONS

All abbreviations of frequently used periodicals, serials, and reference works follow *SBL Handbook of Style: For Biblical Studies and Related Disciplines*, 2nd edn. (Atlanta: SBL Press, 2014). For periodicals, serials, and reference works not addressed in *SBL Handbook of Style*, see below.

ABull	*Art Bulletin*
AGRW	*Associations in the Greco-Roman World: A Sourcebook*. Edited by Richard S. Ascough, Philip A. Harland, and John S. Kloppenborg. Berlin / Waco: de Gruyter / Baylor University Press, 2012.
AncSoc	*Ancient Society*
BBS	*Behavioral and Brain Sciences*
BGU	*Aegyptische Urkunden aus den Königlichen (later Staatlichen) Museen zu Berlin.* Edited by W. Schubart et al. 20 vols. Berlin: Griechische Urkunden, 1895–2014.
BHGNT	Baylor Handbook on the Greek New Testament
CIG	*Corpus inscriptionum graecarum.* 4 vols. Berlin 1828–77.
CIL	*Corpus Inscriptionum Latinarum.* Berlin, 1862–.
C.Ord.Ptol.	*Corpus des ordonnances des Ptolémées: C.Ord.Ptol*. Edited by Marie-Thérèse Lenger. Brussels: Palais des Académies, 1964.
DCLY	*Deuterocanonical and Cognate Literature Yearbook*
DGRA	Smith, William, and J. B. Moyl et al (eds). *A Dictionary of Greek and Roman Antiquities*. 3rd edn. London: John Murray, 1890.
DMAHA	Dutch Monographs on Ancient History and Archaeology
EC	*Early Christianity*
EHS	Europäische Hochschulschriften
ESCJ	Studies in Christianity and Judaism/Etudes sur e christianisme et le judaisme
ESEC	Emory Studies in Early Christianity
FGrHist	*Die Fragmente der Griechischen Historiker.* Edited by Felix Jacoby. Leiden: Brill, 1957–.
GDI	*Sammlung der griechischen Dialekt-Inscriften.* Edited by Hermann Collitz. 3 vols. Göttingen: Vandenhoeck & Ruprecht, 1884–1915.
GHI	P. J. Rhodes and Robin Osborne, *Greek Historical Inscriptions 404–323 BC*. New York: Oxford University Press, 2003.
HBD	*A Dictionary of the Bible*, ed. James Hastings. 5 Volumes. Edinburgh: T&T Clark, 1899–1904.

HTA	Historisch Theologische Auslegung
IDelos	*Inscriptions de Délos: Décrets postérieurs à 166 av. J.-C. (nos. 1497–1524). Dédicaces postérieures à 166 av. J.-C. (nos. 1525–2219).* Académie des Inscriptions et Belles-lettres. Edited by Pierre Roussel and Marcel Launey. Paris: Librairie Ancienne Honoré Champion, 1937.
IDidyma	Rehm, Albert. *Didyma. Zweiter Teil: Die Inschriften.* Edited by Richard Harder. *Deutsches Archäologisches Institut.* Berlin: Verlag Gebr. Mann, 1958.
IEph	*Die Inschriften von Ephesos.* Edited by Hermann Wankel, et al. 8 vols. Bonn: Habelt, 1979–84.
IG	*Inscriptiones Graecae.* Editio Minor. Berlin: de Gruyter, 1924–.
IGR	*Inscriptiones graecae ad res romanas pertinentes.* Edited by R. L. Cagnat, J. F. Toutain, V. Henry, and G. L. Lafaye. 4 vols. Paris: E. Leroux, 1911–27.
ILS	*Inscriptiones latinae selectae.* Edited by Hermann Dessau. 3 vols. 1892–1916.
IPArk	*Prozessrechtliche Inschriften der griechischen Poleis: Arkadien (IPArk).* Österreichische Akademie der Wissenschaften. Philosophisch-historische Klasse. Sitzungsberichte, 607. Vienna: Österreichische Akademie der Wissenschaften, 1994.
JTI	*Journal of Theological Interpretation*
LL	*Links & Letters*
LSAM	*Lois sacrées de l'Asie Mineure. Ecole française d'Athènes.* Edited by Franciszek Sokolowski. Travaux et mémoires 9. Paris: E. de Boccard, 1955.
MBPS	Mellen Biblical Press Series
MCE	Mutual Cognitive Environment
ML	*Mind and Language*
NTM	New Testament Monographs
OGI	*Orientis graeci inscriptiones selectae.* Edited by Wilhelm Dittenberger. 2 vols. Leipzig: Hirzel, 1903–05.
P.Amh.	*The Amherst Papyri, Being an Account of the Greek Papyri in the Collection of the Right Hon. Lord Amherst of Hackney, F.S.A. at Didlington Hall, Norfolk.* Edited by B. P. Grenfell and A. S. Hunt. 2 vols. London: Oxford University Press, 1900–1901.
P.Dem.Berlin	*Demotische Papyri aus den Staatlichen Museen zu Berlin.* Edited by K.-Th. Zauzich et al. 3 vols. Berlin: Akademie Verlag, 1978–92.
P.Dem.Cairo	*Service des Antiquités de l'Égypte, Catalogue Général des Antiquités égyptiennes du Musée du Caire. Die demotischen Denkmäler.* Edited by W. Spiegelberg. 3 vols. Leipzig: W. Drugulin, 1904–32.
P.Dem.Lille	*Papyrus démotiques de Lille.* Edited by H. Sottas et al. 3 vols. 1927–84.
P.Freib.	*Mitteilungen aus der Freiburger Papyrussammlung.* Edited by M. Gelzer et al. 4 vols. 1914–86.

P.Giss.	*Griechische Papyri im Museum des oberhessischen Geschichtsvereins zu Giessen.* Edited by O. Eger, E. Kornemann, and P. M. Meyer. 3 vols. Leipzig-Berlin: 1910–12.
P.Giss.Apoll	*Briefe des Apollonios-Archives aus der Sammlung Papyri Gissenses.* Edited by M. Kortus. Giessen: Universitätsbibliothek, 1999.
PKNT	Papyrologische Kommentare zum Neuen Testament
P.Köln	*Kölner Papyri.* Edited by B. Kramer and R. Hübner et al. 16 vols. Opladen: Westdeutscher Verlag, 1976–.
P.Lond.	*Greek Papyri in the British Museum.* Edited by F. G. Kenyon et al. At present 7 vols. London: The Trustees of the British Museum, 1893–.
P.Mich.	*Michigan Papyri.* Ann Arbor: University of Michigan Press, 1931–.
PNTC	Pillar New Testament Commentary
P.Oxy.	*The Oxyrhynchus Papyri.* Edited by Bernard P. Grenfell. London: Egypt Exploration Fund, 1898–.
P.Panop.Beatty	*Papyri from Panopolis in the Chester Beatty Library Dublin.* Edited by T. C. Skeat. Dublin: Hodges/Figgis, 1964.
P.Sorb.	*Papyrus de la Sorbonne.* 3 vols. Paris: Presses universitaires de France, 1966–2011.
P.Turner	*Papyri Greek and Egyptian Edited by Various Hands in Honour of Eric Gardner Turner on the Occasion of His Seventieth Birthday.* Edited by Peter John Parsons et al. London: Egypt Exploration Society, 1981.
RIDA	*Revue Internationale des droits de l'Antiquité*
RRA	Rhetoric of Religious Antiquity
RT	Relevance Theory
SB	*Sammelbuch griechischer Urkunden aus Aegypten.* Edited by Friedrich Preisigke et al. Wiesbaden: Harrassowitz, 1915–.
SEG	Supplementum epigraphicum graecum
SFEG	Schriften der Finnischen Exegetischen Gellschaft
SIG	*Sylloge inscriptionum graecarum.* Edited by Wilhelm Dittenberger. 4 vols. 3rd ed. Leipzig: Hirzel, 1915–24.
Small. *Nerva*	*Document Illustrating the Principates of Nerva, Trajan, and Hadrian.* Edited by E. M. Smallwood. Cambridge: Cambridge University Press, 1966.
SNTE	Studies in New Testament Exegesis
TANZ	Texte und Arbeiten zum neutestamentlichen Zeitalter
TAPS	*Transactions of the American Philological Society*
ZNW	*Zeitschrift für die Neutestamentliche Wissenschaft*

Chapter 1

INTRODUCTION

Lodged in American cultural memory, *Dragnet* character, detective Joe Friday, famously quips, "just the facts, ma'am." "The facts" are easily confused with mere data. To retrace Ben F. Meyer's rehearsal of R. G. Collingwood's methodological insights, facts emerge at "the end of inquiry" dependent upon historical data and are inferred based on "rational principles."[1] "Why," the rational explanation of "the inside" of a historical event, follows "what," the historical datum.[2] This is elementary historical-critical methodology. Ever the outlier, a survey of "the facts" emerging from studies of 2 Corinthians, demonstrates a curious state of the art; while the historical and literary data are ever contested, the general understanding of the exigencies and aims of 2 Corinthians remain broadly consistent. This is most evident among scholars who supply the prefix social- or socio- to their work. Across the field, 2 Corinthians aims at reconciliation and return, ending a season marked by animosity and absence in which Paul's apostolic status was rejected by some or all the community. Some studies accent the social relationship between Paul and all or part of the community. Others focus on spatiality, emphasizing Paul's drive towards securing an amicable return. Yet, an investigation of the critical study of 2 Corinthians consistently yields the same facts.

Below, I survey studies that attend to the relational dynamics of reconciliation before turning to those that attend to the spatial aspects of Paul's return. What becomes evident is both the dual aim of 2 Corinthians as understood by scholarship and the frequent tacit assumption of a relationship between the crisis in Corinth and Paul's absence. Where exegetes hold together the socio-spatial exigencies/aims of the epistle,

---

1. Ben F. Meyer, *The Aims of Jesus*, ed. Dikran Y. Hadidan, PTMS 48 (Eugene, OR: Pickwick, 2002), 87.
2. Meyer, *Aims of Jesus*, 88.

there is sparse attention to analogies in Graeco-Roman antiquity and thus limited insight from the phenomena attendant to such exigencies/aims. Likewise, attempts to uncover the social texture of the Corinthian conflict never address the socio-spatial dynamics of the letter. With this survey, the ground is cleared to pursue our research questions: What phenomena frequently characterized the exigencies of strife and absence and the aims of reconciliation and return in Graeco-Roman antiquity? In what way do such phenomena resonate with evidence in 2 Corinthians? And if the evidence in 2 Corinthians resonates in any way with such phenomena, how might that resonance supply a salient contextual parameter for the interpretation of discrete textual units perhaps indicative of a broader interpretive framework?

1.1. *Second Corinthians: Review of Relational Dynamics*

The relational strain evident in 2 Corinthians supplies a primary avenue for the interpretation of discrete textual units and a broader interpretive framework of the epistle. A hot spot for research on relational dynamics has long been 2 Cor. 5:14–6:2. Here, however, the research has inquired as to the socio-cultural context of καταλλάγ-cognates primarily in order to understand the origin of Paul's concept of reconciliation[3] and its place within Pauline soteriology.[4] Increasingly, interpreters observe that Paul's discussion of the topic of reconciliation between God and Paul on one hand (5:18-20a) and God and the Corinthians (5:20b–6:2) on the other must be interpreted in light of socio-historical situation, namely Paul's role in reconciliation between God and the community as "ein unverzichtbarer Bestandteil dieses Vorgangshis,"[5] implying Paul's desire to reconcile with his ἐκκλησία (cf. 1:13-14; 6:11-13; 7:2-4; 13:9-10).[6]

---

3. I. Howard Marshall, "The Meaning of 'Reconciliation,'" in *Unity and Diversity in New Testament Theology*, ed. Robert A. Guelich (Grand Rapids: Eerdmans, 1978), 117–32; G. K. Beale, "The Old Testament Background of Reconciliation in 2 Corinthians 5–7 and Its Bearing on the Literary Problem of 2 Corinthians 6.14–7.1," *NTS* 35.4 (1989): 550–81; Ciliers Breytenbach, *Versöhnung: eine Studie zur paulinischen Soteriologi*, WUNT 60 (Neukirchen-Vluyn: Neukirchener Verlag, 1989).

4. Ralph P. Martin, *Reconciliation: A Study of Paul's Theology* (Atlanta: John Knox, 1981).

5. Jens Schröter, *Der versöhnte Versöhner: Paulus als unentbehrlicher Mittler im Heilsvorgang zwischen Gott und Gemeinde nach 2 Kor 2,14–7,4*, TANZ 10 (Tübingen/Basel: Francke, 1993), 2, 341.

6. J.-F. Collange, *Enigmes de la Deuxième Epître de Paul aux Corinthiens: Etude Exégétique de 2 Cor. 2,14–7,4* (New York: Cambridge University Press, 1972), 266; Ralph P. Martin, *2 Corinthians*, WBC 40 (Waco, TX: Word, 1986), 138–9;

1.1.1. *Stages of Conflict: Relational Dynamics and Partition Theories*

The attention to the relational dynamics reflected in 2 Cor. 5:14–6:2 as implied by the topic of reconciliation is paralleled by a broader effort to attend to evidence of relational strain throughout the letter. In general, this aspect of conflict, strain, or enmity supplies most interpreters with the basic exigency of 2 Corinthians, regardless of historical or literary reconstructions. The movement from the topic of reconciliation to the macro-epistolary and rhetorical aims is a leap in scale, representing the scholarly conclusions of several studies concerning the exigency of the letter(s). Bieringer properly claims, "Unabhängig davon, ob sie für Teilung oder Einheit plädieren, sind sich im Grunde alle Exegeten einig daß sich die Briefteile auf dieselbe Gesamtsituation beziehen."[7] The interpreter's perception of *the stage* of the conflict within a particular literary unit—whether some form of rupture is emerging, matured, or retrospective—is central to hypotheses of the letter's integrity or lack thereof.[8]

Adherents of the Semler–Windisch hypothesis—the dominant literary hypothesis during the last quarter of the twentieth century—claim that although traces of hostility can be detected in 2 Corinthians 1–7 (8–9), a subsequent phase of intensified hostility distinct from the ὁ ἀδικήσας conflict (2:5-11; 7:5-16) is evident in 2 Corinthians 10–13.[9] Ralph Martin explains the last four chapters as response to "further troubles."[10] Colin Kruse, likewise, contrasts a "crisis resolved" in chs. 1–9 with "a fresh crisis" in chs. 10–13.[11] Understanding multiple conflicts raises natural

---

Schröter, *Versöhner*, 326; Reimund Bieringer, "Plädoyer für die Einheitlichkeit des 2. Korintherbriefes. Literarkritische und inhaltliche Argumente," in *Studies on 2 Corinthians*, ed. Reimund Bieringer and Jan Lambrecht, BETL 112 (Leuven: Leuven University Press, 1994), 161; John T. Fitzgerald, "Paul and Paradigm Shifts: Reconciliation and Its Linkage Group," in *Paul Beyond the Judaism/Hellenism Divide*, ed. Troels Engberg-Pedersen (Louisville, KY: Westminster John Knox, 2001), 257–8; Ivar Vegge, *2 Corinthians—A Letter about Reconciliation: A Psychological, Epistolographical and Rhetorical Analysis*, WUNT 2.239 (Tübingen: Mohr Siebeck, 2008), 51–2; Thomas Schmeller, *Der zweite Brief an die Korinther*, 2 vols., EKKNT 8 (Neukirchen-Vluyn: Neukirchener Verlag, 2010), 1:329, and others.

7. Reimund Bieringer, "Der 2. Korintherbrief als Ursprüngliche Einheit ein Forschungsüberblick," in Bieringer and Lambrecht, eds., *Studies on 2 Corinthians*, 107, see n. 4; cf. Lars Aejmelaeus, "Der 2. Korintherbrief als Drama von Streit und Versöhnung: Ein Plädoyer für die Briefteilung," *ZNT* 38 (2016): 49.

8. Vegge, *2 Corinthians*, 1–34.

9. Victor Paul Furnish, *II Corinthians*, AYB 32A (Garden City, NY: Doubleday, 1985), 41, and others.

10. Martin, *2 Corinthians*, xlvi.

11. Colin Kruse, *2 Corinthians*, TNTC (Grand Rapids: Eerdmans, 1987), 43.

questions of concerning with whom and over what? Victor Furnish writes, "There is no doubt that apostleship—specifically Paul's authority as the apostle to and for Corinth—is the pervasive underlying theme of canonical 2 Cor."[12] Kruse explains the distinction between the internal ὁ ἀδικήσας conflict and the external conflict with the rivals (chs. 10–13) by hypothesizing continuous, evolving challenge to Paul's authority in Corinth.[13] Persistent challenges to Paul's authority across the multiple conflicts form a substrate across the Semler–Windisch hypothesis. B. J. Oropeza delineates between the settled ὁ ἀδικήσας conflict, complaints about changes to Paul's itinerary, and opponents influencing the community. A recurrent questioning or rejection of Paul's authority and competency links these three conflicts across both letters. Nonetheless, Kenneth Schenck, near the zenith of the Semler–Windisch approach, ties together the two units stating, "Paul has reconciliation on his mind throughout 2 Corinthians."[14]

Advocates of the Hausrath–Kennedy hypothesis—whose popularity surged in the early twentieth century only to quickly diminish especially among anglophone scholars—believe chs. 10–13 evidence an early, significant rupture between Paul and the community, while in chs. 1–7 (8–9) the conflict is resolved and the community largely mollified.[15] For example, Windisch interprets 2 Cor. 7:2b as an emerging accusation while 12:16-18 evidences a later intensification of the charge. Conversely, the same texts according the Hausrath–Kennedy hypothesis interprets 7:2b as residual suspicions occurring after Paul's initial response in 12:16-18. For Kennedy, it was clear that 2 Corinthians 1–9 resulted in the "completeness of reconciliation that had been effected," while the bellicose, universal language of chs. 10–13 implies rebellion throughout the community.[16] Once again, at stake in the Letter of Tears was Paul's apostolic authority,

---

12. Furnish, *II Corinthians*, 34.

13. Colin G. Kruse, "The Relationship between the Opposition to Paul Reflected in 2 Corinthians 1–7 and 10–13," *EvQ* 61.3 (1989): 195–202; see also F. F. Bruce, *I & II Corinthians*, NCBC (Grand Rapids, MI: Eerdmans, 1971), 164–74.

14. Kenneth Schenk, *1 & 2 Corinthians: A Commentary for Bible Students*, Wesley Bible Commentary Series (Indianapolis, IN: Wesleyan Publishing House, 2006), 246.

15. James H. Kennedy, *The Second and Third Epistles of St. Paul to the Corinthians* (London: Methuen, 1900), 94–162; Hans Windisch, *Der zweite Korintherbrief*, KEK 6, 9th edn (Göttingen: Vandenhoeck & Ruprecht, 1924), 221. Conversely, the same texts according the Hausrath–Kennedy hypothesis interprets 7:2b as residual suspicions occurring after Paul's initial response in 12:16-18 (Francis Watson, "2 Cor. X–XIII and Paul's Painful Letter to the Corinthians," *JTS* 35 [1984]: 341).

16. Kennedy, *The Second and Third Epistles*, 94–5, 109.

just as in chs. 10–13.¹⁷ Francis Watson argues that rather than understanding parallel insider–outsider, individual–corporate conflicts in chs. 1–9 and 10–13, respectively, evidence in chs. 10–13 in the form of singular pronouns (τις 10:7, ὁ τοιοῦτος 10:11) and third-person singular verb φησίν (10:10), points towards a ringleader of internal dissent. The chronological prioritizing of chs. 10–13 paired with Watson's claims relieves some awkwardness of attempting to reconstruct historical and social linkages between different areas of strife. Rather than "multiply reconciliations and rebellions,"¹⁸ by identifying chs. 10–13 as the Letter of Tears (2 Cor. 2:4), 2 Corinthians becomes, according to Lars Aejmeleaus, a coherent "Drama von Streit und Versöhnung."¹⁹ Aejmeleaus, quoting Bieringer, notes that the Hausrath–Kennedy hypothesis and most partition theories present Paul "as a successful solver of conflict," rescuing the apostle from the picture of one lurching from consolation to criticism.²⁰

Like the Hausrath–Kennedy hypothesis, the perception of a singular, evolving social conflict in Corinth drives, in part, the Weiss–Bultmann²¹ and Schmithals–Bornkamm hypotheses.²² Significantly, the Weiss–Bultmann hypothesis views 2:14–7:4 and 10–13 as the Letter of Tears, while the Schmithals–Bornkamm understands 2:14–7:4 as a letter preceding Paul's intermediate visit evidencing some strain directed towards his rivals but also didactic aims and chs. 10–13 as the Letter of Tears written after Paul's visit.²³ According to both approaches 1:1–2:13, 7:5-16 represents a later letter that looks retrospectively over the conflict and aims to secure final reconciliation. Bornkamm could not accept that chs. 10–13, which are rife with combat over Paul's credentials, temporally followed the restored peace celebrated in 1:1–2:13, 7:5-16.²⁴ Following the

---

17. Watson, "Painful Letter," 342.
18. Kennedy, *Second and Third Epistles*, xxvi; see also Watson, "Paul's Painful Letter," 332.
19. Aejmelaeus, "Drama von Streit und Versöhnung," 49–54.
20. Aejmelaeus, "Drama von Streit und Versöhnung," 53.
21. 2 Cor. 8; Letter C: 2:14–7:4 (minus 6:14–7:1), 10–13; Letter D: 1:1–2:13, 7:5-16, 9 (Johannes Weiss, *The History of Primitive Christianity*, trans. Frederick C. Grant [New York: Wilson-Erickson, 1937], 1:357). Letter C: 2:14–7:4 (minus 6:14–7:1), 9, 10–13. Letter D: 1:1–2:13, 7:5-16, 8 (Rudolph Bultmann, *The Second Letter to the Corinthians*, trans. Roy A. Harrisville [Minneapolis: Augsburg, 1985], 18).
22. 2:14–7:4 (minus 6:14–7:1); 10–13; 1:1–2:13, 7:5-16; 8; 9 (Dieter Georgi, *The Opponents of Paul in Second Corinthians* [Philadelphia: Fortress, 1996], 9–18).
23. Georgi, *Opponents*, 13–14.
24. Güther Bornkamm, "The History of the Origin of the So-Called Second Letter to the Corinthians," *NTS* 8 (1962): 258, 260.

Schmithals–Bornkamm hypothesis, but representative of Weiss–Bultmann as well, J. A. Crafton claims, "each letter describes the dramatic agon in a conflict in a unique way."[25] Both hypotheses build upon the Hausrath–Kennedy hypothesis by embracing the notion of a singular conflict and further partitioning 2 Corinthians according to perceived stages of relational strain present in a textual unit. Walter Schmithals credited the redactor with grouping the five original letters hidden within canonical 2 Corinthians according to an underlying conflict concerning Paul's place in the community.[26]

1.1.2. *Relational Dynamics and Recent Partition Hypotheses*

More recently, utilizing a five-letter partition theory, Margaret Mitchell and L. L. Welborn have deployed a clear socio-cultural narrative upon 2 Corinthians moving from descent into enmity through reconciliation.[27] Mitchell and Welborn are inheritors of the Weiss–Bultmann and Schmithals–Bornkamm hypotheses, both of which attempt to detect a continuous, evolving social relationship, but now reinforced with insights from the preceding decades of research on relational dynamics in Graeco-Roman antiquity. Mitchell, following Weiss, hypothesizes that as the most proximate communication to 1 Corinthians, 2 Corinthians 8 evidences "historical and rhetorical progression from 1 Corinthians."[28] Mitchell argues that Paul deviates from his statements in 1 Cor. 16:1-4 in two critical ways: (1) he sends Titus rather than himself (1 Cor. 16:5-7; cf. 2 Cor. 1) and (2) he chooses delegates for the collection rather than the Corinthians (1 Cor. 16:3; cf. 2 Cor. 8:22).[29] Mitchell contends 2 Corinthians 8 failed, moving the relationship toward enmity as the community read the letter as an arrogant overreach and suspected financial impropriety as seen in

---

25. Jeffrey A. Crafton, *The Agency of the Apostle: A Dramatistic Analysis of Paul's Response to Conflict in 2 Corinthians*, JSNTSup 51 (Sheffield: JSOT, 1991), 164.

26. Walter Schmithals, "Die Korintherbriefe als Briefsammlung," ZNW 64.3–4 (1973): 287.

27. Mitchell partitions the text: 2 Cor. 8; 2:14–7:4; 10:1–13:10; 1:1–2:13; 7:5-16; 13:11-13; 9 ("Paul's Letters to Corinth: The Interpretive Intertwining of Literary and Historical Reconstruction," in *Urban Religion in Roman Corinth: Interdisciplinary Approaches*, ed. Daniel N. Schowalter and Steven J. Friesen, HTS 53 [Cambridge, MA: Harvard University Press, 2005], 307–38). Welborn partitions the text: 2 Cor. 8; 10–13; 2:14–6:13; 7:2-4; 1:1–2:13; 7:5-16; 9 (*An End to Enmity: Paul and the "Wrongdoer" of Second Corinthians*, BZNW 185 [Berlin: de Gruyter, 2011], xxvi).

28. Mitchell, "Letters," 331.

29. Mitchell, "Letters," 330.

the charges in 2 Cor. 2:14–7:4.[30] This letter (2 Cor. 2:14–7:14) also failed along with the following intermediate visit, thus providing the occasion for 2 Cor. 10:1–13:10 which lead to the punishment of the offender. Paul then sends 2 Cor. 1:1–2:13; 7:5-16; 13:11-13, which mollifies the community. Finally, Paul sends 2 Corinthians 9, intending to consolidate the collection.[31] Calvin Roetzel embraces Mitchell's hypothesis, as a "sophisticated narrative framing of the letter fragments" resulting "in a sequence of exchanges that allows reconciliation…"[32]

Welborn contends that Paul's sharp rhetoric in the letters of 1 Corinthians and 2 Corinthians 8 instigated enmity rather than Paul's initial refusal of patronage.[33] Upon the refusal of Gaius and other wealthy patrons to participate in the delivery of the collection, Paul visited Corinth a second time in which Gaius (= ὁ ἀδικήσας) openly challenged him with accusations of embezzlement.[34] Paul retreated to Ephesus where he sent chs. 10–13,[35] and followed it with a more conciliatory apology (2 Cor. 2:14–7:4) in the hands of Titus. The apology secured support for Paul and punishment for Gaius.[36] Upon hearing of Gaius's censure, Paul sent the letter of reconciliation (1:1–2:13 and 7:5-16).[37] Finally, Paul writes 2 Corinthians 9 to complete the collection.[38] Welborn claims that the letters embedded in 2 Corinthians (not including 2 Cor. 8) effectively restored friendship, which was accomplished through rhetorical maneuvers to aid in reconciliation (not naming opponents/rivals, portrayals of power, self-representation of constancy and friendship) as well as use and adaptation of social conventions.[39] Of course, other criteria (lexical, historical) also enter into the discussion of the integrity of 2 Corinthians. Clearly, however, many current projects employing partition theories focus largely upon a quest to understand 2 Corinthians by uncovering a coherent social narrative wherein textual units elicit evidence of differing stages of relational strife and achieved reconciliation.

---

30. Mitchell, "Letters," 331–3, 334; followed by Paul B. Duff, *Moses in Corinth: The Apologetic Context of 2 Corinthians*, NovTSup 159 (Leiden: Brill, 2015), 82–5.

31. Mitchell, "Letters," 334–5.

32. Calvin Roetzel, *2 Corinthians*, Abingdon New Testament Commentaries (Nashville: Abingdon, 2007), 31–2.

33. Welborn, *Enmity*, 421–4.

34. Welborn, *Enmity*, 425–6.

35. Welborn, *Enmity*, 434–44.

36. Welborn, *Enmity*, 444–60.

37. Welborn, *Enmity*, 461f.

38. Welborn, *Enmity*, 480.

39. Welborn, *Enmity*, 221, 383–4, 442–3, 476.

1.1.3. *Relational Dynamics and Theories of Compositional Unity*

The same emphasis upon relational dynamics is found among several scholars who assert the integrity of 2 Corinthians. Reimund Bieringer and his student Ivar Vegge proffer two important studies. In response to various partition theories, Bieringer claims that in 2 Corinthians there exist three clear issues over which the community and Paul stand in conflict: the ὁ ἀδικήσας (2:5-11; 7:5-16), the opponents (2 Cor. 2:14–7:4; 10–13) and the immoral group within the community (2 Cor. 12:20-21; 13:2).[40] Unlike partition hypotheses that place 2 Corinthians 10–13 before 2 Cor. 2:5-11 and 7:5-16 (Hausrath–Kennedy; Weiss–Bultmann; Schmithals–Bornkamm), Bieringer argues for the unity of 2 Corinthians by interrogating the relationship between the ὁ ἀδικήσας and the opponents, hypothesizing that the ὁ ἀδικήσας conflict functions strategically as perhaps a *captatio benevolentiae* regarding the Collection (chs. 8–9) and "eine Art Modell für die noch ausstehenden Schwierigkeiten."[41] For Bieringer, Paul seizes on the gains of the ὁ ἀδικήσας conflict in order to encourage the community to reconcile further regarding the matter of the opponents (2:4–7:4; 10–13) and immoral group (12:21; 13:2). Accordingly, 2 Corinthians focuses on *complete* reconciliation since some measure of reconciliation has already occurred in the past.[42]

Ivar Vegge builds upon Bieringer's thesis arguing likewise that 2 Corinthians evinces the same three parts of a single conflict.[43] Vegge contends along with Bieringer that the ὁ ἀδικήσας conflict lies largely in the past, thus reasoning that 1:13-14 forms the thesis statement of the epistle as a call for complete reconciliation.[44] However, Vegge argues that 7:5-16 is not a model of reconciliation, but following the examples of psychogogic, rhetorical, and epistolographic practices, Paul depicts an idealized reconciliation in 7:5-16 as a hortative device designed to encourage complete reconciliation between Paul and the community in matters still outstanding (i.e. the immoral group and the opponents).[45] Building upon the work of Stanley N. Olson, who claimed that expressions of confidence are persuasive in function and support the communicator's aims rather than reflections of actual circumstances,[46] Vegge argues that

---

40. Bieringer, "Plädoyer," 156–73.
41. Bieringer, "Plädoyer," 166.
42. Bieringer, "Plädoyer," 161.
43. Vegge, *2 Corinthians*, 66–95.
44. Vegge, *2 Corinthians*, 106, 169–76.
45. Vegge, *2 Corinthians*, 53–70, 71–140.
46. Stanley N. Olson, "Confidence Expressions in Paul: Epistolary Conventions and the Purpose of 2 Corinthians" (Ph.D. diss., Yale University, 1976).

Paul's expressions of confidence in chs. 1–7, 8–9, and 10–13 all contain implicit appeals for complete reconciliation and friendship, thus indicating a consistent epistolary and rhetorical situation.[47] Paul's punitive speech in chs. 10–13 forms a "new kind of tearful letter" that also participates in the ultimate aim of the community's reconciliation with Paul.[48] Thus, the differences in tone do not reflect different situations, but different persuasive tactics aimed at the same goal. Vegge also adds increased emphasis upon the role of the immoral group in the conflict (12:21; 13:2), an element underrepresented by Bieringer and most interpreters. Tying together the various conflicts is the consistent concern about Paul's authority as Corinth's apostle, especially his authority to punish.[49]

Lest it appear that reconciliation as a thread binding together 2 Corinthians applies only to student and teacher, the same claims are found in major commentaries advocating compositional unity with expected variations. Ben Witherington states plainly, "2 Corinthians was written to effect reconciliation between Paul and his converts."[50] Citing Steven Kraftchick, Witherington asserts a "shutdown of mutual affection between Paul and the Corinthians" echoing that "Paul writes to restore this relationship, and to restore their understanding and trust in him as an apostle of God."[51] Employing rhetorical criticism, Witherington claims that all of 2 Corinthians attempts to dispel the assertion that Paul is a false apostle (2:17).[52] Chapters 10–13 evidence a "not unusual," "obligatory" example of pathos at the end of speech needed to persuade the Corinthians to that end, focusing especially on the issue of his opponents as false apostles.[53] Scott Hafemann notes that 2 Corinthians' dual purpose involves consolidating his claims to apostolic legitimacy among the repentant majority (chs. 1–9) and the still rebellious minority (chs. 10–13).[54] Taking

---

47. Vegge, *2 Corinthians*, 141–252.
48. Vegge, *2 Corinthians*, 253–9.
49. Vegge, *2 Corinthians*, 22, 31, 78, 94, 105.
50. Ben Witherington III, *Conflict & Community in Corinth: A Socio-Rhetorical Commentary on 1 and 2 Corinthians* (Grand Rapids: Eerdmans, 1995), 328.
51. Steven J. Kraftchick, "Death in Us, Life in You: The Apostolic Medium," in *Society of Biblical Literature 1991 Seminar Papers*, ed. E. H. Lovering (Atlanta: Scholars Press, 1991), 625, as cited in Witherington, *Conflict & Community in Corinth*, 328.
52. Witherington, *Conflict & Community in Corinth*, 372, 430.
53. Witherington, *Conflict & Community in Corinth*, 430–1; see Craig Keener, *1–2 Corinthians*, NCBC (New York: Cambridge University Press, 2005), 149–50.
54. Scott J. Hafemann, *2 Corinthians: The NIV Application Commentary* (Grand Rapids: Zondervan, 2000), 19–22.

a slightly different angle, David Garland identifies the theme of Paul's defense of his probity as a unifying theme of 2 Corinthians, though this does not infer a question of Paul's apostolic status.[55]

Again, this unifying theme is overlayed upon a reconstruction in which Paul has already secured a repentant majority versus a recalcitrant minority.[56]

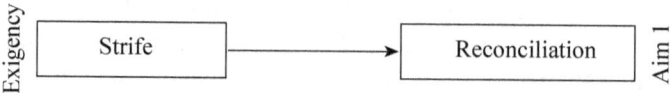

Figure 1. *Relational Dynamics and the Aims of 2 Corinthians*

1.1.4. Conclusions

The aim of this part of our review is not to give a complete accounting of every approach to the relational dynamics found in 2 Corinthians vis-à-vis theories of literary integrity, but rather to offer a description of the degree to which relational discord centered upon Paul's apostleship or probity is essential to the study of 2 Corinthians or its constituent parts. No matter how one slices it or does not, 2 Corinthians is concerned with reconciliation between Paul and the community or components of it.

1.2. Second Corinthians: Review of Socio-Spatial Dynamics

Several interpreters augment the above research trajectory with spatial insights concerning Paul's absence and impending return. The socio-spatial dynamics of 2 Corinthians are evident from the full gamut of literary and historical reconstructions.

1.2.1. Socio-Spatial Dynamics: Rejection of an Intermediate Visit

Certain commentators who reject intermediate events and assert the integrity of the letter emphasize the socio-spatial dynamics present in the letter, attending to Paul's absence (1:15-18), the Letter of Tears as Ersatz to Paul's presence (2:1-4), Titus's previous envoy (2:12-13; 7:5-16), Titus's impending return (chs. 8–9), and Paul's return (chs. 10–13). Representative of this, Heinrich Meyer states, "The aim of the Epistle is stated by Paul himself at xiii. 10, viz. to put the church before his arrival

---

55. D. E. Garland, *2 Corinthians*, NAC 29 (Nashville: Broadman, 1999), 32, 43.
56. Garland, *2 Corinthians*, 28.

in person into that frame of mind, which it was necessary that he should find, in order that he might thereupon set to work among them, not with stern corrective authority, but for their edification."[57] All other matters of import (collection, apostolic authority, rivals) are subordinate to Paul's return.[58] Fredrick J. Long argues similarly.

> The letter prepares for [Paul's] arrival in at least four ways: (1) by defending his previous decision not to visit when planned, but writing a letter instead (1.12–2.11); (2) by exhorting them to a lifestyle befitting the salvation offered in the gospel (5.20–7.3; 12.19–13.1); (3) by securing their complete confidence and cooperation in the collection for Jerusalem (chaps. 8–9; 12.14-18) as a sign for restored relationships with himself; and (4) by creating relational space for himself with the Corinthians by refuting his opponents (10.1–12.13).[59]

Such an emphasis is evident among interpreters who locate Paul's second visit prior to 1 Corinthians (Meyer) and those who reject a second visit entirely (Long).

Paul's impending arrival or its shadow, his absence (cf. 1:15-18; 1:23; 2:1-3), is a favorite point of emphasis among those reject an intermediate visit.[60] Employing rhetorical criticism, Long claims that Paul's "failure to visit" forms the central accusation to which he offers a response.[61] Similarly, other interpreters who reject an intermediate visit often argue that relational strain is primarily tied to Paul's chronic absence and that the discourse aims at clearing ground for his return.[62] Theodore Zahn claims that Paul's intention to address his persistent absence due to a

---

57. Heinrich Meyer, *Critical and Exegetical Handbook to the Epistles to the Corinthians*, trans. D. D. Bannerman, David Hunter, and William Dickson, 2 vols. (Edinburgh: T. & T. Clark, 1884), 2:128.

58. Meyer, *Corinthians*, 2:128.

59. Long, *Ancient Rhetoric*, 2.

60. Ambrosiaster PL 17:173; C. F. G. Heinrici, *Der zweite Brief an die Korinther*, KEK 6, 8th edn (Göttingen: Vandenhoeck & Ruprecht, 1900), 5; P. E. Hughes, *The Second Epistle to the Corinthians*, NICNT (Grand Rapids: Eerdmans, 1962), xvi–xxi; Niels Hyldahl, "Die Frage nach der literarischen Einheit des Zweiten Korintherbriefes," ZWN 64 (1973): 297–8; Bärbel Bosenius, *Die Abwesenheit des Apostels als theologisches Programm: der zweite Korintherbrief als Beispiel für die Brieflichkeit der paulinischen Theologie*, TANZ 11 (Tübingen: Francke, 1994), 7–13, 19–22; Land, *Absence*, 278, passim.

61. Long, *Ancient Rhetoric*, 126–7 passim.

62. For example Hughes, *Second Epistle*, xxvi; Hyldahl, "Frage," 299; Bosenius, *Abwesenheit*, 97–167.

change in itinerary and to announce his return is evident in the traditional structure (chs. 1–7, 8–9, 10–13) of 2 Corinthians, which demonstrates a geographical arrangement from Asia to Macedonia (chs. 1–7) and from Macedonia (chs. 8–9) to Corinth (chs. 10–13).[63] Zahn's influence continues to shape recent studies. Douglas Campbell follows Zahn's contentions that Paul visited Corinth a second time before 1 Corinthians and that the itinerary in 2 Cor. 1:16 chronologically precedes the itinerary in 1 Cor. 16:3-7 and that Paul's second visit precedes 1 Corinthians.[64] It is Paul's change of plans, by sending 1 Corinthians ("the Letter of Tears") in place of a scheduled visit, that leaves Paul open to the criticism of inconsistency (1:17).[65] Christopher Land agrees with Zahn's ordering of the itineraries, but in rejecting any second visit, Land interprets all facets of the crisis reflected in 2 Corinthians as tied in some way to Paul's persistent, unwelcome absence.[66]

Thus, the same reservoir of data may be interpreted as aiming not only at Paul's reconciliation with his community but also addressing his spatial absence and preparing for his return.

1.2.2. *Socio-Spatial Dynamics: Compositional Unity and Intermediate Visit*

Several scholars who assert that 2 Corinthians is constructed upon a spatial axis maintain the integrity of 2 Corinthians but add the presence of an intermediate visit. Murray Harris suggests the "overriding purpose" of the letter is "to prepare the way for an enjoyable third visit to Corinth by removing any obstacles."[67] Drawing from Paul's travel talk, Harris nuances the aims of 2 Corinthians: "In a nutshell he is saying first 'I rejoice over you and have complete confidence in you' (cf. 7:4, 16), then 'I urge you to finish what you have commendably begun' (cf. 8:10-11), and lastly 'I am about to come, so get ready' (cf. 12:14; 13:1, 11)."[68] James M. Scott, employing the traditional structure of 2 Corinthians (chs.

---

63. Theodore Zahn, *Introduction to the New Testament*, trans. John Moore Trout et al., 2nd edn (New York: Scribner's, 1917), 1:307–12.
64. Douglas A. Campbell, *Framing Paul: An Epistolary Biography* (Grand Rapids: Eerdmans, 2014), 74–90.
65. Campbell, *Framing Paul*, 76; see also David R. Hall, *The Unity of the Corinthian Correspondence*, JSNTSup 251 (New York: T&T Clark, 2003), 243–8.
66. Land, *Absence*, 258–9, 278, passim.
67. Murray Harris, *The Second Epistle to the Corinthians: A Commentary on the Greek Text*, NIGTC (Grand Rapids, MI: Eerdmans, 2005), 52; cf. Long, *Ancient Rhetoric*, 2.
68. Harris, *Second Epistle*, 52.

1–7, 8–9, 10–13), concludes, "each aspect of 2 Corinthians prepares for his visit."[69] Chapters 1–7 involves a defense of apostleship including his change in travel plans (1:12–2:13). Chapters 8–9 build on the confidence in 7:5-16 reviving the collection campaign to be completed before Paul's arrival. Chapters 10–13 prepares for Paul's imminent return with greater aggression.[70] Paul Barnett, dividing 2 Corinthians into six units (1:1–2:13; 2:14–6:13; 6:14–7:4; 7:5-16; 8:1–9:15; 10:1–13:14), claims, "the letter is written against the background of an unsuccessful second visit in the light of new difficulties that have now arisen...with the intent to make the Corinthians ready for Paul's last visit, when he and they can be reconciled."[71] For Barnett, the unifying logic to 2 Corinthians involves Paul's return to Corinth and desire to remove obstacles to that end (forgive the wrongdoer, complete the collection, repent of cultic/sexual practices, accept Paul's maintenance principle).[72] Similarly, Thomas Schmeller engages Vegge's argument, countering that the transition to censure in chs. 10–13 cannot be explained by Vegge's schema since the audience and situation were identical in chs. 1–9 and 10–13.[73] Schmeller turns to spatial dynamics to explain the difference in tone. Chapters 1–9 aimed to prepare "for the arrival of Titus and the collection and, on the other hand [10–13], for the arrival of Paul and the final reconciliation."[74] George Guthrie argues that the "geographic context" of 2 Corinthians, which emphasizes the themes of absence and presence, forms the "backbone of the book."[75] Paul negotiates his "relational network" by presenting information concerning "while Paul was absent" (1:1-11), "why Paul was absent" (1:12–2:13), "what Paul has been doing while absent" (2:14–7:4), "when Paul found Titus" (7:5-16), "Titus present to prepare for Paul's coming" (8:1–9:15), and "Paul absent but will be present soon" (10:1–13:13).[76] Thus, the emphasis upon Paul's contentious absence and

---

69. James M. Scott, *2 Corinthians*, NIBCNT (Peabody, MA: Hendrickson, 1998), 5.

70. Scott, *2 Corinthians*, 5, 34, 174, 193.

71. Paul Barnett, *The Second Epistle to the Corinthians*, NICNT (Grand Rapids: Eerdmans, 1997), 17.

72. Barnett, *Second Epistle*, 19.

73. Thomas Schmeller, "No Bridge over Troubled Water? The Gap between 2 Corinthians 1–9 and 10–13 Revisited," *JSNT* 36.1 (2013): 79–80.

74. Schmeller, "Troubled Water," 81; cf. Witherington III, *Conflict & Community*, 328, 351.

75. George Guthrie, *2 Corinthians*, BECNT (Grand Rapids: Baker, 2015), 46–7.

76. Guthrie, *2 Corinthians*, 47–8.

intended return remains robust even among scholars who assent to intermediate events.

1.2.3. *Socio-Spatial Dynamics: Partition Theories*

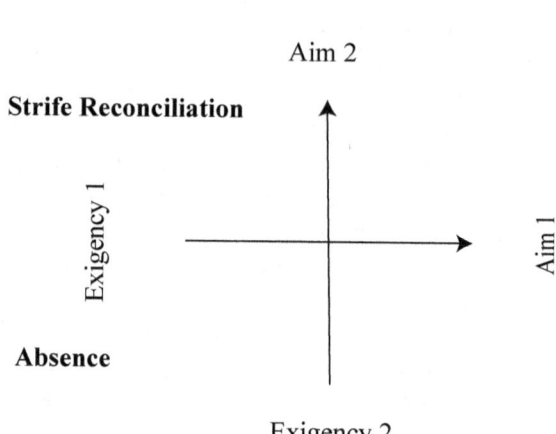

Figure 2. *Socio-Spatial Dynamics and the Aims of 2 Corinthians*

While the previous studies often stress the socio-spatial dynamics of 2 Corinthians in part to argue for its integrity, a similar emphasis is evident in highly partitioned reconstructions. Johannes Weiss stressed that Paul's many letters contained in canonical 2 Corinthians achieved their aim, Paul's return (see Rom. 15:26), the happy nature of which engendered the Epistle to the Romans[77] Welborn, using a similar partition hypothesis, emphasizes the positive psychological effects of Paul's reconciliation with Gaius (i.e. Romans) and return from his "voluntary exile from Corinth," dramatizing Paul's joyous reunion.[78] With a profound knowledge of antique civic structures, Mitchell proffers a significant description: "[Paul's] restoration to a position of respect and authority may be seen in his enfranchisement at Corinth on his final visit there."[79] Ryan Schellenberg agrees that Paul's visits to Corinth involve challenges to his apostolic status, claiming, "few would deny that this theme is

---

77. Weiss, *Primitive Christianity*, 1:357–8.
78. Welborn, *Enmity*, 460, 480–1; cf. L. L Welborn, "Paul's Appeal to the Emotions in 2 Corinthians 1.1–2.13; 7.5-16," *JSNT* 82 (2001): 45.
79. Mitchell, "Letters," 335.

pervasive throughout the canonical letter."⁸⁰ But rather than smoothing all visit talk into a uniform aim of securing Paul's amicable third visit, following Welborn's partition theory, Schellenberg claims, "What we have here, then, are two quite different situations: In 2 Cor. 1:15–2:13, Paul is justifying the postponement of a visit; in 2 Corinthians 10–13, Paul is dealing with the fallout of a disastrous one."⁸¹ Thus, the insistence that Paul aims to return from an acrimonious period marked by his absence is consistent across divergent historical and literary reconstructions as well as complementary to studies of the social dynamics of 2 Corinthians.

1.2.4. *Socio-Spatial Dynamics: Epistolary Theory*

Exegetes attuned to epistolary theory frequently emphasize the socio-spatial substrate of 2 Corinthians, regardless of historical or literary reconstructions. Following Heikki Koskenniemi and Klaus Thraede, who have demonstrated that the letter in antiquity was conceived as a medium to establish and maintain social relationships across geographic distances,⁸² Robert Funk first focused upon Paul's references negotiating his absence and arrival, which he terms as the apostolic *parousia*, and understood them as "a structural element in the Pauline letter."⁸³ Problems with Funk's thesis abound,⁸⁴ yet inasmuch as it has turned a light towards

---

80. Ryan S. Schellenberg, *Rethinking Paul's Rhetorical Education: Comparative Rhetoric and 2 Corinthians 10–13*, ECL 10 (Atlanta: SBL, 2013), 67.

81. Schellenberg, *Paul's Rhetorical Education*, 67.

82. Demetrius, *Eloc.* 227, 231; Heikki Koskenniemi, *Studien zur Idee und Phraseologie des griechischen Briefes Bis 400 n. Chr*, Suomalaisen Tiedeakatemian Toimituksia B/102.2 (Helsinki: Suomalaisen Kirjallisuuden Seura, 1956), 18–63, 88–127; Klaus Thraede, *Grundzüge griechisch-römischer Brieftopik.*, ed. Erik Burk and Hans Diller, Zetemata: Monographien zur klassischen Altertumswissenschaft 48 (Munich: C. H. Beck, 1970), 146–61; David E. Aune, *The New Testament in Its Literary Environment* (Philadelphia: Westminster, 1987), 172–4.

83. Robert Funk, "The Apostolic Parousia: Form and Significance," in *Christian History and Interpretation: Studies Presented to John Knox*, ed. W. R Farmer, C. F. D. Moule, and R. R. Niebuhr (New York: Cambridge University Press, 1967), 266.

84. Particularly, Funk explores the apostolic *parousia* as a "structural element" while Koskenniemi focused on *topoi*, phraseology, and clichés from the tradition of Greek friendship. Funk theorises that the *parousia* motif referred to by Koskenniemi "come[s] to expression as a structural element." This, however, is a terminological and methodological error as Koskenniemi and later Thraede demonstrate how the motif expresses itself—as a motif not a formal structure. Koskenniemi employs the notion of *parousia* as a seminal motif in which he refers to motif of a writer's perspicuous presence through the letter form, further developed by Thraede who notes the "παρουσία-Motiv" as well as the related motifs of "unity in friendship,"

Paul's emphasis on travel and presence, the essay remains essential. Using Funk's typology, Lee A. Johnson claims that the correspondence evinces a greater frequency (1 Cor. 4:14-21; 16:1-11; 16:12; 2 Cor. 8:16-23; 9:1-5; 12:14–13:10; six of thirteen occurrences) and volume (half of the correspondence) of apostolic *parousiai* than other Pauline letters.[85]

Indeed, Funk identifies three instances of apostolic *parousia* in 2 Corinthians (8:16-23; 9:1-5; 12:14–13:10), disqualifying 2 Cor. 1:1–2:13 and 7:4-16, although admitting the passage, "is concerned as a whole with Paul's proposed and previous visits and letters...and thus may be said to be a letter in which the apostolic *parousia* forms the body of the letter [of consolation]."[86] If 1:1–2:13 and 7:4-16 are included, then 2 Corinthians contains five examples of visit talk, far more than any other Pauline letter. Furthermore, Funk acknowledges that all of 2 Corinthians 10:1–13:10, not simply 12:14–13:10, is concerned with Paul's visits, past and future.[87] If one includes 1:3–2:13 and 7:5-16 alongside texts selected by Funk, 33% of 2 Corinthians contains visit talk. If one includes 10:1–13:10, then 58% of 2 Corinthians contains some aspect of visit talk (compare 1 Thessalonians = 21%, Philippians = 9.5%). Thus, Johnson's claim that half the correspondence involves Funk's apostolic *parousia* should only apply to 2 Corinthians.

For Johnson, the uniqueness extends to Paul's discussion of his absence and impending arrival: "throughout these numerous and lengthy passages in the Corinthian letters, Paul never expresses his eagerness to see the Corinthians, never hints that something or someone has hindered him from visiting them, never requests prayers from them nor submits his own prayer for his presence in Corinth, and never acknowledges that such a visit to Corinth would be of benefit to him."[88] This is evidence of Paul's "problematic relationship with that community" and a loss of social power.[89] However, Johnson aims to demonstrate, contra Funk, that Paul's letters were not weak substitutes for his presence, but involved tactical decisions to exercise or regain his authority.[90]

"unity of spirit," and the εικών ψυχῆς motif, which are left relatively untouched by Funk (Terrance Y. Mullins, "Visit Talk in the New Testament Letters," *CBQ* 35 [1973]: 350–8; Lee A. Johnson, "Paul's Epistolary Presence in Corinth: A New Look at Robert W. Funks' Apostolic Parousia," *CBQ* 68 [2006]: 481–501).

85. Johnson, "Presence in Corinth," 486–9, 497.
86. Funk, "Apostolic Parousia," 251 n. 1.
87. Funk, "Apostolic Parousia," 250; Johnson, "Presence in Corinth," 488.
88. Johnson, "Presence in Corinth," 497, see 489–95.
89. Johnson, "Presence in Corinth," 489, 501.
90. Johnson, "Presence in Corinth," 497–9.

Ryan Schellenberg cautions that it is important to specify what Paul's choice of letters over visit means in Corinth. He states:

> Paul did make a choice, but his options were very limited. As Johnson herself is aware, it was Paul's 'stormy relationship with the Corinthians' that led to his uniquely epistolary approach to this community and that made another visit untenable. In other words, the Corinthians' lack of receptivity effectively eliminated the possibility that Paul could travel confidently to Corinth (cf. 2 Cor 2:1-3; 12:20-21).[91]

Thus, for Schellenberg, when Johnson's argument is viewed in light of Paul's need for hospitality (if only to work as an artisan and continue his journey) rather than vis-à-vis Funk's taxonomy, it becomes evident that Paul's absence is based on his lack of welcome, "a rather humiliating reality that he does his best to portray in a positive light" (2 Cor. 1:15-17, 23).[92]

Peter Arzt-Grabner and Kristina Kreinecker also observe the unique nature of Paul's absence in 2 Corinthians, focusing upon the excuse for absence, a feature also found in Funk's apostolic *parousia*. Arzt-Grabner highlights a feature of private letters claiming, "[letter writers] emphasize that they would prefer to visit them in person. According to the actual situation, those letter writers explain more or less extensively why it was, and still is, impossible for them to visit."[93] Kreinecker comments, "clauses that try to explain why a person could not come, are more than just explanations of a fact, but mirror in themselves also the state of the relationship between the sender and the addressee."[94] Arzt-Grabner's analysis elicits three dominant explanations for an absence:[95] illness,[96] pressing duties,[97]

---

91. Ryan S. Schellenberg, "'Danger in the Wilderness, Danger at Sea': Paul and the Perils of Travel," in *Travel and Religion in Antiquity*, ESCJ 21 (Waterloo, ON: Wilfrid Laurier University Press, 2011), 155.

92. Schellenberg, "Perils of Travel," 155, see nn. 31, 32.

93. Peter Arzt-Grabner, "'I was intending to visit you, but...': Clauses Explaining Delayed Visits and Their Importance in Papyrus Letters and in Paul," in *Jewish and Christian Scripture as Artefact and Canon*, ed. Craig A. Evans and H. Daniel Zacharias (London: T&T Clark, 2009), 224.

94. Christina M. Kreinecker, "Emotions in Documentary Papyri: Joys and Sorrow in Everyday Life," *DCLY* 2011.1 (2012): 455; cf. Timothy Luckritz Marquis, *Transient Apostle: Paul, Travel, and the Rhetoric of Empire* (New Haven: Yale University Press, 2013), 51.

95. Here, following Kreinecker's summary of Artz-Grabner, "Emotions," 454.

96. P.Freib. 4.56.2-9; P.Oxy. 12.1488.20-25; 46.3313.6-8; *BGP A* 9.90.

97. *P.Lond.* 7.1979, 17-19; *P.Mich.* 3.203.

and other unforeseen obstacles.[98] The common denominator between these explanations involves pinning an absence upon an external obstacle or uncontrollable situation, which preserves a positive outlook of the relationship (cf. 1 Thess. 2:18; Rom. 1:13; 15:22).

Concerning parallels, Arzt-Grabner concludes, "the examples are very well comparable to Pauline passages, but 2 Cor. 1.23 is different."[99] The nearest parallel according to Arzt-Grabner is P.Oxy.Hels. 48, where a certain Ammon writes to his business partner Dionysius, informing him that "I did not come to you" because "in writing to my [Ammon's] sister, you did not remember me once" (ll. 5-8). Artz-Grabner suggests that both 2 Corinthians and P.Oxy.Hels. 48 exemplify that delay announcements could demonstrate that an author wished to handle situations differently through the letter than in person.[100] However, Ammon states the reason for his absence—a perceived slight from the recipient. It would seem equally reasonable that when the locus of blame is placed upon internal relational constraints, the excuse for absence indicates a measure of social strain manifesting in spatial distance—a conclusion consistent with those of Johnson, Schellenberg,[101] and Arzt-Grabner's comments elsewhere.[102] Thus, from an epistolary perspective, the spatial substrate of 2 Corinthians implies social dynamics complementary to those already discussed.

Finally, Long argues for the forensic species of Paul's discourse in part by appealing to other forensic epistles. "Epistolary forensic discourses were sent as letters and would generate [a] judicial setting. This was

---

98. No transport in P.Oxy. 14.1773.5-16; P.Mich. 15.751.26-30; Cannibalism (!) P.Oxy. 42.3065, 16-17; Molestation in P.Fay. 123.

99. Arzt-Grabner, "Delayed Visits," 228–9; Marquis refers to 1:23f. as Paul's travel apology, *Transient Apostle*, 50–8.

100. Arzt-Grabner, "Delayed Visits," 231.

101. As one of the leaping off points for Marquis's theory of travel as a "floating signifier," he analyses Paul's travel talk as a whole in comparison with Horace's excuse for not visiting Maecenas in *Ep*. 1.7. Marquis acknowledges the importance of the writer's excuse for not visiting as crucial to understanding the relationship between sender and recipient (51), the commonplace of blaming absence on external situations (55), even noting that Horace breaks from convention by admitting his lack of visit was because he, Horace, was a liar (53). Marquis, however, claims that this sort of deviation from convention, and Horace's selection of the epistolary *topos* of travels plans provides Horace and thus Paul a "discursive space to shift social positions" (56). This elaborate scheme could be simplified by observing the blatant similarity—both Paul and Horace make it clear that the failure to visit is due to relational tension, a rare but extant indication of growing distrust (Marquis, *Transient Apostle*, 50–8).

102. Peter Arzt-Grabner, *2 Korinther*, PKNT 4 (Göttingen: Vandenhoeck & Ruprecht, 2014), 165–6.

particularly the case when *the defendant* was in exile."[103] Long proceeds to analyze "demegoric and forensic apologetic literary letters" from antiquity for comparison, highlighting the use of forensic rhetoric both by Demosthenes from exile (*Ep.* 2) and Isocrates in appeal for Agenor's restoration (*Ep.* 8).[104] While Long never claims that Paul writes 2 Corinthians as an exile, like Demosthenes or Agenor, he demonstrates that Paul was not alone in employing apologetic rhetoric to secure an amicable return.

1.2.5. *Conclusions*

The trajectory of research understands 2 Corinthians as (a) letter(s) that aim(s) at reconciliation and return responding to the complex exigency of Paul's absence and the strife directed towards him by some in the community. For some interpreters, the accent is upon the social dynamics of relational strain, non-reciprocity, or enmity. Others attend to the spatial substrate of the social dynamics in the text. Yet, the socio-spatial aim of the epistle is agreed upon broadly regardless of differences in literary or historical reconstruction. Frequently, Paul's role as Corinth's apostle is at stake within socio-spatial matrix. This observation does not minimize the exegetical importance tied to rival historical and literary reconstructions. However, in an area of study which often proves so fluid and unstable, the dual exigency of strife and absence as well as Paul's fundamental aim at reconciliation with and return to the ἐκκλησία in Corinth supplies a measure, however small, of solid ground. With this we turn to socio-historical studies, a crucial subsidiary of the historical-critical method to describe the state of the art regarding the social and spatial dynamics behind 2 Corinthians, which results in a clear lacuna between the socio-spatial trajectory of research and socio-historical approaches on 2 Corinthians.

1.3. *Sources of Conflict: Insights from the Social World*

The turn to socio-cultural frames in correspondence studies is best understood in part as an effort to move beyond the global, opposition theories advanced by the likes of F. C. Baur and (to a degree) Wilhelm Lütgert and the resulting picture of orthodoxy-heresy combat in Corinth. Johannes Munck, who took aim at Baur, claimed that the conflict (in 1 Corinthians) arose not from a monolithic theological framework, but a "Hellenistic *milieu*...a mixture of philosophy and sophistry, typical of that

---

103. Long, *Ancient Rhetoric*, 39, italics original.
104. Long, *Ancient Rhetoric*, 103–9.

age."[105] His thesis implicitly challenged Lütgert and all other theologically based theories,[106] what became referred to as historical criticism's "idealist fallacy"[107] or "methodological docetism."[108] The ensuing shift in research from opponents' identity to socio-cultural frames characterize socio-historical or socio-cultural research. These studies fostered many advances in the areas of social *realia*, social history, social organization, cultural scripts, and prompted socially framed exegesis of the New Testament.[109] As the research paradigm emerged, the classicist Edwin Judge sounded the clarion call:

> The relations between Paul and his collaborators and rivals, especially in Corinth, constitute a crux of our subject. In spite of an array of detailed analyses, no solution has yet generally commended itself as the key to the matter. What seems inescapable, however, is that Paul is caught in a social trap of some sort. 'Idealistic' explanations seem bound to fail here, if anywhere. But the trouble is to identify the social conventions that marked out the battlefield.[110]

The resulting correspondence studies based largely on the "new consensus"[111]—the paradigm that asserts social stratification resulted in a

---

105. Johannes Munck, *Paul and the Salvation of Mankind*, trans. Frank Clark (Richmond: John Knox, 1959), 152–3. While Munck here comments upon 1 Cor. 1–4, elsewhere he argues likewise for the entire correspondence: "[the Corinthians] made themselves a picture of the Christian leader, even before I Corinthians, as a man who had honour and power in this world (I Cor. 1–4); and II Corinthians show that the continuing conflict with the church, reaching its climax during the intermediate visit, was over this very question" (184).

106. "We cannot approve the traditional point of departure of Pauline research where the opponents, if they are not Judaizers, automatically become spiritual men with no third possibility" (Munck, *Paul*, 176). For brief, explicit criticisms of Bousett and Lütgert, see 155–6, 174–5.

107. Bengt Holmberg, *Paul and Power: The Structure of Authority in the Primitive Church as Reflected in the Pauline Epistles* (Philadelphia: Fortress, 1980), 201–3.

108. Robin Scroggs, "The Sociological Interpretation of the New Testament: The Present State of Research," *NTS* 26 (1980): 165.

109. John H. Elliot, *What Is Social Scientific Criticism?*, ed. Dan O. Via (Minneapolis: Fortress, 1993), 18–20.

110. E. A. Judge, "The Social Identity of the First Christians: A Question of Method in Religious History," in *Social Distinctives of the Christians in the First Century: Pivotal Essays by E. A. Judge*, ed. David M. Scholer (Peabody, MA: Hendrickson, 2008), 133.

111. Abraham Malherbe, *Social Aspects of Early Christianity* (Philadelphia: Fortress, 1983), 31.

socio-cultural rather than theological *agon*—argued that criticisms of Paul emerged from a socially pretentious or ascendant contingent who argued that Paul failed to measure up to the canons of ideal leadership in matters of money, rhetoric, or masculinity.

1.3.1. Money Matters

Scholars have long perceived the significance of maintenance in the Corinthian crisis. One line of thought represented by Gerd Thiessen asserts that questions of Paul's apostolic legitimacy are tied to the rejection of Corinthian support (1 Cor. 9; 2 Cor. 11:7-12; 12:13, 14-15).[112] Theissen contends Paul battled against *followers* of itinerant missionaries in 1 Corinthians and against *actual* itinerants in 2 Corinthians, in both cases of a Palestinian type,[113] in which Paul was forced to defend his apostolic legitimacy as a newer, urban "community organizer (1 Cor. 9; 2 Cor. 11:7; 12:13) in the face of a traditional type of charismatic mission, which accepted support" according to dominical command (Mt. 10:8-10; Lk. 10:7).[114] The discrepancy between Paul's labor and the Palestinian charismatics' poverty and acceptance of maintenance thus generates the criticism.

Rather than violating an early intra-communal standard, another line of inquiry contends that Paul infringed broad Graeco-Roman expectations concerning support. R. F. Hock argued that Paul's refusal to enter a household as a client and his preference for a slavish trade (1 Cor. 9) were offensive to upper-class sentiments and cast disdain upon the community.[115] In play across the corpus is Paul's self-understanding of his apostleship in the form of the Cynic discussion of the ideal working philosopher. Particular to the Corinthian conflict, Paul's self-representation of a working philosopher was employed paradigmatically, advocating group ethics as well as apologetically in response to his

---

112. Gerd Theissen, *The Setting of Pauline Christianity: Essays on Corinth*, trans. John H. Schütz, 2nd edn (Eugene, OR: Wipf & Stock, 2004), 42–8; see also Ernst Käsemann, "Die Legitimität des Apostles: Eine Untersuchung zu II Korinther 10–13," *ZWN* 41 (1942): 36; Holmberg, *Paul and Power*, 90–1; Martin, *2 Corinthians*, 344–5; Thomas Schmeller, *Hierarchie und Egalität: Eine sozialgeschichtliche Untersuchung paulinischer Gemeinden und griechisch-römischer Vereine*, SBS 162 (Stuttgart: Katholisches Bibelwerk, 1995), 59; Georgi, *Opponents*, 238–42.

113. Theissen, *Essays on Corinth*, 41, 42, 65 n. 54.

114. Theissen, *Essays on Corinth*, 57–8.

115. Ronald F. Hock, *The Social Context of Paul's Ministry: Tentmaking and Apostleship* (Philadelphia: Fortress, 1980), 65; see also Abraham Malherbe, "Antisthenes and Odysseus, and Paul at War," *HTR* 76.2 (1983): 168–9.

wealthy detractors (1 Cor. 4:10-13; 9:1-27).[116] The re-emergence of the same issues in 2 Cor. 11:7-11, and the acceptance of maintenance by the rivals (11:12-15) indicates that Paul's financial practice was central to the Corinthian conflict.[117]

Similarly, Peter Marshall introduces the institution of enmity to Corinthian studies and contends that the correspondence manifests a single exigency: "in each passage [1 Cor. 9; 2 Cor. 11:7-15; 12:13-18] the point of contention is identical—Paul's refusal of support when he was in Corinth."[118] Unlike Hock, Marshall argues at issue is neither the Cynic ideal nor Paul's general policy regarding manual labor but the social implications "implied by giving and receiving."[119] Thus Marshall reasons, "the offer made to Paul was not disinterested" but would obligate Paul to an asymmetrical friendship.[120] Marshall's thesis has enjoyed an enormous influence on subsequent scholarship.[121]

Numerous iterations concerning the nature of the Corinthians' offer and Paul's refusal exist. Schellenberg even argues that Paul never refuses maintenance, but rather the Corinthians never made an offer.[122] Nevertheless, almost all attempts to interpret 1 and 2 Corinthians happily echo Bengt Holmberg's sentiment: "money looms large in the [Corinthian] conflict."[123] Indeed, while the frequency of publications of monographs

---

116. Hock, *Tentmaking*, 60–1.

117. Hock, *Tentmaking*, 139.

118. Peter Marshall, *Enmity at Corinth: Social Conventions in Paul's Relations with the Corinthians*, WUNT 2/23 (Tübingen: Mohr Siebeck, 1987), 174–5.

119. Marshall, *Enmity*, 173.

120. Marshall, *Enmity*, 233.

121. John K. Chow, *Patronage and Power: A Study of Social Networks in Corinth*, JSNTSup 75 (Sheffield: JSOT, 1992), 107–10; Dale B. Martin, *Slavery as Salvation: The Metaphor of Slavery in Pauline Christianity* (New Haven: Yale University Press, 1990), 81–5, 137–40; David Horrell, *The Social Ethos of the Corinthian Correspondence: Interests and Ideology from 1 Corinthians to 1 Clement*, SNTW (Edinburgh: T. &. T. Clark, 1996), 200–216, 220–9; Timothy B. Savage, *Power Through Weakness: Paul's Understanding of the Christian Ministry in 2 Corinthians*, SNTSMS (Cambridge: Cambridge University Press, 1996), 90–4; Welborn, *Enmity*, 132–52.

122. Ryan S. Schellenberg, "Did Paul Refuse an Offer of Support from the Corinthians?," *JSNT* 40.3 (2018): 312–36.

123. Holmberg, *Paul and Power*, 95. For a dissenting voice see Lars Aejmelaeus, "The Question of Salary in the Conflict Between Paul and the 'Super Apostles' in Corinth," in *Fair Play: Diversity and Conflicts in Early Christianity: Essays in Honour of Heikki Räisänen*, ed. Ismo Dunderberg, Christopher Tuckett, and Kari Syreeni, NovTSup 53 (Leiden: Brill, 2002), 343–76.

and articles on the topic has cooled recently, the line of inquiry continues to supply an explanation of the source of conflict between Paul and the community and thus a matter from which Paul sought reconciliation.

1.3.2. Rhetoric

Following Munck's sophistic alternative to the Tübingen School, a flood of research further inspired by emergence of rhetorical criticism sought to interpret texts in 1 and 2 Corinthians in light of the artifactual remains of the Second Sophistic. As early as 1961, Judge claimed ancient audiences would have perceived Paul as a sophist.[124] More studies interacting with a rhetorical background soon followed.[125]

Monographs by interpreters such as Stephen Pogoloff employed source material from ancient Greece and the second and third centuries in order to establish that the phrase σοφία λόγου (1 Cor. 1:17) refers to "sophisticated speech."[126] Similarly, Duane Litfin argues from source material dating to ancient Greece (e.g. Plato, Isocrates, Aristotle) as well as the first century BCE through the third century CE (e.g. Cicero, Quintilian, Dio Chrysostom, Philostratus) that σοφία refers to "the Greco-Roman rhetorical tradition."[127] Pogoloff concludes that while in 1 Corinthians 1–4 Paul was over-valued as a rhetor and the object of divisive allegiance, in 2 Corinthians Paul is now rejected "as an inferior rhetor" an ἰδιώτης τῷ λόγῳ (11:7).[128] Litfin contends, however, that the negative evaluation of Paul's speaking style and the social capital wedded to it run through the correspondence (1 Cor. 1–4; 2 Cor. 1:12; 2:17; 4:2, 7; 10:3-4).[129] Bruce Winter argues that the sophistic movement was a primary impediment to Paul's work in Corinth. Winter argues in part that 1 Corinthians indicates Paul's "anti-sophistic" proclamation to Corinth drew criticism from the community, ultimately resulting in his detractors recruiting rhetorically

---

124. E. A. Judge, "The Early Christians as a Scholastic Community," *JRH* 1 (1960): 125–6.
125. Hock, *Tentmaking*, 50–3; Malherbe, *Social Aspects*, 46–59; L. L. Welborn, "On the Discord in Corinth: I Corinthians 1–4 and Ancient Politics," *JBL* 106 (1987): 102.
126. Stephen M. Pogoloff, *Logos and Sophia: The Rhetorical Situation of First Corinthians*, SBLDS 134 (Atlanta: Scholars Press, 1992), 109.
127. Duane Litfin, *St. Paul's Theology of Proclamation: 1 Corinthians 1–4 and Greco-Roman Rhetoric*, SNTSMS 79 (Cambridge: Cambridge University Press, 1994), 189.
128. Pogoloff, *Logos and Sophia*, 153.
129. Litfin, *Proclamation*, 160–73, 210–12, 249–50 passim.

adroit replacement apostles who criticize a crippling deficiency in Paul's oratorical delivery (2 Cor. 10:10; 11:6).[130]

Anthony Thiselton refers to these monographs as instigating "a flood of research on the Corinthian epistles" which "offers a consensus on 'rhetoric', 'audience', 'performance' and social status at Corinth."[131] The argument that Paul responds to criticisms of his poor oratorical abilities vis-à-vis sophistic sensibilities has travelled by full circle by being recognized by some classicists.[132]

1.3.3. The Ideal Mediterranean Male

While several commentators are content to point to the issue of maintenance and oratory, or some combination of the two, recently, a complementary third rubric has emerged that points to Paul's failure to measure up to the canons of ideal, masculine leadership. Albert Harrill claims that in 2 Cor. 10:10 the criticism involves invective concerning Paul's appearance and speaking ability according to the "physiognomic principle that a weak body signifies a slave" and thus making him unfit to rule.[133] Similarly, Jennifer Larson claims that Paul's *gravitas* as an ideal leader is questioned in the areas of deportment and oratory (2 Cor. 10:10), courage to discipline (10:1), reliability (1:17-18), and body inviolability (11:23-25).[134] Jennifer Glancy engages 2 Cor. 11:23-25 and, taking aim at John Fitzgerald, claims that Paul's presentation of his "catalogue of punishments" demonstrates not Stoic-like endurance, but somatic ignominy and penetrability.[135] Glancy connects Paul's boast in his "whippable body" to

---

130. Bruce W. Winter, *Paul and Philo Among the Sophists: Alexandrian and Corinthian Responses to a Julio-Claudian Movement*, 2nd edn (Grand Rapids, MI: Eerdmans, 2002), 141–79, 203–39 passim.

131. Anthony Thiselton, *Thiselton on Hermeneutics: Collected Works with New Essays* (Grand Rapids, MI: Eerdmans, 2006), 597; cf. Oh-Young Kwon, "A Critical Review of Recent Scholarship on the Pauline Opposition and the Nature of Its Wisdom (σοφία) in 1 Corinthians 1–4," *CBQ* 8.3 (2010): 386–427.

132. Ian Henderson, "The Second Sophistic and Non-Elite Speakers," in *Perception of the Second Sophistic and Its Times*, ed. Thomas Schmidt and Pascal Fleury (Toronto: University of Toronto Press, 2011), 23–35. But see Schellenberg, *Paul's Rhetorical Education*, 151–7.

133. J. A. Harrill, "Invective Against Paul (2 Cor 10:10), the Physiognomics of the Ancient Slave Body, and the Greco-Roman Rhetoric of Manhood," in *Antiquity and Humanity: Presented to Hans Dieter Betz on His 70th Birthday*, ed. Adela Yarbro Collins and Margaret M. Mitchell (Tübingen: Mohr Siebeck, 2001), 192, 211 passim.

134. Jennifer Larson, "Paul's Masculinity," *JBL* 123.1 (2004): 85–97.

135. Jennifer A. Glancy, "Boasting of Beatings (2 Corinthians 11:23–25)," *JBL* 123.1 (2004): 99–135.

10:1-11, a passage that echoes questions concerning Paul's ability to discipline the community. Together the texts point to a larger criticism: "Paul was perceived as the sort who was subject to the rod, not the sort likely to wield a rod."[136] Glancy echoes the earlier conclusions of Scott Andrews, who likewise argued Paul's peristasis catalogue (11:23b-33) intentionally points to his lack of status and masculine courage (ἀνδρεία), which is representative of the criticisms against Paul in 10:10 (strength) and 11:6 (oratory).[137] Similarly, Calvin Roetzel argues that Paul's "weakness" in 2 Cor. 10:1-11 and 11:30–12:10 originates with his detractors' criticism of his cowardly and womanish behavior.[138]

These articles have provided a broader rubric through which to understand the social dynamics behind the conflict in Corinth under which may still be subsumed criticisms concerning rhetoric and maintenance. While these articles only engage a few passages, such texts (1:17-18; 10:1-11; 11:23b-33) have widely been viewed as lynchpins to understanding the social dynamics to the conflict. Finally, the emphasis upon the ideal, Mediterranean male has given renewed impetus to the view that Paul stands accused of martial impotence (10:1-11; 13:1-10), a view long proffered but now grounded in a socio-historical framework.[139]

1.4. *The Problem*

While these studies have probed the social dynamics behind the conflict in 2 Corinthians (and 1 Corinthians), none explicitly focuses upon nor systematically explores the social significance of the spatial dynamics in 2 Corinthians, namely, Paul's absence and desired amicable return within Graeco-Roman antiquity. If the socio-spatial trajectory of research

---

136. Glancy, "Boasting," 130.

137. Scott B. Andrews, "Too Weak Not to Lead: The Form and Function of 2 Cor 11.23b-33," *NTS* 41.2 (1996): 263–76. For Andrews, the point of such a boast is challenge upper class ideals of leadership (274).

138. Calvin Roetzel, "The Language of War (2 Cor. 10:1-6) and the Language of Weakness (2 Cor. 11:21b–13:10)," *BibInt* 17 (2009): 80, 88, passim.

139. Weiss, *Primitive Christianity*, 1:342–3; Floyd V. Filson, "The Second Epistle to the Corinthians," in *IB*, 381–8; D. W. Oostendorp, *Another Jesus: A Gospel of Jewish-Christian Superiority in II Corinthians* (Kampen: J. H. Kok, 1967), 17–27; Watson, "Painful Letter," 42–5; Barnett, *Second Epistle*, 457–78, 597, 605, 608; Lars Aejmelaeus, *Schwachheit als Waffe. Die Argumentation des Paulus im "Tränenbrief" (2.Kor. 10–13)*, SFEG 78 (Göttingen: Vandenhoeck & Ruprecht, 2000), 54–99; D. D. Walker, *Paul's Offer of Leniency (2 Cor 10:1)*, WUNT 2/152 (Tübingen: Mohr Siebeck, 2002), 242–57; Vegge, *2 Corinthians*, 262–332; Schmeller, *Zweite Brief*, 2:130; Schellenberg, *Education*, 280; Land, *Absence*, 208–11.

is correct, socio-historical studies have turned a light upon possible exigencies of the social conflict in Corinth, while largely taking Paul's absence as happenstance. This is all the more surprising considering the consensus in Corinthian studies that Paul's absence from Corinth is not due to peripatetic overtime, but follows from and is characterized by a rather nasty clash between Paul and one or some of his detractors (2 Cor. 1:23; 2:1; 12:14, 21; 13:1-2).[140] Welborn's reference to Paul's "voluntary exile from Corinth" and Mitchell's reference to civic enfranchisement appear to attach identifiable social descriptions to Paul's absence and return, although the expressions, while rooted in the antique Mediterranean world, seem more stylistic than substantive.[141] Only recently has Adam White taken Welborn's phrase as a clue for further research. Though White does not commit to a literary hypothesis, Welborn's influence is clear as White contends that 2 Cor. 1:1–2:11, 7:5-16 "reframes [Paul's] actions as a form of 'voluntary exile.'"[142] While the scope of White's work and primary emphasis on the rhetoric of exile in some ways limits the possibility of interaction, White's work (article and recent book on discipline in Pauline communities[143]) along with this monograph (and its antecedent) represent a new direction of study. Thus, between the socio-spatial trajectory of research and the socio-historical probing of the social conventions behind the conflict exists space to explore and to identify "a recognizable form of social interaction" to which strife and reconciliation, absence and return might relate.[144]

140. Reimund Bieringer, "Zwischen Kontinuität und Diskontinuität: Die beiden Korintherbriefe in ihrer Beziehung zueinander nach der neueren Forschung," in *The Corinthian Correspondence*, ed. Reimund Bieringer, BETL 125 (Leuven: Leuven University Press/Peeters, 1996), 11.

141. After completing the bulk of my research and writing, I was made aware of the research of Adam White, who generously shared his now published article with me, which expounds upon Welborn's phrase "voluntary exile." Although we independently arrived at similar conclusions on the nature and social significance of Paul's absence and insights concerning the literary tropes employed by those sharing Paul's social location, my approach differs in scope, attention to absence and conflict in the non-elite world, the import of 1 Corinthians to the conflict, the nature of the conflict during Paul's intermediate visit, and Paul's appropriation of displacement discourses. For interaction with White (particularly Adam White, "Paul's Absence from Corinth as Voluntary Exile: Reading 2 Corinthians 1:1–2:13 and 7:5-16 as a Letter from Exile," *JSNT* 43 [2020]: 44–66), see especially Chapter 5.

142. White, "Paul's Absence," 45.

143. Adam White, *Paul, Community, and Disciple: Establishing Boundaries and Dealing with the Disorderly*, Paul in Critical Contexts (New York: Lexington Books/Fortress Academic, 2021).

144. Land, *Absence*, 37.

1.5. Methodology: Relevance-theoretic Considerations

Based on the socio-spatial exigencies and aims of 2 Corinthians, the present work aims to methodically study the socio-cultural phenomena often attendant to such exigencies and aims, investigate to what degree such phenomena resonate with evidence in 2 Corinthians, and finally to demonstrate how attention to the nature of Paul's absence and desire to return might supply salient contextual parameters previously unconsidered for the interpretation of discreet textual units. For aid and further warrant in this venture we turn to relevance theory (RT) introduced by Dan Sperber and Deirdre Wilson.[145]

Within biblical studies, RT functions as an emerging tool for translation,[146] hermeneutics,[147] exegesis,[148] and theology.[149] RT attempts to develop Gricean pragmatics,[150] agreeing that (1) the linguistically and

---

145. Dan Sperber and Deirdre Wilson, *Relevance: Communication and Cognition*, 2nd edn (Oxford: Blackwell, 1995); Robyn Carston, *Thoughts and Utterances: The Pragmatics of Explicit Communication* (Malden, MA: Blackwell, 2002); Deirdre Wilson and Dan Sperber, *Meaning and Relevance* (New York: Cambridge University Press, 2012); Billy Clark, *Relevance Theory*, Cambridge Textbooks in Linguistics (New York: Cambridge University Press, 2013).

146. Ernst-August Gutt, "Translation and Relevance" (Ph.D. diss., University of London, 1989); Ernst-August Gutt, *Relevance Theory: A Guide to Successful Communication in Translation* (Dallas: SIL; New York: UBS, 1992); Karen H. Jobes, "Relevance Theory and the Translation of Scripture," *JETS* 50.4 (2007): 773–97.

147. Kevin Vanhoozer, "From Speech Acts to Scripture Acts: The Covenant of Discourse and the Discourse of the Covenant," in *After Pentecost: Language and Biblical Interpretation*, ed. Craig G. Bartholomew, Colin Green, and Karl Möller, Scripture and Hermeneutics 2 (Grand Rapids, MI: Zondervan, 2001), 1–49; Anthony C. Thiselton, *New Horizons in Hermeneutics* (Grand Rapids: Zondervan, 1992), 2.

148. Tim Meadowcroft, "Relevance as a Mediating Category in the Reading of Biblical Texts: Venturing Beyond the Hermeneutical Circle," *JETS* 45.4 (2002): 611–27; Gene L. Green, "Lexical Pragmatics and Biblical Interpretation," *JETS* 50.4 (2007): 799–812; Stephen Pattemore, *The People of God in the Apocalypse: Discourse, Structure, and Exegesis*, SNTSMS 128 (New York: Cambridge University Press, 2004); Gene L. Green, "Relevance Theory and Biblical Interpretation," in *The Linguist as Pedagogue: Trends in Teaching and Linguistic Analysis of the Greek New Testament*, ed. Stanley E. Porter and Matthew Brook O'Donnell (Sheffield: Sheffield Phoenix, 2009), 217–40; Gene L. Green, "Relevance Theory and Theological Interpretation: Thoughts on Metarepresentation," *JTI* 4.1 (2010): 75–90; Fredrick J. Long, *II Corinthians: A Handbook on the Greek Text*, BHGNT (Waco, TX: Baylor University Press, 2015), xxiv–xxvi, xxxviii–xxxix.

149. Green, "Metarepresentation."

150. Sperber and Wilson, *Relevance*, 37.

lexically encoded material of an utterance is underdetermined and does not completely encode a communicator's meaning, (2) human communication inherently contains expectations which guide a hearer to meaning through an inferential process, (3) inferential communication is not a "field of play" but the precise and predictable expression and recognition of a communicator's intentions.[151] Thus, Sperber and Wilson offer an impressive thesis:

> The central claim of relevance theory is that the expectations of relevance raised by an utterance are precise enough, and predictable enough, to guide the hearer towards the speaker's meaning. The aim is to explain in cognitively realistic terms what these expectations of relevance amount to, and how they might contribute to an empirically plausible account of comprehension.[152]

Our study is relevance-theoretic in orientation and thus does not require a complete elucidation of RT. Most crucial for our purposes is Sperber and Wilson's conception of the mutual cognitive environment. When a person can potentially mentally represent a fact or assumption as true or likely true, it is said to be manifest. An individual's cognitive environment "is the set of all the facts [and assumptions] that he can perceive or infer: all the facts [and assumptions] that are manifest to him."[153] Accordingly, human communication works not because of an impossible duplication of thoughts, but because humans can share a cognitive environment, and that sharing itself is manifest to both communicator and audience, referred to as a mutual cognitive environment (MCE).[154]

Stephen Pattemore, commenting on RT, claims the aim of communication is to modify the "representation of the world" of another; that is, "to enlarge the scope of what is mutually manifest to both communicator and audience."[155] For Sperber and Wilson, this is possible because the communicator leads the audience on an inferential path by a series of inputs or stimuli, clues, and cues. That inferential pathway is always based on context, arising from the MCE, particularly the communicator's understanding of it, and the deployment of code and contextual

---

151. Deirdre Wilson and Dan Sperber, "Relevance Theory," in *Handbook of Pragmatics*, ed. G. Horn and L. Ward (Oxford: Blackwell, 2004), 607–8.
152. Wilson and Sperber, "Relevance Theory," 607–8.
153. Sperber and Wilson, *Relevance*, 39.
154. Sperber and Wilson, *Relevance*, 38–46.
155. Stephen Pattemore, *People of God*, 15.

information that is the most salient to the audience and thus likely to lead to proper interpretation.[156] When an input combined with existing background knowledge, or context, yields new and important information efficiently, known as cognitive effects, it is said to be relevant.[157] Such an input may strengthen existing assumptions, contradict existing assumptions, or combine with existing assumptions to yield new cognitive effects.[158]

Unlike code theory where context is viewed unidirectionally as a word is placed within a static context generating a decodable message, RT asserts context is constructed in a dynamic, dialogical process in which new inputs are linked to existing contextual information.[159] As is obvious in life and discipline, there are a plethora of contexts in which an utterance could be meaningful. However, RT argues that the human mind is architectured for efficiency, finding the most cognitive effects for the least processing effort.[160] Thus, RT's First (or Cognitive) Principle states, "human cognition tends to be geared to the maximisation of relevance."[161] In ostensive-inferential communication, the universal cognitive tendency towards efficiency means that the presumption of relevance is shared between communicator and audience. This is encapsulated in the Second (or Communicative) Principle: "Every act of ostensive communication communicates a presumption of its own optimal relevance."[162] Both principles are what Sperber and Wilson originally referred to singularly as "principle of relevance."[163] Thus, words do not acquire meaning through, in or by a static context, rather utterances activate the construction of salient contexts from the MCE within which they are meaningful.[164]

---

156. Sperber and Wilson, *Relevance*, 43.

157. Sperber and Wilson, *Relevance*, 48.

158. Sperber and Wilson, *Relevance*, 108–17; Clark, *Relevance Theory*, 102, 364–5.

159. Sperber and Wilson, *Relevance*, 132–71.

160. For detailed discussion, see Dan Sperber and Deirdre Wilson, "Pragmatics, Modularity and Mind Reading," *ML* 17 (2002): 3–23.

161. Sperber and Wilson, *Relevance*, 260–1.

162. Sperber and Wilson, *Relevance*, 260–1.

163. Dan Sperber and Deirdre Wilson, "Précis of Relevance: Communication and Cognition," *BBS* 10 (1987): 697.

164. Sperber and Wilson, *Relevance*, 141–2; Peter Auer, "From Context to Contextualization," *LL* 3 (1995): 11–28.

1.6. *Plan of Study*

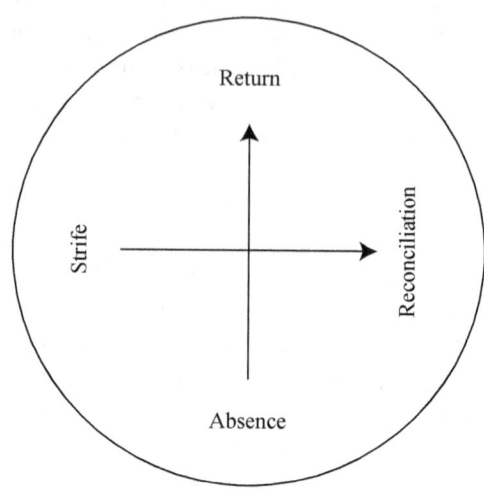

Figure 3. *Unknown Mutual Cognitive Environment in Relation to Political Displacement*

In Part I, I describe, as faithfully as possible, the contents of the mutual cognitive environment in relation to Paul's aim of reconciliation and return and consistent with the exigencies of strife and absence. This move is complementary to Clifford Geertz's thick description, except with a cognitively precise understanding of the function of context in communication.[165] Chapter 2 describes the type of phenomena that were often attendant to reconciliation and return in Graeco-Roman antiquity. For the phenomena, I supply the broad etic descriptor of political displacement. As well, Chapter 2 engages our level of confidence concerning the implied audience's—a non-elite, economically modest political community in Corinth in the mid-first century CE—and the implied author's familiarity with such phenomena.[166] In Chapter 3, the

---

165. Clifford Geertz, "Thick Description: Toward an Interpretive Theory of Culture," in *The Interpretation of Cultures: Selected Essays* (New York: Basic Books, 1973), 3–30.

166. Here I follow the argument of Richard Last, *The Pauline Church and the Corinthian Ekklēsia: Greco-Roman Associations in Comparative Context*, SNTSMS 164 (New York: Cambridge University Press, 2016), 83–113. For studies concerning the socio-economic level of Pauline communities, see Steven J. Friesen, "Prospects for a Demography of the Pauline Mission: Corinth among the Churches," in Schowalter and Friesen, eds., *Urban Religion in Roman Corinth*, 351–70; Peter Oakes, *Reading*

description of the MCE is employed comparatively to ascertain the degree to which the phenomena resonate with evidence in 2 Corinthians. Thus, I explore whether Paul and his audience viewed these phenomena as merely inferable from the wider world (i.e. manifest) or whether and to what degree the phenomena of political displacement relate to Paul's absence and the acute Corinthian crisis (i.e. more manifest), evaluating the appropriate level of confidence on Barclay's historical plausibility scale from virtually certain to incredible. Here I argue that Paul's exit from Corinth followed a failure to discipline his detractors in the face of affront (2 Cor. 12:21; 13:2) as promised (1 Cor. 4:18-21), leading to a series of judgments (2 Cor. 10:1, 10) and a rejection of Paul's communal legitimacy (2 Cor. 10:7; 13:3), suggesting his defeat and displacement from Corinth. Chapter 4 demonstrates the explanatory power of viewing Paul as responding to a moment of political displacement from Corinth, arguing that the seemingly unrelated judgments of financial impropriety (2 Cor. 7:2; 12:14-18) and inconsistency in travel habits (1:15-17) should be understood as arising predictably from the events described in Chapter 3. As well, I consider the quasi-formal consequences of accusations of malignant character (1:12, 17-18; 5:13; 12:16) in Paul's ἐκκλησία in Corinth (cf. 1 Cor. 5:9-13) vis-à-vis the community's symbolic withdrawal from relations with Paul. I conclude that the evidence gathered and analyzed in Part I indicates that Paul experienced a recognizable instance of political displacement from which he writes to secure an amicable return.

In Part II, by employing relevance-theoretic principles, I demonstrate the salience of Paul's political displacement from Corinth (Part I) for the interpretation of discreet textual units in 2 Corinthians. In Chapter 5, I interpret three accounts of apostolic ordeals occurring in four passages (1:3-11; 2:12-13 and 7:5-16; 11:30-33). The accounts echo both the themes and criticisms emerging from Paul's response to his challengers during the intermediate visit as well as tropes and schemas used by other displaced persons and Israel's exilic tradition. Finally, in Chapter 6, I interpret 2 Cor. 13:1-10, Paul's final appeal for an amicable return. I conclude that one route by which Paul attempts to achieve an amicable return involved the interweaving of displacement tropes, intelligible to the wider Mediterranean world and consistent with Israel's exile tradition, reworked through Paul's Christo-logic.

Romans in Pompeii: Paul's Letter at Ground Level (Minneapolis: Fortress, 2009); Bruce W. Longenecker, *Remember the Poor: Paul, Poverty, and the Greco-Roman World* (Grand Rapids, MI: Eerdmans, 2010), and others. Below I attempt to address the concerns of those critical of the presuppositions of the "new consensus."

Part I

Paul and Political Displacement in Corinth

In Part I, I describe the phenomena often associated with strife and absence and antecedent to the dual epistolary aim of full reconciliation and return. Those phenomena point to the ubiquitous practice of political displacement. From a relevance-theoretic perspective, by outlining the practice, I establish the presence of political displacement in the MCE, simultaneously familiarizing the reader with the phenomena associated with political displacement. Not only did political displacement exist within the MCE, but also in two areas in 2 Corinthians—Paul's intermediate visit and subsequent absence (Chapter 3) and the accusations of embezzlement, levity, and diseased character brought against Paul (Chapter 4)—evidence indicates that Paul stands under communal judgment of the type and nature consistent with the practice of political displacement. This hypothesis is further substantiated by evidence of the community's withdrawal from Paul.

Chapter 2

POLITICAL DISPLACEMENT IN GRAECO-ROMAN ANTIQUITY

Based upon the review of literature and methodology, the objective is twofold. First, I intend to demonstrate that the dual aim of reconciliation and return frequently implied that an individual's absence in the context of strife implied or embodied the community's judgment against them. Second, I describe the cultural, political, and communal phenomena antecedent to an attempted amicable return, for which I supply the etic descriptor, political displacement. From a relevance-theoretic perspective, these objectives demonstrate the manifestness of political displacement; that is, our confidence concerning Paul and the Corinthians' level of awareness of the practice. This in turn makes possible further inquiry by enabling the researcher to attend to evidence of the phenomena in 2 Corinthians.

Political displacement refers to the exit of an individual or a group from a political community for inimical reasons, sometimes enforced through communal penalty such that an individual's absence implied or embodied a judgment against them. Of course, displacement resulted from a broad range of exigencies—war, colonization, food shortage, or economic opportunity. The narrow scope of our study allows extended focus upon exits and removals arising from intra-personal and intra-communal conflicts. The term *exile* is frequently deployed to denote such situations, but not without risk of anachronism. As Jan Felix Gaertner comments, the keywords associated with exile were elastic and could easily refer to expulsion or voluntary departure.[1] A similar trend exists

---

1. Jan Felix Gaertner, "The Discourse of Displacement in Greco-Roman Antiquity," in *Writing Exile: The Discourse of Displacement in Greco-Roman Antiquity and Beyond*, ed. Jan Felix Gaertner, Mnemosyne 83 (Leiden: Brill, 2007), 2. See also Ernst Ludwig Grasmück, *Exilium: Untersuchungen zur Verbannung in*

in the translation of the Hebrew word *golah* and related lexemes.² Thus, the descriptor, political displacement, refers to voluntary and enforced absences in response to internecine hostility.

RT's emphasis on the audience's role in interpretation makes the aim of this chapter something other than retrieving Paul's source material or reconstructing his noetic state.³ Rather, our interest is whether the implied author and audience were aware of the phenomena linked to political displacement and to what degree. Here, it is necessary to explore contextual material accessible to those that lived beneath elite economic or poverty scales. Thus, while elite political culture supplies significant evidence of ancient life, it must be asked to what degree such material may be used in understanding Paul and the Corinthians' mutual cognitive environment.

This chapter demonstrates that the dual aim of reconciliation and return belonged to those whose absence implied or embodied a judgment against them or, in some instances, judgments against the community (§2.1). Furthermore, the phenomena of political displacement intersected certain socio-cultural institutions and conventions (§2.2), political theory (§2.3), and penology (§2.4). These features pervaded many non-elite political communities (§2.5), and second temple communities (§2.6) including Paul's Corinthian ἐκκλησία (§2.7).

2.1. The End of Exile: Reconciliation and Return

Not all reconciliations involved return and not all returns involved reconciliation. However, when ancient witnesses refer to both elements, as a topic of discourse or a discursive aim, the reference is native to political dissidents across Graeco-Roman antiquity and often presumed a social rupture manifesting in spatial distance.

2.1.1. Reconciliation and Return as Elite Topic and Aim

Copious examples exist of reconciliation facilitating the return of displaced persons in elite society from Classical Greece to the Early Empire. In suing for Agenor's return, Isocrates (fl. ca. 436–338 BCE)

---

der Antike, ed. Alexander Hollerbach, Hans Maier, and Paul Mikat, Rechts- und Staatswissenschaftliche Veröffentlichungen der Görres-Gesellschaft 30 (Munich: Ferdinand Schöningh, 1978), 20–9.

2. Mark J. Boda et al., eds., *The Prophets Speak on Forced Migration*, Ancient Israel and Its Literature (Atlanta: SBL, 2015).

3. See Part II.

employs the gloss, κατάγω (restoration), referring to the socio-spatial return of the exile.[4] Similarly, Demosthenes's (fl. ca. 384–322 BCE) *Epistle 2* is entitled ΠΕΡΙ ΤΗΣ ΙΔΙΑΣ ΚΑΘΟΔΟΥ ΔΗΜΟΣΘΕΝΗΣ. In the letter aimed at his return, Demosthenes pleads, "So, since, quite rightly, you have become reconciled [διήλλαχθε] with all others involved in these charges, be reconciled [διαλλάγητ'] with me also, men of Athens; for I have done no wrong against you."[5] In the context of the Struggle of the Orders, Dionysius writes that the Senate commanded envoys, "to reconcile the people [φιλίαν τῷ δήμῳ] to the patricians…and to bring the fugitives home speedily."[6] According to Dionysius (fl. ca. 60 BCE–7 BCE), Marcius Coriolanus (fl. fifth century BCE) wrote to Minucius, concerning Marcius's exile, stating, "concerning friendship and reconciliation [φιλίας καὶ διαλλαγῶν], which you desire for me to conduct to the people in the hopes of return discuss it no more."[7] Dio Chrysostom (fl. ca. 40–ca. 115 CE) marks his return from relegation with a formal announcement of friendship by the Apameians.[8] The thought is consistent with Philo's (fl. ca. 20 BCE–ca. 50 CE) treatise on Joseph in which Joseph's reconciliation (καταλλαγάς) with his brothers precedes their resettlement in Egypt.[9]

2.1.2. *Greek Reconciliations and Returns*

In the Greek period, civil strife and mass expulsions were resolved through returns and formal reconciliations. In these cases, return was often affected by victory. The famous return of the democrats and Athenian reconciliation in 403 BCE remains exemplary.[10] A decree (between 365–359 BCE) marking the conditions of the return of exiled factions in Dikaia is introduced as "[concerni]ng the reconci[lia]tions as [Lykios and] the conciliators pro[vid]ed."[11] Frequently, reconciliations allowing the return of exiles were referred to by the term διάλυσις in the epigraphic

---

4. Isocrates, *Ep. 8*, 1-4.
5. Demosthenes, *Ep. 2*, 16-17.
6. Dionysius of Halicarnassus, *Rom. ant.* 6.69.4.
7. Dionysius of Halicarnassus, *Rom. ant.* 8.29.3.
8. Dio Chrysostom, *Conc. Apam.* 16.
9. Philo, *Ios.* 40-42.
10. Aristotle, *Ath. pol.* 39.1; Xenophon, *Hell.* 2.4.39-43.
11. E. Voutiras and K. Sismanides, "Δικαιοπολιτῶν Συναλλαγαί. Μια Νέα Επιγραφή Από Τη Δίκαια," in *Ancient Macedonia: Seventh International Symposium* (Thessaloniki: Institute for Balkan Studies, 2007), 257–9, ll. 2–3; trans. Benjamin D. Gray, "Exile and the Political Cultures of the Greek Polis, c. 404–146 BC" (Ph.D. diss., Oxford University, 2011), 363.

record.¹² In Mytilene, a reconciliation states, "the people [should pray] on the twentieth of the month [Maimakter (?) to all] the gods that the reconciliation (τὰν διάλυσιν) will be for the salvation and flou[rishing of all the citizens], for those who ha[ve returned and for those] in the city."¹³ A second-century BCE decree, *SB* 8.989, provided amnesty (l. 2), allowing for those who quit the community (ἀναχωρέω, l. 7) to return (καταπορεύομαι, l. 8) to their prior occupations and avoid prosecution (cf. P.Teb. 1.5.1-13; *OGI* 90.19-20).

2.1.3. *As Aim in the Papyri*

The dual aim is evident in private correspondence in the papyri. A letter from the second century CE (*BGU* 3.846) by a man named Antonius Longus aimed at reconciliation with his mother (παρακα[λ]ῶ σαι, μήτηρ, δ[ι]αλάγητί μοι, l. 10). The letter aims at reconciliation (l. 10) likely to manifest in a spatial return (l. 16). Undervalued is the spatial separation between Antonius and his mother representative of the social rupture between the two parties. Antonius employs negated forms of εἰσέρχομαι explaining his absence was due to a relational conflict (ll. 7–8). Antonius writes to his mother that he did not enter (εἰσέρχομαι) the metropolis (Arsinoe) because he was convinced that his mother would not meet him there, nor come (εἰσέρχομαι) to Karanis (mother's home?) because of his shame (ll. 5–9). The reason for absence clearly indicated in the expression, "I know that I have sinned" (l. 11), later echoing a charge of financial wrongdoing (ll. 15–16).

A similar exhortation for social reconciliation and geographical return is seen in the conclusion of the body of a second-century CE letter from a woman named Tays, an apparent runaway or banished slave,¹⁴ to Apollonius in P.Giss.17 (=P.Giss.Apoll.13). She pleas for reconciliation and return (ὥστε διαλλάγηθι ἡμεῖν κ[αὶ π]έμ[ψ]ον ἐφ' ἡμᾶς, ll. 13–14; cf. ll. 9–10). Here, the exigencies of strife and absence to be resolved are unofficial, likely occurring in a non-elite context. As the letters of Demosthenes indicate, in an elite context, letter writing also supplied an indispensable means of achieving reconciliation and return, often employed as a component of often coordinated campaigns which might include the strategic choice of exile and the lobbying of friends, family, and legates (see Appendix I).

---

12. Gray, "Exile," 85–114; see Aristotle, Ath. pol. 39.1.
13. *GHI*, 85B, ll. 39–42; trans. Gray, "Exile," 95.
14. Fitzgerald, "Paul and Paradigm Shifts," 250–1.

2.1.4. Conclusions

Thus, reconciliation and return often involved attempted closure to a period marked by hostility characterized in part by absence (cf. Eph. 2:11-22). That absence could be voluntary or involuntary. In most cases, the absent party was on the receiving end of the staying party's animus with the exception of the Struggle of the Orders (and perhaps P.Giss.17 and SB 8.989). This at least suggests some ancients employed exit and absence as means of protest and/or judgment against untenable circumstances (Mt. 10:14; Lk. 10:10-12; cf. Acts 13:51). Yet, in every case, those absent functioned as the socially or politically weaker party at least in the situation leading up to their exit. The nature of the rupture may be official and elite (Demosthenes) or unofficial and non-elite (*BGU* 3.846; P.Giss.17).

Without question, words matter. Lexical evidence provides important clues to situations of displacement behind the text. In our case, only one unit of 2 Corinthians appears to resonate with such language (5:1–6:2). However, to reduce this study to keywords fails to account for the full nexus of displacement. Classicists resist reducing similar studies to a purely lexical approach.[15] This is, in the present case, because to build out from a few lexica in 2 Corinthians would be to miss the nexus of political displacement that involves a host of constituent interactions, conventions, and institutions that may never manifest in keywords like exile. Unlike studies of reconciliation, reconciliation and return are not purely lexical or grammatical artefacts, but cultural artefacts spanning a wide swath of Graeco-Roman antiquity. To the phenomena that occasioned social ruptures marked by exit and absence we now turn.

2.2. Socio-cultural Institutions and Conventions: Enmity, Ordeals, and Absences

Broadly speaking, Graeco-Roman institutions and conventions often manifested a socio-spatial element. Personal relationships not partisan ideology influenced most decisions and supplied an organizing principle for communities.[16] In this manner, the institutions of friendship and enmity offer key entry points to political displacement. Of course, reconciliation

---

15. E.g. Andrew T. Alwine, *Enmity and Feuding in Classical Athens* (Austin: University of Texas Press, 2015), 42.
16. David F. Epstein, *Personal Enmity in Roman Politics, 218–43 B.C.* (New York: Croom Helm, 1987), 31; Ronald Syme, *The Roman Revolution* (New York: Oxford University Press, 1939), 11.

refers to the transformation of a relationship from enmity to friendship.[17] Both friendship and enmity were thoroughly reciprocal relationships, as cited by Marshall with the well-known maxim "to help a friend and harm an enemy."[18] Classicists note that while friendship could achieve homeostasis, the retaliatory logic of enmity often resulted in an escalating feud.[19] To be sure, enmities came in different shapes and sizes. Yet, enemies often had ends in mind other than the off-ramp provided by reconciliation. Enmity, like friendship, was action oriented.[20]

> Enmity was typically characterized by open displays of hostility, such as public renunciation of friendship; various forms of social ostracism, including both physical exclusion (shunning or more seriously exile) and non-communication (silent treatment); slanderous attacks on someone's honor, whether through defamation of character or challenging the validity of military or public service; confiscation of property and denial of civil rights; prosecution in the courts; and in some instances even physical violence and death.[21]

Much of the teleology of ritual enmity (prosecution, denial of civic rights, exclusion, loss of property) is central to the mechanisms of displacement as outlined below. M. I. Finley also observes a spatial component to enmity. The most effective way to undermine opponents was "by moral obloquy, by financial penalties, and, best of all, by physically removing them from the community through exile or death."[22]

The harshness of enmity did not diminish its import. While David Epstein and others refer to enmity as "private warfare," it also supplied a meaningful form of social interaction, what John Winkler refers to as "the electricity of that social machine."[23] Andrew Alwine describes classical Athens as "an 'enmity culture,' a society rife with hostile relationships that members of a community openly recognized and to

---

17. LSJ, sv. καταλασσω; Ciliers Breytenbach, *Grace, Reconciliation, Concord: The Death of Christ in Graeco-Roman Metaphors*, SNTS 135 (Boston: Brill, 2010), 172.

18. Marshall, *Enmity*, 35, passim, from Aristophanes, *Birds* 420f; Plato, *Phdr.* 240A.

19. M. I. Finley, *Politics in the Ancient World* (New York: Cambridge University Press, 1994), 118.

20. Alwine, *Enmity*, 31, passim.

21. Edward M. Keazirian, *Peace and Peacemaking in Paul and the Greco-Roman World* (New York: Peter Lang, 2013), 131.

22. Finley, *Politics*, 119.

23. John J. Winkler, *The Constraints of Desire: The Anthropology of Sex and Gender in Ancient Greece* (New York: Routledge, 1990), 55.

which they attached considerable importance for evaluating individuals' honor and standing in the community."[24] It is a fitting description for the wider Graeco-Roman world.[25] The social bloc and solidarity provided through friendship was matched in the proving grounds supplied by enmity. "Enmity was a fact of life," contends Alwine, "and a man's ability to overcome his enemies could be considered part of a definition of living well."[26] Euripides questions rhetorically, "Is there any god-given privilege nobler in the sight of men than to hold one's hand in triumph over the heads of foes?"[27] Alwine also points to Xenophon's *Hiero*, "I think that the most pleasant thing of all is to take things from enemies against their will."[28] Such forms of domination possessed personal satisfaction, in part, because they supplied increased honor and status according to the court of reputation.

Social status and esteem existed in the critical gaze of the community, resulting in the constant renegotiation of both "through competitive displays of bravado and superiority."[29] According to Carlin Barton, enmity relationships and other forms of threat and adversity were essential elements to Roman "contest culture" in which ordeals and trials (ἀγών, δοκιμή, πεῖρα, *labor, discrimen, contentio*) functioned as essential indicators of personal character, place within the social hierarchy, and the standing of a community itself.[30] This is evidenced in the Roman view that a male (*mas*) or human (*homo*) makes himself a man (*vir*) through energetic and courageous responses to adversity or affront.[31] Cicero (*Tusc.* 2.18.43) famously connected the virtue of courage to manhood (*vir*): "it is from the word for 'man' that the word virture is derived; but man's peculiar virtue is fortitude, of which there are two main functions, namely scorn of death and scorn of pain. These we must practice…if we wish to be men." Ordeals often furnished by enmity provided the opportunity to display character and claim status. "As gold is proven by fire," writes the Christian Minucius Felix, appropriating Roman norms (fl. ca. 200–240 CE), "so we are by ordeals."[32] Euripides (fl. ca. 484–ca. 407 BCE) writes in the context of an impending clash, "It is unmanly [ἀνανδρία] to

---

24. Alwine, *Enmity*, 26.
25. Epstein, *Enmity*; Marshall, *Enmity*, 35–67.
26. Alwine, *Enmity*, 37.
27. Euripides, *Bacch.* 877–80.
28. Xenophon, *Hier.* 1.34, trans. Alwine, *Enmity*, 37.
29. Alwine, *Enmity*, 40.
30. Carlin Barton, *Roman Honor: The Fire in the Bones* (Berkeley: University of California Press, 2001), 31, 35.
31. Barton, 38–47; cf. Isocrates, *Antid.* 217; Xenophon, *Hier.* 7.1-10; Livy 1.41.3.
32. Minucius Felix, *Oct.* 36.9, trans. Barton, *Roman Honor*, 34.

give up the greater thing and take the lesser."[33] Conversely, according to Seneca, after hiding in his mother's stratagem (*matris dolos*) to escape battle, Achilles "confessed himself a man by taking up arms."[34] Adversity could take many forms, but the need for an ordeal to define one's social space inherently highlights the necessity and value of conflict and enmity relationships for ancient society. Enmity, adversity, and threat provided opportunity to engage in therapy by ordeal—the moment, Barton writes, "when one gambled what one was."[35]

2.2.1. Zero-Sum Agonism

Honor and shame were not mental abstractions, but inherently tethered to communitarian views of character and public actions.[36] Te-Li Lau comments, "In the honor–shame culture of the Roman world, one's goal was understandably to obtain the largest possible share of creditable attention (honor) while avoiding the least possible experience of discreditable attention (shame)."[37] The contest for the limited goods of honor and status implied zero-sum logic, which was unforgiving for those on the losing side.[38] It is also required that agonistic interactions, which could occur in virtually any situation, possessed some finely calibrated, stock aspects providing basic criteria to judge whose performance was most honorable. Here, Bruce Malina's anthropological scripts regarding challenge and riposte supply insight on ordeals from the vantage of the evolution of an enmity relationship.[39] He writes, "the challenge is a claim to enter the social space of another."[40] Accordingly, at least three phases occur in a challenge-response:

33. Euripides, *Phoen.* 509–10.
34. Seneca, *Tro.* 212-14.
35. Barton, *Roman Honor*, 35, italics suppressed.
36. Te-Li Lau, *Defending Shame: Its Formative Power in Paul's Letters* (Grand Rapids, MI: Baker Academic, 2020), 44.
37. Lau, *Defending Shame*, 136.
38. For the earliest reference of the "zero sum game" in the contest for honor, see Alvin W. Gouldner, *Enter Plato: Classical Greece and the Origins of Social Theory* (New York: Basic Books, 1965), 49–60; for discussion on the idea limited quality of honor and "all the desired things of life," see Bruce Malina, *The New Testament World: Insights from Cultural Anthropology*, 3rd edn (Louisville, KY: Westminster John Knox, 2001), 89–90; for ancient sources reflecting anxiety over the limited amount of honor, cf. Plutarch, *Aud.* 44B; *An seni* 787D; Josephus, *Vita* 25.
39. Malina, *Insights*, 33–6, 40–3.
40. In an enmity relationship, the reason for the challenge would be negative—to dislodge an opponent from their social space and thus gain honor (Malina, *Insights*, 33).

(1) the challenge in term of some action (word, deed, or both) on the part of the challenger; (2) the perception of the message by both the individual to whom it is directed and the public at large; and (3) the reaction of the receiving individual and the evaluation of the reaction on the part of the public.[41]

There was always the possibility that the receiver failed to act assertively. Malina writes, "the receiver can react by offering nothing by way of response; he can fail or neglect to respond, and this would imply dishonor for the receiver."[42] For Barton, this reality made much of Roman life a high-wire act in which elites were faced constant exposure to challenge.[43] "The higher the wire," writes Robert Castor, "the more exposed to *pudor*—the more enviable your position and the more admirable your performance."[44] Of the loser in an ordeal or enmity relationship, Marshall states, "failure almost always meant the destruction of a man's status and reputation in public estimation."[45] Alwine writes of hostile exchanges, "turning the other cheek would have been a dangerous policy."[46] The essential need was appropriate action in response. For Aristotle (*Rhet.* 1.12.20), those who "have been wronged by many but have never prosecuted," quickly become "Mysian booty." The same was true in Rome. Too much inhibiting shame resulted in paralysis in the moment of truth. Quintilian (*Inst.* 12.5.3) criticizes, "modesty which is a form of fear deterring the soul from doing what it should, and resulting in confusion of mind, regret that our task was ever begun, and sudden silence." From Malina's scripts to primary evidence, action was required, bashfulness despised.

2.2.2. Absence as Response to Shame

A basic spatial element pervaded the stock evaluative criteria of the Graeco-Roman world. Cultural scripts indicate the negative judgments associated with absence in relation to a contest. "Above all," writes Barton, "a Roman was ashamed of being ineffective and impotent […]."[47] Withdrawal (social or geographic) was understood as an admission of and therapeutic response to some source of shame, often impotence or defeat.[48]

---

41. Malina, *Insights*, 33.
42. Malina, *Insights*, 35.
43. Barton, *Roman Honor*, 199–200.
44. Robert A. Castor, "The Shame of the Romans," *TAPS* 127 (1997): 11.
45. Marshall, *Enmity*, 69.
46. Alwine, *Enmity*, 23.
47. Barton, *Roman Honor*, 232.
48. Barton, *Roman Honor*, 256–8.

In defeat, withdrawal could function as a response to or embodiment of the shame of impotence. With athletics forming a microcosm of ancient agonistic values (i.e. no second-place awards), Pindar comments upon young Greeks who lost in the Olympics. For losers, there is no happy homecoming, but "staying clear of their enemies they shrink down alleyways bitten by failure."[49] After the defeat at the Caudine Forks, Livy (fl. ca. 59 BCE–17 CE) writes of the retreating Roman soldiers, "shame beyond grief compelled them to flee the conversation and company of other men."[50] The soldier who was beaten by a gardener in Apuleius's *Metamorphosis* (fl. ca. 123–170 CE), hid because of the shame of his "impotence and inaction" (*impotentia deque inertia*).[51] From exile due to defeat by Clodius, Cicero (fl. ca. 106–43 BCE) laments, "I hate crowds and shun my fellow creatures, I can hardly bear the light of day."[52]

Withdrawal could also supply a response to the shame of illicit or reprobate conduct, forms of moral impotence. In Plautus's (fl. ca. 254–184 BCE) *Casina*, Olympio cries of his conspiracy with Lysidamus, "I don't know where to flee, where to hide, or how to conceal this disgrace."[53] Livy tells of ten prisoners of war who remained in Rome, breaking oath with their captor Hannibal, "the men were subjected to all manner of criticism and humiliation, so much so that some immediately committed suicide and the others spent the rest of their lives not only avoiding the forum but virtually avoiding daylight and the streets."[54] Cicero states similarly of the ascendant Publius Sulla's conduct after corruption charges, "Who afterwards saw Sulla other than in deep depression, cast down and crushed? Who ever suspected that he was avoiding men's gaze and the light of day more out of resentment than from shame? ...[A]lthough he might legally have remained in Rome, he virtually condemned himself to exile."[55] Tacitus writes of Tiberius, "in doubt whether to enter the capital or no,— or, possibly, affecting the intention of arrival because he had decided not to arrive. After landing frequently at neighbouring points and visiting the Gardens by the Tiber, he resorted once more to his rocks and the solitude of the sea, in shame at the sins and lusts."[56] Losing in athletic compe-

---

49. Pindar, *Pyth.* 8.83-87.

50. Livy 9.6.9-10, trans. Barton, *Roman Honor*, 255; for the spatial removal of soldiers who experienced defeat or capture, see Livy 25.6.7-9; Josephus, *B.J.* 6.362.

51. Apuleius, *Metam.* 9.41; for withdrawal in response to shame caused by moral misdeeds, see Tacitus, *Ann.* 6.7; cf. Suetonius, *Aug.* 65.2.

52. Cicero, *Att.* 52.1.

53. Plautus, *Cas.* 875-877.

54. Livy 22.61.10.

55. Cicero, *Sull.* 74.

56. Tacitus, *Ann.* 6.5.1.

tition, defeat in battle or social contest, or illicit conduct often resulted in withdrawal as a remedy for shame.

Such scripts were accessible to Paul. He and the Corinthians knew that in the games, "only one receives the prize" (1 Cor 9:24). Even a conservative reconstruction of Paul's cognitive environment yields clear links between shame and absence. Genesis 2:25 describes Edenic existence as lacking shame. Yet, following Adam and Eve's sin, the shame associated with the awareness of their nudity moves them to cover themselves. In response to God's inquiry as to Adam and Eve's location, Adam responds, "I was afraid because I am naked, so I hid" (3:10). The reference to covering-hiding actions implies an awareness of shameful conduct as perceived by human and divine gaze.[57]

Paul appropriates similar language in his narratival undressing of Peter. Peter, Paul recounts, "withdrew [ὑποστέλλω] and separated [ἀφορίζω] himself." Paul makes clear this wasn't in response to illicit conduct according to divine scrutiny, but "fearing those of the circumcision" (Gal. 2:12). Peter, according to Paul, feared the evaluation of "those from James," knowing his interethnic commensality appeared to them truly shameful.

2.2.3. *The Shame of Flight in Combat*

Similarly, the act of leaving was regarded as intensely shameful. This may be seen first in the context of an exit from a contest or combat.[58] In Aristotle's moral psychology, shame arises from evil deeds stemming from a character fault. Paradigmatic of such deeds is, "throwing away one's shield or taking to flight" which is due to the vice of cowardice.[59] To flee a conflict rather than fight was itself shameful. Lysias's retreat was described as a αἰσχρῶς φεύγων (2 Macc. 11:12). Maximus Valerius (fl. ca. 14–37 CE) writes of the son of Scaurus:

> A body of Roman horsemen who were routed by a Cimbrian attack at the river Athesis fled in terror to Rome, deserting Consul Catulus. One of them, participating in their panic, was the son of M. Scaurus, the light and ornament of his country, who sent him the following message: he would rather come upon the bones of his son killed in action than see him in person guilty of so disgraceful a flight; therefore, if he had any remnant of shame left in his heart, he would avoid the sight of the father from whom he had degenerated.[60]

---

57. Lau, *Defending Shame*, 64.
58. See J. E. Lendon, *Empire of Honour: The Art of Government in the Roman World* (Oxford: Oxford University Press, 1997), 243–52.
59. Aristotle, *Rhet.* 2.6.3.
60. Maximus Valerius 5.4.

Not only should Scaurus's son remain absent in response to his shameful deed, but also the act of fleeing itself was intensely disgraceful.

Scarus's response demonstrates that the shame of flight from an ordeal often cascaded to others in the community. Therapy by ordeal was as much communal in nature as it was individual. Barton comments, "the values of the community—the very existence of the community—were formed in Rome by those who were willing to risk all."[61] Thus, Cicero, quoting Ennius, states, "The commonwealth of Rome is founded firm. On ancient customs and on men of might."[62] Polybius (fl. ca. 208–ca. 125 BC) comments that Rome was founded not upon words (λόγος) but "through many struggles and contests [διά δέ πολλῶν πραγμάτων καί αγώνων]."[63] Thus, such failure in the moment of truth threatened the communal fabric and in the case of Rome, the imperial myth.

Similar communal importance was attached to the valor of notable figures in other political communities would be present in the implied author's cognitive environment (cf. 4 Macc. 11:20-22; 17:11-16).[64] This is evident in the Old Testament in what Susan Niditch terms "bardic tradition." The bardic tradition is styled as "part of a larger narrative patterns that are typical of a cross-cultural range of epic stories about heroes."[65] Here, scenes of clash and ordeal function to provide important scenes in the life story of a hero in which the best man wins taking the spoils including macho respectability.[66]

For example, the narrative arch of the judge Gideon moves forward through a series of ordeals. The divinely acclaimed, "mighty man of valor" (δυνατὸς τῇ ἰσχύι) is anything but in the opening scenes in which Gideon worries over the weakness (ταπεινός) of his clan, and lack of status or stature (μικρὸς) in his family (Judg. 6:14). Even following his theophany, Gideon's defenestration of local Baalism occurs at night, because he feared (φοβέω) his father's house and the men of the city (Judg. 6:27). Gideon begins to live up to his appellation in his initial defeat of the Midianites, but not before needing more affirmation by putting YHWH to the test (Judg. 6:36-40). His subsequent pursuit of the fleeing Midianites across the Jordan results in a lack of hospitality from the town of Succoth, who doubt his ability to capture the kings Zebah and

61. Barton, *Roman Honor*, 87.
62. Cicero, *Resp.* 5.1.1; for a list of exempla, see *Resp.* 1.1.1.
63. Polybius, 6.10.14, my translation.
64. Barton, *Roman Honor*, 87 n. 273.
65. Susan Niditch, *War in the Hebrew Bible: A Study in the Ethics of Violence* (Oxford: Oxford University Press, 1993), 90.
66. Niditch, *War*, 105.

Zalmuna (Judg. 8:6, 15). Niditch comments, "[the people of Succoth] challenge his manhood and power."[67] Gideon eventually defeats the Midianite kings and, once condemned, Zebah and Zalmuna state, "Arise yourself and face us, because as a man is, so is his might [ὅτι ὡς ἀνὴρ ἡ δύναμις αὐτοῦ]" (Judg. 8:21). The arc is largely complete as the little one from the weak clan becomes the mighty man who dispatches kings through divine aid resulting in Israel's rest.

Even with the significant discrepancy between the MT and the LXX in 1 Samuel 17 (2 Kgdms), the Goliath episode evidences many identifiable marks of an ordeal. Niditch comments, "Drama is high and the concept of war as sport or contest is prevalent, as is the concern with prestige."[68] The narrator's description of Goliath's awesome physical appearance—an ἀνὴρ δυνατός (17:4)—and challenge to limited war set the stage (17:1-10). In the LXX, the Israelite army fails to respond: "they were amazed and greatly afraid" (17:12). The MT texts adds, "they fled [נוס] from him" (17:24). The logic is present in the LXX: "the people hid...just as people who are ashamed hide when they flee a battle" (2 Sam. 19:4). The paralysis of the Israelite encampment is evident in both traditions. Niditch comments, "a dare cannot be ignored unless the object of the challenge and implicit insult wishes to admit cowardice, womanishness, and defeat."[69] The challenge is met by David, whose stature (17:33) contrasts Goliath's and whose faithful daring (1 Sam. 16:18) contrasts Saul's dis-ease and fear. The result is Goliath's death, Philistine flight (נוס, 17:51), and Israelite triumph along with David's heightened status. Such tales have more in common with Graeco-Roman epic than other OT war texts.[70]

Paul can represent his past conduct in similar shades. Prior to his call and conversion, he marauded the countryside searching to destroy any threats to the "traditions of the fathers" (Gal. 1:13-14; 1 Cor. 15:9; Phil. 3:6; cf. Acts 8:1; 9:1-2; 22:4-5). His self-reported violent zeal for communal orthodoxy married with his social ascent and credentials portray Paul as a communal hero or at least well on his way.

While Paul eventually counted such markers as a loss to knowing the Messiah (Phil. 3:8), he certainly did not lose his taste for confrontation in defending the boundaries and norms of the Messianic community. In general, Paul's letters are evidence of his response to such threats. Specifically, the Antioch incident demonstrates Paul's confrontational role. Regarding Peter, he writes, "I opposed him to his face, because he stood

---

67. Niditch, *War*, 93.
68. Niditch, *War*, 93.
69. Niditch, *War*, 93.
70. Niditch, *War*, 105.

condemned" (Gal. 3:11), publicly confronting him before an audience (3:14). Paul frames the contest in Antioch, according to John Barclay, as "a clash between two regulative structures."[71] The clash between two sets or norms is adjudicated, in part, through Paul's public confrontation with Peter arguing for the community to align with "the truth of the good news" (Gal. 2:14). The results of that public ordeal are then appropriated for the audience of Galatians regarding the ongoing conflict.

2.2.4. The Shame of Flight and Absence beyond Combat

Beyond military combat, leaving a contest remained shameful. Cicero's ordeal with Clodius resulted in his flight from Rome. Writing from the early days of voluntary exile, Cicero laments,

> It was my duty either to avoid the impending danger by taking a Commissionership or to oppose it by careful provision or to fall bravely. Nothing could have been more miserable, dishonourable, and unworthy of me than *this*. So, I am overwhelmed by shame as well as grief. Yes, I am ashamed to have been found wanting in courage and carefulness.[72]

Cicero does not flee from something he regards as shameful, but just as Scarus expected his son to fight the Cimbrians, so too Cicero counts his lack of courage to face Clodius by electing to go into exile as an act of shame. Similarly, Dio Chrysostom states, "I reflected that Croesus, the king of the Lydians, was advised by Apollo, when a certain mischance fell, to leave his kingdom and go voluntarily into exile, and not to feel himself disgraced if he should be looked upon by men as a coward."[73] Dio's reflection functions as sublimation for his own exile, thus indicating the shame normally associated with flight and the degree to which absence indicated a lack of masculine virtue.

Voluntary, shameful exits would be present in Paul's cognitive environment. Clues in the text imply that David's retreat from Jerusalem before Absalom's insurrection should be interpreted as shameful. David's weakening, folly, and indecisiveness following the Bathsheba affair supply a helpful framing to David's retreat. He is deceived by Amnon and fails to act decisively in response to Tamar's rape (2 Sam. 13:1-22). He banishes Absalom after his revenge killing (2 Sam. 13:23-39) but withholds reconciliation from him after allowing Absalom to return to Jerusalem,

---

71. John M. G. Barclay, *Paul & the Gift* (Grand Rapids, MI: Eerdmans, 2015), 367–68.
72. Cicero, *Fam.* 14.3.1-2.
73. Dio Chrysostom, *Exil.* 6.

unaware of the brewing populist insurgency (2 Sam. 14:1–15:6). And once Absalom travels to Hebron to begin a rebellion, David is once again deceived by a son (15:7-12). It is the picture of a flaccid man, asleep at the wheel.

Clearly, the Deuteronomist depicts David's flight as the lived reality of the divine judgment proclaimed by Nathan. In this way, "David's expulsion from Jerusalem is therefore described almost as a trial by ordeal."[74] It is a judgment David accepts, embracing signs of penitence during his retreat procession (2 Sam. 15:31). The retreat from Jerusalem appears, in part, as an inversion of the Goliath episode as Shimei hurls stones and insults at the retreating David (2 Sam. 16:13).[75] Conquest, though temporary, and shaming are evident in Absalom's raping of David's concubines on the very rooftop where David observed Bathsheba (2 Sam. 16:22). At stake is not merely status, but legal rank within the community, a question of who the rightful king is (2 Sam. 15:10). It is David's retreat from Jerusalem that raises questions about his kingship (2 Sam. 19:3). To be sure, the retreat and return narrative depict David in positive ways as he awakens from his covenantal and sapiential slumber.[76] This supplies an initial piece of evidence that displacement presented a liminal condition from which writers could rescue and re-present those who leave.

Paul himself could depict flight and social withdrawal as shameful. In his clash with the Galatians, he depicts them as "quickly deserting" the gospel under the pressure of the interlopers (Gal. 1:6). Paul remembers fonder times when the community embraced Paul, standing firm in hospitality though his condition to them was a test (πειρασμός, 4:14). Under their current test, Paul is far from complementary. The Galatians buckling under the pressure of the rivals finds a parallel in Peter's withdrawal from gentile believers at the arrival of the Judaizers (2:12-13). Lau contends, Paul's description of Peter's withdrawal (ὑποστέλλω, 2:12), "connotes shameful cowardice" or "hiding and shrinking away" in the face of challenge.[77]

---

74. Victor Harold Matthews, Mark W. Chavalas, and John H. Walton, *The IVP Bible Background Commentary: Old Testament*, electronic edn (Downers Grove, IL: InterVarsity, 2000), 2 Sam. 15:26.

75. Victor P. Hamilton, *Handbook on the Historical Books* (Grand Rapids, MI: Baker Academic, 2001), 350.

76. See now Steven T. Mann, *Run, David, Run! An Investigation of the Theological Speech Acts of David's Departure and Return (2 Samuel 14–20)*, Siphrut 10 (Winona Lake, IN: Eisenbrauns, 2013).

77. Lau, *Defending Shame*, 95, 96.

2.2.5. Conclusions

A common denominator shared by rather disparate examples is the spatial substrate in which exit and absence in response to strife or adversity implies or embodies judgment. Whether the judgment was formal and ratified by a community in the case of exile or informal in the instances of the athletes, Apuleius's soldier, or Scarus's son, absence involved the assessment that in the moment of truth, one had been found wanting. If enmity, affronts, and adversity provided the opportunity for aggressive, boundary defining actions, then absence reflected the judgment (by observers, opponents, oneself) that one's behavior or character was beyond the pale. Absence in the context of an ordeal implied an acknowledgment that one had failed the test and often involved the tacit acknowledgment of impotence and a lack of virtue in one form or another. Such a judgment came with scars most clearly observed in the injury affixed to an individual's status. It is from within these conventions the need in part arises for reconciliation and return as testified to by Cicero's campaign for restoration.[78] Such scripts and conventions existed not simply in the Graeco-Roman world at large, but, to the best of our knowledge, were native to Paul.

2.3. Political Theory: Displacement within Political Communities

Conflict occurred within communities both to their benefit and detriment. Across many types of political communities, competition for honor (φιλοτιμία) not only generated acts of euergetism but also naturally fueled rivalry. In such a climate, private enmities could metastasize into episodes of internecine strife.[79] That enmity could mature into a serious communal issue comes as no surprise considering our discussion above. Enmity was not a free-floating abstraction but tied to the machinery of political communities. Many of the aims of an enmity relationship (e.g. financial penalties, loss of civic rights, exile) involve not simply actions in public but public actions occurring within a political group's jurisdiction, using the institutions (e.g. courts) of political communities. Herein a political community refers descriptively to a wide range of groups (family, association, *polis*, empire) who effectively organize themselves with some sense of both belonging, whether such territoriality is real or abstract, and an ambit of jurisdiction, particularly manifest in the power to discipline

---

78. Cicero, *Att.* 3.8.4; 3.9.3; *Fam.* 5.4; see Kelly, *Exile*, 119–20.
79. Aeschines, *Tim.* 1.2; cf. 1.1.

members. Below we consider the theoretical aspects of displacement in the context of political communities.

2.3.1. Discord and Displacement

That enmity relationships could precipitate communal conflict evokes the ancient discussion of internecine strife. The polysemous term στάσις often referred to competing conceptions of the community and the antagonisms that followed. While the LSJ refers to στάσις as a "party formed for seditious purposes, faction,"[80] Finley claims στάσις involved any attempt in antiquity to bring about "a change in some law or arrangement, and any change meant a loss of rights, privileges or wealth to some group, faction or class, for whom the *stasis* was accordingly seditious."[81] Thus, Henning Börm comments "*stasis* involved huge risks" in securing control of a political community.[82] The complex social linkages that stitched together communities often meant that the social networks of the combatants became involved in hostile relationships, thus setting off factionalism.[83] Factions pursued the very thing individuals sought—the acquisition of honor and power—although often to the destruction of the community.[84] For Aristotle, στάσις, whether in a democracy or oligarchy, resulted from parties not receiving what they believed they were due, whether this inequality was linked to predatory behavior of officials or the distribution of honor and power in the *polis*.[85]

While enmity formed an important institution, from the Classical period to the early Empire, internecine strife was the dread of ancient moralists and an existential threat to be avoided across Graeco-Roman political theory.[86] Hans van Wees writes that the obsession to avoid internecine strife lay at the center of Homer's *Iliad* and *Odyssey*: "the

---

80. LSJ, s.v. "στάσις."

81. Finley, *Politics*, 106; cf. Gray, "Exile," 115.

82. Henning Börm, "Stasis in Post-Classical Greece: The Discourse of Civil Strife in the Hellenistic World," in *The Polis in the Hellenistic World*, ed. Henning Börn and Nino Luraghi (Stuttgart: Franz Steiner, 2018), 56.

83. Alwine, *Enmity*, 34; cf. Hans-Joachim Gehrke, *Stasis: Untersuchungen zu den inneren Kriegen in den griechischen Staaten des 5. und 4. Jahrhunderts v. Chr.*, Vestigia 35 (Munich: Beck, 1985), 339.

84. Gehrke, *Stasis*, 343–50; cf. Thucydides 3.82-83; Polybius 15.21; Gehrke also claims that the 'Bipolarität' and 'Exclusivität' of factionalism was an intensified expression of the zero-sum aspect of agonistic culture (245–49, 351); for a current discussion of the causes of στάσις, see Gray, *Exile*, Chapter 3.

85. Aristotle, *Pol.* 5.1.3–5.2.11; see White, *Discipline*, 25–6.

86. Börm, "Stasis," 71–2.

poems concentrate on episodes which illustrate the causes and disastrous consequences of internal conflict."[87] Aelius Aristides (fl. 117–181 CE) demonstrates the ancient view of στάσις as an existential threat, commenting, "that if we have faction, it [ἡ πατρίς] is lost."[88] When applied to the body metaphor, discord was the pathology of the body politic.[89]

At a seminal level and across the Graeco-Roman era, the reflexive response to communal discord was displacement often against the weaker, defeated party.[90] Andrew Lintott, commenting upon discord in the Greek *polis*, writes, "the outcome of *stasis* was usually exile of the leading members of the defeated group."[91] Similarly, Gordon Kelly has collated extant accounts of exile from 220–44 BCE and, as Adam White observes, "with few exceptions, every one of them refers to issues of political strife."[92] Concerning a band of exiles, Isocrates comments to the rulers of the Mytileneans, "you had expelled them because you feared for the welfare of the city."[93] Aristotle (fl. 384–322 BCE) comments that exile serves as medicine (ἰατρεία) to factional strife in the body politic.[94] Tacitus (fl. ca. 56–ca. 120 CE), citing inter-city fighting between Pompeii and Nuceria that occurred at a gladiatorial match, tells of the eventual exile of the patron of the games, Livineius Regulus, as well as the instigators.[95] Dio Chrysostom counsels the city of Tarsus likewise, "Well, if you

---

87. Hans van Wees, "Stasis, the Destroyer of Men," in *Sécurité collective et ordre public dans les sociétés anciennes. Sept exposés suivis de discussions*, Entretiens sur l'Antiquité classique 54 (Geneva: Fondation Hardt, 2008), 4.

88. Aelius Aristides, *Or.* 24.37; see 23.31, 54; 24.21; Tacitus, *Agr.* 32.1; Polybius 23.11; Livy 6.42.9-12, 40.8; Dionysius of Halicarnassus, *Ant. rom.* 2.76.3; 6.86.5; 7.42.1; 7.60.2; Josephus, *Mos.* 264; Bacchylides, *Lyricus* Fr. 24; Gehrke, *Stasis*, 1 n. 3, 2, 5.

89. Xenophon, *Mem.* 2.3.18; Cicero, *Off.* 3.5.22; Livy 2.32.9-12; Plutarch, *Frat. amor.* 2.13 (479B); Dio Chrysostom, *2 Tars.* 20, 22–3; see Roger Brock, *Greek Political Imagery from Homer to Aristotle* (London: Bloomsbury, 2013), 69–76.

90. Grasmück explains, "Wo der Zwang (ἀνάγκη) regierte und die Gefahren des Umsturzes ständig drohten, waren auch Emigration und Verbannung an der Tagesordnung" (*Exilium*, 36).

91. Andrew Lintott, *Violence, Civil Strife, and Revolution in the Classical City* (Baltimore: Johns Hopkins University Press, 1982), 257; see Robert Garland, *Wandering Greeks: The Ancient Greek Diaspora from the Age of Homer to the Death of Alexander the Great* (Princeton: Princeton University Press, 2014), 79–80.

92. Gordon Kelly, *A History of Exile in the Roman Republic* (New York: Cambridge University Press, 2006), 161–219; White, *Discrip*, 33 n.24.

93. Isocrates, *Ep. 8*, 3–4.

94. Aristotle *Pol.* 1284b21-22; cf. Lysias 12.5.

95. Tacitus, *Ann.* 14.17.

believe them to be detrimental to you and instigators of insurrection and confusion, you should expel them altogether and not admit them to your popular assemblies."[96] In his concluding remarks to Nicea, Dio exhorts the city "to expel discord, contentiousness, and jealousy" for the sake of civic flourishing.[97]

Classicists routinely refer to political displacement as a "safety-valve" employed to resolve civic discord.[98] This function can be understood in at least two directions. First, in the zero-sum game of ancient agonism and the pervasive drive for ὁμόνοια or *concordia*, there existed little space for dissent, challenge to communal norm, and losers in social struggles.[99] Aristotle comments ὁμόνοια is a shared emotion of civic friendship, prevailing "when the citizens agree as to their interests, adopt the same policy, and carry their common resolves into execution."[100] For Cicero, *concordia* is the harmonious agreement "among dissimilar elements, brought about by a fair and reasonable blending together of the upper, middle, and lower classes, just as if they were musical tones."[101] The deified political abstractions of *concordia* and ὁμόνοια were long recognized as elemental to social order and often claimed as slogans by the victors in στάσις or *discordia*. For instance, L. Opimius, hardly a purveyor of civic peace, constructed a temple to Concord after massacring C. Gracchus and driving his supporters into exile.[102]

Second, within the political necessity for concord, "displacement was an effective means of rendering a rival or oppositional force harmless, without creating martyrs and thus provoking new resistance."[103] Thus, for those on the winning side of a conflict, exile provided a means of demonstrating dominance and restoring concord without resorting to bloodletting. The losers in a civic conflict were not constrained through cultural logic to resort to armed conflict but could be sentenced to or elect for exile.[104] The possibility of exile "lowered the stakes in political disputes" saved

---

96. Dio Chrysostom, *2 Tars.* 21.
97. Dio Chrysostom, *Nicaeen.* 8, my translation.
98. Garland, *Wandering*, 80, 138; Gray, "Exile," 50; Kelly, *Exile*, 13; referring to colonization, Finley, *Politics*, 110.
99. For a discussion of the relationship between ὁμόνοια and *concordia* see Arnaldo Momigliano, "Camillus and Concord," *ClQ* 34.3/4 (1942): 117–20.
100. Aristotle, *Nic. Eth.* 9.6.2.
101. Cicero, *Resp.* 2.17.69.
102. Appian, *Bell. civ.* 1.26; Plutarch, *Ti. C. Gracch.* 17; Cicero, *Sest.* 140; Kelly, *Exile*, 12 n. 37.
103. Grasmück, *Exilium*, 35, my translation.
104. Kelly, *Exile*, 7–14; Garland, *Wandering*, 81.

communities from otherwise predictable bloodshed and expedited a return to concord.[105] Two notable examples will suffice for now. From exile in Ertruria, Cataline rehabilitates his reputation, claiming that he was not "complicit in such a dreadful crime, but in order that the state might be a peace." When Cicero's enmity with Clodius fully metastasized, his friends counselled him to leave Rome rather than fight, believing that by doing so, he would become "a savior of his nation,"[106] which became a favored trope upon his return.[107]

Thus, exit and absence in the context of internecine conflict, whether enforced or voluntary, often implies or embodies a communal judgment that one is both a threat to civic order and defeated by stronger elements. Yet, such evaluations were not monolithic. Contrary to the implications from attention merely to socio-cultural conventions and institutions, the link between communal well-being and voluntary exit provided space for the absent and their supporters to argue for the virtue of such actions.

2.3.2. The Political Calculus of Displacement

While exit and absence in the context of communal conflict often implied judgment, displacement simultaneously provided ancients with a politically expeditious tool to drive opponents from power. According to Ernst Grasmück, the general political theory suggested, "Wenn es gelang, persönliche Gegner oder die Führer der Opposition außer Landes zu treiben dann ließ sich jede Art von Widerstand leichter unter Kontrolle bringen."[108] Likewise Sara Forsdyke comments, "power in the archaic polis was largely a function of the ability to expel one's opponents."[109] Many examples across Graeco-Roman antiquity may be cited.[110] Sulla,

---

105. Kelly, *Exile*, 13.
106. Plutarch, *Cic.* 31.4-5.
107. Cicero, *Dom.* 98.
108. Grasmück, *Exilium*, 35.
109. Sara Forsdyke, *Exile, Ostracism, and Democracy: The Politics of Expulsion in Ancient Greece* (Princeton: Princeton University Press, 2005), 111; cf. Grasmück, *Exilium*, 19 n. 32.
110. M. I. Finley observes that the most effective way to undermine opponents was "by moral obloquy, by financial penalties, and, best of all, by physically removing them from the community through exile or death" (*Politics*, 119). Demosthenes attributes his exile to the enmity (ἔχθρα) of his unnamed opponents (Demosthenes, *Ep.* 2, 26). A declaration of enmity—*renuntiatio amicitiae*—with the Roman emperor effectively ended careers and sometimes resulted in exile. Gallus, appointed as prefect of Roman Egypt, diminished Augustus's honor through gossip about the emperor, erecting images of himself, and inscribing his achievement on the pyramids. The offence resulted in confiscation of his property and eventual exile which he

having heard that his fellow consul, Publius Sulpicius, along with Marius had intrigued against him, returned to Rome with his army and "drove from the city the twelve persons responsible for these revolutionary and vicious measures."[111] The same practice is observable in the early Principate as issues of succession were frequently solved through displacement, as the case of Agrippa Postumus demonstrates.[112] Often, displacement was achieved through legal institutions. Tiberius, hoping to dispose of Antistius Vetus after he was acquitted of an adultery charge, responded immediately with the charge of sedition, tying him to the plans of Rhescuporis.[113] He was quickly condemned to exile. Agrippina believed Lollia to be a rival for the emperor's hand and had her exiled by having her charged with "traffic[ing] with Chaldaeans and magicians, and application to the image of the Clarian Apollo for information as to the sovereign's marriage."[114] The situation was similar during the reign of Nero, with several executions or exiles following treason condemnations on specious grounds.[115]

2.3.3. Displacement, Ethos, and Communal Memory

The spatial removal of opponents for political objectives seems axiomatic; however, the use of political displacement was deeply entrenched in the ancient conceptions of space, politics, and memory. Looking over the landscape of Graeco-Roman politics, Finley questions, "why in antiquity

---

avoided by suicide (Suetonius, *Aug.* 66; Dio Cassius 53.23.6). Similarly, Tacitus writes of Decimus Silanus, Augustus's granddaughter's paramour, "though subjected to no harsher penalty than forfeiture of the imperial friendship (*amicitia Caesaris*), realized that the implication was exile" (Tacitus, *Ann.* 3.24.5–7). In defense of Sulla, Cicero rhetorically questions the prosecution, "do you wish to drive an enemy into exile?" suggesting the intelligibility of the practice (Cicero, *Sull.* 91). Cicero himself would find himself in exile because of personal enmity with Clodius (Plutarch, *Cic.* 30–31). Philo presents the downfall and exile of Flaccus at the hands of his gloating enemies (Philo, *Flacc.* 18). For the evolution of an enmity relationship, see Alwine, *Enmity*, 28, 39.

111. Velleius Paterculus 2.19.1.

112. See Andrew Pettinger, *The Republic in Danger: Drusus Libo and the Succession of Tiberius* (Oxford: Oxford University Press, 2012), 103–22.

113. Neil Raj Singh-Masuda, "Exilium Romanum: Exile, Politics and Personal Experience from 58 BC to AD 68" (Ph.D. diss., University of Warwick, 1996), 178–9; Tacitus, *Ann.* 3.38.4.

114. Tacitus, *Ann.* 12.21.

115. Singh-Masuda, "Exilium," 179; for the trials and convictions of Thrasea Paetus, Helvidius Priscus, Paconius Agrippinus, and Curtius Montanus, see Tacitus, *Ann.* 16.18-19.

was it important to 'destroy' political opponents and not just their political positions?"[116] Finley claims with agreement from David Epstein that personal relationships, not ideology, dominated social and political life in the ancient world.[117] From this vantage point, the most effective means to defeat someone was to deprive them of the face-to-face interaction necessary to sustain social power.

From another angle, the personal nature of ancient politics indicates not that ideology was inconsequential, but that persons could be considered the embodiment of certain values/ethos. Paul Zanker demonstrates that a key aspect of the imperial ethos was the careful control and inflection of Augustus's portraiture, building campaigns, and other aspects of a complex web of imperial images.[118] Regarding the link between image and ideology, we are most familiar with those aspects that survive, such as statuary and monuments.[119] The same association between values and person may be seen in Dio's oration to the emperor: "he who most closely imitates your ways [τρόπος] and shows the greatest possible conformity with your habits [ἦθος] would be by far your dearest comrade and friend."[120] From wax images of deceased relatives in the Roman *domus* to the statuary of a city to epigraphs to historiography, these images and writings projected not only social power, but also virtuous *exampla* worthy of emulation.[121] It stands to reason that as well as the highly personal aspect of ancient politics, the person and the projections of the person were imbued with ideological value.

From such a perspective, displacement is helpfully understood alongside its post-mortem relative, memory sanctions. John Kloppenborg synthesizes the monumental impulse—the ubiquitous inscribing of names and construction of statuary—practiced across Graeco-Roman political communities, describing the practice as "the ancient equivalent of group portraits: they not only indicated who belonged, but also articulated

---

116. Finley, *Politics*, 118.
117. Epstein, *Enmity*, 31; Finley, *Politics*, 119; cf. Syme, *Roman Revolution*, 11.
118. Paul Zanker, *The Power of Images in the Age of Augustus*, trans. Alan Shapiro (Ann Arbor: University of Michigan Press, 1990), 98–100, 101–66, 167–238.
119. See R. R. R. Smith, "Cultural Choice and Political Identity in Honorific Portrait Statues in the Greek East in the Second Century A.D.," *JRS* 88 (1998): 56–93.
120. Dio Chrysostom, *1 Regn.* 44.
121. Sinclair Bell, "Introduction: Role Models in the Roman World," in *Role Models in the Roman World: Identity and Assimilation*, ed. Sinclair Bell and Inge Lyse Hansen, vol. 7 of *Supplements to the Memoirs of the American Academy in Rome* (Ann Arbor: University of Michigan Press, 2008), 1–39.

hierarchies."[122] John Ma comments, "within cities, the construction of memory may have been the means or the prize in struggles or personal agendas."[123] To remove a name or topple a statue was to condemn a person to oblivion. According to Harriett Flower, just as memory sanctions attempted to remove the epigraphic record of a person's presence from the community posthumously, exile attempted likewise through eviction of the living to redraw the ideological boundaries and social memory of the community.[124] Flower comments, "physical space was didactic, so memory sanctions upon physical space would amend a new generation's understanding of the past as found in monumentalization."[125]

Displacement and erasure sometimes occurred simultaneously, indicating the close relation. After electing for *interdictio*, Clodius razed Cicero's house—the fundamental marker of a person's identity within a community's memory space—and constructed an altar to *Libertas* on the site, which celebrated his victory over the Cimbri.[126] Flower comments, "the shrine and the portico Clodius built were both a kind of personal victory monument and the manifesto of a popular political program."[127] Apparently, the practice was not unique. Modestinus (fl. ca. 200–ca. 250) writes, "we must know that persons who have been relegated or deported on the ground of treason are to have their statues pulled down."[128] The toppling of Favorinus's statue in Corinth may indicate a similar approach.[129]

---

122. John S. Kloppenborg, *Christ's Associations: Connecting and Belonging in the Ancient City* (New Haven, CT: Yale University Press, 2019), 135.

123. John Ma, "The City as Memory," in *The Oxford Handbook of Hellenic Studies*, ed. George Boys-Stones et al. (Oxford: Oxford University Press, 2009), 256.

124. Harriett I. Flower, *The Art of Forgetting: Disgrace and Oblivion in Roman Political Culture* (Chapel Hill: University of North Carolina Press, 2006), 5.

125. Flower, *Forgetting*, 6.

126. Cicero, *Dom.* 127–129. "The identification of the house with an individual is manifest in the recorded instances of *damnatio memoriae*, which included the destruction of the home as a part of the programmatic eradication of a person's memory" (Betinna Bergmann, "The Roman House as Memory Theater: The House of the Tragic Poet in Pompeii," *ABull* 76.2 [1994]: 225).

127. Flower, *Forgetting*, 102.

128. Modestinus, *Digest* 48.19.24, trans. by Alan Watson, Theodor Mommsen, and Paul Krueger, *The Digest of Justinian*, 4 vols. (Philadelphia: University of Pennsylvania Press, 1985), 851; see Tacitus, *Ann.* 3.17.

129. Dio, [*Cor.*] 20–22; Philostratus, *Vit. phil.* 1.8; cf. Ovid, *Fasti* 6.642; Zanker, *Images*, 137–9.

Examples confirm the use of political displacement as an instrument to establish or reproduce favored civic ideals. As Erich Gruen observes, Claudius's *deportatio* of the Jews in 49 CE, and later the astrologers in 52, was the response to a contrived στάσις in order to demonstrate *pietas* and "proscribe a certain social order."[130] Far from posing a threat to civic order, the newly named *Pater Patriae* deemed it necessary to banish the Julias under adultery laws in order to preserve moral order within his social program.[131] Thus, just as the poets and other artists were enlisted in the propagandic campaign supporting the *mores maiorum*, Augustus expelled members of his household whose behavior was in contradiction to the prescribed communal identity. Ovid (fl. 43 BCE–17/18 CE) claimed his relegation to Pontus was due to *carmen et error*.[132] The reference to *carmen* is patently his *Ars Amatoria*, undoubtedly offensive to Augustus's moral initiatives. His successor, Tiberius, likewise used exile to combat profligacy among the elite.[133] The same use of displacement can be seen in Domitian's attempt at a moral redux.[134] Thus, since absence in such a context formed a judgment against individuals and groups, it also supplied a useful mechanism to disempower rivals, functioning as a judgment *against* the policies or ethos embodied by absent persons and *for* the dominant, prescribed moral order.

2.3.4. Conclusions

Across antiquity, the reflexive response to communal strife was political displacement. Scholars claim that political displacement provided a crucial function within political communities by allowing an expedited return to concord without the necessity of bloodshed, while still demonstrating dominance over the defeated. Beyond the level of political theory, displacement was an effective weapon to dispatch and control opponents and silence critics. Not only did political displacement consign people to oblivion vis-à-vis the community, in some instances it removed a proscribed ethos attendant to the person, reinforcing a desired social program. Thus, at the level of the community, political displacement

---

130. Erich S. Gruen, *Diaspora: Jews amidst Greeks and Romans* (Cambridge, MA: Harvard University Press, 2002), 39–41; Suetonius, *Claud.* 25.4; Tacitus, *Ann.* 12.52.

131. Suetonius, *Aug.* 55.1; Tacticus, *Ann.* 3.24.2-3; cf. Richard A. Bauman, *Crime and Punishment in Ancient Rome* (New York: Routledge, 1996), 42.

132. Ovid, *Trist.* 2.207.

133. Suetonius, *Tib.* 35.1-2.

134. Bauman, *Crime*, 72; Cassius Dio 67.3.3; Seneca, *Dom.* 8.3-4.

evinces the spatial substrate that lay beneath the complex intersection of power, judgment, and communal identity. It is entirely plausible that Paul and his audience would have familiarity with aspects of the political theory described above. However, further conclusions will be reserved after further study below.

2.4. Penology: Enforced Absences

Codified forms of political displacement practiced in Graeco-Roman political communities (*polis*, Republic, Principate) resulted in an "enforced absence."[135] While diverse lexically and temporally, enforced absences across antiquity possess commonalities helpful to this study. The official forms of judgment move our exploration of the MCE from broad social institutions, cultural scripts, and political theory to the specific warrants for, consequences of, and apparatuses involved in political displacement. In the context of a communal conflict and ordeal, the judgment associated with absence may be entirely informal. However, in political communities, as evident above, attempts to displace prominent figures frequently involved juridical avenues resulting in punitive sanctions.

2.4.1. Greece

The employment of displacement or exile emerged from within Archaic society likely as a severe form of popular justice within highly dyadic, segmented societies as well as a means of avoiding retribution for a capital crime.[136] The rise of the *polis* in eighth-century Greece marks the beginning of the use of displacement as an official form of social control.[137] Three prominent forms of enforced absence were φυγή, ἀτιμία, and ostracism.

The penalty of exile (φυγή) comprised the basic form of enforced displacement in which persons were ejected from their home *polis*, often as an expression of a commuted death sentence.[138] *Polis* courts and assemblies applied the sentence of φυγή for a range of serious and sometimes amorphous offences.[139] The penalty would often include the seizure of

---

135. Sarah T. Cohen, "Exile in the Political Language of the Early Principate" (Ph.D. diss., University of Chicago, 2002), 18.
136. Forsdyke, *Exile*, 114.
137. Forsdyke, *Exile*, 34–43.
138. Grasmück, *Exilium*, 20–9; Stephen Todd, *The Shape of Athenian Law* (Oxford: Oxford University Press, 1993), 139.
139. Gray, "Exile," 41–5.

property, the loss of civic rights, and the displacement of the criminal's family.[140]

The sentence of ἀτιμία or outlawry contained the conditions of φυγή, but included the possibility that the offender could be killed with impunity outside of the home *polis*.[141] As well, refuge in another *polis* was denied to an outlaw on pain of death, resulting in the outlaw's permanently removal of civic rights.[142] The conduct deserving of ἀτιμία involved serious civic crimes similar with φυγή.[143] So harsh was the sentence that, according to Forsdyke, the decree of ἀτιμία was a surrogate for the death penalty.[144] The related penalty of ἀτιμία *qua* civic disenfranchisement involved only the loss of coveted civic rights and property. While disenfranchisement did not stipulate geographical displacement, it included social ostracism likely resulting in voluntary exile.[145]

The practice of ostracism allowed the citizenry to oust any potential threat to democratic Athens for ten years through a vote of at least 6,000 written-upon potsherds.[146] The ostracized person would retain his property and regain his citizenship upon return.[147] Thus, ostracism reflects potential displacement for non-violent, even exceptional citizens,[148] however, extant ostraca suggest other candidates were accused of a range of moral and legal offences.[149] Forsdyke elucidates the relationship between more informal and codified aspects of displacement, commenting, "the difference between flight out of fear of persecution or prosecution and an actual decree of banishment is usually not important, since formal sentence would typically follow flight (since flight was taken to be an indication of guilt), and often the two occurred simultaneously."[150]

---

140. Gray, "Exile," 41–2; Garland, *Wandering*, 135.
141. Grasmück, *Exilium*, 16–20.
142. Grasmück, *Exilium*, 20.
143. Gray, "Exile," 45–6.
144. Forsdyke, *Exile*, 24; see Demosthenes, *Mid*. 43; Kaitlijn Vandorpe, "'Protecting Sagalassos' Fortress of the Akra: Two Large Fragments of an Early Hellenistic Inscription (with an Appendix by Marc Waelkens)," *AncSoc* 37 (2007): 123–5.
145. Gehrke, *Stasis*, 214; Forsdyke, *Exile*, 21; Gray, "Exile," 47.
146. Grasmück, *Exilium*, 23–5; Finley, *Politics*, 55; Forsdyke, *Exile*, 187–258, 349–54.
147. Forsdyke, *Exile*, 191.
148. Gray, "Exile," 41, 51; see Aristotle, *Pol*. 1284a3-b34; Diodorus 19.1.1-4.
149. Forsdyke, *Exile*, 195–7.
150. Forsdyke, *Exile*, 23–4.

2.4.2. Roman Republic

The origins of Roman exile are unknown from the Regal Period and the early Republic, but likely were rooted in conceptions of private or popular justice, avoidance of retribution, and communal purity, not unlike Greek origins. Gordon Kelly claims that the practice of *aquae et ignis interdictio* emerged by the late third century.[151] Both Polybius and Cicero claimed the unique qualities of *interdictio*, the former remarking that voluntary exile was granted to citizens in the process of being found guilty in capital cases,[152] the latter that *interdictio* was not legal penalty but a means of avoiding punishment before conviction.[153]

The sentence of *aquae et ignis interdictio* was passed by the tribune of the plebs *ex post facto* once a person was charged with a capital crime had fled Roman territory, an expanding sphere throughout the Republic with the eventual enfranchisement of all Italy after the Social War.[154] Flight was a means of obstructing new accusations as well as formal conviction.[155] The warrants for *interdictio* included military defeat and cowardice,[156] arson,[157] violence and treason,[158] homicide,[159] testimonary fraud,[160] and insurrection,[161] embezzlement from state contracts,[162] and maladministration.[163] At some point in the late Republic, either under Sulla's reforms[164] or Caesar's dictatorships, *interdictio* became an official legal penalty for a number of crimes.[165]

Interdictio, like aspects of Greek displacement, involved the removal of civic rights, prohibition from entering Roman territory, and usually

---

151. Kelly, *Exile*, 4.
152. Polybius 6.14.6-8.
153. Cicero, *Caec.* 34.100; see Sallust, *Bell. Cat.* 51.23-23, 40-42.
154. Kelly, *Exile*, 28, 93.
155. Strachan-Davidson, *Problems*, 2:4; Kelly, *Exile*, 18; on the frequent use of excuses for nonappearance to delay and obstruct a trial, see 27 n. 41.
156. *Gran. Licin.* 33.6-11C, 24C.
157. Dio 40.55; Ulpian, *Dig.* 12.5.1.
158. Cicero, *Phil.* 1.9.21-23.
159. Suetonius, *Jul.* 42.
160. Modestinus, *Dig.* 48.10.33.
161. Asconius 36.9C.
162. Livy, *Histories of Rome* 24.4.9-10.
163. Caelius, *Fam.* 8.8.2-3.
164. Cohen, "Exile," 31–40.
165. Kelly, *Exile*, 39–45; Bauman, *Crime*, 19–22.

the confiscation of property.[166] As well, citizens were not to provide aid to an *interdictus*. The sentence provided impetus for the *interdictus* to seek citizenship in another community, although citizenship could not be removed only surrendered upon accepting it from another community.[167] The geographic exit of an individual accompanied by the loss of property and status was devastating. Accordingly, "[an *interdictus*] lost everything that made life valuable or even bearable: he became civilly dead."[168]

Voluntary exile functioned as a surrogate of the death penalty among Roman citizens making *interdictio* a "conditional death sentence."[169] This implies that such an option was reserved for the elite.[170] The surrogacy of the sentence of exile and death can be most easily seen in a line from Polybius regarding the policies of Charops: "The people of Phoenice by a majority, either terrorized or seduced by Charops, condemned all the accused not to exile, but to death as enemies of Rome. So all these people went into exile."[171]

The sentence of *relegatio* was the innovation of the late Republic, in which citizens were temporarily excluded for sub-capital crimes.[172] *Relegatio* did not result in the loss of *civitas* or confiscation of property.[173] Undesirables could be banished from Rome through edict of *relegatio* generally defined as a temporary exclusion.[174] This was the fate for several undesirables including Greek philosophers, Epicureans, Chaldeans, and Jews.[175]

---

166. Strachan-Davidson, *Problems*, 23–50; Grasmück, *Exilium*, 65–6; Kelly, *Exile*, 37.

167. Strachan-Davidson, *Problems*, 2:37–40; Grasmück, *Exilium*, 101; Kelly, *Exile*, 18, 45–7; for the *ius exulare* as encouragement to settle in states friendly to Rome, see 54–65.

168. *DGRA*, s.v. "Exsilium."

169. Singh-Masuda, "Exilium," 21, 30; Bauman, *Crime*, 6, 20; Kelly, *Exile*, 1, 6; see now Strachan-Davidson, *Problems*, 2:23–40.

170. Cohen, "Exile," 31–2; cf. *Dig.* 48.8.3.5.

171. Polybius, *Hist.* 22.6.

172. Cohen, "Exile," 41.

173. Strachan-Davidson, *Problems*, 2:65–6.

174. Mommsen, *Strafrecht*, 48, 965–79; Strachan-Davidson, *Problems*, 1:109, 2.64–8; Grasmück, *Exilium*, 100; Kelly, *Exile*, 65; Cohen argues, contra Mommsen and Kelly, that magistrates did not use *coercito* in the application of relegation but appealed to legislative bodies ("Exile," 48–53).

175. Mommsen, *Strafrecht*, 48 n. 1; Kelly, *Exile*, 65–7. Relegation continued into the early empire often with consequences similar to *deportatio*. Claudius introduced a new form of *relegatio* that sentenced people to remain within three miles of Rome (Bauman, *Crime*, 56; Seneca, *Claud.* 23.2).

2.4.3. *The Principate*

Claudia Cohen comments that exile was generally reserved for the higher classes in the Principate, just as in the Republic, rather than forced labor or death.[176] Whereas non-elites may be sentenced to work in the mines, elites were exiled.[177] Both forms of sanction were surrogates to the death sentence.[178]

Relegatio, just as in the waning days of the Republic, involved sub-capital offences in which the *relegatus* retained their citizenship.[179] The power of relegation extended to provincial governors and most often involved relegation from a place (province, Rome, emperor's presence) rather than confinement to a location.[180] In 18–17 BCE, Augustus extended the punishment of *relegatio* to include life-long banishment for illicit sexual intercourse through the *lex Iulia de adulteriis coercendis*.[181] As mentioned above, this initiative was tied to the *mores maiorum*. To enforce the law, Augustus formed a standing court to try cases of adultery and *stuprum*. According to Richard Bauman, the court "had the longest life and the heaviest workload of any jury court in the Principate."[182] The emphasis upon social hygiene provided a helpful pretense for driving away opponents.[183]

In 12 CE Augustus ordered that the banished be restricted to islands no more than fifty miles from Italy.[184] While interdiction was still employed, the territorial expansion of the empire made it nearly impossible for an offender to quit the state and exit Roman jurisdiction.[185] This reality, paired with the autocratic and often temperamental rule of the *princepes*, resulted in the supersession of *interdictio* with the frequent deployment

---

176. Cohen, "Exile," 56.
177. For evidence of non-elite exile in the Principate, see Suetonius, *Aug.* 51; Singh-Masuda, "Exilium," 3 n. 4.
178. Cohen, "Exile," 56 n. 128.
179. Cohen, "Exile," 57.
180. Cohen, "Exile," 57.
181. Strachan-Davidson, *Problems*, 2:66–7; Bauman, *Crime*, 24.
182. Bauman, *Crime*, 24.
183. Ronald Syme, *The Augustan Aristocracy*, 2nd edn (Oxford: Clarendon, 1989), 9; Singh-Masuda, "Exilium," 126.
184. Singh-Masuda, "Exilium," 16; Cohen, "Exile," 65; contra Mary V. Braginton, "Exile under the Roman Emperors," *CJ* 39.7 (1944): 394.
185. Strachan-Davidson, *Problems*, 2.27, 37–38; Grasmück, *Exilium*, 101; Bauman, *Crime*, 41; for a detailed discussion, see, Kelly, *Exile*, 93–108; Cohen, "Exile," 66–70.

of *deportatio (in insulam)*.[186] The offences warranting deportation were largely synonymous with those warranting interdiction.

Deportatio evidenced deviations from previous displacement practices. Established under Tiberius in 23 CE, deportation involved confinement to a particular location, often an island, along with the loss of civic rights.[187] Unlike the customs associated with interdiction, the *deportatus* could not voluntarily quit the community to join another, but were stripped of their *patria potestas*.[188] Thus, with the rise of Principate, voluntary exile ceased as an option at the imperial level.[189] Dissolved of citizenship and unable to join another community, such persons were consigned to a state of near non-personhood.[190] In as much as political displacement was tied to the death penalty in the Graeco-Roman world, and paraded as a humane replacement for it in the Republic, the Principate often utilized exile for the purpose of conducting executions out of the public eye, or encouraging suicides through the threat of prosecution.[191] The early Empire employed the policy with devastating effect, resulting in the liquidation of large portions of the old aristocracy.[192]

2.4.4. Conclusions

Attention to the penological aspect of displacement within elite political communities illustrates that enmity relationships, affronts, and internecine strife often resulted in enforced absences ratified by a community's juridical apparatus. The multiple forms of enforced absence possess four common features. First, enforced absences involved official judgments made by communities or rulers concerning actions, violations of the communal contract or ethos, that threatened the welfare and stability of the community. The punitive aspect does not detract from the reality that elites used displacement as a weapon to silence rivals and reinforce a preferred social program. Second, most forms of enforced absence

---

186. Mommsen, *Strafrecht*, 967–80; Bauman, *Crime*, 21; Singh-Masuda, "Exilium," 8–9, 188–89, Marcian, *Dig.* 48.19.2, 48.22.6 and 14.

187. Tacitus, *Ann.* 4.13; Strachan-Davidson, *Problems*, 2:65, 67.

188. However, the marriage of a *deportatus* remained valid (Singh-Masuda, "Exilium," 126, 190; Pliny, *Ep.* 4.11.3; Marcian, *Dig.* 32.1.2; 48.20.7).

189. Cohen, "Exile," 70.

190. Singh-Masuda, "Exilium," 191–2.

191. Tacitus, *Ann.* 1.6; 1.53; 6.29; 15.28; Seutonius, *Tib.* 50, 53, 54; *Calig.* 28; *Dom.* 10.2–3; Seneca, *Polyb.* 13.4; Bragington, "Exile," 404–5; Singh-Masuda, "Exilium," 111–14, 177–8, 216–20.

192. Bragington, "Exile," 392.

involved the erasure of a person's official civic status. What appears as dishonor, disgrace, and humiliation from the vantage of socio-cultural institutions and conventions appears as the formal revocation of individuals' official place in the community, further demonstrated by property seizure and prohibition against communal aid.[193] Third, enforced absences often served as a surrogate for the death penalty, linking displacement and death. Fourth, the formal legal aspects of political displacement often retain the concept of a voluntary absence in response to hostility, perhaps most familiar to broad cultural scripts of leaving an ordeal. Those who faced long odds could, in some instances, voluntarily leave a community, often with little to no distinction from those who were formally expelled. Again, it is plausible if not probable that Paul and the Corinthians were familiar with some of these practices, especially those operative in the middle of the first century. Yet, any conclusions must await further study of non-elite political communities.

2.5. Absence as Judgment among Non-Elite, Graeco-Roman Political Communities

Graeco-Roman private or voluntary associations (*collegium*, σύνοδος, πλῆθος, κοινόν, θίασος) supply an important avenue of inquiry. C. F. G. Heinrici originally proposed that the Corinthian churches were constructed along the lines of Greek associations.[194] An impressive number of monographs and theses demonstrate that Heinrici's initial supposition provides a meaningful approach to the study of early Christian communities.[195] Here the scope of study is limited to the practice of exit and absence in conflict as a form of judgment in small, often non-elite social groups. Particularly of interest is whether and to what degree the socio-cultural scripts, political theory, penology described above was present in non-elite strata.

---

193. On the relationship between rank and status, see E. A. Judge, *Rank and Status in the World of the Caesars and St Paul* (Christchurch: University of Canterbury, 1982), 9.

194. C. F. G. Heinrici, "Die Christengemeinden Korinths und die religiösen Genossenschaften der Griechen," *ZWT* 19 (1876): 465–526; cf. E. A. Judge, *The Social Pattern of Christian Groups in the First Century* (London: Tyndale, 1960), 40–8.

195. See now Richard Ascough, "What Are They Now Saying about Christ Groups and Associations?," *CurBR* 13.2 (2015): 207–44.

2.5.1. Associations and Elite Life

While it is true that some people (slaves in particular) in antiquity aspired to exit a community, perhaps as an expression of judgment against intolerable circumstances and those responsible, it is equally true that many non-elites found in associations a necessary, if not desirable, political community.[196] According to Eva Ebel, the majority of urban males either participated in associations or were familiar with their practices.[197] These associations, although largely composed of non-elites, systematically reproduced elite syntax and institutions in non-elite settings.[198] Officially, associational *nomoi* often publicly mimicked structures and laws of the *polis* or empire.[199] Onno van Nijf claims that most members of voluntary associations had little access to official civic life and thus found in voluntary associations an accessible, alternative means to participating

---

196. On flight as a means of avoidance and escape, see Garland, *Wandering*, 145–9; Jerry Toner, *Popular Culture in Ancient Rome* (Malden, MA: Polity, 2009), 171–2. The appeal of exiting a community is implied in the Oracles of Astrampsychus. Inquirers could ask, "Shall I be a fugitive?," "Will my flight be undetected?," and "Am I to be separated from my wife?" Answers according to the oracle-monger included, "You will not see your country," and "Your flight is not to be undetected" (G. M. Browne, *The Papyri of the Sortes Astrampsychi* [Meisenheim am Glan: Verlag Anton Hain, 1974], 22, 36, 56). On evidence for the spatial containment of slaves and debtors, see Sandra R. Joshel, "Geographies of Slave Containment and Movement," in *Roman Slavery and Roman Material Culture*, ed. Michelle George, Phoenix Supplementary 52 (Toronto: University of Toronto Press, 2013), 99–128.

197. Eva Ebel, "Regeln von der Gemeinschaft für die Gemeinschaft? Das Aposteldekret und antike Vereinssatzungen im Vergleich," in *Aposteldekret und antikes Vereinswesen: Gemeinschaft und ihre Ordnung* (Tübingen: Mohr Siebeck, 2011), 317–18.

198. Erich Ziebarth claims, "Der Geschäftsgang war durchaus dem des Staatslebens nachgebildet, wie die Urkundensprache der Vereine zeigt" (*Das griechische Vereinswesen* [Leipzig: Hirzel, 1869], 144); Jean Pierre Waltzing asserts, "Dans la hiérarchie des colleges romains, la cité avait encore servi de modèle. Le municipe ou la colonie avait ses patrons, ses magistrats, son sénat et sa plebe: il en était de meme des colleges" (*Étude historique sur les corporations professionnelles chez les romains depuis les origines jusqu'à la chute de l'Empire d'Occident*, 4 vols. [Louvain: Charles Peeters, 1895–1900], 362); Franz Poland suggests, "daß es in den Verreinen zwar ganz analog den staatlichen Formen herging" (*Geschichte des griechischen Vereinwesens* [Leipzig: Teubner, 1909], 333, see also 424–5); Ramsay MacMullen, *Roman Social Relations: 50 B.C. to A.D. 284* (New Haven, CT: Yale University Press, 1974), 76–7; Grasmück, *Exilium*, 32 n. 120; Konraad Verboven, "The Associative Order: Status and Ethos of Roman Businessmen in [the] Late Republic and Early Empire," *Athenaeum* 95 (2007): 889, and others.

199. Grasmück, *Exilium*, 32.

in a civic forum that offered the same trappings as elite society.[200] For non-elites, Koenraad Verboven writes, "the associations created a social environment with constraints and possibilities that for the vast majority of the population constituted the social order par excellence, forging social identities integrated into urban society but not derived from civic criteria."[201] According to Alicia Batten, the reproduction of elite civic life was more than skin deep, but involved the democratization of elite values.[202] She states, "regulations for life in the association upheld important codes that were connected to broader societal values."[203] The public nature of *nomoi* indicates associations advertised themselves as guarantors of the elite civic order.[204] Such evidence does not indicate civic decline, a lack of attachment to the *polis*, and the compensatory nature of associations, nor that associations were insular from civic life, but rather that associations participated enthusiastically with the political framework, even aggressively appropriating civic honorifics and advertising imperial connections.[205] Thus, sufficient reason exists for understanding associations as occupying a crucial space between elite and non-elite society.[206]

200. Onno van Nijf, *The Civic World of Professional Associations in the Roman East*, DMAHA (Amsterdam: Gieben, 1997), 3–23, 243–7; Philip A. Harland, *Associations, Synagogues, and Congregations: Claiming a Place in Ancient Mediterranean Society* (Minneapolis: Fortress, 2003), 25–53.

201. Verboven, "Associative Order," 871.

202. Alicia Batten, "The Moral World of Greco-Roman Associations," *SR* 36.1 (2007): passim.

203. Batten, "Moral World," 135; see Martial 10.79; Frederick W. Danker, "On Stones and Benefactors," *CTM 86* (1981): 352–3; Lendon, *Honour*, 100–103.

204. Ziebarth, *Vereinswesen*, 177; Grasmück, *Exilium*, 33; John S. Kloppenborg, "The Moralizing of Discourse in Greco-Roman Associations," in *"The One Who Sows Bountifully": Essays in Honor of Stanley K. Stowers*, ed. Caroline Johnson Hodge et al., BJS 356 (Providence, RI: Brown University, 2013), 225–6.

205. Harland, *Claiming a Place*, 89–112, 115–36, 137–60; for further discussion concerning the interpretation of mimicry of elite political culture, see John S. Kloppenborg, "Associations, Christ Groups, and Their Place in the Polis," *ZNW* 108.1 (2017): 12–25.

206. Philip A. Harland, "Connections with Elites in the World of the Early Christians," in *Handbook of Early Christianity: Social Science Approaches*, ed. Anthony J. Blasi, Paul-André Turcotte, and Jean Duhaime (Walnut Creek, CA: Alta Mira, 2002), 385–408; for benefaction as an important connection between elite and association life, see Waltzing, *Corporations professionnelles*, 1:425–46, 299–430; Philip A. Harland, "Associations and the Economics of Group Life: A Preliminary Case Study of Asia Minor and the Aegean Islands," *SEÅ* 80 (2015): 5–10; Verboven, "Associative Order," passim.

2.5.2. Associations: Honor, Competition, Ordeals, and Absences

As microcosms of elite culture, voluntary associations both valued the agonistic spirit and feared internecine strife. On the one hand, association life presented members with a clear hierarchy that one could ascend and a superior community.[207] The opportunity to acquire status among non-elites leads Jon Lendon to conclude *collegia* were "communities of honour" like their elite counterparts.[208] As a representative example, an association devoted to Aphrodite set up an inscription (302/301 BCE) in honor of the leader (ἄρχων) in order to, in part, instruct ambitious members the proper way to rise through the association's ranks.[209] Richard Last demonstrates that officers' activities were heavily surveilled and scrutinized in a manner consistent with δοκιμασία trials in ancient Greek politics.[210] Only after an officer's conduct was thoroughly vetted was s/he publicly recognized.[211] The valorization and memorialization of such behavior, most often involving patronage, both facilitated group survival through reciprocity (honor for support) and also advertised the association's attractiveness to outsiders.[212] Patronage also provided the possibility of gaining competitive honor for the association. The *Iobbochhoi* at Athens (164/165 CE) celebrate the support of Claudius Herodes, well-known orator of the Roman senatorial order. The injection of money into the association moves the association to inscribe νῦν εὐτυχεῖς, νῦν πάντων πρῶτοι | τῶν Βακχείων.[213] Thus, "like everyone else," writes Ramsay Macmullen, "[associations] sought status" both internally and as a community in relation to other associations.[214]

Conversely, competition for honor necessitated ordeals as proving grounds leading to confrontations and ordeals.[215] The clearest evidence is found in extant charters. P.Lond. 7.2193 (ca. 69–58 BCE) evidences

---

207. Waltzing, *Corporations professionnelles*, 1:363–8.
208. Lendon, *Honour*, 97–102.
209. *SIG* 1098; cf. the exaggerated but insightful account in Apuleius, *Met.* 7.9.
210. Richard Last, "Money, Meals, and Honour: The Economic and Honorific Organization of the Corinthian Ekklēsia" (Ph.D. diss., University of Toronto, 2013), 107–10.
211. *IG* 1271.1-14; 1327.4-16; 1329.3-19.
212. Last, "Corinthian Ekklēsia," 150–4.
213. *IG* 1368.27-28.
214. MacMullen, *Roman Social Relations*, 253.
215. See John S. Kloppenborg, "Greco-Roman Thiasoi, the Ekklēsia at Corinth, and Conflict Management," in *Redescribing Paul and the Corinthians*, ed. Ron Cameron and Merrill P. Miller (Atlanta: Society of Biblical Literature, 2011), 187–218; Philip F. Venticinque, "Family Affairs: Guild Regulations and Family Relationships in Roman Egypt," *GRBS* 50 (2010): 273–94.

the presence of enmity culture, recording the possibility of factionalism (σχίματα) as well as infighting, violence within a banquet, spouse stealing, lawsuits, and challenges to the leader's authority. An association from Lanuvium (136 CE) suggests the possibility of disturbances (*seditionis*) by seat stealing and abusive speech[216] and the *Iobbochhoi* at Athens presume a similarly raucous gathering culminating in abuse and requiring the presence of bouncers.[217] The papyri P.Mich. 5.243 (ca. 14–37 CE) acknowledges the possibility of intrigue (ὑπονομεύω) and adultery (οἰκοφθορέω), along with absenteeism (a passive form of aggression), refusal to supply aid to members in distress, and prosecution of a member in public courts.[218] While many of the behaviors are transcultural, from the vantage of an enmity or contest culture, the prohibited actions are reflective of the assertiveness often used to determine one's place in the communal hierarchy. While the by-laws displayed the best of associational order and warned participants to avoid the worst, there is little reason to doubt that competition resulting in affronts occurred. Beyond enmity lexica, the vote to admit members provided an opportunity for exclusion. Robin Lane writes of the Athenian Iobacchoi, "The minor Iobacchus… had his Iobacchic vote and once a month he could exclude the people he hated most from the company which he most enjoyed."[219] If attempts to deprive another of their social space were successful (seat stealing, adultery, challenges to authority, intrigue, voting against rivals), it stands to reason that such a figure would incur shame like that of Apuleius's gardener, Scaurus's son, or Cicero. However, such events would never be memorialized.[220]

As in elite society, associations prioritized concord as a crucial element for group survival. Among the *Iobacchoi*, the frequent references to disturbance (θόρυβος) and disorder (ἀκοσμέω) betray the association's fixation that everything be said and done in all order (πᾶσα εὐκοσμία).[221] The epigraphic record indicates associations valued ὁμόνοια as a virtue among members,[222] leaders,[223] and between communities with translocal

---

216. *CIL* 14.2112.
217. *IG* 1368.
218. Venticinque, "Guild Regulations," 285–8.
219. R. L. Fox, *Pagans and Christians* (Harmondsworth: Viking Penguin, 1986), 88.
220. For a possible instance of *damnatio memoriae*, see Van Nijf, *Associations*, 94, 126–7.
221. *IG* 1368; see also *IG* 1334; *IGR* 4.1430.
222. SEG 33.1165; *IG* 4985.
223. IDidyma 486.

ties.²²⁴ The need for concord and obedience to the *nomoi* was two-fold. Positively, concord allowed for the establishment of trust necessary for the joint ventures undertaken in associations.²²⁵ As well, concord made unlikely the threat of Roman intervention.²²⁶

Although the epigraphic record is formal, official, and incomplete, when competition and enmity led to a breakdown in concord, absences in which socially weak, overpowered, and defeated individuals exited were likely the result. A snapshot of such absences appears from the non-elite text, Artimedorus's *Oneirocritica* (second century CE):²²⁷ "A man dreamt that he had a mouth and large, beautiful teeth in his rectum through which he spoke...and did everything that is usually done by a mouth. Because of certain unguarded remarks, the man had to flee his homeland and went into exile."²²⁸ The outcome of the dream reflects the possibility among non-elites of enmity and affront resulting in absence. We are thus on solid ground to conclude that associations were rife with kinds of enmities and ordeals that aimed at or resulted in the informal displacement of individual as found in elite sources.

2.5.3. *Enforced Absences: Temporary Exclusions and Permanent Expulsions*

The official nature of *nomoi* supplies a more complete accounting of enforced absences. Associations employed enforced absences for the most serious offences against the community. The range of punishments involved fines, temporary exclusions, and expulsions. Plenary gatherings often adjudicated punishments indicating the autonomy of associational quasi-legal apparatuses.²²⁹ The most common form of group discipline for

---

224. SEG 26.826.

225. *Nomoi* fostered "an ethos of trust and solidarity that no doubt functioned as an instrument of recruitment" (Kloppenborg, "Moralizing of Discourse," 226; cf. Venticinque, "Guild Regulations," 285–92).

226. Waltzing, *Corporations professionnelles*, 1:115–16; Sarolta A. Takács, "Politics and Religion in the Bacchanalian Affair of 186 B.C.E.," *HSCP 100* (2000): 301–10; Venticinque, "Guild Regulations," 287–8; cf. Tacitus, *Ann.* 14.17; on the overvaluing of elite sources on this topic, see the important discussion by Harland, *Claiming a Place*, 161–73.

227. Arthur S. Ousley, "Notes of Artemidorus' 'Oneirocritica,'" *CJ 592* (1963): 66–7.

228. Artemidorus, *The Interpretation of Dreams: Oneirocritica*, trans. R. J. White (New Jersey: Noyes, 1975), 5:68.

229. Ilias Arnaoutoglou, "Roman Law and Collegia in Asia Minor," *RIDA* 49 (2002): 43. Such evidence supports Harland's larger thesis that many associations

violating *nomoi* was the fine, providing an important stream of revenue for associations.[230] For more serious offences, associations utilized temporary exclusions, often to extract unpaid fines or dues and permanent expulsion, thus terminating a revenue stream.[231] Undoubtedly, inasmuch as associations provided non-elites with the opportunity to acquire status, discipline involved the reduction or removal of communal standing. In the Greek period, this was made explicit in the disenfranchisement (ἄτιμος ἔστω) of a member who failed to pay a fine in the Delphic phratry of Labyadia.[232] While the fine was the main strategy to limit disorder, Kloppenborg observes the increased role of exclusions and expulsions in the first century BCE and the first two centuries CE.[233]

The *Iobbachoi*, although an elite association, provide excellent evidence of expulsionary practices.[234] For absenteeism, often an indication of factional intentions, and refusal to pay the fine, the offender was severed (ἐργαθεῖν) from the gatherings. The same fate befell those who did not pay the entry fee, those who assaulted another member, those who reported

---

were integrated into the larger civic structure, rather than heavily regulated and monitored as potentially subversive. See Harland, *Claiming a Place*, 161–73; contra Richard Ascough, *Paul's Macedonian Associations*, WUNT 2/161 (Tübingen: Mohr Siebeck, 2003), 42–6. Ascough follows the traditional understanding of associations as externally regulated and monitored. Welborn follows Ascough and others claiming that the church court system in Corinth thus could only adjudicate, "the most trivial of civil offences" (*End to Enmity*, 42). For evidence that associations adjudicated issues of theft, see P.Dem.Lille 29.9-10, 25-26; P.Dem.Berlin 3115 D 1.5-7; for violence, see P. Dem.Lille 29.13-14, 21-22; P.Dem.Cairo 30606.8, 20-21, 24-25; P.Dem.Cairo 31179.24-26; P.Lond. 2710.15-16; P.Mich. 5.243.3; *CIL* 14.2112; *ILS* 7212.2.25-28; *SIG* 3.1109.72-91; for adultery, see P.Dem.Lille 29.25; P.Dem.Cairo 31179.22; P. Mich. 5.243.8, from Yonder Moynihan Gillihan, *Civic Ideology, Organization, and the Law in the Rule Scrolls: A Comparative Study of the Covenanters' Sect and Contemporary Voluntary Associations in Political Context*, ed. Florentino García Martínez, STDJ 97 (Boston: Brill, 2012), 88 n. 35. See also Verboven, "Associative Order," 886. For evidence of special juridical gatherings, see P.Dem.Cairo 30606; *ILS* 7212.1.26–2.2; *IG* 2.1275; *IG* 2.1369; SEG 31.122; *IG* 1368.

230. Poland, *Geschichte*, 492–8; Harland, "Economics of Group Life," 9–16.

231. Ziebarth, *Vereinswesen*, 172; Poland, *Geschichte*, 448; Grasmück, *Exilium*, 32–3.

232. *CID* 1.9B.40-45.

233. Kloppenborg, "Disaffiliation," 10–11; contra Eva Ebel, *Die Attraktivität früher christlicher Gemeinden: Die Gemeinde von Korinth im Spiegel griechisch-römischer Vereine*, WUNT 2/178 (Tübingen: Mohr Siebeck, 2004), 185–7, who argues that expulsions from associations were largely nonexistent across antiquity.

234. *IG* 2.1368.A.

the assault to public courts, or officials who failed to expel the assailant. During a gathering, the presiding officer was furnished with a wand (θύρσος) to place upon a disorderly person, who would be dismissed from the ritual, by force if necessary.

Similarly, the association of the *Heroistai*, dated to first century BCE, punished failure to pay a fine with temporary exclusion.[235] An association linked to Bendis excluded members for violating an entrenchment clause.[236] Another association, dated to the second-century CE, offer the following *nomoi*: "But if anyone of those should be seen where fighting or disturbances [θόρυβος] occur, he shall be expelled [ἐκβάλλω] from the club, being fined twenty-five Attic drachmae or being punished with double the blows in addition to judgment."[237]

Likewise, for the Herakliasts near Athens (ca. 100 CE), the penalty for fighting included a vote (ψῆφον?) to expel (ἐκβιβάζω) the perpetrator and the imposition of fine. Failure to pay this fine resulted in permanent expulsion (ἐξέρανος) and thus the removal of association rank.[238] The association of Sebek at Tebtynis (157 BCE) agreed that if a member falsely accused another of being a leper, "his fine is 100 *debens* and they shall expel him from the House."[239] The same two-phase punishment befell an adulterer in another Egyptian association (147 BCE).[240] In the fragmentary inscription IEph 1386, dated to the first century CE, violation of a rule results in a two-stage punishment, a fine and then expulsion, potentially accompanied by a curse.[241] In an association in Philadelphia, illicit sexual behavior resulted in exclusion or perhaps expulsion.[242]

While the best epigraphic evidence is found in Attica, Kloppenborg argues, "there is no good reason to doubt that other associations in Asia, Syria, Egypt, North Africa, Italy and elsewhere adopted practices to control conflict and dissent."[243] His argument is bolstered by the presence of a dream concerning association life in *Oneirocritica*:

---

235. *IG* 2.1339.5–15, 57; see Kloppenborg, "Disaffiliation," 11.
236. *IG* 2.1361.13–15.
237. *IG* 2.1369.40–44, trans. Kloppenborg, "Disaffiliation," 11.
238. SEG 31.122.
239. P.Dem.Cairo 30606, trans. Kloppenborg, from Harland, "Regulations of a Demotic Cult Association," *Associations in the Greco-Roman World*, 2015, http://www.philipharland.com/greco-roman-associations/?p=2984.
240. P.Dem.Cairo 31179.22.
241. IEph 1386.3–5.
242. *SIG* 985.25–50.
243. Kloppenborg, "Disaffiliation," 12.

Someone who belonged to a club and a phratry dreamt that he lifted up his clothes in front of his fellow club members and urinated on each one of them. He was expelled (ἀπελαύνω) from the phratry for being unworthy of it. For it is understandable that those who act in such a drunken manner should be hated and expelled (ἀπελαύνω).[244]

The dream and its outcome alongside the evidence above suggest that exit and absence in the context of conflict implied or embodied a form of judgment in non-elite associational life like that of elite political culture.

For those who found themselves driven from an association, either through personal affront or the legal machinery of the community, the result, according to Kloppenborg, would have been a non-elite form of social death. The possibility of erasure from the role "evoke the anxiety of oblivion, of never having been there at all." The loss of status and rank also involved the elimination of an important source of economic support and security.

2.5.4. Conclusions

The evidence suggests that non-elite private associations largely metabolized and appropriated elements of the larger socio-political superstructure and disciplinary apparatus. By reproducing elite values, associations provided non-elites with the arena for the acquisition of elite-like honor through ordeals. Unsurprisingly, strife and enmities developed, in which foes undoubtedly aimed to undermine and remove their opponents. The epigraphic and papyrological records indicate that associations prioritized harmony, and thus fined, excluded, and expelled members whose behavior contributed to the breakdown of the community.

2.6. Second Temple Political Communities

Carved into nearly every page of the Old Testament are the marks of displacement. While individuals might have fled or fought during certain events as in the bardic tradition, cosmic and national exile permeate the Hebrew Scriptures and exist inextricably tied to Israel's purity maps. Distinct from the Graeco-Roman tradition, this displacement focused not upon individual flight, but upon national expulsion. And national exile is not due to civic unrest or superior foes, but due to covenantal breach against Israel's divine king, YHWH.[245] Various Jewish communities

---

244. Artemidorus, *Oneir.* 4.44.
245. White, *Discipline*, 114–15.

inherited and appropriated this tradition within a covenantal framework to nourish a unique identity during the complexities of the second temple period.

All discussions of displacement among pre-rabbinical, second temple communities are indebted to William Horbury, whose seminal article demonstrates that offences warranting the covenantal death penalty were consistently reinterpreted and appropriated as extirpation.[246] Horbury argues the headwaters of this reinterpretation begin in Ezra 10:8 in which Ezra threatens those who absent themselves from communal summons will have their property *ḥerem*-ed and will be "separated [נדל] from the community of exiles."[247] Horbury also cites Josephus's account of the Shechamites who received Jews banished from Jerusalem, whose offences were capital in nature and the account in 3 Maccabees of apostate Jews from Alexandria, whom the faithful shunned and refused to render aid (3 Macc. 2:33).[248]

2.6.1. Dead Sea Communities

Due to the healthy skepticism about the pre-70 CE polity of the Pharisees, the best evidence in Israel comes from the Dead Sea. Enforced absences are evident among the Dead Sea communities, which have also been analyzed both as voluntary associations and salient analogies to Pauline churches.[249] The basic term at Qumran for expulsion from the community is שָׁלַח, the same verb used for Adam's expulsion from the Garden (Gen. 3:23).[250]

Where execution would be the expected ruling, expulsion was the prescription. In the Damascus Document, the clear demand for execution of the Sabbath-breaker in Num. 15:35 is met with the updated ruling, "he shall not be put to death."[251] The expulsion liturgy in 4QD^a fr. 11 5c-18 supplies an apt example in which capital crimes were penalized by expulsion in a ceremony accompanied by curses.[252] With implications for disciplinary practices in Corinth (1 Cor. 5:1-13), Horbury claims that

---

246. Horbury, "Extirpation and Excommunication," *VT* 35.1 (1985): 13–38.
247. Horbury, "Extirpation and Excommunication," 14, 19, 21.
248. Horbury, "Extirpation and Excommunication," 22–3.
249. Gillihan, *Rule Scrolls*, and others.
250. Horbury, "Extirpation and Excommunication," 23.
251. CD 12.4-6, translated by Horbury, "Extirpation and Excommunication," 28.
252. "And all [17] [those who dwell] in Camps shall assemble in the third month, and they shall curse the one who turns to the right [18] [or to the left from th]e Torah. 4 QDa fr. 11.17-18, trans. Gillihan, *Rule Scrolls*, 270–1, cf. 392.

concerning the prescription for the death penalty, whereas the MT reads, "you shall purge the evil from your midst," the LXX sometimes and regularly in the Targums Onkelos, Pseudo-Jonathan, and the Sifre, read "the evil man" (Deut. 13:6[5]).[253] Aharon Shemesh, likewise, argues that the Covenanters offered a sectarian *halakic* interpretation of the biblical punishment of כרת as permanent expulsion, rather than its standard interpretation, execution.[254] Like the visible nature of membership in other ancient communities, White highlights that members' conduct was scrutinized and names were recorded in a scroll.[255] Members who were expelled from the community or left would be removed from the roll.[256]

2.6.2. *Diaspora Communities*

Most Jews remained in the Diaspora from which we possess sparse evidence. Alongside the account of the shunning practice of Alexandrian Jews, other evidence from the diaspora supports pre-rabbinical forms of displacement. Horbury draws attention to Philo, who, after praising the Phineas's execution of Zimri, states the Moses merely banished the diviners in Deut. 28:10, when they were sentenced to death according to Lev. 20:6, 27.[257]

The strongest evidence of this emerges from the diasporic reaction against the Christian mutation of Judaism. The Fourth Gospel, with its likely Asia Minor provenance, refers three times (Jn 9:22; 12:42; 16:2) to the notion of characters—and by extension the audience—as being expelled from the synagogue (ἀποσυνάγωγος) as deviant Jews (cf. Jn 9:34). As Johannine communities continued and encountered internecine power struggles, they soon embraced their own practices of banishment and shunning (1 Jn 2:19; 2 Jn 10; 3 Jn 10).

Paul himself refers to being banished (ἐκδιώκω) and censored in speaking to Gentiles by certain, local Jews (1 Thess. 2:16). In one sense, this may refer to a final step in the synagogue disciplinary process in which a figure found guilty five times and punished with thirty-nine

---

253. Horbury, "Extirpation and Excommunication," 28.
254. Aharon Shemesh, "Expulsion and Exclusion in the Community Rule and the Damascus Document," *DSD* 9.1 (2002): 59–63; cf. James T. South, *Disciplinary Practices in Pauline Texts* (Lewiston, NY: Mellen, 1992), 50–1; see CD 12.4-6.
255. White, *Discipline*, 121; 1QS 2.19-22.
256. CD 19–20; see White, *Discipline*, 121.
257. Philo, *Spec. Leg.* 1.60; see Horbury, "Extirpation and Excommunication," 29.

lashes was finally expelled from the synagogue.[258] A second possibility is that Paul simply refers to a generic event, one lacking the official marks of synagogue expulsion.[259] If the passage is authentic, it is more likely, with the reference to preaching to Gentiles, that Paul refers to the specific instance of unofficial banishment from Thessalonica (not unlike the narration in Acts 17:1-10).[260] Paul refers to the visit to Thessalonica resulting in banishment as comprising a great ordeal (ἀγών, 2:2) and the resulting exit seems to have touched an apologetic nerve for the apostle (1 Thess. 2:1-20).

The greatest amount of evidence emerges from the small, elite communities represented by the writings at Qumran, while the least evidence is found concerning the diaspora practices. The use of expulsion as a surrogate for the death penalty evokes similar practices in elite Graeco-Roman political communities. That practice is tied genealogically to the Old Testament, but it also fits within a broader punitive matrix and appears intelligible across a wide swath of ancient communities. Like evidence from other communities, second temple communities marked deviance and demonstrated power, in part, through socio-spatial judgments, including official expulsion, shunning, and popular expulsions.

2.7. Conflict, Absence, and Judgment in Paul's Corinthian Ἐκκλησία

While the evidence from voluntary associations and second temple communities supports the existence of political displacement, such epigraphic and papyrological evidence is biased towards a few locations, such as Qumran, Athens, Rome, Ostia (epigraphic), and Egypt (papyrological). Thus, caution is required. There is no methodological warrant to subsume all similar social groupings under the same rubric asserting the presence of the same social phenomena, nor is their warrant to assume *a priori* Paul's Corinthian ἐκκλησία either shared such a broad view or distinguished itself as taxonomically different in this area.[261] While the evidence suggests a general substrate linking conflict, absence, and judgment, the question remains whether Paul's Corinthian ἐκκλησία connected absence with judgment in a complementary way.

258. John M. G. Barclay, *Jews in the Mediterranean Diaspora: From Alexander to Trajan (323 BCE–117 CE)* (Berkeley: University of California Press, 1996), 394.

259. Carol J. Schlueter, *Filling Up the Measure: Polemical Hyperbole in 1 Thessalonians 2.14-16*, JSNTSup 98 (Sheffield: JSOT, 1994), 72–3.

260. Todd D. Still, *Conflict at Thessalonica: A Pauline Church and Its Neighbours*, JSNTSup 183 (Sheffield: Sheffield Academic, 1999), 126–49.

261. See now Kloppenborg, "Place in the Polis," 28.

First Corinthians 5:1-13 is as fascinating as it is a labyrinth of controversy. The passage breaks easily into two main units (5:1-8, 9-13). The first unit involves the punishment of single offender (5:1-5) and the grounds for the punishment (5:6-8) and the second unit (5:9-13) corrects an errant interpretation of the Previous Letter simultaneously providing a general principle for punishments of future offenders.[262] Contextually, the passage belongs to the broader segment 5:1–6:20, which form particular test cases of Paul's authority to order communal life, notably while absent (see 4:18-21).[263] A fundamental question is, to what sanction does Paul refer in 5:1-5 and how does it relate to Paul's generalized principle in 5:9-13?

2.7.1. Displacement in Corinth

The nature of the punishment demanded in 1 Cor. 5:1-5 supplies a notorious crux for interpreters. From the perspective of analogous political communities, perhaps most surprising is the trajectory of research. In fact, the study of discipline in Pauline communities in general and 1 Corinthians 5 almost entirely overlooks the foregoing evidence, save Qumran.[264] Accordingly, interpreters often argue between the punitive action resulting in curse/death[265] or the temporary exclusion of the

---

262. South, *Disciplinary Practices*, 60; Jacob Kremer, *Der erste Brief an die Korinther*, RNT (Regensburg: F. Pustet, 1997), 99–111, and others.

263. Gordon Fee, *The First Epistle to the Corinthians*, NICNT (Grand Rapids: Eerdmans, 1987), 194.

264. White, *Discipline*, 2–4.

265. Ernst Käsemann, "Sentences of Holy Law in New Testament," in *New Testament Questions of Today*, trans. W. J. Montague, 2nd edn (London: SCM, 1969), 70–1; Bruce, *I & II Corinthians*, 54–5; Göran Forkman, *Limits of the Religious Community: Expulsion from the Religious Community within the Qumran Sect, within Rabbinic Judaism, and within Primitive Christianity*, ConBNT 5 (Lund: Gleerup, 1972), 144, 146–7; Calvin Roetzel, *Judgement in the Community: A Study of the Relationship Between Eschatology and Ecclesiology in Paul* (Leiden: Brill, 1972), 120–4; J. D. M. Derrett, "'Handing Over to Satan': An Explanation of 1 Cor 5:1-7," *RIDA* 21 (1979): 22; Adela Yarbro Collins, "The Function of 'Excommunication' in Paul," *HTR* 73 (1980): 251–63; Gerald Harris, "The Beginnings of Church Discipline: 1 Corinthians 5," *NTS* 37 (1991): 17; Hans von Campenhausen, *Ecclesiastical Authority and Spiritual Power in the Church of the First Three Centuries*, trans. J. A. Baker, 2nd edn (Peabody, MA: Hendrickson, 1997), 134–5; David Raymond Smith, *"Hand This Man over to Satan": Curse, Exclusion, and Salvation in 1 Corinthians 5*, ed. Mark Goodacre, LNTS 386 (London: T&T Clark, 2008), 178–80; Dieter Zeller, *Der erste Brief an die Korinther*, KEK 5 (Göttingen: Vandenhoeck & Ruprecht, 2010), 202.

offender.²⁶⁶ Both arguments have merit but ultimately leave much to be desired.

Those who rightly question the curse/death thesis highlight the improbability that 1 Cor. 5:5 refers to the offender's death. The final purpose clause in 1 Cor. 5:5, ἵνα τὸ πνεῦμα σωθῇ ἐν τῇ ἡμέρᾳ τοῦ κυρίου, appears to have the offender's restoration in view.²⁶⁷ There remains debate about whether τὸ πνεῦμα belongs to the man,²⁶⁸ the community,²⁶⁹ or both.²⁷⁰ Importantly, we should add to the discussion that displacement, as shown above, functioned primarily to save the community, a sentiment that rises to the surface in 1 Cor. 5:6-8. Whatever the view, it is unlikely that Paul views the death of the man to affect salvific (σῴζω) aims, whether for the offender or the community.²⁷¹ Conversely, given Paul's use of the σάρξ/πνεῦμα binary—the former term often refers to a complete orientation away from God—it is unlikely that the preceding phrase εἰς ὄλεθρον τῆς σαρκός refers to physical death.²⁷²

The evidence from the social world makes the death penalty even more unlikely. Analogous voluntary social formations did not conduct capital punishment in antiquity.²⁷³ Moreover, the penalty for incest was

---

266. G. W. H. Lampe, "Church Discipline," in Farmer, Moule, and Niebuhr, eds., *Christian History and Interpretation*, 349–53; Fee, *First Epistle*, 210–14; Judith Gundry Volf, *Paul and Perseverance: Staying In and Falling Away*, WUNT 2/37 (Tübingen: Mohr Siebeck, 1990), 113–20; South, *Disciplinary Practices*, 43–65; Witherington, *Conflict and Community in Corinth*, 158–9; Martin, *Corinthian Body*, 174; Brian Rosner, "'Drive out the Wicked Person': A Biblical Theology of Exclusion," *EvQ* 71.1 (1999): 30–4; Thiselton, *First Epistle*, 396; Matthias Konradt, *Gericht und Gemeinde: Eine Studie zur Bedeutung und Funktion von Gerichtsaussagen im Rahmen der paulinischen Ekklesiologie und Ethik im 1 Thess und 1 Kor*, BZNW 117 (New York: de Gruyter, 2003), 315–17; Robert Moses, "Physical and/or Spiritual Exclusion? Ecclesial Discipline in 1 Corinthians 5," *NTS* 59 (2013): 172–91.

267. Fee, *First Epistle*, 208 nn. 66, 67, who argues that εἰς supplies the result not the purpose of the act.

268. Thiselton, *First Epistle*, 399.

269. Collins, "Excommunication," 260.

270. Martin, *Corinthian Body*, 174.

271. Konradt, *Gericht und Gemeinde*, 316.

272. Fee, *First Epistle*, 212; Rosner, "Drive Out," 32–3; cf. Rom. 5:16-24; 8:5-17.

273. The more severe penalties did not likely entail execution, but curses (*LSAM* 19; *SIG* 985). The clearest reference to execution is in *SIG* 997, in which violations of

relegatio ad insulum in the principate.²⁷⁴ Finally, a curse pronouncement, although grammatically ambiguous but historically plausible, is unreliable evidence for the death penalty. Curses were ubiquitous in antiquity and did not necessitate the death of the target.²⁷⁵ Importantly, curses accompanied exiles and expulsion liturgies.²⁷⁶ Deviations from definitions of the proper community incurred a curse which was accompanied by the standard range of punitive actions.²⁷⁷ Similarly, when Paul "curses" as he likely does in 1 Cor. 16:22, it does not imply physical death.²⁷⁸ There, Paul uses ἀνάθεμα, the term used in the LXX to translate חֵרֶם about half of the time (e.g. Deut. 13:16[15]). Elsewhere, Paul employs ἀνάθεμα in exclusionary contexts (Gal. 1:8-9; Rom. 9:3). Once again, there was a broad trend and particular Jewish practice of employing expulsion as a surrogate for capital cases.

While enigmatic, it remains likely that the final-purpose clause refers primarily to the community's restoration and plausibly, also, to the man's repentant return. South states, "the offender is to be thrust out of the community and into the realm where Satan rules. By this act, presumably, he will come to see the awful consequences of letting 'the flesh' rule his life and will repent."²⁷⁹ However, the ambiguous possibility of return cannot be equated with temporary exclusion. No conditions—payment of fines, restitution—are given as in associational *nomoi*,²⁸⁰ nor is the length of time

---

the sacred fish or tackle resulted in the offender being thrown into the sacred fishpond to "perish in terrible destruction by being eaten by fish." Here, the evidence exists as a threat to deter certain behavior whereas 1 Cor. 5:3-5 is a prescription. See Batten, "Moral World," 138–9.

274. Andrew D. Clarke, *Secular and Christian Leadership in Corinth: A Socio-Historical and Exegetical Study of 1 Corinthians 1–6* (Leiden: Brill, 1993), 77.

275. John G. Gager, ed., *Curse Tablets and Binding Spells from the Ancient World* (New York: Oxford University Press, 1992), 21–2.

276. 4QDa fr. 11.17–18; Plato, *Leg.* 881d–e; 909c, 955b.

277. Group-oriented curses are found in the ancient context of civic constitutions (Plato, *Leg.* 9.871B; *SIG* 987.35-36; *GDI* 5653C.10-12), association regulations (*AGRW* 121; *IGR* 3.137, *AGRW* 299, IDelos 1520.53-69), and potsherds used in Athenian ostracisms (Forsdyke, *Exile*, 156–8).

278. See now John Fotopoulos, "Paul's Curse of the Corinthians: Restraining Rivals with Fear and Voces Mysticae (1 Cor 16:22)," *NovT* 56 (2014): 275–309.

279. South, *Disciplinary Practices*, 55.

280. Kloppenborg, "Disaffiliation," 10–12.

specified as with DSS.²⁸¹ Ebel, who compares 5:1-13 to *nomoi*, concurs, "Diese Maßnahme ist...keinesfalls als ein vorübergehender Aschluß zu deuten."²⁸² Despite the optimism of some interpreters, as South concedes, there is in fact, "no guarantee that expulsion will have the desired effect."²⁸³ Thus, the sanction is best described as an indefinite expulsion.

2.7.2. Death and Displacement in Corinth

The evidence stressed by the advocates of the curse/death interpretation points to expulsion, rather than the death sentence or temporary exclusion. A certain deathliness broods over 1 Cor. 5:1-13. Ernst Käsemann's interpretation highlights this approach, claiming, "'handing over to Satan,' is identical with exclusion from the community," only to claim the phrase "obviously entails the death of the guilty."²⁸⁴ Supporters of the curse/death interpretation draw attention to the term ὄλεθρος in 5:5.²⁸⁵ Ὄλεθρος and its cognates often refer to death in the LXX (Exod. 12:23; Josh. 3:10; 7:25; Jer. 2:30). However, it also was used with a metaphorical reference for exile (Jer. 5:6; Ezek. 6:14). Turning to 5:9-13, the six vices in 5:11, *sans* πλεονέκτης, likely draws from six passages in Deuteronomy that call for the death penalty for serious breaches of covenant fidelity.²⁸⁶ Paul leaves little doubt of this link in 5:13b as he employs the modified quotation "remove the evildoer from among you," an adapted imperative for the death penalty in many Deuteronomic texts and elsewhere.²⁸⁷

Yet, the deathliness of the passage is best explained by the use of enforced absences as a surrogate for the death penalty in Second Temple Judaism and across Graeco-Roman antiquity (§2.4; §2.6). As discussed above, across the Second Temple period, the death penalty was routinely replaced with expulsion.²⁸⁸ It is instructive that the LXX can use verbal form of ὄλεθρος (ολεθρεύω) to translate חָרַם to refer the death penalty for idolatry (Exod. 22:19[20]). Paul both refers to the punishment of the

---

281. 1QS 6.25–7.25; 4Q 266/270; cf. Shemesh, "Expulsion and Exclusion," 59; Horbury, "Extirpation and Excommunication," 28.

282. Ebel, *Gemeinden*, 185.

283. South, *Disciplinary Practices*, 65; cf. Gundry Volf, *Perseverance*, 116.

284. Käsemann, "Holy Law," 71.

285. Fee, *First Epistle*, 55.

286. Deut. 12:1-5; 17:2-7; 19:16-20; 21:18-21; 22:21-30; 24:7; Brian Rosner, *Paul, Scripture and Ethics: A Study of 1 Corinthians 5–7* (Leiden: Brill, 1994), 69.

287. Rosner, "Drive Out," 27; see Deut. 13:6; 17:7; 19:19; 21:21; 24:7; Judg. 20:13.

288. Shemesh, "Expulsion and Exclusion," 59–63; cf. South, *Disciplinary Practices*, 50–1; see CD 12.4-6.

incestuous man with the term ὄλεθρος (5:5) and specifies that an εἰδωλολάτρης is to be punished by means other than death (5:11). This suggests that expulsion served as a surrogate for the death penalty in Corinth. Furthermore, similar to the offence in 1 Cor. 5:1-8, the punishment for fornication was expulsion in the Damascus Document[289]—one of the five specific expulsion-worthy offences of the Community Rule.[290] Finally, Horbury observes that Paul's interpretive translation of the conclusion for the prescription of the death penalty in 5:13 follows a Palestinian tradition in which expulsion replaced death.[291] Such a tradition would be largely intelligible from the broader Graeco-Roman phenomena associated with an enforced absence.

In 5:9-13, Paul supplies the clearest indication of a broader communal penology in Corinth. Using rare imperatival infinitives in 5:10 and 11, Paul prohibits the community from associating (συναναμείγνυμι) or dining with (συνεσθίω) offenders who falls under the rubric of the vice-list (5:11). Some commentators make a distinction between the punitive action prescribed in 5:3-5 and thus make a minimalist interpretation of the prohibition in 5:11, suggesting it involved a brief avoidance,[292] or partial expulsion.[293] Others understand the prohibition to be exhaustive.[294]

The answer lies in the relationship between 5:1-8 and 9-13. In 5:9-13, Paul generalizes the acute case in 5:1-5. As James South claims, μὴ συναναμίγνυσθαι...μηδὲ συνεσθίειν must be interpreted within the wider context. He asserts, "Vv 9-13 show that this was not Paul's reaction to a specific case, but rather the application of what he had taught them before, of a principle that applied to other forms of deviant behavior as well."[295] The use of the qualitative, demonstrative pronoun, τοιοῦτος in 5:5 indicates, according to Jerome Murphy-O'Connor, the exemplary nature of the case.[296] That Paul generalizes a host of deviant behaviors with the

---

289. "And the one who approaches his wife for fornication which is not according to the law shall leave and not return again" (4Q270 7 i 12-13), trans. Shemesh, "Expulsion and Exclusion," 63 n. 41.

290. Shemesh, "Expulsion and Exclusion," 63, 70; Gillihan hypothesizes that because in biblical law כרת possessed ambiguity (i.e. how to fulfill it), the *halakic* interpretation provided clarity (*Rule Scrolls*, 221).

291. Horbury, "Extirpation and Excommunication," 28.

292. von Campenhausen, *Ecclesiastical Authority*, 134–5.

293. Forkman, *Limits*, 150.

294. Lampe, "Church Discipline," 342–3; cf. F. W. Grosheide, *Commentary on the First Epistle to the Corinthians: The English Text with Introduction, Exposition and Notes*, NICNT (Grand Rapids: Eerdmans, 1953), 129–30; Zeller, *Erste Brief*, 208.

295. South, *Disciplinary Practices*, 60.

296. Murphy-O'Connor, "I Corinthians, V, 3-5," *RB* 84 (1977): 244.

same pronoun, τοιοῦτος, in 5:11 suggests that Paul in fact wishes to apply the consequences of the πόρνος (5:9) to the behaviors denoted on the vice list. Likewise, the descriptions of the offender in 5:1 and those referred to in the vice lists (5:10-11; cf. 6:9-10) share similarities.[297] Whereas Paul refers to the offender in 5:1 with the present tense ἔχειν (5:1), indicating the habituated nature of the offence,[298] so too Paul refers to the stereotypical offender in the vice-lists with the nominative, singular and plural forms respectively. The grammatical form has not been lost on exegetes, who frequently conclude that the nominative form denotes a type of person manifesting habituated, deviant character.[299] Thus, the imperatival infinitives in 5:11 parallel the imperatival infinitive in 5:5 such that παραδοῦναι = μὴ συναναμίγνυσθαι/συνεσθίειν.

Considering the likely generalization in 5:9-13 of the acute case in 5:1-8, the prohibitions to not eat with nor associate with those on the vice list reinforce the likelihood that Paul prescribes expulsion for both the offender and as a general policy for other deviants. Rather than interpret 5:9-13 as a separate, less serious case, it is important to observe the connection between the verbs indicating spatial removal by the verbs αἴρω (5:2), ἐκκαθαίρω (5:7), ἐξαίρω (5:13) and the infinitives indicating social withdrawal (5:11).

Spatial exclusion and social withdrawal were complementary aspects of political displacement across antiquity. In Athens, citizens were neither to eat with, nor associate with, exiles, for fear of bringing a curse into the wider community:

---

297. A generation ago, Paul's vice catalogues were assumed to be the cultural reproduction of ancient moralists detached from the epistolary occasion (Hans Conzelmann, *1 Corinthians: A Commentary on the First Epistle to the Corinthians*, trans. James W. Leitch, Hermeneia [Philadelphia: Fortress, 1975], 100–101). This position has been challenged and replaced by a number of studies that demonstrate the offences were actual behaviors present in the community (Peter S. Zaas, "Catalogues and Context: 1 Corinthians 5 and 6," *NTS* 34 [1988]: 622–9; B. J. Oropeza, "Situational Immorality? The Relevance of Paul's 'Vice Lists' for the Corinthian Congregation," *ExpTim* 110.1 [1988]: 9–10).

298. Chow, *Patronage and Power*, 132.

299. "These 'vices' are indeed listed as *characteristics*, or *continuous practices*, as against lapses from which an offender subsequently turns away" (Thiselton, *First Epistle*, 413, see 439; see Fee, *First Epistle*, 225–6). Ebel claims the nominatives refer to "character qualities and behavior even outside the meetings" (*Gemeinden*, 183, my translation.). Ebel notices that the lists of prohibited, deviant behaviors shared many similarities with associational *nomoi* save the use of nouns rather than participles or conditional constructions (*Gemeinden*, 182–83).

And if any free man voluntarily eat or drink or hold any similar intercourse with such a one, or even give him merely a greeting when he meets him, he shall not enter any holy place or the market or any part of the city until he be purified, but he shall regard himself as having incurred a share of contagious guilt.[300]

Romans were prohibited from aiding exiles under pain of death.[301] Similarly, the Covenanters forbade support of expelled members for capital crimes:

And the expelled man shall depart. Anyone who shares food from their property, or inquires about his welfare, or accompanies him, let his deed be recorded by the authority of the Examiner with an engraving instrument, and his judgment will be complete.[302]

For those technically under the death penalty, similar prohibitions among second temple Jews included prohibitions against participating in the Passover (Exod. 12:43 in Tg. Onq. and Tg. Ps.-J.), receiving aid because of an enemy (Exod. 23:5 in Tos. B.M. 2.33), or offering an oblation (Lev. 1:2 in Tg. Ps.-J and Sifra).[303]

Paul is not prescribing limits to interaction beyond which social intercourse is acceptable.[304] The separation—for both the offender and other deviants—is to be totalizing and represents a rejection of membership.[305] Paul's communities and other analogous associations could not spatially displace someone from a sphere beyond communal gatherings. To police the interaction of members beyond the confines of the gathering indicates that the punishment involves a complete withdrawal of relations.[306] This would be comparable to the most severe form of punishment to be handed out by a voluntary association. Thus, social withdrawal (μὴ συναναμίγνυσθαι/συνεσθίειν) is the surrogate to the death sentence in Paul's Corinth.

---

300. Plato, *Leg.* 881d-e; cf. 909c, 955b.

301. *Prisc. Inst. Gramm.* 8.4.16; Cicero, *Planc.* 97; *Fam.* 14.4.2; Paulus, *Sententiae* 5.26.3; see Kelly, *Exile*, 30, 38; Strachan-Davidson, *Problems*, 1:36.

302. 4QDa fr. 11:14c-16b trans. Gillihan, *Rule Scrolls*, 271.

303. Horbury, "Extirpation and Excommunication," 29.

304. Contra Wolfgang Schrage, *Der erste Brief an die Korinther*, 4 vols., EKKNT 7 (Neukirchen-Vluyn: Neukirchener, 1991), 1:386; cf. Fee, *First Epistle*, 226.

305. Lampe "Church Discipline," 342–3; Kremer, *Erste Brief*, 109.

306. For the devastating effects of expulsion, see Harris, "Church Discipline," 16–17.

2.7.3. An Eschatological and Identifiable Approach to Judgment

The socio-spatializing of judgment is evident elsewhere in the immediate context of 1 Corinthians (see §3.3). In a similar vice-list in 1 Cor. 6:9-10, Paul, twice employing metaphor of eschatological disinheritance, claims that behaviors in the vice-list result in a future exclusion from the Kingdom of God (6:9, 11).[307] Paul does not press the logic of punitive action, presumably since he has already outlined basic penology in 5:9-13. Instead, he aims to persuade his audience to embrace his communal ethic based on new baptismal identities (6:11). First Corinthians 6:9-11 depicts the fate, not of the Corinthians, but of οἱ ἄδικοι (6:9).[308] Thus, exclusion–expulsion possesses a *now–then* distinction based upon an *inside–outside* binary. Just as the community is to judge τοὺς ἔσω (5:12; cf. 11:27-34) who violate the community's ethos with indefinite expulsion *now*, God will judge the τοὺς ἔξω (5:13) with eschatological exclusion *then* (6:9-10). Interpreted alongside 5:9-13, it indicates that the indefinite expulsion delivered by the community in the present anticipates eschatological exclusion in the future, likely to interdict final judgment (cf. 11:29-32).[309]

2.7.4. Conclusions

By interpreting 1 Cor. 5:1-13 within the broader displacement matrix, a surprising lacuna in approaches to the text, new insights emerged furthering the intelligibility of the passage. In 1 Cor. 5:1-13 and 6:9-10 (cf. 2 Cor. 2:5-11) the practice of political displacement in Corinth functioned in ways complementary to the broader Graeco-Roman world.

Kloppenborg summarizes aptly:

> Pauline groups adopted judicial practices that imitated the polis... In 1Cor 5,1-13...Paul imagines an assembly at which the matter is considered, with Paul 'virtually present' and offering his judgment, resulting in expulsion of the wrongdoer. The procedure of meting out punishments, including... expulsion is paralleled in the practices of many associations, and these in turn mimic the practices of the civic assembly.[310]

---

307. See Michael Peppard, "Brother against Brother: Controversiae about Inheritance Disputes and 1 Corinthians 6:1–11." *JBL* 133.1 (2014): 179–92.

308. Gundry-Volf, *Perseverance*, 134–6.

309. N. T. Wright, *Paul and the Faithfulness of God*, Christian Origins and the Question of God 4 (Minneapolis: Fortress, 2013), 976–80.

310. Kloppenborg, "Place in the Polis," 33–4.

Accordingly, expulsion in Corinth was rhetorically linked to the death penalty and likely involved the removal of communal rank and status. As well, displacement in Corinth involved the complete withdrawal of communal support. Yet, our analysis of 1 Cor. 5:1-13 relied equally upon contextual information found in second temple texts. Furthermore, the indefinite nature of expulsion in Corinth, the eschatological dimension attached to it, and the emphasis upon habituated character supply unique features. Thus, while only attending to a text referring to official, enforced sanction, Paul and community were aware of and practiced some basic features of political displacement.

2.8. *Summary and Conclusions*

After demonstrating that the aims of reconciliation and return belonged to those whose absence implied or embodied judgment against them (§2.1), this chapter has attempted to outline the basic features of the etic descriptor, political displacement when viewed from three perspectives: socio-cultural institutions and conventions, political theory, and communal penology. First, enmity culture provided the context of an ordeal in which people (men in particular) demonstrated the virtues of aggression, daring, and violence to establish their position in the social hierarchy. According to broad socio-cultural expectations, absence or flight in the context of a contest indicated shame and often defeat resulting in dishonor (§2.2). From the vantage of political theory, absence often involved a remedy to communal discord and the restoration of ὁμόνοια at one level, and on another level the desire to drive an opponent from the community to reshape a community's memory and ethos (§2.3). Attention to Graeco-Roman penology brings to light the legal, codified actions of political communities in which communities expelled members whose behavior threatened the welfare of the group. Such enforced absences often included the formal removal of an individual's communal rank and frequently functioned as a surrogate for the death penalty (§2.4). An analysis of voluntary associations indicates the presence of enmity culture, ordeals, an emphasis upon group concord, and quasi-legal expulsions among non-elites comparable to if not dependent upon elite culture (§2.5). Appropriating the Hebrew Bible's death sentence and purity maps, second temple communities employed displacement practices largely intelligible within wider Graeco-Roman practices (§2.6). Finally, the Corinthian ἐκκλησία was familiar with attempted displacement, which shared elements of second temple and other Graeco-Roman communities' practices, oriented around Pauline eschatology (§2.7).

Methodologically, the aim was twofold. First, I desired to know whether the elements associated with political displacement were manifest within the mutual cognitive environment (MCE). The evidence allows the reader to conclude with confidence that members of Paul's Corinthian ἐκκλησία would be reasonably familiar with the phenomena associated with political displacement, as well as likely any financially and socially non-elite political community living in Corinth in the middle of the first century CE. Second, I wished to familiarize the reader with the constellation of phenomena associated with political displacement to perceive any evidence of the practice in 2 Corinthians. With this in mind, we turn to Second Corinthians to understand the occasion for Paul's absence.

Chapter 3

THE INTERMEDIATE ORDEAL

With the practice of political displacement established within the mutual cognitive environment (MCE), this chapter analyzes crucial texts used for reconstruction to delineate the precise occasion for Paul's absence from his community in Corinth, interrogating the textual evidence in light of Chapter 2. This chapter seeks to answer two interrelated questions: What situation(s) occasioned Paul's hostile absence from which he attempted to secure an amicable return and how might a "thick description" of the situation elucidate the Corinthian crisis? I argue that Paul's absence from Corinth was in direct response to an affront expressed by a contingent *within the community* during the intermediate visit and that his detractors and others interpreted Paul's behavior as indicative of his impotence, defeat, and displacement from Corinth.

To guard against Procrustean impulses, our own form of the illegitimate totality transfer, the evidence found in the Corinthian archive will be measured against the evidence in Chapter 2, using the sliding scale of hypotheses ranging from "certain" to "incredible" devised by E. P. Sanders for historical Jesus study and appropriated by John M. G. Barclay for mirror-reading Galatians.[1] Barclay correctly urged scholars to be more candid in the plausibility of their conclusions. He claimed explorations of biblical material against relevant contextual parameters remain worthy even if they cannot be proven beyond doubt. Barclay's taxonomy ranged from "certain or virtually certain" through "highly probable," "probable," "possible," "conceivable," to "incredible." This scale will suffice in supplying added rigor in weighing the evidence.

---

1. E. P. Sanders, *Jesus and Judaism* (London: SCM, 1985), 326–7; John M. G. Barclay, "Mirror-Reading a Polemical Letter: Galatians as a Test Case," *JSNT* 31 (1987): 85.

3.1. Four Roadblocks

Initially, four common suppositions challenge our inquiry. First, an influential minority of scholars contend *a priori* that Paul is always in control of, if not aloof from, the Corinthian conflict. Specific to 2 Corinthians, these researchers accept the reality of an intermediate visit, but contend Paul would never flee the scene of a challenge. R. Mackintosh, at the beginning of the twentieth century, tied Paul's intermediate visit to communal discipline, claiming that the death sentence exhorted in 1 Corinthians 5 was not executed. Paul thus visited to carry out the judgment. So certain of Paul's undiminished authority, Mackintosh imagines, "the lightning from St. Paul's eye might well blast the soul pertinaciously guilty of a scandalous life."[2] From the same era, G. G. Findlay, asserting Paul visited prior to 1 Corinthians, dismissed the idea of a retreat from challenge, though acknowledging the social cost of such an event: "St. Paul is not the man to have retreated before a personal attack, shooting Parthian arrows by letters from a distance; such a defeat would have been irreparable."[3] E. B. Allo, too, is concerned that the main rupture between Paul and the community occurred, "après son depart."[4] Any sense that Paul responded to a conflict by leaving, "aurait atteint en lui non pas l'homme seul, mais la dignité de l'Apôtre."[5] Schmithals, in part, dismisses an "inglorious retreat" because such behavior could "not even remotely correspond to the same Paul who wrote [2 Cor.] 11:23-33."[6] Forms of this critique remain present in scholarship, as Murray Harris remarks in his influential commentary, "[Paul] was not the sort of man who would retreat before opposition only to resort to a letter and the intervention of his delegate Titus to gain what he himself had failed to achieve."[7] Thus, the conflict with the community reached an inflection point only *after* his exit from Corinth.[8] In one sense, this line of critique implies that Paul remained impervious to the phenomena outlined in Chapter 2. Yet, these

---

2. R. Mackintosh, "The Brief Visit to Corinth," *Expositor* 6 (1908): 231.
3. G. G. Findlay, "Paul the Apostle," in *A Dictionary of the Bible*, ed. James Hastings (Edinburgh: T. & T. Clark, 1909), 3:711.
4. E. B. Allo, *Saint Paul: Seconde Epître aux Corinthiens*, ÉBib (Paris: Gabalda, 1937), ix, also 55, 61–2, 72, 76.
5. Allo, *Seconde Epître*, 61–2.
6. Schmithals, *Gnosticism*, 104.
7. Harris, *Second Epistle*, 59, 226–7; see also Hughes, *Second Epistle*, 59–64.
8. Following the reconstruction of Heinrich Ewald, *Die Sendschreiben des Apostels Paulus* (Göttingen: Dietrich, 1857), 226–7.

scholars carry an acute awareness of what would be at stake if Paul did in fact exit Corinth in response to affront.

Second and related to the first roadblock, commentators commonly interpret Paul's absence as an offence *against* the community, claiming the existence of a desire for Paul's presence rather than his continued absence.[9] The headwaters to this tradition are found in Ambrosiaster, who claims Paul wrote 2 Cor. 1:23 that "they might not think themselves to be unworthy and despised by him."[10] Chrysostom, similarly claims that 1:23 and the immediate context responds to the charge, "because of this you did not desire to return to us—because you hate us."[11] Although this discussion rarely engages socio-historical background, we may proffer a question as a refinement in light of Chapter 2: Do Paul's interlocutors, to which he responds, view Paul's absence as a form of (passive) aggression (like that of plebeians, slaves, and absent association members) or is it in response to communal aggression?

Third, most scholars who claim that intermediate events involved a challenge to Paul's authority followed by a tense absence often interpret this event *sui generis* and thus do not consider Paul's absence as an intelligible cultural artefact.[12] There is no shortage of dramatic narratives of Paul's encounter at and retreat from Corinth, but these are entirely untethered from the world sketched in Chapter 2. To this we recall that for those interpreters attuned to the social world, who also perceive the community's irritation with Paul concerning his conduct (oratory, maintenance, masculinity), Paul's absence is largely happenstance and of historical, not interpretive, significance.

Fourth and likely connected to the third supposition, the consensus understands the ὁ ἀδικήσας and/or the external rivals to be the central, although veiled catalysts, to the troubles in Corinth. As such, any animus is the responsibility primarily of an individual and/or outsiders rather than the community proper.[13] Historically, exegetes have often analyzed the

---

9. G. S. Duncan, *St. Paul's Ephesian Ministry* (London: Hodder, 1929), 173, 179; R. H. Strachan, *The Second Epistle of Paul to the Corinthians*, 7th edn (London: Hodder & Stoughton, 1964), 64; Jean Héring, *The Second Epistle of Saint Paul to the Corinthians*, trans. A. W. Heathcote and P. J. Allcock, 2nd edn (London: Epworth, 1967), 55; Furnish, *II Corinthians*, 144.

10. ne putarent se indignos esse, et contemni ab illo (PL 17:173).

11. ὅτι διὰ τοῦτο οὐκ ἠθέλησας ἐλθεῖν ἐμίσησας γάρ ἡμᾶς (PG 61:455); see §1.2.4.

12. C. K. Barrett, *A Commentary on the Second Epistle to the Corinthians* (New York: Harper, 1973), 7, 89, 213; Bieringer, "Plädoyer," 172–3, and others.

13. Cf. Bieringer, "Kontinuität," 11.

crisis primarily through the lens of the opponents and found evidence of a binary contest between rival, early Christian missions and thus a combat largely unique vis-à-vis the wider social world (§1.3).

With those objections in mind, first, I aim to better understand Paul's absence by establishing the most reliable evidence concerning Paul's most recent presence in Corinth, what is known as the intermediate visit (§3.2). Second, I interpret the nature and character of that visit and absence (§3.3). Third, I evaluate the evidence considering the material brought forth in Chapter 2 to better understand the nature of Paul's visit to and absence from Corinth (§3.4).

3.2. The Intermediate Visit

A consensus of interpreters believes that Paul made an intermediate visit to Corinth. However, a small contingent continues to hold to only two visits.[14] Beginning in 1830, Friedrich Bleek claimed that 2 Cor. 12:14 and 13:1 implied Paul visited twice prior to 2 Corinthians.[15] Supported by many in the years prior to World War I and by a few today, Bleek posited that the second visit occurred prior to 1 Corinthians, following Erasmus and Chrysostom.[16] In 1857, Heinrich Ewald claimed that the visit occurred between the canonical epistles.[17] Karl Weizsäcker modified Ewald's hypothesis, claiming a conflict occurred therein between the community and Paul.[18] Following World War I to the present, the Ewald–Weizsäcker hypothesis has gained broad assent.[19] The hypothesis has proven so persuasive that in a field as contested as the Corinthian

---

14. See §1.2.1.

15. Friedrich Bleek, "Erörterungen in Beziehung auf die Briefe Pauli an die Korinther," *TSK* 3 (1830): 615.

16. Bleek, "Erörterungen," 615; Albert Klöpper, *Kommentar über das zweite Sendschreiben des Apostels Paulus an die Gemeinde zu Corinth* (Berlin: Reimer, 1874), 34; Zahn, *Introduction*, 1:263; Meyer, *Corinthians*, 2:130–1. Contemporary interpreters include, Hughes, *Second Epistle*, 52; Hall, *Unity*, 243–5; Campbell, *Framing Paul*, 83–4.

17. Ewald, *Sendschreiben*, 223–7.

18. Karl Heinrich von Weizsäcker, *Das apostilische Zeitalter der christlichen Kirche* (Freiburg: Mohr, 1892), 287–94 passim.

19. Max Krenkel, *Beiträge zur Aufhellung der Geschicht und der Briefe des Apostels Paulus* (Branschweig: Scuwetschke, 1895), 154; Kirsopp Lake, *The Earlier Epistles of St. Paul: Their Motive and Origin* (London: Rivingtons, 1911), 145, 149–51; Allo, *Seconde Epître*, 49–50; Strachan, *Second Epistle*, 62–70; Héring, *Second Epistle*, 13; Bruce, *I & II Corinthians*, 182; Barrett, *Second Epistle*, 18; Furnish, *II Corinthians*, 54–4; Martin, *2 Corinthians*, xlvi–xlvii; Margaret E. Thrall,

correspondence, it appears in Bieringer's "Miminalkonsens."[20] The results of Bieringer's survey remain accurate today.[21] Yet, caution is necessary since some scholarly trends, notably opponent theories, have a history of gaining wide assent on rather shallow evidentiary grounds. We begin by evaluating the texts Bleek considered persuasive, 2 Cor. 12:14 and 13:1.

3.2.1. *Second Corinthians 12:14, 13:1-2*

In 2 Cor. 12:14, Paul writes, τρίτον τοῦτο ἑτοίμως ἔχω ἐλθεῖν. The phrase can be interpreted as a reference to a third *intention* or *preparation* if τρίτον τοῦτο modifies ἑτοίμως ἔχω.[22] Hyldahl translates 12:14, "siehe, dies dritte Mal bin ich bereit, zu euch zu kommen (wie die zwei vorigen Male auch, als ich indessen nicht kam)."[23] Conversely, τρίτον τοῦτο may be taken with ἐλθεῖν and thus refer to a third trip to Corinth. For example, Harris responds that the phrase involves two distinct thoughts, "he is coming on a third visit, and he is now ready to come."[24] By appealing to classical sources as well as Acts 21:13, Max Krenkel demonstrates that both translations are grammatically possible, concluding that context, not grammar, must be determinative.[25]

The debate concerning 2 Cor. 12:14 is largely preliminary to the discussion of the more exegetically determinative passage, 13:1-2. There, Paul states, τρίτον τοῦτο ἔρχομαι πρὸς ὑμᾶς, in reference to his impending

---

The Second Epistle to the Corinthians, 2 vols., ICC (Edinburgh: T. & T. Clark, 1994), 1:56; Vegge, *2 Corinthians*, 82–93; Schmeller, *Zweite Brief*, 1:39–40; Arzt-Grabner, *2 Korinther*, 149–50; Guthrie, *2 Corinthians*, 20–1.

20. Bieringer, "Kontinuität," 11.

21. "Mit fast allen neuen Interpreten wird ferner ein Zwischenbesuch vertreten" (Schmeller, *Zweite Brief*, 1:39).

22. Hyldahl, "Frage," 303; Troels Engberg-Pedersen, "2 Korintherbrevs indledningsspørgsmål," in *Tro og historie: festskrift til Niels Hyldahl i anledning af 65 års fødselsdagen den 30 december 1995*, ed. L. Fatum and M. Müller, FBE 7 (Copenhagen: Museum Tusculanums Forlag, 1996), 76; Land, *Absence*, 223–4. Carlson aptly highlights how Hyldahl and Engberg-Pedersen seem to appeal to word order to justify their interpretations of 12:14 while rejecting word order for their preferred interpretations in 2:1 ("On Paul's Second Visit to Corinth: Πάλιν, Parsing, and Presupposition in 2 Corinthians 2:1," *JBL* 135.3 [2016]: 609 n. 50); cf. Ferdinand C. Baur, *Paul, the Apostle of Jesus Christ*, trans. Eduard Zeller, 2 vols., 2nd edn (London: Williams & Norgate, 1876), 1:302–6.

23. Hyldahl, "Frage," 303.

24. Harris, *Second Epistle*, 882.

25. Krenkel, *Beiträge*, 186.

return. Grammatical ambiguity exists here as well since the expression may refer to a definite future event[26] or merely a present intention.[27] Thus, as in 12:14, context must be determinative. The argument naturally proceeds to 13:2 which states in three parallel phrases as demonstrated by Hughes:[28]

προείρηκα	καὶ	προλέγω
ὡς παρὼν τὸ δεύτερον	καὶ	ἀπὼν νῦν
τοῖς προημαρτηκόσιν	καὶ	τοῖς λοιποῖς πᾶσιν

The content of Paul's warning is, "that when I come I will not spare [you] again."[29]

The minority position proffers two significant reasons for denying a second, intermediate visit. First, Vegge demonstrates that at the grammatical level, scholars who interpret 13:1 as only referencing one prior visit claim the expression in 13:2, ὡς παρὼν τὸ δεύτερον καὶ ἀπὼν νῦν, modifies προλέγω only and understand the perfect προείρηκα to refer to the warnings in 1 Cor. 4:18-21.[30] In spite of three-fold parallelism, the passage is read as unfolding in a linear fashion.

---

26. Krenkel, *Beiträge*, 187–9; Alfred Plummer, *A Critical and Exegetical Commentary on the Second Epistle of St. Paul to the Corinthians* (New York: Scribner's Sons, 1915), 371; Windisch, *Zweite Korintherbrief*, 412–13; Bultmann, *Second Letter*, 240; Barrett, *Second Epistle*, 332–3; Barnett, *Second Epistle*, 598; Schmeller, *Zweite Brief*, 2:364, and others.

27. Baur, *Paul*, 1:306; Engberg-Pedersen, "2 Korintherbrevs," 76; Long, *II Corinthians*, 247; for discussion of Engberg-Pederson's interpretation, see Vegge, *2 Corinthians*, 82 n. 50.

28. From Hughes, *Second Epistle*, 476.

29. The ὅτι is likely recititative (D. Hans Lietzmann, *An die Korinther I–II*, HNT 9 [Tübingen: Mohr Siebeck, 1949], 160; Barnett, *Second Epistle*, 600 n. 38; Vegge, *2 Corinthians*, 92 n. 85, and others); the trans. follows Windisch and Schmeller with εἰς τὸ πάλιν modifying οὐ φείσομαι (Windisch, *Zweite Korintherbrief*, 415; Schmeller, *Zweite Brief*, 2:369).

30. Vegge, *2 Corinthians*, 83; Baur, *Paul*, 1:307; cf. Hyldahl, "Frage," 305; Long infers the clause modifies προλέγω both with his translation (246), and his grammatical comment, "ὡς. Introduces a correspondence clause…comparing and supporting his current forewarning" (*2 Corinthians*, 246–7).

3. The Intermediate Ordeal

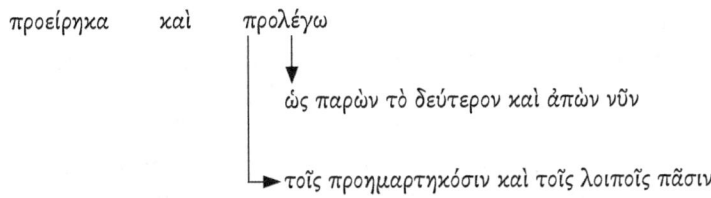

As well, Hyldahl claims καὶ functions concessively and should be translated, "jedoch tatsächlich."[31]

Second, some claim that with the phrase ὡς παρὼν τὸ δεύτερον (13:2) refers to an epistolary visit, which counted as Paul's second visit to Corinth. Appealing to cultural context, Long claims that the participles παρών and ἀπών are technical terms referring to epistolary conventions like those used by Seneca and other writers in which a letter might count as a visit.[32] Thus, Paul speaks as present yet absent now, just as he had in 1 Corinthians. Others, like Baur and Hyldahl, claim ἀπών–παρών refers to an "imagined" visit without reference to epistolary conventions.[33] Most often, these exegetes understand the phrase in 13:2a as reference to 1 Corinthians.[34] Recently, Christopher Land has proposed alternatively that 13:2 should be translated "as one who is approaching for the second time and at a distance for the moment."[35] Land asserts that παρών may be glossed as "near" or "at hand," indicating the Paul has warned the community previously through 1 Corinthians and now on his impending approach to Corinth.[36]

Initially, it is proper to question whether it would be sensible for Paul to link the seriousness and definiteness of "two or three witnesses" via cardinals with corresponding ordinals that only refer to mere attempts

---

31. Hyldahl, "Frage," 304; cf. Kennedy, *Second and Third Epistles*, 3.
32. Long, *II Corinthians*, 247–8, 250; cf. Long, *Ancient Rhetoric*, 238.
33. Baur, *Paul*, 1:307; cf. Hyldahl, "Frage," 304; Bosenius, *Abwesenheit*, 13.
34. Hyldahl, "Frage," 304–5; Long, *Ancient Rhetoric*, 238. However, Bosenius claims Paul's "imaginary" second visit is 2 Corinthians: "Unter Verwendung des ἀπών-παρών-Motivs entwickelt Paulus in der ersten Hälfre von 13,2 den Gedanken, daß er, wenn er den 2 Kor verfaßt, nun gleichsam (ὡς)—in der Imagination—schon das zweite Mal (τὸ δεύτερον) bei den Briefandressaten anwesend (παρών) ist, obwohl er realiter doch aus der Abwesenheit heraus (ἀπὼν νῦν) schreibt" (*Abwesenheit*, 13). Also Heinrici, *Der Zweite*, 425.
35. Land, *Absence*, 229.
36. Land, *Absence*, 229 n. 94.

to visit.[37] Furthermore, the parallelism in 13:2 suggests that the differentiation between the perfect προείρηκα and present προλέγω indicates that respective verbs belong to distinct participial phrases.[38] Guthrie states, "the two warnings correspond to two points in time."[39] Thus, προείρηκα links with παρὼν τὸ δεύτερον, referring to the prior warning and προλέγω with ἀπὼν νῦν, referring to the current warning.[40] This was Chrysostom's understanding of the grammar.[41] Thus, the passage may be interpreted as follows:

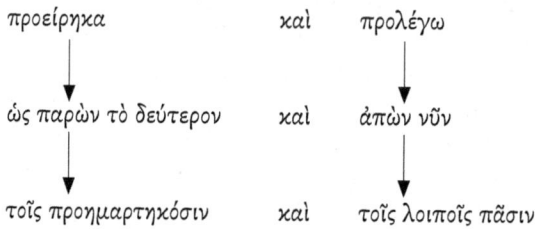

This observation makes unnecessary the claim that καὶ ἀπὼν νῦν is concessive. Rather, the construction ὡς...καὶ should be understood as correlative and translated as...so (καὶ = οὕτος).[42] This fits better with the immediate context (2 Cor. 10:1-11; 13:10), indicating that the use of ὡς παρών...καὶ ἀπὼν νῦν emphasizes the continuity of the warnings through contrasting media as a riposte to accusations of inconstancy

---

37. Krenkel, *Beiträge*, 189; a number of scholars argue that 13:1a refers to three separate visits on the basis of Paul's use of Deut. 19:15, claiming that each of Paul's visits corresponds with a "witness" against the community in 13:1b–2 (Windisch, *Zweite Korintherbrief*, 413; Barrett, *Second Epistle*, 333, and others); yet the clear link between ordinals and cardinals in 13:1–2 does not supply sufficient evidence that each "witness" is in fact a visit (Bultmann, *Second Letter*, 241; Furnish, *II Corinthians*, 575).

38. Schmeller, *Zweite Brief*, 2:368.

39. Guthrie, *2 Corinthians*, 632; Zahn, *Introduction*, 1:271 n. 13.

40. Windisch, *Zweite Korintherbrief*, 414; Barnett, *Second Epistle*, 599–600; Martin, *2 Corinthians*, 470; Harris, *Second Epistle*, 909; Schmeller, *Zweite Brief*, 2:368; Guthrie, *2 Corinthians*, 632; Carlson, "Πάλιν," 608.

41. εἰ γὰρ ἐπὶ στόματος δύο μαρτύρων καὶ τριῶν σταθήσεται πᾶν ῥῆμα, παρεγενόμην δεύτερον καὶ εἶπον, λέγω δὲ καὶ νῦν διὰ τῆς Ἐπιστολῆς· ὥσπερ γὰρ παρὼν ἔλεγον, οὕτω καὶ ἀπὼν νῦν γράφω (PG 61:640).

42. See BDAG, s.v. "ὡς" 2a; Mt. 6:10; 7:51; Gal. 1:9; Acts 7:51; Phil. 1:20; Furnish, *II Corinthians*, 569–70; Harris, *Second Epistle*, 909; Vegge, *2 Corinthians*, 83.

between his personal and epistolary presence (cf. 10:1-11).⁴³ Similarly, Last's rendering is unnecessarily redundant, since both participle clauses would essentially say that Paul is absent, which Last admits only to claim such a construction adds emphasis.⁴⁴ However, the ἀπών–παρών *topos* in 10:1-11 and 13:1-10, of which 13:2 is a part, focuses upon the accused dissonance between Paul's physical presence and absence not a discussion concerning Paul's "approach" and "distance," which results in an unintelligible interpretation.

Regarding the claim that Paul wished for his letter *to count* for a visit in an imaginary or technical sense, I can find no convincing examples in antiquity. While literary and personal letters functioned as surrogates for visits by making absence into presence,⁴⁵ emphasizing the perspicuous effects of the author to the audience through reception⁴⁶ or the audience to the author during composition,⁴⁷ this *topos* never actually seems equated with a visit.⁴⁸ The oft-cited papyrus *BGU* 4.1080.1-10 demonstrates the point. A father writing to his son recalls the news of his son's wedding and states, "And we by hearing [about the wedding], indeed being absent (ἀπόντες), we rejoiced as being present (ὡς παρόντες) at the occasion, wishing you well for the things to come" (ll. 6–8). The report of the wedding causes the father to rejoice as if he were present, and the *topos* likely functions to communicate the philophronetic regards vividly. Nothing suggests that the father wants credit for attending the wedding, only that he rejoiced as if present. Perhaps in 1 Cor. 5:3 Paul goes beyond mere epistolary convention, with the *topos* claiming that he is present by the Spirit in the expulsion of the incestuous offender as claimed by

---

43. See Hans-Joseph Klauck, *2 Korintherbrief*, NEchtB 8 (Würzburg: Echter, 1986), 100.

44. Land, *Absence*, 229.

45. Koskenniemi, *Idee und Phraseologie*, 18–63, 88–127, 175–84; Thraede, *Grundzüge*, 55–61, 97–102, 146–61; Hans-Joseph Klauck, *Ancient Letters and the New Testament: A Guide to Context and Exegesis* (Waco, TX: Baylor University Press, 2006), 191–4; see Demetrius, *Eloc.* 227, 231.

46. Plautus, *Pseud.* 35–36, 63–64; Plato, *Phaed.* 228E; Seneca, *Epist.* 40.1; Ovid, *Trist.* 5.1.79–80; Cicero, *Ad Fam.* 16.16.2; P.Mich. 8.482; P.Lond. 1926.16-18.

47. Cicero, *Att.* 12.53; *Fam.* 2.9.2; 15.16.1.

48. It is significant that that Arzt-Grabner cites no instances of an imaginary or technical, epistolary visit with the ἀπών–παρών antithesis in non-literary letters, see *2 Korinther*, 450; since letters did not count as visits, it makes unnecessary the claim that since the modifier τῷ πνεύματι is missing in 13:2 unlike 1 Cor. 5:3, that the former text does not invoke Paul's imaginary presence, contra Krenkel, *Beiträge*, 180–1; Vegge, *2 Corinthians*, 84, and others.

Thiselton.⁴⁹ Yet, there is no evidence that this would be understood as counting for a (second) visit.

Even if this were not the case, that the terms ἀπών–παρών refer to technical epistolary conventions remains unlikely since in the immediate context the ἀπών–παρών antithesis refers to the accused dissonance between Paul's epistolary and personal presence (10:1-11; 13:1-10). Paul uses the *topos* in 1 Cor. 5:3 (ἀπὼν τῷ σώματι παρὼν δὲ τῷ πνεύματι) to encourage the discipline of the incestuous member. However, if this was in view in 13:2, Paul's argument concerning the consistency of his behavior through different media would amount to a *non sequitur*, since Paul would essentially argue that his behavior now through 2 Corinthians is consistent with his epistolary presence in 1 Cor. 5:1-13, a point upon which his detractors would happily agree (2 Cor. 10:1, 10). Moreover, the papyri often employed ἀπών and παρών to refer to the actual absence and presence of an individual, as in 2 Cor. 10:1-11; 13:10.⁵⁰

Second Corinthians 13:1-2 most likely implies two previous visits. Based upon the principle of parsimony, an intermediate visit is preferable to either an earlier second visit since one is never mentioned in 1 Corinthians or an epistolary visit.⁵¹ Douglas Campbell has recently resurrected the claim that Paul's second visit occurred prior to 1 Corinthians.⁵² His argument is intriguing on many levels, but ultimately fails his own criterion of parsimony. Simplicity of explanation according to epistolary data would need to account for why Paul's detractors could assert themselves on the idea Paul "is not coming to you" (1 Cor. 4:18) if, as Campbell claims, Paul had recently announced an impending double-visit (2 Cor. 1:15-16) through the Previous Letter (1 Cor. 5:9). This Campbell does not do. Nor does he attempt to explain how the criteria of Paul's proleptic visit in 1 Cor. 4:19-21 becomes fodder for his detractors who look back on Paul's second visit (2 Cor. 10:1-11; 13:1-10).

3.2.2. *Second Corinthians 2:1, 12:21*

According to most interpreters, 2 Cor. 2:1 and 12:21 implies a previous visit to Corinth with the use of ἔρχομαι and the iterative adverb, πάλιν. Second Corinthians 2:1 supplies the reason for his absence. "For I myself decided this," Paul writes, τὸ μὴ πάλιν ἐν λύπῃ πρὸς ὑμᾶς ἐλθεῖν. The verse

---

49. Thiselton, *First Epistle*, 390–2.
50. ἐμνήσθητέ μου περὶ τῆς | ἀσφαλείας τῆς οἰκίας ἡμῶν, ὡς καὶ πολλάκις διὰ γραμμάτων καὶ ἐπιστο|λῶν καὶ κατ' ὄψιν παρὼν ἐνετιλάμην (P.Oxy. 7.1070.49-50); for ἀπών, see *BGU* 16.2636.10; *SB* 22.15779.10, from Arzt-Grabner, *2 Korinther*, 450.
51. Weizsäcker, *Zeitalter*, 288.
52. Campbell, *Framing Paul*, 74–80.

3. The Intermediate Ordeal

is parallel to 1:23 in which Paul states, "that in order to spare you (φειδό-μενος), I have not yet (οὐκέτι) come to Corinth."[53] Together, both passages supply Paul's unique epistolary excuse for absence (see §1.2.4). The use of φείδομαι in 13:2 and 1:23 (and 2:1) suggests that both passages are connected lexically, rhetorically, and perhaps historically, suggesting that Paul's absence involves a threat of punitive sanction, a threat made during the intermediate visit.

The primary question in 2:1 centers upon πάλιν and what specifically it modifies. Chrysostom connected πάλιν primarily with ἐν λύπῃ,[54] although the painful event refers to Paul's composition of 1 Corinthians.[55] Conversely, Theodoret claimed πάλιν modified only ἐλθεῖν—thus Paul simply desired not to return since that trip would be characterized grief.[56] Today, the vast majority of exegetes understand that πάλιν modifies ἐν λύπῃ[57] or the entire infinitival clause[58] rather than simply modify ἐλθεῖν,[59] thus concluding ἐν λύπῃ refers to a painful trip other than the founding mission.

Stephen Carlson argues that πάλιν is simply too ambiguous to argue for or against an intermediate visit.[60] Often critics press word order to make the case for or against an intermediate visit. For example, Bultmann claims, "as the position indicates πάλιν does not merely belong with ἐλθεῖν...rather πάλιν ἐν λύπῃ belong together."[61] In response, Carlson refers to Troels Engberg-Pedersen's argument concerning 2 Cor. 1:16 in which word order does not provide sufficient exegetical evidence. There, Paul writes, καὶ πάλιν ἀπὸ Μακεδονίας ἐλθεῖν πρὸς ὑμᾶς, in which πάλιν clearly modifies ἐλθεῖν rather than the phrase immediately to its right, ἀπὸ

---

53. Hyldahl incorrectly argues that the adverb οὐκέτι should be translated "anymore" in the context of Paul's reference to his founding visit in 1:19 ("Frage," 287–98). Both Barrett and Furnish insist that οὐκέτι with an aorist does not mean "anymore" but a reference to a specific trip that was aborted (Barrett, *Second Epistle*, 84; Furnish, *II Corinthians*, 138).

54. Τὸ, Πάλιν, δείκνυσι καί ἤδη λυπηθέντα εκείθεν, PG 61:455.

55. PG 61:420-21.

56. Τὸ δὲ πάλιν, τῇ παρουσίᾳ, οὐ τῇ λύπῃ συνέζευκται, PG 82:385.

57. Windisch, *Zweite Korintherbrief*, 77–8; Bultmann, *Second Letter*, 45; Furnish, *II Corinthians*, 140; Thrall, *Second Epistle*, 163–5; Harris, *Second Epistle*, 215–16; Schmeller, *Zweite Brief*, 1:121–2.

58. Vegge, *2 Corinthians*, 87; Land, *Absence*, 225.

59. Heinrici, *Zweite Brief*, 87–9; Engberg-Pedersen, "2 Korintherbrevs," 75–6; cf. Baur, who argues for an epistolographic error (*Paul*, 1:306).

60. Carlson, "Πάλιν."

61. Bultmann, *Second Letter*, 45; cf. Schmeller, *Zweite Brief*, 1:122.

Μακεδονίας.⁶² Thus, Carlson reasons that πάλιν in 2:1 simply cannot bear the weight of any theoretical reconstruction.⁶³

Second Corinthians 12:20-21 continues to be an underinterpreted text in the Corinthian conflict, which may supply further evidence of an intermediate visit.⁶⁴ The notion of a second, painful visit seems implied in 12:21, where in a third μή πως clause with φοβοῦμαι supplied elliptically—here without πως suggesting the reality of the situation⁶⁵—Paul writes, πάλιν ἐλθόντος μου ταπεινώσῃ με ὁ θεός μου πρὸς ὑμᾶς. Unsurprisingly, the question of word order in relation to the scope of πάλιν comes to the fore. Windisch and Hans Lietzmann remain consistent with their interpretation of 2:1, claiming πάλιν modifies what immediately follows it, ἐλθόντος μου.⁶⁶ Others contend that πάλιν modifies ταπεινώσῃ⁶⁷ or the entire clause,⁶⁸ since the genitive absolute ἐλθόντος μου is grammatically subordinate and unlikely to be modified by the emphatic πάλιν.⁶⁹

Unlike 2 Cor. 2:1, clearer evidence indicates πάλιν modifies ταπεινώσῃ rather than ἐλθόντος μου. Plummer argues that because Paul's return has already been mentioned in 12:20 with ἐλθών—a term that can easily mean return—the use of πάλιν would be "superfluous rather than emphatic."⁷⁰ This indicates that πάλιν does not modify ἐλθόντος μου, but instead ταπεινώσῃ and refers to a prior encounter. Some commentators connect Paul's previous humiliation directly to the ὁ ἀδικήσας conflict (2:5-11; 7:5-16) and λύπη in 2:1.⁷¹ However, in 12:21b and 13:2, a group is in view, not an individual.⁷² In 12:21b Paul's potential humiliation is tied

---

62. Carlson, "Πάλιν," 605–6; cf. Engberg-Pederson for what he claims as a general rule, "Pointen er, at hvis der i en sætning med palin optræder en vedføjet løsere bestemmelse af verbet, fx af adverbial karakter, så vil palin lægge sig til verbet og ikke til den løsere bestemmelse, selv om det står tættere på den løsere bestemmelse" ("2 Korintherbrevs," 75).

63. Carlson, "Πάλιν," 608.

64. Vegge, *2 Corinthians*, 92.

65. Harris, *Second Epistle*, 901.

66. Windisch, *Zweite Korintherbrief*, 409; Lietzmann, *Korinther I–II*, 158.

67. Plummer, *Second Epistle*, 369; Martin, *2 Corinthians*, 464–5; Furnish, *II Corinthians*, 562; Vegge, *2 Corinthians*, 340; Schmeller, *Zweite Brief*, 2:359.

68. Meyer, *Corinthians*, 2:493.

69. Harris, *Second Epistle*, 901.

70. *Second Epistle*, 369; cf. Harris, *Second Epistle*, 901.

71. Barrett, *Second Epistle*, 330; Bultmann, *Second Letter*, 238–9; Martin, *2 Corinthians*, 465; Vegge, *2 Corinthians*, 340.

72. Munck, *Paul*, 188; Marshall, *Enmity*, 261. The tension between the singular entity in 2:5-11 and the corporate entity in 12:21; 13:2 leads J. M. Gilchrist to conclude that Paul conducted two disciplinary visits, one prior to 2 Cor. 1–9 and another prior

το πολλούς προημαρτηκότων καὶ μὴ μετανοησάντων ἐπὶ τῇ ἀκαθαρσίᾳ καὶ πορνείᾳ καὶ ἀσελγείᾳ ᾗ ἔπραξαν,[73] a group,[74] over whom he fears he will grieve upon his return. In 13:2, it is this same group (τοῖς προημαρτηκόσιν) that Paul recounts warning (προείρηκα) when present on his second visit (παρὼν τὸ δεύτερον). Again, although the position of πάλιν alone does not solve the quandary, the use of ἐλθών in 12:20 and the presence of the immoral group in 12:21 and 13:2 supplies enough contextual information to make it clear that Paul encountered the group on a previous visit, believed the group to still be in existence at the time of writing, and entertained the possibility that he would encounter them again.

This however creates a second-order problem. In what sense might God humble Paul *again*?[75] Universally, exegetes acknowledge a pejorative meaning of ταπεινόω in 12:21.[76] Moreover, cognates of ταπεινόω and associated terms are linked to the detractors' negative evaluation of Paul's personal presence during the intermediate visit (10:1, 10) and his policy of not demanding support (11:7; cf. 11:20-21). Some suggest that Paul's hypothetical humiliation refers to a repetition of similar negative conditions found on his intermediate visit.[77] This is true to the extent that it reflects the rejection of Paul's leadership by the immoral group. Yet, fundamentally, Paul pronounces that his return will be *unlike* his previous visit (10:2, 11; 13:2), and consistent with the Christological pattern

to 2 Cor. 10–13 based in part upon the difference between a singular offender (2:5–11; 7:5–16) and immoral group (12:21–13:2) ("Paul and the Corinthians: The Sequence of Letters and Visits," *JSNT* 34 [1988]: 53). Last argues that the offender in 2:5-11 refers to a group (*Absence*, 103). More likely, Paul made one intermediate visit on which both encounters likely occurred, although historical primacy should be granted to the immoral group, not the ὁ ἀδικήσας conflict.

73. The phrase πολλοὺς τῶν προημαρτηκότων καὶ μὴ μετανοησάντων may refer to a subset of former sinners and unrepentants (partitive genitive) (Land, *Absence*, 226) or "the many who previously sinned and did not repent" (epexegetic genitive) (Harris, *Second Epistle*, 902–3; Schmeller, *Zweite Brief*, 2:360).

74. Harris argues that the single definite article shared by both participles indicates the two groups are "not to be distinguished" but that "we should differentiate between" the two tenses (*Second Epistle*, 903; cf. Schmeller, *Zweite Brief*, 2:360).

75. In order to deny the reality of an intermediate visit, Land unreasonably contends Paul's initial humiliation refers to his missionary visit when he found future members living as unbelievers (Land, *Absence*, 226 n. 80).

76. Grundmann, "Ταπεινός," *TDNT*, 8.17.

77. Grundmann, "Ταπεινός," 8:17; Barrett, *Second Epistle*, 331; Klauck, *2 Korintherbrief*, 99; Aejmelaeus, *Schwachheit*, 345–6; or simply humiliation of a failed mission (Marshall, *Enmity*, 376; Garland, *2 Corinthians*, 537; Guthrie, *2 Corinthians*, 622–3).

(13:3b-4). Whereas Paul "spared" the profligate group in the intermediate visit, he will not do so upon his return (13:2). This leads several interpreters to contend that the humiliation which will occur is fundamentally different from that of the intermediate visit. Paul will be humiliated by the group's refractoriness and as well his demonstration of apostolic authority by καθαίρεσις rather than οἰκοδομή (10:8; 13:10).[78] Such an arrival would surely amount to an apocalyptic moment in the life of Paul (see 13:4), though it would disclose the inferiority of his work in Corinth (1 Cor. 3:13-15). Thus, while ταπεινόω may be said to be experienced again, the actual content of Paul's humiliation is somewhat different.[79]

This interpretation suggests that in 12:21, when employed with πάλιν, the term ταπεινόω is intentionally polysemous in which the past and hypothetical referents point to different realities. The added contextual evidence in 12:21 indicates that Paul's usage of λύπη in 2:1, a near parallel, may also be polysemous.[80] This seems possible since Paul employs the verb φείδομαι in 13:2 as a warning to the immoral group and also in 1:23—a parallel to 2:1—as a reason for his absence, indicating the hypothetical referent in 2:1 involves Paul's punitive action.[81] If this is the case, 12:21 (and potentially 2:1) testifies to the intermediate visit with negative expressions, although, the qualities associated with the future hypothetical return are of a punitive order. However, an important qualification is necessary: whereas punitive actions were achieved regarding the ὁ ἀδικήσας through the Severe Letter (2:5-11; 7:5-16), the potential of punitive actions remain regarding the immoral

---

78. Lietzmann, *Korinther I–II*, 159; cf. W. G. Kümmel, *Introduction to the New Testament*, 17th edn (Nashville: Abingdon, 1975), 213; Furnish, *II Corinthians*, 567; Barnett, *Second Epistle*, 596; Schmeller, *Zweite Brief*, 2:359; scholars contending Paul's humiliation is only tied to his disciplinary action include: Bultmann, *Second Letter*, 239; Martin, *2 Corinthians*, 465; Brian J. Peterson, *Eloquence and the Proclamation of the Gospel in Corinth*, SBLDS 163 (Atlanta: Scholars Press, 1998), 136; Vegge, *2 Corinthians*, 341.

79. Martin differentiates Paul's second humiliation not only by its punitive character, but also by its source. God, rather than the community (incorrectly the ὁ ἀδικήσας), will supply Paul's hypothetical humiliation (*2 Corinthians*, 465).

80. "This minor difference between the two occasions (actual and hypothetical) means that the phrase ἐν λύπῃ has an implicit dual reference" (Thrall, *Second Epistle*, 165 n. 256; cf. Schmeller, *Zweite Brief*, 1:122).

81. That λύπη in reference to the hypothetical visit refers to punitive action against the community (Ewald, *Sendschreiben*, 256; Thrall, *Second Epistle*, 1:165, and others).

group (13:2). The lexical, grammatical, and rhetorical connections make it possible, although not certain, that the ὁ ἀδικήσας conflict is historically related to the immoral group. However, the surest footing for the events during Paul's second visit is found 12:21–13:2.[82]

3.2.3. Conclusions

The simplest explanation for the available evidence is that Paul visited Corinth twice before 2 Corinthians, making his upcoming return his third visit (2 Cor. 12:14; 13:1). The first occasion was the founding visit (1 Cor. 2:1-5; 2 Cor. 1:19; cf. Acts 18:1-18), and the second is implied at least four times in 2 Corinthians. The lack of any evidence of a second visit in 1 Corinthians leads to the conclusion that the visit occurred between the epistles.

With the majority of interpreters, it is possible that the intermediate visit is included as the first leg of the itinerary announced in 2 Cor. 1:15-16,[83] which may supersede the itinerary in 1 Corinthians 16.[84] The best evidence for an intermediate visit is found in 13:1-2 supplemented by 12:21.[85] The evidence points most conclusively to at least one interaction with the immoral group, which resulted in a threat to punish on Paul's return (12:21; 13:2). The ὁ ἀδικήσας may have occurred during the visit and the rivals may have been present, but this is conjecture. Our study emphasizes the determinative quality of 13:1-2 alongside 12:21 and the derivative nature of 12:14 and 2:1 (cf. 1:23). Yet, if we may take Bieringer's minimal consensus as representative, it is the rivals' presence and the ὁ ἀδικήσας conflict that are given ontological status during the visit, with no mention of the immoral group.[86] Thus, our analysis of the evidence represents an affirmation of and a departure from the current consensus.

---

82. Carlson, "Πάλιν," 610, 613; Campbell, *Framing Paul*, 88–9.

83. Windisch, *Zweite Korintherbrief*, 75; Barrett, *Second Epistle*, 7–8; Martin, *2 Corinthians*, xlvi–xlvii; Harris, *Second Epistle*, 63; contra, Furnish, *II Corinthians*, 54–5, 143–5, 151. Guthrie contends that Paul's intermediate visit is not included in the itinerary and that he cancelled the itinerary entirely (*2 Corinthians*, 20).

84. Windisch, *Zweite Korintherbrief*, 60; Bruce, *I & II Corinthians*, 180; Thrall, *Second Epistle*, 1:71; Harris, *Second Epistle*, 62; contra Duncan, *Ephesian Ministry*, 174–6.

85. Kennedy, *Second and Third Epistles*, 3.

86. Bieringer, "Kontinuität," 11; cf. Schmeller, *Zweite Brief*, 1:38–40.

3.3. The Character of the Intermediate Visit and Subsequent Absence

The reality of Paul's intermediate visit provokes inquiry as to the nature or character of Paul's second visit to Corinth.[87] In a field as contentious as 2 Corinthians, scholars widely agree that Paul aims to return from an especially acrimonious intermediate visit, in which an anonymous offender challenged Paul (2:5-11; 7:5-16). Bieringer summarizes this "minimal consensus" writing, "After 1 Corinthians, there is a second visit of Paul to Corinth, not mentioned in Acts. During this visit, there is a dispute that escalates into an altercation in which someone does something wrong to another (probably Paul). The Corinthians do not side with Paul. Paul realizes that his attempts to solve the problems have failed and he leaves."[88] Weizsäcker foreshadowed if not influenced this situation as he largely abandoned 12:14 and 13:1-2 in his reconstruction of the intermediate conflict (Der Zwist) in favor of 2:1-11, 7:5-16.[89] Any consideration of chs. 10–13 focused upon the presence and identity of Paul's rivals, who according to most are present during the intermediate visit "lurking in the background."[90]

All the same, the notion that upon his arrival in Corinth, Paul met with some expression of opposition and responded by exiting naturally evokes the phenomena presented in Chapter 2. In particular, the oft-colorful reconstructions echo the language of ordeals that resulted in a voluntary, shameful absence. For example, Weiss claims, "one of them [the Corinthians]...flung insolent insults in his face." Weiss reconstructs Paul's exit: "with feeble words and the loss of personal dignity, he abandoned the field...leaving almost by flight."[91] Writes F. F. Bruce of the encounter, "the opposition came to a head, and one member of the church in particular took the lead in defying his authority. Paul was deeply humiliated...and withdrew."[92] D. E. Garland describes Paul's exit as, "a hasty retreat" following an "attack by someone in the community."[93]

---

87. Cf. Baur, *Paul*, 1:304.
88. Bieringer, "Kontinuität," 11, my translation.
89. Weizsäcker, *Zeitalter*, 287–90, 294–303.
90. Colin G. Kruse, "The Offender and the Offence in 2 Corinthians 2:5 and 7:12," *EvQ* 88.2 (1988): 133, 135–6. Bieringer summarizes: "Kurz nach der Ankunft von 1 Kor kommen in Korinth externe Gegner an" ("Kontinuität," 11).
91. Weiss, *Primitive Christianity*, 1:343, 345.
92. Bruce, *I & II Corinthians*, 164.
93. Garland, *2 Corinthians*, 27.

Welborn claims, "Paul's rectitude and honor suffered a crushing blow... [he] departed Corinth in utter humiliation."[94]

The descriptions could continue. Yet, Bieringer accurately distills the majority view: the visit was an utter failure, primarily because of a conflict with the ὁ ἀδικήσας (2:5-11; 7:5-16) and the influence of the opponents (chs. 10–13).[95] The effect of this hypothesis is to place the locus of the conflict upon a single community member or outside the community, with the church proper bearing only tangential and passive responsibility. However, as we have established, the clearest evidence of the nature of the visit emerges from the evidence of Paul's interaction with the immoral group (12:21; 13:1-2). It is only by extension through lexical, grammatical, and rhetorical linkages that one may posit that the ὁ ἀδικήσας conflict occurred during the visit as well.

Yet, we wish to place to the side the ὁ ἀδικήσας conflict and the search for the rivals, exploring what might have happened if critical scholarship began the reconstruction of Paul's visit with 12:21 and 13:1-2, the most historically determinative texts. This is warranted for three reasons. First, these texts (12:21–13:2) are the most exegetically determinative for the visit, yet are rarely valued as such concerning its nature. Second, Vegge has demonstrated the dissonance between the portion of the community (οἱ πλείονες, 2:6) which appropriated Paul's call for discipline through the Severe Letter and Paul's praise of the entire community's innocence (ἁγνός) in the matter (πρᾶγμα, 7:11), thus indicating the rhetorical function of 2:5-11, 7:5-16 as an idealized account of a complete reconciliation for hortatory ends.[96] Welborn rightly highlights that the entire account is suffused with a good measure of political amnesia, purposefully concealing the nature of the conflict.[97] Thus, the highly stylized ὁ ἀδικήσας conflict is limited in historically reliable insights. What seems clear is Paul's use of the conflict and its idealized resolution through the Severe Letter and Titus's emissary as riposte to the accusations in 1:17. Such features (amnesty, coordinated campaigns involving letters and envoys) are generally consistent with others seeking reconciliation and return (see Appendix I and II). Third, while it is possible that the ὁ ἀδικήσας acted during the visit, that Paul was the ὁ ἀδικηθείς (7:12, see Appendix II), and that the rivals worked as the hidden hands behind the affair, such a conclusion only renders the visit as generally negative, in turn creating

---

94. Welborn, *Enmity*, 426.
95. Bieringer, "Kontinuität," 11.
96. Vegge, *2 Corinthians*, 95–140, 175–6.
97. Welborn, "Identification," 151–2 passim.

interpretive space for imaginative renderings of the exchange. Those renderings then form or should form the terminus to inquiry, lest one build conjecture upon conjecture or employ an in-the-gaps approach, which posits that an unexplainable datum in 2 Corinthians becomes explainable considering a hypothetical reconstruction of the visit.

3.3.1. *Prioritizing Knowns Over Unknowns*

Second Corinthians 12:21–13:2 functions within a contextual unit, 12:14–13:10 (12:19-21 functions transitionally between 12:14-19 and 13:1-10), marked by a heightened emphasis upon his impending return to Corinth (12:14).[98] To many exegetes, it is surprising that in a letter seemingly dominated by concerns about the ὁ ἀδικήσας conflict and external opponents, Paul reveals a new front in the conflict with a group.[99] Bachmann states, "alles, was Paulus da bisher als mangelhaft an der Gemeinde empfunden hat, auf einem ganz anderen Gebiete liegt, als auf dem des sittlich-sexuellen Lebens, nämlich auf dem der persönlichen Beziehungen zu Paulus."[100] Most commentators marginalize the import of the group in the crisis of authority, predictably placing emphasis upon the opponents and the ὁ ἀδικήσας.[101] Windisch and Barrett reason that 12:21 reflects lingering issues from 1 Corinthians (5:1-13; 6:12-20) that have little to do with crisis.[102] Others claim a connection with the opponents in which the immoral group was susceptible to the influence of or strategically aligned with the opponents.[103] Still others link the group to the ὁ ἀδικήσας conflict.[104] Thus, it is not that interpreters are unconvinced of

---

98. "Die Verteidigung geht weiter, vgl. V. 16–18.19; aber der beherrschende Gedanke ist der neuen Besuch" (Windisch, *Zweite Korintherbrief*, 398).

99. Bieringer, "Plädoyer," 169–70, 73.

100. Philipp Bachmann, *Der zweite Brief des Paulus an die Korinther*, KNT 8 (Leipzig: Deichert, 1909), 404; Plummer, *Second Epistle*, 368.

101. Bieringer, "Plädoyer," 170–3.

102. Windisch, *Zweite Korintherbrief*, 411–12; Barrett, "Paul's Opponents in II Corinthians," *NTS* 17 (1971): 247–9.

103. The opponents influenced the group (Bachmann, *Zweite Brief*, 170–1; Furnish, *II Corinthians*, 567–8; Aejmelaeus, *Schwachheit*, 55–6; Harris, *Second Epistle*, 904; Schmeller, *Zweite Brief*, 2:361, 368). The group partnered with opponents on pragmatic grounds in their struggle against Paul (Karl Prümm, *Diakonia Pneumatos: Der zweite Korintherbrief als Zugang zur apostolischen Botschaft. Auslegung und Theologie*, 2 vols. [Rome: Herder, 1967], 1:758). The opponents operated in opposition to Paul already in 1 Corinthians (Hall, *Unity*, 18, 29, 243).

104. The ὁ ἀδικήσας was a representative of the group (Weiss, *Primitive Christianity*, 1:343; Watson, "Painful Letter," 343–4; Barnett, *Second Epistle*, 380 n. 45, 597–8). The group opposing the sentence of the ὁ ἀδικήσας in the Severe Letter (2:6)

the existence of an immoral group during the intermediate visit, rather, they are fundamentally unsure as to how to understand the group in light of the historical-critical tradition. Campbell is on the right path, stating, "all we know from the epistolary data is that Paul was concerned during the second visit with sexual immorality."[105] To nuance Campbell, we know Paul encountered a plurality of sexually immoral members during his visit. Since the clearest evidence of a negative encounter during the intermediate visit is found in 12:21–13:2, it is evident that scholars have essentially worked backwards, prioritizing a relatively unknown (the identity/theology/chronology of the rivals) and a possibility (the ὁ ἀδικήσας conflict), resulting in detailed reconstructions only to relegate the import of a known (the existence of the immoral group). This results in relativizing the most prominent clues.

3.3.2. *The Interpretive Significance of the Presence of the Immoral Group*

It is of central importance to understand how Paul and the community understood the existence of the immoral group and how the community interpreted Paul's interaction with the group during his visit. Addressing these issues in turn we ask initially, how was the existence of the profligate group understood by Paul and the community?

In 12:21, the immoral group is referred to by the expression πολλοὺς τῶν προημαρτηκότων καὶ μὴ μετανοησάντων ἐπὶ τῇ ἀκαθαρσίᾳ καὶ πορνείᾳ καὶ ἀσελγείᾳ ᾗ ἔπραξαν. Most interpreters suggest that since the perfect and aorist participles are modified by a singular article, the phrase refers to persistent sexually immoral behavior that was not amended at a particular event.[106] The opportunity for repentance may refer to 1 Corinthians, Paul's confrontation with the group during the intermediate visit, or the Severe Letter that resulted in the repentance of some (2:1-11; 7:5-16).[107] If so, then the preposition προ- in 12:21 and 13:2 would mark a period prior to the intermediate visit.[108]

(Meyer, *Corinthians*, 2:172). With an added emphasis on the role of the ὁ ἀδικήσας, Welborn, regarding 12:21, relegates the immoral group to a figment of Paul's anthropological imagination, and without warrant, argues 13:2 refers to the ὁ ἀδικήσας (*Enmity*, 186-7, 193).

105. Campbell, *Framing Paul*, 88–9; contra Bieringer, "Kontinuität," 29.

106. Plummer, *Second Epistle*, 320; Hughes, *Second Epistle*, 473; Barrett, *Second Epistle*, 332; Harris, *Second Epistle*, 903, and others.

107. Plummer, *Second Epistle*, 370; Hughes, *Second Epistle*, 473; Barnett, *Second Epistle*, 597 n. 16; Harris, *Second Epistle*, 903.

108. Meyer, *Corinthians*, 2:496; C. K. Barrett, "Opponents," 247–8; contra, Harris who emphasizes προ- refers to "the period during and after his 'painful' visit" (*Second Epistle*, 903).

The profligacy of the immoral group in 12:21, 13:2 likely finds its root in a power struggle already underway in 1 Corinthians, as Barrett and Windisch suppose. Bultmann rejects that the preposition προ- in οἱ προημαρτηκώς refers to the period prior to the intermediate visit, claiming, "in that case, special offenses against Paul would have to be intended, not the sexual vices enumerated."[109] This is similar to Bachmann's contention that 2 Corinthians is characterized by "der persönlichen Beziehungen zu Paulus" not moral failures in the community.[110] Bultmann understands only the ὁ ἀδικήσας conflict as an example of such an offence. Similarly, Campbell, who correctly identifies the content of the intermediate visit, rests a fair amount of his argument upon questioning whether such profligacy would really amount to much of an issue since it was "presumably a fairly generic issue" hardly worthy of either a visit or any negative characterizations of it had it occurred.[111]

However, Bultmann and Campbell on the one hand and Windisch and Barrett on the other along with most misunderstand that sexual conduct across the correspondence remains germane to the conflict concerning Paul's governance of the community. Lexically, the term πορνεία and the overlapping semantic domains of ἀκαθαρσία and ἀσέλγεια (2 Cor. 12:21) most easily refer back to a series of communal issues in 1 Cor. 5:1–6:20. Gordon Fee claims that the three issues in 1 Cor. 5:1–6:20 (the incestuous brother, lawsuits, sexual immorality) function as test cases of Paul's apostolic authority in the context of an emerging power struggle.[112] That struggle centers upon "the arrogant ones" who question Paul's authority to order community life *in absentia* and whom Paul warns to enact discipline upon his return (4:18-21). The import of sexual boundaries in that struggle is substantiated by Paul's mention of the contents of his Previous Letter in 1 Cor. 5:9, "not to associate with sexually immoral people." As Barclay observes, Paul had a long history of attempting to establish boundaries in Corinth "quite different from those the Corinthians are willing to accept."[113] Far from an innocent misunderstanding, it is more likely, as Wolfgang Schrage suggests, that Paul's detractors malignantly misinterpreted his "previous" words.[114] Thus, with the scandal of

109. Bultmann, *Second Letter*, 240.
110. Bachmann, *Zweite Brief*, 404.
111. Campbell, *Framing Paul*, 87–8.
112. Fee, *First Epistle*, 194; cf. Weiss, *Primitive Christianity*, 1:342–3.
113. John M. G. Barclay, "Thessalonica and Corinth: Social Contrasts in Pauline Christianity," in *Pauline Churches and Diaspora Jews* (Grand Rapids, MI: Eerdmans, 2011), 191.
114. Schrage, *Erste Brief*, 1:388–9; contra John C. Hurd, *The Origins of 1 Corinthians* (London: SPCK, 1965), 52 n. 1.

the incestuous man (5:1-13) and the theologically rationalized sexual immorality among some members (6:12-20), sexual conduct forms a crucial fault-line in the emerging crisis of authority.[115]

Alongside evidence of sexual misconduct, several of the communal problems reflected in 1 Corinthians indicate that the live wires in the Corinthian conflict possessed a high valuation of assertiveness and intra-mural status-games (1:10-11; 6:1-11; 11:17-33; 14:1-33). As Barclay argues, the Corinthians' conversion involved elevation of status to that of πνευματικοί and τέλειοι (1 Cor. 2:6–3:3).[116] The empowerment by the Spirit led to a differentiation between themselves and outsiders (ψυχικοί), but it was a differentiation without exclusivity as many remained fully integrated into pre-conversion networks.[117] As a result, many conversions never manifested a "significant social and moral realignment."[118] The competitive status differentiation was also turned within the community similar to the evidence found among voluntary associations. Stephen Chester argues that many in Corinth reproduced, through a practical consciousness of life in voluntary associations, a typical competitive drive for honor.[119] By agnostically attaching themselves to early Christian party mascots (1:10-11), pursuing litigation among members (6:1-11), competing for honor at the Lord's Supper (11:17-33), and through the demonstration of spiritual gifts (14:1-33), many in the community evidently employed status-games unrestrained by the explicit rules which regulated the destructive aspects of competitive honor in other political communities.[120]

First Corinthians raises these stakes, as Paul exhorts the community to abandon such status-games, not through an overt set of statutes as in associations, but through the paradigm of his own cruciform autobiography

---

115. Because 6:12-20 is more vague than 5:1-13 and 6:1-11 it is subject to over and under-reading. However, considering the topic of the Previous Letter (5:9), it is proper to conclude that 6:12-20 refers to a persistent abuse in the realm of sexual ethics (Joseph A. Fitzmyer, *First Corinthians*, AYB 32 [New Haven, CT: Yale University Press, 2008], 261). This argument is grounded by studies that demonstrate the Strong's immorality was moored by the elitist secular aphorism πάντα μοι ἔξεστιν (6:12) (Dale B. Martin, *The Corinthian Body* [New Haven, CT: Yale University Press, 1995], 174–9; Bruce W. Winter, *After Paul Left Corinth: The Influence of Secular Ethics and Social Change* [Grand Rapids: Eerdmans, 2001], 86–91).

116. Barclay, "Thessalonica and Corinth," 192.

117. Barclay, "Thessalonica and Corinth," 200.

118. Barclay, "Thessalonica and Corinth," 200.

119. Stephen J. Chester, *Conversion at Corinth: Perspectives on Conversion in Paul's Theology and the Corinthian Church* (New York: T&T Clark, 2005), 233.

120. Chester, *Conversion at Corinth*, 227–66.

(4:16; 9:1-26; 11:1).[121] Paul's interventions in 1 Corinthians certainly undermined a number of socio-religious practices valued by some in the community, which if followed would come at significant cost.[122] It would be unsurprising if Paul's recommended social ethos was found offensive and untenable by some.[123] In reality, the presence of some of these behaviors in 1 Corinthians indicates likely opposition to Paul's recommended communal ethos. The slogan πάντα ἔξεστιν (6:12-13; 10:23) with its ideology authorized conduct in matters of food and sex. The empowerment of the Spirit made the πνευματικοί not only impenetrable to any pollutant, but also provided, according to Barclay, "a sense of immunity and of indifference to apostolic warnings."[124]

Notwithstanding the frequent dismissal of 1 Corinthians as evidence necessary to interpret 2 Corinthians,[125] that Paul would find a group in open defiance of his deliberations that were undoubtedly preached on his first visit, exhorted in the Previous Letter, and attached to his apostolic persona in 1 Corinthians is evidence that the immoral group by its existence supplied a brazen challenge to Paul's apostolicity. It is not uncommon for scholars to assert that Paul's deliberations in 1 Corinthians were not well received.[126] However, the presence of the immoral group is the most ostensive evidence of such a reaction. Weiss comments, "we now see that the theoretical justification of fornication with which Paul has had to contend in the first letter [6:12-20]...had a very serious background in fact... This group had for a long time resisted Paul's rigorous attitude."[127] Without necessarily assenting to Weiss's partition theories, it is probable

---

121. Margaret M. Mitchell, *Paul and the Rhetoric of Reconciliation: An Exegetical Investigation of the Language and Composition of 1 Corinthians* (Louisville, KY: Westminster John Knox, 1991), 247, passim.

122. Horrell, *Social Ethos*, 218; Duff, *Moses*, 68.

123. Jerome Murphy-O'Connor, *Paul: A Critical Life* (New York: Oxford University Press, 1997), 303.

124. Barclay, "Thessalonica and Corinth," 193.

125. Most easily witnessed through Barrett's maxim, "the second epistle must not be interpreted in terms of the situation presupposed in the first" (*Paul*, 64; see Witherington, *1 and 2 Corinthians*, 74; Mitchell, *Reconciliation*, 244 n. 328). The maxim even evolves into an *a priori* methodological mandate (Furnish, *II Corinthians*, 50).

126. "It is clear from 2 Corinthians that Paul's rhetorical strategy of appealing to himself as the respected example to be imitated was not well received in Corinth" (Mitchell, *Reconciliation*, 303).

127. Weiss argues the ἀδικήσας belonged to the arrogant of 1 Corinthians who were linked "with the lax, immoral attitude of the church" (*Primitive Christianity*, 1:342). Weizsäcker similarly places the ὁ ἀδικήσας as a member of the Christ-party and thus understood the conflict as protracted (*Zeitalter*, 298–9); cf. Meyer, *Corinthians*, 2:172; Barnett, *Second Epistle*, 597.

that both the immoral members in 1 Corinthians and the group in 2 Cor. 12:21 and 13:2 correspond more or less to the same persons and certainly the same attitude of defiance.

The evidence concerning the immoral group in the context of the correspondence resonates with the socio-cultural institutions, conventions, and political theory surveyed in Chapter 2 and encourages us to understand Paul's encounter with the immoral group as an identifiable form of social interaction. First, the participants, community, and Paul likely interpreted the existence of the immoral group as an honor challenge. However, most have not shared such an interpretation, primarily because of the devaluing of 12:21–13:2 and secondarily because of Malina's model, which claims, "the challenge–response game, can only take place between social equals."[128] This leads Vegge, who initially grants that the immoral group represents a challenge only to echo Malina and claim that because of Paul's unequal status, "his personal status (and honour) is, therefore, not drawn into any serious doubt."[129] Not only does this assume that the discursive construal of Paul's authority is certain and equivalent to the authority acknowledged by his readers, which is not the case (2 Cor. 10:7; 13:3a), it is also inaccurate. Zeba A. Crook argues that this portion of Malina's model needs revision, demonstrating that challenges and ripostes occurred between people of unequal status.[130] Similarly, Lendon writes, "the status or the identity of the critic did not matter: the shouted abuse of the base, anonymous lampoons and verses, anonymous gossip, and anonymous slander all excited acute concern. Insult also argued weakness, the inability to defend honor."[131]

Revisiting Malina's comments from Chapter 2, he states, "a challenge is a claim to enter the social space of another."[132] Similarly, following Paul's manifold interventions in which he commands sexual purity and establishes himself as an exemplar of sexual restraint (1 Cor. 7:7, 32-35), the presence of the immoral group signals an affront to Paul's role in the community. Since deference was a chief sign of acknowledging another's honor, anything short of capitulation could result in pique.[133] In a world in which the smallest slight, such as failing to dismount a donkey or mule at the passing of a superior, preventing a man from fishing or blowing smoke

---

128. Malina, *Insights*, 35.
129. Vegge, *2 Corinthians*, 285, see 281–3, 284–5.
130. Zeba A. Crook, "Honor, Shame, and Social Status Revisited," *JBL* 128.3 (2009): 599–604; cf. Barton, *Roman Honor*, 62; Aullus Gellius, *Noct. att.* 7.14.3.
131. Lendon, *Honour*, 51.
132. Malina, *Insights*, 33.
133. Lendon, *Honour*, 50–1; Susan P. Mattern, *Rome and the Enemy: Imperial Strategy in the Principate* (Berkeley: University of California Press, 1999), 171–94

into a room, was evidence of affront or offence, it is hard to imagine the presence of the immoral group during the visit as anything less than an honor challenge.[134] Yet, the presence of the immoral group is not simply a failure at acquiescence. Deference to authority implied obedience.[135] By their presence, the immoral group defied Paul's authority and represented an intentional, symbolic challenge regarding Paul's social power to order group life.

Second, such a public encounter before the community resonates with the ancient ordeal. Barton insightfully states, "Romans were eager to interpret any and every confrontation as an ordeal, an opportunity for the exercise of will."[136] Initially, this is supported by evidence that valued public spectacle in which communal hierarchy was defined. First Corinthians 4:18-21, in which Paul threatens his detractors with martial action in person, although his aim is hortatory, echoes such a high-wire scene.[137] The immoral group's presence during the visit indicates any interaction would indeed appear as a contest, a boundary-defining moment of truth.[138] While challenges might involve personal space and one's boundaries, the challenge of the founder/leader of a group amounts to a contest concerning the group's social constitution, an issue clearly unsettled throughout the correspondence. Indeed, Paul's use of his own epistolary *persona* as communal exemplar (1 Cor. 4:16; 5:3; 7:7; 11:1) reflects the ancient understanding that persons were considered the embodiment of their policies and representative of social programs (§2.3.3).

Third, in light of the ongoing struggle to define the community's proper social ethos and Paul's warnings in 1 Cor. 4:18-21, the immoral group's presence indicates an intelligible expression of enmity and within the communal paradigm indicates a breakdown in the political community (§2.3.1). In as much as the "new consensus" contends that Corinth was a stratified community with an unruly contingent possessing elite-like pretensions, such a challenge is not unlike other recorded στάσεις in which elites vied for power (§2.3.1-2),[139] present also in non-elite communities (§2.5.2).

---

134. On failure to dismount, see Dio 24.22.10; Suetonius, *Nero* 5.1; preventing a fishing trip, see Ulpian, *Dig.* 47.0.13.7; smoke, Javolenus, *Dig.* 47.10.44, from Lendon, *Honour*, 51, and Ramsay MacMullen, *Changes in the Roman Empire: Essays in the Ordinary* (Princeton: Princeton University Press, 1990), 190–3.

135. Lendon, *Honour*, 60–1.

136. Barton, *Roman Honor*, 32.

137. Witherington, *Conflict and Community*, 148; Vegge, *2 Corinthians*, 264.

138. Barton, *Roman Honor*, 35.

139. Cf. Gehrke, *Stasis*, 328–39.

3.3.3. *The Roots of the Intermediate Visit (1 Corinthians 4:18-21)*

Moving forward, it is necessary to ask how the community or elements within interpreted or construed Paul's threat of martial action (13:2) and subsequent exit. Initially, Paul's ultimatum (13:3a) and reason for absence (1:23) suggests a position of strength, but when framed by Paul's challenge to a group of detractors in 1 Cor. 4:18-21, echoes of a negative interpretation become unavoidable in 2 Cor. 10:1-11, 12:21, and 13:1-10.[140] Below we analyze Paul's proleptic challenge and promise of martial discipline in 1 Cor. 4:18-21 before turning to 2 Cor. 10:1-11 and 13:1-10 in order to analyze the evidence of the community's negative evaluation of the intermediate visit.

The intermediate visit and the terms used to qualify it in 2 Corinthians most likely find their origin in 1 Corinthians.[141] From the vantage of Paul's ongoing relationship with the Corinthians, 1 Cor. 4:18-21 demonstrates a growing animus and Paul's promise of martial efficacy.[142] To those who have judged Paul negatively, he promises to come and administer discipline (4:18-21).[143] In the first unit (1:10–4:21) that judgment involves Paul's rhetorical abilities which were maligned by some in the community (cf. 2:1-5; 3:1-4; 4:1-5; 2 Cor 11:6),[144] while those of Apollos were favored (3:1-4; 16:12).[145] This may point to a source of the factionalism found in 1:10,[146] with the preference for certain forms of rhetoric split along socio-economic lines.[147] Inasmuch as 1 Cor. 4:18-21 straddles two textual units, the warning takes aim both for those who critique Paul's speech (1:10–4:16) and those addressed in the test cases of apostolic authority (5:1–6:20), which includes sexual misconduct.[148]

---

140. Cf. Carlson, "Πάλιν," 613.

141. My argument here is largely indebted to Vegge, whose points I aim to further (*2 Corinthians*, 262–6).

142. Weizsäcker originally tied the motivation of the intermediate visit to 1 Cor. 4:18–21 (*Zeitalter*, 293–4).

143. Contra Martin, who argues along with others that Paul is not actually the target of any criticism in 1 Corinthians, which only happens—along the same lines—with the arrivals of the interlopers in 2 Corinthians (*Corinthian Body*, 52).

144. Winter, *Paul and Philo Among the Sophists*, 155–60; contra Martin, *Corinthian Body*, 52, who argues with others that Paul is not actually the target of any criticism in 1 Corinthians, which only happens—along the same lines—with the arrivals of the interlopers in 2 Corinthians.

145. Schrage, *Erste Brief*, 1:144; Winter, *Paul and Philo*, 172–8.

146. Welborn, "On the Discord in Corinth', 102; Winter, *Paul and Philo*, 173.

147. Martin, *Corinthian Body*, xvii, 56, 67; cf. Theissen, *Essays on Corinth*, 97–8.

148. Land, *Absence*, 263.

Regarding his detractors, Paul states in 1 Cor. 4:18, "some [τινες] have become arrogant as if I am not coming to you." Not only do some inappropriately judge Paul before the Lord comes (4:5b), they also judge him in *absentia*. Paul indicates that questions concerning his social power are tied to his absence.[149]

While Paul repeatedly claims future judgment is to be anticipated in the present in Corinth (1 Cor. 5:1-13; 6:1-11; 11:29-32), he simultaneously claims he is exempt from any present judgment (4:3-5). Interpreters suggest that some in Corinth consider Paul's absence inconsiderate[150] or evidence of a lack of courage.[151] Yet neither suggest why Paul's absence contributes to a challenge to his authority. Scott Hafemann remarks, "the objection was also being raised by some that although Paul was the founder of the church at Corinth, his absence now meant that his authority was no longer valued for the entire church but only those whom he had personally won for the Lord."[152] Perhaps this was the case, which may further suggest that a shift in the community composition equated to something of a demographic timebomb, in which elite-like pretensions were destined to clash with Paul's prerogatives. Whatever the case, the "arrogant ones" find in his absence the necessary social space to criticize him and embrace an alternative ethos.[153] Implied is that members from this group do not wish for Paul's return (cf. 16:12).[154] That Paul's absence was viewed as opportunity for a revision of the community's social ethos is implied in his numerous attempts to impose his discursive representation as paradigmatic of the group's ethos (4:16; 9:1-26; 11:1) and his epistolary presence in the summons to punitive action (5:3).[155]

---

149. Kremer, *Erste Brief*, 96.

150. Nils A. Dahl, "Paul and the Church at Corinth According to 1 Corinthians 1:10–4:21," in *Christian History and Interpretation: Studies Presented to John Knox*, ed. W. R Farmer, C. F. D. Moule, and R. R. Niebuhr (Cambridge: Cambridge University Press, 1967), 325–9.

151. Weizsäcker, *Zeitalter*, 288; Schrage, *Erste Brief*, 1:361; Kremer, *Erste Briefe*, 96; Vegge, *2 Corinthians*, 263.

152. Scott J. Hafemann, *Suffering & Ministry in the Spirit: Paul's Defense of His Ministry in II Corinthians 2:14–3:3* (Grand Rapids: Eerdmans, 1990), 60.

153. "Der Gedanke wäre: Wenn die Katze aus dem Haus ist, tanzen die Mäuse" (Zeller, *Erste Brief*, 194).

154. As implied in the request for Apollos not Paul to return (Winter, *Paul and Philo*, 177–8).

155. Mitchell comments, "the appeal to example, and especially that of Paul is the deliberative unifying appeals found throughout 1 Corinthians" (*Reconciliation*, 247).

Paul responds with a threat drawing upon a combination of the presence–absence and word–deed motif. The passage is structured as follows:

I. Arrogance in Paul's Absence (4:18)
II. Paul's Coming Scrutiny of δύναμις not λόγος (4:19)
III. The Nature of the Kingdom of God (4:20)
IV. Warning in Advance of Visit (4:21)

Paul turns the tables, wishing to scrutinize not the words (λόγος) but the power (δύναμις) of the "arrogant ones" (τῶν πεφυσιωμένων) when he arrives (4:19b). The criterion for the scrutiny involves the word–power antithesis, of which Anthony Thiselton states, "its central point is therefore *the ability to carry a deed through effectively*."[156] In 4:20, Paul emphasizes that the Kingdom of God is defined primarily by its δύναμις not λόγος, a point pressed already in 1 Cor. 2:1-5 concerning the contrast between oratorical flair and Paul's critique of eloquence. The word–power antithesis involves a seeming challenge to his detractors to actualize their criticisms, if they dare. In the context of factitious behavior and the criticism of Paul's oratorical prowess (1:10–4:21), Paul offers an ultimatum. "There is a choice open to the congregation," writes Eva Lassen. "Paul concludes his long discussion of dissension and revolt in 1 Cor. 1:10–4:21 with the questions 'What do you wish? Shall I come to you with a rod or with love in a spirit of gentleness?'"[157] As Corinth's apostle, Paul himself promises to meet the "arrogant ones" with disciplinary action in the form a ῥάβδος as evidence of Paul's apostolic power but if they relent through Paul's epistolary intervention (4:14) and Timothy's visit (4:17), his return will be characterized by πραΰτης (4:21). This is clearly language of a proleptic challenge.[158] Vegge claims Paul frames "a potential power-encounter" to occur upon Paul's return.[159] Paul raised the stakes concerning control of the community upon his impending visit by threatening his detractors with an apostolic therapy by ordeal—a demonstration of Paul's efficacious, disciplinary presence to define his proper place as Corinth's apostle.

To what disciplinary action ῥάβδος refers is uncertain. However, in a recent article White concludes with a host of German scholars that ῥάβδος

---

156. Thiselton, *First Epistle*, 370, italics original; similarly Zeller, *Erste Briefe*, 195.
157. Eva Maria Lassen, "The Use of the Father Image in Imperial Propaganda and 1 Corinthians 4:14–21," *TynBul* 42.1 (1991): 136.
158. Witherington, *Conflict and Community*, 148; Vegge, *2 Corinthians*, 264.
159. Vegge, *2 Corinthians*, 264.

refers metaphorically to excommunication.[160] At an elementary level, claims Jacob Kremer, it is a vivid example of Paul tying his authority to the use of punitive violence ("von strafender Gewalt Gebrauch").[161] Fundamentally, ῥάβδος along with 4:18-21 points to another example of present judgment in light of eschatological realities, here involving a demonstration of Paul's authority over his challengers (see below, §2.7.3). In light of the often ruinous outcomes of internecine conflict, Eckhard Schnabel unassumingly echoes this longstanding component of Graeco-Roman political theory, stating, "Möglicherweise denkt Paulus an den Ausschluss der Christen aus der Gemeinde, die für Rivalitäten verantwortlich sind."[162] This would be predictable in light of the reflexive response to communal strife.

Interestingly, Paul demands a form of expulsion in the next unit (5:1-13), an enforced absence. There Paul invokes his presence τῷ πνεύματι (5:3) to expel a person, which according to Fee, "probably harks back to the 'arrogance' of those who say he is not returning."[163] Paul's judgment (κρίνω) of the incestuous man is in the name of [our] Lord Jesus (5:3).[164] The community, once convened, "and with my spirit along with the power of our Lord Jesus" (5:4), is to "hand over this one to Satan" (5:5). The parallelism between Paul's current judgment and the community's proleptic judgment conditioned by the "power" of the Lord indicates that even Paul's virtual presence evidences the institutional power to push out a defiant sinner. Thus, the expulsion τῷ πνεύματι that Paul summons regarding the incestuous man harkens what he threatens to do παρών "while present" regarding the arrogant ones.

This interpretation is consistent both with our study in which power in antique society often involved the ability to expel one's opponents and the practice of exclusions or expulsions, which occurred in analogous communities (§2.3.2; §2.5.3). Perhaps most importantly, Paul frames the terms of the contest to demonstrate his authority on a presence–absence

---

160. White, "The Rod," 404–6; similarly Johannes Weiss, *Der erste Korintherbrief*, KEK 5, 9th edn (Göttingen: Vandenhoeck & Ruprecht, 1910), 122; Kremer, *Erste Brief*, 97; Eckhard J. Schnabel, *Der erste Brief des Paulus an die Korinther*, HTA (Brunnen: Brockhaus, 2006), 268; Zeller, *Erste Brief*, 196.

161. "Paulus setzt mit der bildhaften Ausdrucksweise jedenfalls voraus, daß er in der Gemeinde von seiner Autorität und, wenn nötig, auch von strafender Gewalt Gebrauch machen kann" (Kremer, *Erste Brief*, 97).

162. Schnabel, *Erste Brief*, 268.

163. Fee, *First Epistle*, 205.

164. For extended discussion of the grammatical function of the adverbial phrases in 5:4, see Thiselton, *First Epistle*, 392–4.

axis. Paul who is absent now, facing some measure of criticism, will come to Corinth and, if necessary, make absent through martial action the arrogant ones thus demonstrating his apostolic power as divinely authorized and the counterfeit nature of those who critique the apostle.

3.3.4. *The Construal of the Intermediate Visit (2 Corinthians 10:1-11)*

While the absence–presence, word–deed motif in 1 Cor. 4:18–21 looks forward to Paul's second visit to Corinth, Paul's detractors in 2 Corinthians likely evaluate the intermediate visit with a similar absence–presence, word–deed motif. The evidence of the community's negative evaluation of Paul's behavior during the intermediate visit is most evident in 2 Cor. 10:1-11 and 13:1-10. The connection between both units is evident through the ἀπών–παρών antithesis and other parallels.[165] The antithesis refers not simply to his confrontation with the immoral group, but a schema produced by his detractors or opponents claiming a fundamental dissonance between Paul in person and Paul in absence (cf. 2 Cor. 1:17). Thus, while presently, we inquire how Paul's audience interpreted this confrontation, there are at least two more recent layers present in the text: the claim that Paul is two *personae* following the Severe Letter (and 1 Corinthians) and Paul's response. While it is necessary to attend to all layers present, our interest is primarily upon the evaluation of Paul present (παρών) during the intermediate visit.

Second Corinthians 10:1-11 evidences a shift in tone and intensity from chs. 8–9, leaving interpreters grasping at straws. Yet, 10:1-11 (and 13:1-10) lies bare the intermediate visit as construed by some in the community.

I. Criticism of Presence and Threats of Martial Action (10:1-6)
   A. Entreaty and Absence–Presence Criticism (10:1-2)
   B. Threats of War in Corinth (10:3-6)
II. Paul's Authority (Re)Established in Corinth (10:7-11)
   A. Claim to Authority (10:7)
   B. Authority Questioned in Absence–Presence Criticism (10:8-10)
   C. Authority (Re)Established through Martial Action (10:11)

It is reasonable to suppose that 10:1–13:10 focuses upon not only Paul's return, but also upon those who view his exit and return negatively, that

---

165. For links between both units, see Hans-Georg Sundermann, *Der schwache Apostel und die Kraft der Rede. eine rhetorische Analyse von 2 Kor 10–13*, EHS 23.575 (Frankfurt: Peter Lang, 1996), 47.

is, those who remain unreconciled to Paul whether through the Severe Letter (2:6; 12:20-21; 13:2), or from the visit itself if 10:1-11 belong to the Severe Letter.

In 2 Cor. 10:1, 10, Paul echoes negative characterizations of his presence in Corinth. Paul quotes or paraphrases his detractors, "[I am] abject [ταπεινός] when face to face, but when absent I am courageous" (10:1). Moreover, "his bodily presence is weak" (ἡ παρουσία τοῦ σώματος ἀσθενὴς) and "his word is of no consequence" (ὁ λόγος ἐξουθενημένος, 10:10). It is generally agreed that the expressions ταπεινός, ἀσθενής, and ὁ λόγος ἐξουθενημένος reflect criticisms of Paul's actions *in* Corinth (i.e. ἐν ὑμῖν, 10:1).[166] There is debate about whether the source of the criticism comes from inside the community[167] or from the rivals[168] and whether the singular pronouns (τις, ὁ τοιοῦτος) and verb (φησίν) refer to an individual (i.e. ὁ ἀδικήσας[169] or a prominent rival[170]) or generically to the group in 10:2.[171] Second Corinthians 13:1-10 indicates that Paul responds to parallel criticism *from the community* with the recurrent use of the second person plural (cf. 13:3-4; 10:7-8).[172] Thus, the singular pronouns (τις, ὁ τοιοῦτος) and verb (φησίν) most likely function generically, perhaps referring to the community at large or the remaining detractors.[173] However, it is possible the singular pronouns refer to a prominent figure whose criticisms are representative of a larger contingent.

Further debate centers upon the qualities or behavior to which ταπεινός and ἀσθενής refer. Clearly, the terms are pejorative in nature—a meaning entirely at odds with most New Testament and the patristic usages (Lk. 1:52; Rom. 12:15; Jas 1:9; 4:6; 1 Pet. 5:5; *1 Clem.* 30:2; 55:6; 59:3; *Barn.* 14:9). Commentators question whether the criticisms refer to Paul's general deportment or his particular conduct during the intermediate visit. Overwhelmingly, those who appeal to the social

---

166. Aejmelaeus, *Schwachheit*, 54; Schmeller, *Zweite Brief*, 2:128, and most others; contra Betz, *Der Apostel Paulus und die sokratische Tradition: Eine exegetische Untersuchung zu seiner "Apologie" 2 Kor 10–13*, BHT 45 (Tübingen: Mohr Siebeck, 1972), 45–57.

167. Barnett, *Second Epistle*, 453–5; Campbell, *Framing Paul*, 113; to a degree, Vegge, *2 Corinthians*, 270.

168. Weizsäcker, *Zeitalter*, 309; Plummer, *Second Epistle*, 280, 283–84; Bultmann, *Second Letter*, 190; Furnish, *II Corinthians*, 464, 466, 468.

169. Watson, "Painful Letter," 343–6, and others Welborn, *Enmity*, 103, 122–4.

170. Barrett, *Second Epistle*, 256, 260–1; Martin, *2 Corinthians*, 307–8, 311.

171. Vegge, *2 Corinthians*, 270–1.

172. Vegge, *2 Corinthians*, 270.

173. Barnett *Second Epistle*, 453; Watson, "Painful Letter," 343–4.

3. The Intermediate Ordeal

world claim that the criticisms against Paul refer to a chronic deficiency in the apostle's personal physical presence. These exegetes claim the defect involves his poor physical appearance or condition,[174] insistence on plying an ignoble trade for support,[175] pneumatic speech,[176] or rhetorical ability and style.[177]

Convincing reasons exist to suppose, however, that Paul echoes criticisms of the specific character of the immediately preceding visit, rather than of general deportment.[178] Chapters 10–13 are dominated by the concern of Paul's impending arrival (cf. 10:11; 12:14, 20-21; 13:1-10). Within the unit, Paul emphasizes the specific, potentially martial nature of his return (10:2, 3-6, 11; 13:2, 3b-4, 10) implying a similar emphasis on the specific topic of the previous visit. Paul argues that his supposed abasement ἐν ὑμῖν (10:1) will be transformed by God's resurrection power will be manifest εἰς ὑμᾶς (13:4). This seems warranted by Paul's clear characterization of that visit as ταπεινόω...πρὸς ὑμᾶς (12:21), which is echoed in the accusation against Paul, "who [is] lowly [ταπεινός] when face to face, but when absent I am courageous" (10:1). Likewise, Paul responds to the charge of being ταπεινός and ἀσθενής in person, promising, "the sort of people we are in word [λόγος] by letters when we are absent, such we will also be in deed [ἔργον] when we are present" (10:11).[179] If Paul means these words with any seriousness, it is unlikely that he is referring to a longstanding criticism. Paul would then capitulate to his detractors, promising to demonstrate a quality, like rhetoric or

---

174. Betz, *Paulus*, 45–57, 96; Harrill, "Invective."

175. Hock, *Tentmaking*, 50–65; for the inverse, that Paul's letters financially burdened his audience, see Sundermann, *schwache Apostel*, 66–7.

176. Richard Reitzenstein, *Hellenistic Mystery-Religions: Their Basic Ideas and Significance*, ed. Dikran Y. Hadidian, PTMS (Pittsburgh: Pickwick, 1978), 461; Käsemann, "Die Legitimität des Apostles," 35; Lietzmann, *Korinther I–II*, 142; Oostendorp, *Another Jesus*, 17; Schmithals, *Gnosticism*, 176–9; Bultmann, *Second Letter*, 188, 190; Martin, *2 Corinthians*, 312; H. Wayne Merritt, *In Word and Deed: Moral Integrity in Paul*, ESEC (New York: Peter Lang, 1993), 127–8; Aejmelaeus, *Schwachheit*, 94–5.

177. Allo, *Seconde Epître*, 249; Hughes, *Second Epistle*, 362; Marshall, *Enmity*, 385–6; David E. Fredrickson, "Paul's Bold Speech in the Argument of 2 Corinthians 2:14–7:16" (Ph.D. diss., Yale University, 1990), 36–48; Pogoloff, *Logos and Sophia*, 147–8; Peterson, *Eloquence*, 92; Winter, *Paul and Philo*, 204–13, 221–3; in part, Welborn, *Enmity*, 105–22.

178. Weizsäcker, *Zeitalter*, 299; Bachmann, *Zweite Brief*, 350; Aejmelaeus, *Schwachheit*, 54; Schmeller, *Zweite Brief*, 2:145.

179. Schmeller, *Zweite Brief*, 2:147 n. 161; cf. Aejmelaeus, *Schwachheit*, 96–7.

maintenance, previously rejected on theological grounds and, stranger still, would in the case of rhetoric refer to oratory as ἔργον.[180] Thus, when considering the judgment against Paul in 10:1, 10 in relation to the intermediate visit, the common explanations linked to the social world fail to convince (§1.3.1; §1.3.2).

The charges that Paul is ταπεινός, ἀσθενής, and ὁ λόγος ἐξουθενημένος more likely echo the community's judgment of Paul's behavior during the intermediate visit, most notably his failure to affect communal discipline in response to the affront by the immoral group as he promised in 1 Cor. 4:18-21 (cf. §1.3.3).[181] This is signaled through Paul's admission that he only warned the immoral group upon his visit (13:2). Apparently, this group was not swayed by 1 Corinthians and called Paul's bluff. Paul responded with only another warning. In the simplest terms Francis Watson concludes, "Paul therefore did not carry out the intention for his second visit expressed in 1 Cor. iv. 18-21."[182] This lies at the heart of the evaluation of Paul's conduct in 2 Cor. 10:1, 10 and beyond (13:1-10). Thus, the criticism is not simply that Paul does not perform according to the community's desire, but that he did not act as he promised. Thus, *while Paul argued he is exempt from communal judgment in 1 Cor. 4:4 in response to some measure of criticism, it is evident in 2 Cor. 10:1-11 (13:1-10) that he is the target of judgment based on the criteria laid out in 1 Cor. 4:18-21.*

Notably, Harris, who rejects the possibility of Paul's exit after a confrontation with the ὁ ἀδικήσας on the grounds that "he was not the sort of man to retreat before opposition," essentially agrees with Watson.[183] In regards to the charges in 10:1, 11, he states, "a contributing factor to the charge of 'weakness in person' may have been his inability during his recent 'painful visit'...to discipline those guilty of immorality and bring them to repentance...an inability he himself calls a humiliation."[184] Thus, however uncomfortable Harris is with the notion of Paul in flight, he

---

180. Vegge, *2 Corinthians*, 321–2; Schellenberg, *Education*, 279–80; contra Schmeller, *Zweite Brief*, 2:146.

181. Weiss, *Primitive Christianity*, 1:342–3; Oostendorp, *Another Jesus*, 17–27; Watson, "Painful Letter," 42–5; Vegge, *2 Corinthians*, 262–3; Schmeller, *Zweite Brief*, 2:130, 145; Schellenberg, *Education*, 280–1. Similarly, Filson, "Second Epistle," 381–8; Barnett, *Second Epistle*, 457–78, 597, 605, 608; Aejmelaeus, *Schwachheit*, 52–99; Savage, *Power*, 64–9; Walker, *Offer*, 242–57; Larson, "Paul's Masculinity," 92; Harris, *Second Epistle*, 669–71; Land, *Absence*, 208–11.

182. Watson, "Painful Letter," 343.

183. Harris, *Second Epistle*, 59.

184. Harris, *Second Epistle*, 671.

finds it reasonable to conclude that Paul found a group in defiance of his gospel's ethos and left without affecting discipline. Harris's somewhat contradictory contention indicates that the full significance of Paul's inaction has yet to be explored and understood.

3.3.5. Martial Inaction in Ancient Sources

From the evidence found in the social world, the criticisms echoed in 2 Cor. 10:1, 10 are largely what we would expect emerging from a community ordeal, a challenge of authority. As demonstrated in the overview of ordeals, in the face of adversity and affront, individuals were expected to display assertiveness, masculine courage, and energetic response (§2.2). Paul seemingly promised as much in 1 Cor. 4:16-21, in a letter that provides few other objective criteria for gauging status or restraining conduct as found in analogous communities. Vegge observes that martial restraint could be perceived as weakness.[185] A salient parallel comes from Plutarch (fl. ca. 50–120 CE), who writes of Cicero,

> Cicero...began to deliberate...what he should do with the men. For he shrank from inflicting the extreme penalty...because of the kindliness [ἐπιείκεια] of his nature... For...he himself would be thought unmanly and weak [ἄνανδρος καὶ μαλακός], especially as the multitude already thought him very far from courageous.[186]

Importantly, Plutarch connects Cicero's martial restraint both to his character and the community's broader evaluation of him. Dio Cassius (fl. ca. 150–235) claimed that leniency towards a subordinate could be viewed as a virtue in the case of emperors. Yet, for the rest "such conduct is thought to argue their weakness [ἀσθένεια], whereas to attack and to exact vengeance is considered to furnish proof of great power [δύναμαι]."[187] Dio's remark connects the evaluation of weakness and strength specifically to the question of a martial response to an affront from an unequal. Plutarch remarks that for Marius, the measure of a man was "conquest and mastery in all things and at all times...not weakness and effeminacy [ἀσθένεια καὶ μαλακία]."[188] Similarly, in 4 Maccabees the typical weakness (ἀσθενόψυχος, 15:5) of a woman is contrasted with the mother's masculine courage (ἀνδρειόω, 15:23) demonstrated during her sons' ordeal before Antiochus.

---

185. Vegge, *2 Corinthians*, 280; cf. Philo, *Somn.* 2.95; Dio Chrysostom, *Conc. Apam.* 24; Josephus, *B.J.* 5.335.
186. Plutarch, *Cic.* 19.7 cited also by Vegge.
187. Dio Cassius 58.5.4.
188. Plutarch, *Cor.* 15.5.

As demonstrated in Chapter 2, this framework was available to Paul through the stories of Gideon and Goliath and present in his own narration of his assertive, public challenge to Peter.

From the vantage of the virtue economy Graeco-Roman, masculinity and femininity were not simply issues of anatomy, but better understood as a precarious, hierarchical continuum, on which one's location was dependent upon displays of masculine virtues.[189] The perilous nature of one's place on the continuum demanded constant vigilance and demonstration of all the affairs under one's care. Any loss of control in the affairs under one's governance pushed a person down the hierarchical continuum towards effeminacy.[190] Such cultural evaluations likely drive the criticisms that Paul is abject and weak following the intermediate visit.

One reason for martial action in response to an affront from one of lower status occurs, according to Aulus Gellius (fl. ca. 123–170 CE), "when the dignity and the prestige of the one who is sinned against must be maintained, lest the omission of punishment bring him into contempt and diminish the esteem in which he is held."[191] The resulting evaluation of Paul implies the diminution of honor in the eyes of the community. Often, physical force was seen as necessary to repel a challenge. Lendon comments, "a man needed the power to hurt to defend his honour, to protect himself against slights and humiliations."[192] For instance, Cicero states to Caesar that he conducted civil war "to repel insult from yourself."[193] Euripides writes one would "feel shame" (αἰσχύνομαι) at the inability to repel an assault.[194] Ramsay MacMullen summarizes the alternative even for superiors: "if you simply accepted insulting behavior, you lost face. That was serious. You became Nothing—as even an emperor might."[195] The evaluation of Paul as weak in his reluctance to act as he threatened signals that the detractors viewed him similarly—as a disgraced, impotent leader. What Paul lacks, so his detractors say, is the power to assert himself against his challengers as promised.

When Paul responded to a brazen affront to his authority, he only warned the immoral group again and left Corinth and so incurred such an

---

189. Stephen D. Moore and Janice Capel Anderson, "Taking It Like a Man: Masculinity in 4 Maccabees," *JBL* 117 (1998): 250, 269.

190. Marilyn B. Skinner, "Ego Mulier: The Construction of Male Sexuality in Catallus," *Helios* 20 (1993): 111.

191. Aulus Gellius, *Noct. att.* 7.14.3.

192. Lendon, *Honour*, 106.

193. Cicero, *Lig.* 18; cf. Cicero, *Sull.* 46; *Cat.* 4.20; Caesar, *Bell. gall.* 8.24.

194. Euripides, *Phoen.* 510, here in the context of war.

195. MacMullen, *Changes*, 194; see Dio 79.20.1-3.

evaluation—he was weak (ἀσθενής) and submissive (ταπεινός) in person because his threatening word came to nothing (ὁ λόγος ἐξουθενημένος). Not only does this reflect a larger cultural context, but also indicates Paul is evaluated on the presence–absence, word–deed rubric, which he proffered in 1 Cor. 4:18-21, the very criterion for the proleptic ordeal. This suggests not only that the criticisms reflect Paul's words in 1 Cor. 4:18-21, but that the immoral group understood its existence during the intermediate visit in that light. Thus, the final phrase ὁ λόγος ἐξουθενημένος in an overwhelming martial context is not a reference to Paul's poor oratorical improvisation.[196] Rather, it refers to the reality that Paul's threatening words never materialized into punitive action (see 1 Macc. 3:14; 2 Chron. 36:16).[197] This is likely reflected in Paul's comment, "I will not be put to shame [αἰσχυνθήσομαι] lest I seem as [only] to frighten in my letters" (10:8-9).[198] Vegge aptly questions, "where is the Paul who in 1 Cor. 4:18-21 threatened to demonstrate the power of the kingdom of God by coming with the stick?"[199] In context of Paul's martial threat in 1 Cor. 4:18-21 and the cultural expectations outlined above, the criticism was both justifiable and devastating.

Paul's failure to fulfill his martial threat in person materializes in the inverse accusations that Paul is bold (θαρρέω, 10:1, 2) when absent and weighty (βαρύς, 10:10) and powerful (ἰσχυρός, 10:10) through his letters. These terms refer in part to the kind of martial qualities Paul promised in 1 Cor. 4:18-21, qualities which ancients valued in their leaders in moments of adversity and affront. Rather than the missives' rhetorical or pneumatic flare found lacking during the visit, the accusation is that Paul is an epistolary tiger. The verb θαρρέω generally means, "to have confidence and firmness of purpose in the face of danger or testing."[200] It is used consistently as a summons to resolute action in occasions of distress and anxiety.[201] Paul's detractors remark that he evinces courage from a safe distance but such boldness vanishes at the actual moment of testing. In response, Paul threatens to be bold (θαρρέω) in his return (10:2), which is ultimately explained in 10:3-6 as a military assault on Corinth.

---

196. Contra Winter, *Paul and Philo*, 221–3.

197. For such a connotation, see Schellenberg, *Education*, 284–5; Oostendorp, *Another Jesus*, 20.

198. Bachmann, *Zweite Brief*, 348–50. On the awkwardness of the transition between 10:8-9, see Schellenberg, *Education*, 267–8.

199. Vegge, *2 Corinthians*, 266.

200. L&N §25.156.

201. Aeschylus, *Suppl.* 732; Homer, *Il.* 1.85; Sophocles, *Oed. col.* 649; Exod. 14:13; 20:20 (LXX); Zech. 8:13 (LXX); Bar. 4:5.

Paul's retort thus centers upon the question of martial action against disobedience in the community just as in 1 Cor. 4:18-21, although now in light of the criticized second visit.[202]

Furthermore, his detractors claim his letters are βαρύς and ἰσχυρός (10:10). The terms function in 10:10 synonymously and both may refer to martial or juridical action and personal authority.[203] Plutarch's *Lives* frequently uses the more common βαρός as a masculine virtue in martial or administrative contexts. In reference to a person's authority and competence to judge, Plutarch employs the related term βαρός, writing, "The city made trial of its other generals and counsellors for the conduct of the war, but since no one appeared to have weight [βαρός] that was adequate or authority that was competent for such leadership, it yearned for Pericles, and summoned him back to the bema and the war-office."[204] Of Cato, Plutarch comments, "he displayed a dignity and severity [βαρός] which fully corresponded, for in the administration of justice he was inexorable, and in carrying out the edicts of the government was direct and masterful."[205] Plutarch remarks of "the weight [βαρός] and dignity of [Cato's] character" demonstrated not simply in legal contests but "in battles and campaigns against the enemy."[206] Cato's βαρός resulted in unparalleled φοβερωτέραν of Roman power. Similarly, Polybius comments that the "powerful [βαρός] nature of the Roman forces" threw the Sicilians into terror and dismay, causing them to revolt from the Carthaginians and side with the Romans.[207] Thus, βαρός frequently denotes necessary administrative and martial qualities that at times prompted fear and dismay in onlookers.

The accusations that Paul is θαρρέω, βαρύς, and ἰσχυρός correlate with such a martial and administrative context when placed in the wider context of Paul's threat of punitive action in 1 Cor. 4:18-21 and the more immediate context of 2 Cor. 10:1–13:10. Paul's previous letters project martial strength against members of the community that does not materialize in his personal presence.[208] Barnett comments, "these critics appear to be contrasting the ineffectual discipline attempted by Paul

202. Garland, *2 Corinthians*, 438.
203. Harris, *Second Epistle*, 698–9.
204. Plutarch, *Per.* 37.1.
205. Plutarch, *Cat. Mai.* 6.3.
206. Plutarch, *Cat. Mai.* 1.4-6; *Cor.* 2.1.
207. Polybius 1.16.4.
208. Plummer, *Second Epistle*, 275, 281–2; Weiss, *Primitive Christianity*, 1:343; Filson, "Second Epistle," 383; Watson, "Painful Letter," 343–4; Barnett, *Second Epistle*, 461, 476–7; Aejmelaeus, *Schwachheit*, 54; Vegge, *2 Corinthians*, 263–7, 320–5; Schmeller, *Zweite Brief*, 2:130; Schellenberg, *Rethinking*, 280.

during the second ('painful') visit with the success of the 'Severe Letter' written afterward in place of the expected return visit."²⁰⁹ Yet the plural ἐπιστολαί points to 1 Corinthians as well. Thus, Plummer states Paul was viewed as "at once a coward and a bully."²¹⁰ Interestingly, Posidonius of Apamea (fl. ca. 135–ca. 51 BCE) comments that unchecked βαρύτης in political leaders can lead citizens to desperation and στάσις.²¹¹ This would fit with our reconstruction that the confrontation during the intermediate visit involved a frustration over the costs of Paul's social program in 1 Corinthians. Far from a complement to Paul's rhetorical style²¹² or aggressiveness²¹³ via letter, Paul is criticized for his epistolary bravado (cf. 2 Cor. 1:24; 2:5) that becomes impotence in person.²¹⁴ Tacitus appeals to a similar formula when he wishes to demonstrate the utter incompetence and inferiority of the Helvetti, who "were bold before the crisis came, but grew timid in the face of danger."²¹⁵ The gist of the criticism, then, is that Paul does not have the power to actualize his martial threats and broader program when confronted in person, as demonstrated during the intermediate visit. Thus, Roetzel insightfully comments that Paul was scorned "as a coward who ran away when challenged but wrote 'brave' letters from a distance."²¹⁶

When the criticisms in 10:1, 10 are no longer viewed as referencing a chronic lack in Paul's conduct (rhetorical proficiency, support policy)—however, not inconsistent with such so-called deficiencies—it becomes evident that Paul was hoisted by his own petard, facing the judgment that he was not made of ideal, masculine, timber due to his inability to act forcefully as threatened in 1 Cor. 4:18-21. The accusations refer to a judgment of Paul's leadership qualities considering the intermediate visit. With the aid of 1 Cor. 4:18-21, the judgment against Paul in 2 Cor. 10:1-11 indicates the reality of an interaction between Paul and the community occurring in the interim between 1 and 2 Corinthians, the type of which often linked spectacle and exit with judgment (§2.2) and might precede

209. Barnett, *Second Epistle*, 461.
210. Plummer, *Second Epistle*, 275.
211. Diodorus 34.2.33 = *FGrHist* 87 F 108c.
212. Contra Welborn, *Enmity*, 110.
213. Contra Aejmelaeus, *Schwachheit*, 55, 94.
214. Plummer, who initially concludes that βαρεῖαι καὶ ἰσχυραί refer to a positive evaluation of Paul's letters, reconsiders, stating, "they might mean that in his letters he was tyrannical and violent" (*Second Epistle*, 282).
215. Tacitus, *Hist.* 1.68; cf. Cicero, *Fam.* 7.6 = Ennius, *Trag.* 261.
216. Roetzel, "The Language of War," 80.

attempts at reconciliation and return. Crucially, these accusations are tied to if not dependent upon Paul's behavior during and exit following his visit, which concerns primarily neither a lone wolf, nor the rivals, but a contingent of the community.

3.3.6. *Political Legitimacy, Absence, and Judgment*

Routinely, interpreters perceive that Paul's apostolic (or Christian) legitimacy is in doubt in 2 Corinthians is most evident in 10:7b and 13:3a (cf. 2:16–3:4).[217] There is good reason for such interpretations. In 10:7b, Paul states, "if anyone is persuaded in himself to be of Christ, let this one consider again concerning himself that just as he is of Christ, so also are we." The impression is that Paul responds to a rejection of his legitimacy. However, it is unclear whether the figure (τις) is an individual or a generic reference. Unsurprisingly, opponent theories and the ὁ ἀδικήσας factor into hypotheses for the identity of τις (10:7). However, the communal nature of the criticism is made clear in the parallel passage 13:3a in which Paul acknowledges the community questions his legitimacy, "since you seek [ζητεῖτε] proof that Christ is speaking in me."[218] Paul's point in 10:7 would then be that if any of his detractors consider themselves Χριστοῦ εἶναι then such an assertion is possible only if Paul is rightfully recognized as Corinth's apostle, an interpretation consistent with 13:5-6, which evidences a dialogical relationship between Paul and the community's political legitimacy.[219] If the community or a contingent could make the further challenge concerning Paul's legitimacy based on his behavior, there is no need to foist the responsibility upon the rivals or the ὁ ἀδικήσας.

The employment of δοκιμ- cognates especially in 13:1-10 (10:18), place the discussion of Paul's legitimacy squarely within ancient political communities' evaluation of leadership. Δοκιμασία trials existed in ancient

---

217. Scholars question whether Paul's Christian status is in question (Käsemann, "Die Legitimitat des Apostels. Eine Untersuchung zu II Korinther 10–1," 36; Oostendorp, *Another Jesus*, 18–19) or his apostolic status (Meyer, *Corinthians*, 2:399–400; Plummer, *Second Epistle*, 280; Weiss, *Primitive Christianity*, 1:344; Bultmann, *Second Letter*, 185; Barnett, *Second Epistle*, 470–1; Vegge, *2 Corinthians*, 305–6, Schmeller, *Zweite Brief*, 2:140). When scholars understand chs. 10–13 as the Severe Letter, the singular pronoun refers to the ὁ ἀδικήσας (Klauck, *2 Korintherbrief*, 79; Aejmelaeus, *Schwachheit*, 82).

218. Vegge furthers this interpretive line, which makes contradictory his claim that no one in the community is challenging Paul's legitimacy (*2 Corinthians*, 306–7).

219. Barnett, *Second Epistle*, 470–2; §6.2.1.

Greece as a means of vetting officials' conduct before taking office.²²⁰ Last demonstrates that association officers' activities were heavily surveilled and scrutinized in a manner consistent with δοκιμασία trials in ancient Greek politics.²²¹ The cognate continued to be used in reference to similar elections to offices or acceptance into communities among voluntary associations.²²² Paul encourages a scrutinizing approach to others' leadership in the Corinthian ἐκκλησία (1 Cor. 3:13-14; 11:19; 16:3, 18b), but, as discussed, he rejects the notion that he could face such scrutiny until the *parousia* (1 Cor. 4:3-5). However, some detractors did not accept Paul's claim to immunity after the intermediate visit.

In that light, we ask, on what criteria is Paul judged as ἀδόκιμος (13:6)? Rather than appeal to the broader social world to find analogies concerning the revocation of communal status/rank, scholars routinely suspect that Paul lacks some good that functions as a standard for apostleship. The oft-unstated premise is that in absence of this apostolic quality, the revocation of his legitimacy is possible, what Schmeller refers to as rejection of Paul's "Vollmacht zur Mission (10:8) und den Erfolg der Mission (10:12-18)."²²³ In general, interpreters link the question of Paul's status to whatever is perceived to be the larger criticism in 2 Corinthians 10–13. Sometimes that good is understood as a unique in-group qualification with little relationship to the broader society. Unsurprisingly, opponent theories factor prominently into these hypotheses (esp. 10:7),²²⁴ with commentators claiming the rivals staked legitimacy and superiority upon relation to the earthly Jesus,²²⁵ pneumatic phenomena,²²⁶ or acceptance of support.²²⁷ Others hint that Paul's deficiency involves the usual suspects—the dearth of a valued status indicator, like rhetorical proficiency or appropriate occupation.²²⁸

There are two disqualifying evidences to these approaches. First, all theories are quite forced considering the immediate context. The

---

220. See Gabriel Adeleye, "The Purpose of the 'Dokimasia,'" *GRBS* 24 (1983): 295–306; see §2.5.2; §4.4.1.

221. Last, "Money, Meals, and Honour," 107–10.

222. *IG* 12.3.330 C; *IG* 1368.53-5 from Last, *Corinthian Ekklēsia*, 194–5.

223. Schmeller, *Zweite Brief*, 2:140.

224. For example, Betz, *Apologie*, 132–7.

225. Hughes, *Second Epistle*, 356; Furnish, *II Corinthians*, 476.

226. Bultmann, *Second Letter*, 187–8.

227. Notably reaching for passages quite a distance from 10:7 and 13:3a (11:7-12; 12:13, 14-18; 1 Cor. 9), Käsemann, "Legitimität," 36; Georgi, *Opponents*, 238–42; Theissen, *Essays on Corinth*, 42–8; Thrall, *Second Epistle*, 2:621–2.

228. See Oropeza, *Second Corinthians*, 576–7.

surrounding discourse (10:1-11; 13:1-10) is focused upon Paul's impotent response to affront and his threat of martial efficacy in return. In 10:1-6, Paul responds to those who reckon (λογίζομαι, 10:2) that he walks according to the flesh with a threat of martial action and call to obedience (10:3-6). In 10:7-11, Paul once again takes on those who reckon (λογίζομαι, 10:7) they are of Christ, ultimately arguing to those who reckon (λογίζομαι) that Paul is weak in person that the martial threats and injunctions via missive will be realized in person when Paul returns to Corinth (10:11). The recurrence of λογίζομαι and the content of Paul's argument indicate the entirety of the passage centers on criticisms concerning Paul's inaction during the intermediate visit. A similar focus is evident in 13:1-10, in which the challenge to his apostolicity would be silenced by Paul's martial return (13:3-4, 10). Thus, any hint about the criteria upon which Paul's legitimacy is challenged points towards his lack of martial conduct in the face of affront.

Second, these approaches fail to consider the arena in which a prominent figure's communal rank was revoked. It is as if Paul's communities are *sui generis* in this matter. To be clear, exegetes frequently assert not a diminution of influence or honor, which is already evident in the qualifiers ταπεινός and ἀσθενής, but something far more akin to the potential loss of political status or rank.[229] There are limited examples of revocation of rights when elite males engaged in non-elite activities such as manual labor.[230] Yet, as demonstrated, the revocation of communal rank is largely a unique manifestation of political displacement. There is ample evidence that the criticisms following Paul's intermediate visit resulted in the loss of civic status in other communities. Analogous political communities found such behavior in their leaders untenable for group life. Parallels frequently resulted in formal displacement. In the Greek *polis* absenteeism during an attempted coup resulted in exile.[231] Fleeing the *polis* in a time of revolt or crisis resulted in the sanction of ἀτιμία.[232] In the Republic, cowardice by military officials resulting in defeat could result in *interdictio*.[233] The same principle held true in at least some associations. At Athens, the *Iobbachoi* administered expulsion (ἐργαθεῖν) for officials who failed to bring exclusionary actions against a violent member in violation of the associational

---

229. See §2.4.
230. SEG 18.726.46-8
231. SEG 51.1105B.3-6.
232. IvP I 249.26-30.
233. *Gran. Licin.* 33.6-11C, 24C; Diodorus 3.3.2; Cicero, *Div. Caec.* 63; Valerius Maximus 4.7.3; 6.9.13.

nomoi.²³⁴ Thus, in both matters of honor and administration, communities often expected and demanded that a leader govern with ideal courage and power, enforcing penalties upon the deviant, reprisals upon challengers, thus reinforcing the leader's role and the group's stability. For those who could not enforce the absence of deviants, the judgment associated with absence often fell to them, often resulting in the erasure of a person's position within the community.

More proximately, Paul's behavior during his visit and subsequent absence naturally raise questions of legitimacy according to Paul's words in a manner consistent with cultural logic.²³⁵ Pointing in the right direction, Thrall claims, "Paul has to defend himself against the charge that he is not Christ's spokesman because he has not dealt firmly with delinquents."²³⁶ Yet, Thrall, echoing Theissen's approach, attempts to divine the criteria of such a judgment by appealing both to the assumed contrasting standard embodied by the rivals, further wondering of an unstated early Christian standard: "was there in primitive Christianity, some expectation that an apostle, as Christ's representative, ought to possess some provisional and preliminary powers of judgement and punishment, which he would exercise at the time of his own παρουσία in a particular Christian community?"²³⁷

Rather than a movement-wide standard, the answer is found in Paul's proleptic view to his arrival in Corinth. The challenge to Paul's ways ἐν Χριστῷ Ἰησοῦ (1 Cor. 4:17) was based in part upon his absence in Corinth, a judgment "before the time" (1 Cor. 4:5). Paul's response (4:18-21) implied a question of political legitimacy. As stated, while hortatory in nature, Paul's expression can also be interpreted as a challenge to ordeal. Along with the broader society, Paul viewed such tests as revelatory of a person's true status. However, for Paul, the truth about a person is found in the eschatological ordeal (1 Cor. 3:12-15). Thus, Paul states, τὸ πῦρ [αὐτὸ] δοκιμάσει in 3:13 in reference to the disclosure of the quality or legitimacy of one's work. Thiselton comments that in part "the person concerned shares the rightwised (justified) status of those who are in Christ."²³⁸

---

234. *IG* 1368.84-95.
235. Similarly, Barnett, *Second Epistle*, 601–2; Vegge, *2 Corinthians*, 306–7, 343–4.
236. Margaret E. Thrall, "Super-Apostles, Servants of Christ, and Servants of Satan," *JSNT* 6 (1980): 54.
237. Thrall, "Super-Apostles," 54.
238. Thiselton, *First Epistle*, 313.

Yet, for Paul, eschatological verdicts are often anticipated in present, communal moments of truth.[239] The same revelatory effects of "the Day" are demonstrated in the Lord's Supper (11:17-34). A meal in the present (συνέρχεσθε, 11:17) that proclaims the Lord's death until he comes (ἔλθῃ, 11:26) distinguishes the approved (οἱ δόκιμοι, 11:19) from the unapproved, exposing the latter to present judgment (11:27-30). However, if members would judge themselves rightly, they would avoid eschatological judgment (11:31-32).[240] Similarly, Paul commands the formation of a plenary body for the expulsion of the incestuous brother now (5:3) in light of "the Day of the Lord Jesus" (5:5). Present displacement from the community (5:9-13) anticipates eschatological disinheritance (6:9-10). And it is the saints' eschatological ambit of jurisdiction that warrants the formation of communal courts (6:2) and the illegitimacy of external courts (6:4). Thus, present moments in Corinth (meals, plenary gatherings, judicial hearings) may be suffused with eschatological realism (§2.7.3).

Such moments of discriminating judgment in the Corinthian correspondence are complementary to Moses's leadership ordeals in the Numbers 12–20. In Numbers 12, Aaron and Miriam challenge Moses's role as unique mouthpiece of YHWH. The author remarks that Moses was exceedingly humble (πραΰς, Num. 12:3) before YHWH comes to Moses's defense (Num. 12:4-9). The judgment results in Miriam stricken with leprosy (12:10) and banished (ἀφορίζω) from the camp for seven days (12:14). The rebellion of Korah against Aaron, and Dathan and Abiram's challenge to Moses results in the earth swallowing all three rebels (Num. 16:31-34) as fire consumes their supporters (16:35). Finally, Moses and Aaron's presumptuous and disobedient actions at Kadesh result in both leaders' disqualification from entering the Promised Land (Num. 20:1-13). In each instance, leadership ordeals result in divine judgment resulting in exclusion from the community or sacred space.

Although Paul commands judgments to be withheld "until the Lord comes who will bring to light the secrets of darkness and reveal the purpose of the heart" (1 Cor. 4:5), Paul's threat to come (ἔλθω) in judgment by ordeal in 1 Cor. 4:21 clearly echoes the eschatological ordeal in which the Lord comes (ἔλθῃ) in 4:5. Even the expression ἡ βασιλεία τοῦ θεοῦ (4:20) which often possesses an eschatological sense (1 Cor. 6:9-10; 15:50; Gal. 5:21; Eph. 5:5; 2 Thess. 1:5), here refers to the present.[241] The

---

239. Roetzel, *Judgement*, 109–76.

240. Lanuwabang Jamir, *Exclusion and Judgment in Fellowship Meals: The Socio-Historical Background of 1 Corinthians 11:17–34* (Eugene, OR: Pickwick, 2016), 227, see 223–5.

241. Fitzmyer, *First Corinthians*, 225; Kremer, *Erste Briefe*, 96.

hint of eschatological realism in Paul's arrival parallels the examples above.[242] Thus, in 1 Cor. 4:18-21, legitimacy within the kingdom of God is measured by δύναμις in person, not λόγος, and inadvertently constructs a criterion by which Paul may face scrutiny. In that context, if Paul did not wield eschatological δύναμις, the evaluation of Paul as weak in person and bold from afar already implies the charge of eschatological illegitimacy. Thrall's hunch is likely correct, although the issue of legitimacy springs from Paul's own words concerning his arrival in 1 Corinthians rather than an apostolic norm. In Paul's Corinthian church, not unlike the wider world, test and judgment of legitimacy (communal ranks) were concomitant, although Paul's discourse is shot through with his eschatology.

Moreover, it is Paul who leaves Corinth while the immoral group continues to operate, perhaps along with replacement apostles at the behest of the detractors. Paul's riposte in 1 Cor. 4:18-21 reflects the territoriality of the conflict, in which he promised to meet recalcitrance with the metaphorical ῥάβδος, most likely referring to a sanction through exclusion or expulsion. We have already demonstrated that across antiquity expulsions and voluntary exits often resulted in the complementary sanction of the erasure of a person's civic rank.

Consistent with the politics of displacement, Paul's references to intra-communal judgment both in the present and also the eschaton in 1 Corinthians consistently refer to approval and legitimacy in terms of presence or remaining (1 Cor. 3:14; cf. 13:13) and illegitimacy in terms of incineration of work (3:15), expulsion (5:1-13), exclusion (6:9-10), and weakness/illness/death (11:28-30).[243] Yet, in the context of the intermediate ordeal, an occasion loaded with spatial, punitive, and status-related significance, it is Paul who leaves.[244] Weiss comments, "So that 'day of judgment'…had run its course, with results that were sufficiently disastrous for him."[245] Not only does Paul not act punitively in the eschatologically colored visit, he leaves rather than his challengers. In consideration of the accusations against Paul, it would be quite logical for the community to question Paul's political legitimacy without appeal to the rivals or some early Christian standard since his behavior (inaction and exit) was a sign of illegitimacy both in 1 Corinthians and according to a broader cultural logic. This seems confirmed in Paul's assertion that

---

242. See Funk, "Apostolic Parousia," 264–6; Roetzel, *Judgement*, 162 n. 4.

243. Conversely, if Last's interpretation of 1 Cor. 11:18-34 is correct, judgment involves not simply the loss of members, but the removal of current officers and the election (αἵρεσις) of others, *Corinthian Ekklēsia*, 183–212.

244. See Duff, *Moses*, 90–1.

245. Weiss, *Primitive Christianity*, 1:343.

he will reclaim if necessary his legitimacy in his punitive return (2 Cor. 10:11; 13:3-4).[246]

Elsewhere, Paul could employ withdrawal language (ὑποστέλλω, Gal. 2:12) as implying not only cowardice, but condemnation (καταγιγνώσκω, Gal. 2:11). He knew what it meant to arrive in a city and publicly confront wrongdoing with authority, as with Peter. He also knew what it meant to be driven from a contest, responding with sensitivity to what that implied (1 Thess. 2:1-20). What emerges as unique in the Corinthians correspondence is Paul withdrawing from an internecine challenge. If inaction and exit pointed to judgment and illegitimacy, then Paul's withdrawal from the intermediate ordeal suggests it is Paul who stands under the judgment of political and eschatological illegitimacy. Paul was supposed to bring the exclusionary rod to Corinth, but instead he received the rod according to his detractors, as evidenced in the judgment of illegitimacy.

3.4. *Evaluating the Evidence*

In response to our initial question concerning whether some in the community evaluated Paul's absence from Corinth as a form of painful affront or a response to communal strife; the evidence indicates the latter. Furthermore, in order to challenge those interpretations that understand the intermediate visit as an event *sui generis*, we ask, to what social phenomenon does the above interpretation point? In light of the exigencies of strife and absence and the aims of reconciliation and return, this chapter has demonstrated a resonance with the known mutual cognitive environment concerning political displacement. Paul's non-martial presence, subsequent exit, and continuing absence likely appeared to observers as a form of political displacement. This assertion resonates with frequent scholarly descriptions of the intermediate event, but draws upon other texts and emphasizes Paul's response in light of the social world.

First, it is certain or virtually certain that maturing enmity relationship between Paul and his detractors manifested in an affront during the

---

246. I am unconvinced that the community or a part thereof actually demanded that Paul demonstrate his martial strength in 13:3a. While possible, it would again seem odd if Paul either tentatively promises to capitulate to his detractors' demands, or if the community desires Paul's punitive action within its walls as proving grounds for his authority. Paul likely responds to the status/rank consequences made explicit in 1 Cor. 4:18-21 and the implicit necessity to address the criticisms through masculine assertiveness. Contra Barnett, *Second Epistle*, 601–2; Vegge, *2 Corinthians*, 306–7, 343–4.

intermediate visit. Our basic understanding of the challenge–riposte script indicates that observers would understand Paul's inaction and exit as shameful behavior, a dishonor indicating his martial impotence.

Second, it is certain or virtually certain that the participants perceived the encounter from the added vantage of an eschatological ordeal, a perspective encouraged by 1 Cor. 4:18-21. In the zero-sum world of ancient society, Paul's inaction and exit suggest his defeat. This fits both with the terms of the contest as defined in 1 Cor. 4:18–21 and the broader scripts concerning absence following an ordeal. Thus, Weiss is not far from the mark: "[Paul] had suffered a grievous humiliation (II Cor. 12:21), a heavy defeat, all the more striking and disgraceful since he had announced inquiry and judgment in lofty and threatening terms (I Cor 4:19ff)."[247] If ordeals revealed the truth about a person, the evidence suggests Paul's detractors considered his behavior revealed his martial weakness.

Third, it is probable that Paul's exit and absence evoked the political calculus found in other communities. As demonstrated, the preferred solution to communal unrest such as described above in Corinth was the forced or voluntary exit of at least one side in the conflict as a safety-valve for internecine strife. At its simplest, the evidence suggests that Paul's arrival in Corinth was met with conflict concerning his authority to order group life to which he responded with only a threat followed by his exit. In this light, Paul's volitional exit and martial inaction would also appear as a displacement, an insight confirmed by 1 Cor. 4:18-21. This interpretation is germane to the aims of internecine rivals who frequently sought to drive away opponents both to consolidate power and to redraw the ideological boundaries of the community (§2.3). Such a contest for the social program of the Corinthian community is evident in 1 Corinthians in which the live wires in the Corinthian conflict long demonstrated an infatuation with aggressive, assertive, domineering behavior (1 Cor. 3:1-4; 4:18; 5:1-8; 6:1-11, 12-20; 8:1–11:1; 11:17-33; 14:1-33; 2 Cor. 12:20-21). The contest between Paul and the immoral group involved rival visions for the community's social ethos. Following the intermediate ordeal, evidence indicates the presence of replacement apostles in Corinth, who, at least symbolically, occupy Paul's territory in Corinth (10:12-16) displaying the sort of culturally conditioned virtues lacking in Paul (11:1-21). When the rivals are viewed in this manner rather than the hidden hand behind most of Paul's troubles, the scenario suggests a move among some in the community to consign Paul's apostleship and its ethos

---

247. Weiss, *Primitive Christianity*, 1:343.

to oblivion in favor of a more culturally acceptable Jesus and apostleship, an impulse already evident in 1 Corinthians.

Fourth, it is certain or virtually certain that the rejection of Paul's apostolicity amounts to a rejection of political legitimacy based upon his conduct during the intermediate visit. The loss of or challenge to Paul's political legitimacy (10:7; 13:3a) resonates broadly with the frequent results of exile, the erasure of one's civic status. However, it remains incredible to suggest Paul was an exile in the sense of an official, enforced absence. There is no lexical or juridical evidence to support this. More proximately, Paul's discussion of eschatological trials and the eschatological realism with which he inflects his upcoming visit, suggests that Paul's behavior therein would naturally raise questions of his legitimacy. Thus, whereas most removals of civic rank involved enforced absence, we have no conclusive evidence of a true juridical proceeding regarding Paul's conduct. Rather, allowing for nuances within different political communities, the visit was the trial and Paul's behavior (inaction and absence) prompted the judgment.

Following Paul's intermediate visit and exit, Paul's absence was characterized by the judgment that he was an impotent, illegitimate leader. We have demonstrated that such exits and judgments, whether formal or informal, occurred across political communities in the Graeco-Roman world. The evidence indicates the occurrence of such a judgment against an absent leader in a middling political community in Corinth in the middle of the first century CE.

3.5. Conclusions

We conclude along with the scholarly consensus that Paul visited Corinth between the canonical epistles. However, the strongest evidence emerges from Paul's interaction with the immoral group (2 Cor. 13:2; cf. 12:21; 13:1), rather than texts concerning the ὁ ἀδικήσας conflict (2 Cor. 2:5-11; 7:5-16). In moving the center of study away from the ὁ ἀδικήσας conflict or the rivals and to the interaction with the immoral group, our study elucidates the account of Paul's political displacement. Thus, contrary to a longstanding interpretive tradition, we contend Paul's interlocutors did not view his absence as an offence against the community, but as a response to enmity expressed by an element within. Moreover, against a prominent minority interpretation, Paul indeed left Corinth in the face of affront. This indicates that the conflict is not simply a culturally conditioned misunderstanding about the nature of apostleship from which Paul remains aloof, but a far more serious challenge to Paul's apostleship in Corinth.

The immoral group represented a longstanding challenge to Paul's authority to order the social ethos of the community (1 Cor. 4:18-21; 5:9; 6:12-20). In view of Paul's threat of therapy by ordeal against his detractors (1 Cor. 4:18-21), the immoral group's existence during the intermediate visit represented an explicit challenge to Paul's authority (12:21; 13:2). The evidence indicates that Paul responded to the challenge by offering further threats of future martial action and his subsequent exit (13:2) rather than expelling his challengers as promised. The detractors and perhaps the community at large interpreted Paul's inaction and exit as evidence of impotence (10:1, 10) according to both Paul's words in 1 Cor. 4:18-21 and also the canons of effective, masculine leadership.

When the intermediate event is reattached to the social world in which it occurred, such behavior echoes widely held values and scripts associated with dishonor. It is highly probable that observers would view such behavior as evidence of defeat and displacement. This is affirmed by evidence found in the broader cultural logic and Paul's statements in 1 Corinthians, including both the challenge of Paul's communal status (10:7; 12:3) and the presence of replacement apostles in 2 Corinthians.

On the one hand, our approach justifies the consensus view concerning the exigencies and aims of 2 Corinthians by identifying a recognizable form of social interaction in which the exigencies gain greater nuance and the aims become more salient. On the other hand, the behaviors argued in this chapter occurring within a political community resonate with the warp and woof of political displacement with significant explanatory power previously unconsidered. At its simplest, the evidence points to a communal leader who in the context of an honor challenge and during an ordeal failed to repel an affront as promised, but rather warned and exited, whose political legitimacy remains in doubt in his absence. Such a figure—defeated, absent, judged as illegitimate—was highly recognizable. While Paul regained momentum in Corinth through the Severe Letter and ongoing diplomacy—also features of displacement—it is clear he remains absent (2 Cor. 1:17) and only partially reconciled (1:13-14). Methodologically, our reconstruction suggests not only that political displacement exists within the MCE, but with this chapter's evidence in view, it likely supplies a highly efficient context for interpreting certain passages in 2 Corinthians.

Chapter 4

Testing the Hypothesis: Embezzlement, Levity, and Deviant Character

This chapter aims to test the explanatory power of the hypothesis brought forth in Chapter 3—that Paul's martial weakness during the intermediate visit and subsequent absence amounted to an intelligible occurrence of political displacement—by examining the echoes of the charges of embezzlement (2 Cor. 7:2; 12:16-18) and levity (2 Cor. 1:17) against Paul. Thus, this chapter explores the connection between Paul's intermediate visit and subsequent absence with the seemingly disparate echoes of these other judgments against Paul. Despite the near total consensus concerning the charge of embezzlement and frequent commentary on the charge of levity, the relationship between these charges and that of Paul's weakness in person (2 Cor. 10:1-11) is undervalued, save the general rubric of inconsistency, and the cultural schema of the flatterer-parasite. This chapter contends that the charges of embezzlement and levity arise singularly from Paul's intermediate visit as interpreted in Chapter 3, further substantiating the claim that behind Paul's aim of an amicable return lies a culturally conditioned judgment that he lacked the criteria of an ideal, assertive leader. Furthermore, if these judgments are evaluated not only considering cultural values, but in the context of a non-elite political community in Corinth, as done thus far, then the voices behind these judgments demonstrate their aim not for Paul's return but continued absence. In this way, the judgments against Paul substantiate the reconstruction and interpretation in Chapter 3.

First, exegesis of the passages which refer directly (2 Cor. 7:2; 12:16-18) and indirectly (2 Cor. 2:11) to the accusation of embezzlement (πλεονεκτέω) demonstrates the presence of the charge and its contextual linkage to issues of Paul's discipline of the community or lack thereof. Second, by drawing upon evidence concerning public ordeals or tests, we argue the charge of embezzlement and the collapse of Paul's credibility arise predictably after the intermediate visit, thus filling a gap in knowledge currently occupied by inventive theories. Third, the charge of ἐλαφρία and deciding κατὰ σάρκα (1:17) are best understood respectively as accusations concerning Paul's conduct and deviant character, arising from Paul's martial inaction and confirmed by his ongoing absence evidencing his inability to exercise authority in person. Echoes of these accusations indicate that as in Chapter 3 and as was frequent across antiquity, Paul's absence following his visit implied and embodied judgments against him beyond those of his impotence and illegitimacy. Fourth, if we take seriously the formation of a nascent political community, a view encouraged in 1 Cor. 5:1-13 and elsewhere, then the judgment that Paul is an embezzler, lacking martial gravitas, and possessing devious character constitutes a more concrete argument that he is unfit to lead the community, a view complemented by the community's withdrawal of support of Paul since the intermediate visit.

4.1. Πλεονεκτέω in 2 Corinthians

A near total consensus agrees that Paul echoes accusations of embezzlement of the collection funds in 2 Cor. 7:2b and 12:16-18 (with a possible allusion in 1:12).[1] Below we aim to observe and interpret the passages that make explicit (7:2; 12:16-18) and implicit (2:11) mention of the charge, establishing its presence, import, and odd contextual links to texts referring to Paul's discipline of the community.

4.1.1. Second Corinthians 7:2b

Following an appeal to reconcile (7:2a), Paul rejects a three-fold accusation in 7:2b: "We have wronged no one, we have ruined no one, we have defrauded no one" (οὐδένα ἠδικήσαμεν, οὐδένα ἐφθείραμεν, οὐδένα ἐπλεονεκτήσαμεν). Most interpreters claim that Paul pleads innocence to the charge of a financial crime marked specifically by the verb πλεονεκτέω in 7:2b.[2] As expected, some see in 7:2b a vague echo of the charge which

---

1. Betz, *2 Corinthians 8 and 9*, 97, 208; Klauck, *2 Korintherbrief*, 22, 62–3, 97–8; Martin, *2 Corinthians*, 424; Schmeller, *Zweite Brief*, 1:83, 384–5, 2:351–2; Welborn, *Enmity*, 164–208; Schellenberg, *Education*, 74–5, and most others; see Aejmelaeus, "Salary," 366–70.

2. Windisch, *Zweite Korintherbrief*, 221; Harris, *Second Epistle*, 517; Vegge, *2 Corinthians*, 192; Schmeller, *Zweite Brief*, 1:385; Welborn, *Enmity*, 454, and others; contra Witherington, *Conflict & Community*, 408, and Fredrickson, "Bold Speech," 302–3.

is more pronounced in 12:16-18 (Semler–Windisch)³ and also those to whom 7:2b refers to issues already resolved in chs. 10–13 (Hausrath–Kennedy et al.),⁴ while those holding to the unity of 2 Corinthians claim that the charge in 7:2b is consistent with 12:16-18.⁵

Contrary to the majority of interpreters, the tripartite anaphora most likely refers to a single charge involving a financial crime. It has been proposed that ἀδικέω refers to Paul's stern action in judicial proceedings (1 Cor. 5:1-13; 2 Cor. 2:5-11),⁶ that φθείρω refers to financial ruin caused by Paul's deliberations in 1 Corinthians⁷ or his doctrinal corruption of the community,⁸ and that πλεονεκτέω refers to fraud regarding the collection. However, within classical political theory, all three terms could refer complementarily to financial offenses. The nominal πλεονεξία, a grasping for more, was equated with ἀδικέω⁹ and both were opposed to ἴσος/ἰσότης and δικαιόω, which was ensured by laws.¹⁰ The papyri demonstrate that victims of property crimes denoted by the verb πλεονεκτέω reference legal recourse with δικ-root terms.¹¹ In SB 24.16134.15-17, a petitioner describes the offenders as τῶν δὲ δηλουμένων πλε|ονεκτούντων καὶ οὐ θελόν|των δικαιοπραγεῖν ("blatant defrauders and those who do not wish to act justly").¹²

---

3. Barrett, *Second Epistle*, 203, 324; Martin, *2 Corinthians*, 219; Thrall, *Second Epistle*, 1:482; cf. comments by Vegge, *2 Corinthians*, 192 n. 219.

4. Plummer, *Second Epistle*, 213–14; Filson, "Second Epistle," 356; Horrell, *Social Ethos*, 230.

5. Vegge, *2 Corinthians*, 192 n. 219.

6. Harris, *Second Epistle*, 517.

7. Strachan, *Second Epistle*, 124–5; cf. Meyer, *Corinthians*, 2:321.

8. Plummer, *Second Epistle*, 213; Jan Lambrecht, *Second Corinthians*, SP 8 (Collegeville, MN: Liturgical, 1999), 119.

9. Plato, *Leg.* 3.691a; Euripides, *Phoen.* 549; πλεονέκτης ὁ ἄδικος (Aristotle, *Eth. nic.* 5.1.8-9 (1129a32), ὁ μὲν γὰρ ἀδικῶν πλέονέχει (Aristotle, *Eth. nic.* 5.3.14 [1131.20]); πλεονεκτικῶς as law-breaking and stealing property (Demosthenes, *Andr.* 56–57); Philo, *Prob.* 159; *Mos.* 2.186; cf. G. J. Boter, "Thrasymachus and ΠΛΕΟΝΕΞΙΑ," *Mnemosyne* 39.3 (1986): 261–81; "In the LXX the word group is used only for בצע and עשק, which originally denote 'unlawful gain'" (Gerhard Delling, "Πλεονέκτης, Πλεονεκτέω, Πλεονεξία," *TDNT* 269); cf. Jer. 22:17; Ezek. 22:27.

10. Archytas, fr.D25b; Plato, *Rep.* 359c; Dio Chrysostom, *Avar.* 10; cf. Boter, "ΠΛΕΟΝΕΞΙΑ"; Fredrickson, "Bold Speech," 304.

11. P.Oxy. 34.2708.11-14; 65.4481.8; P.Amh. 2.78.11-14. Importantly, all Arzt-Grabner's examples of πλεονεκτέω in the papyri occur within a legal context except P.Panop.Beatty 2.97. Yet, even there the term refers to embezzlement of property tax by giving old, potentially fraudulent *solidi* (Arzt-Grabner, *2 Korinther*, 248–9).

12. See P.Turner 34.13, 23 in which τοὺς πλεονεκτο[υμ]ένους is contrasted with the epistrategos's δικαίᾳ δεξιᾷ (Arzt-Grabner, *2 Korinther*, 249 n. 331).

The term φθείρω often refers to the result of a misdeed as the conjectures above suggest. In 1 Cor. 3:17 φθείρω refers to damage done to the community warranting divine judgment. In the papyri, φθείρω could express *the result* of financial misdeeds.[13] Bultmann suspects a connection with the anaphoric expression, pondering, "ruined (by πλεονεξία?)."[14] In fact, πλεονεξία was commonly claimed to destroy communities.[15] Dio comments that πλεονεξία "overthrows and destroys [διαφθείρει] the flourishing of families and cities."[16] Plutarch comments that πλεονεξία and στάσις leads to the destruction (διαφθείρω) of communities as the enemies of concord (ὁμόνοια).[17] Seneca (fl. ca. 4 BCE–65 CE) offers an origin story about the loss of the golden age in which the "bond which holds mortals together" was broken by *avaritia*, leading to poverty and bloodshed.[18] Among widely dispersed good ruler *topoi*, πλεονεξία was the worst vice, singularly disqualifying for a leader.[19]

Thus, the three expressions are complementary and likely point to the most precise articulation of the charge of pecuniary misdeeds.[20] While πλεονεκτέω possesses a broad semantic range, the use of ἀδικέω and φθείρω constrain the meaning of the charge, pointing to a deceptive or unlawful attempt to acquire money that threatened the welfare of the community. Paul's lack of communal support (1 Cor. 9; 2 Cor. 11:7-12; 12:13) limits the possibilities of the accusation to the collection effort, although this remained uncompleted (2 Cor. 8:10; 9:2). This is supported by the usage of the charge of πλεονεκτέω in the papyri, which refers entirely to fraud of common property.[21] In any event, Paul clearly responds to an accusation of anti-citizen, deviant behavior.

13. *SB* 24.1607.31-32; P.Mich. 5.234.8; for financial crimes in which φθείρω has a personal pronoun as a direct object, see P.Sorb. 3.103.9; Arzt-Grabner, *2 Korinther*, 367.

14. Bultmann, *Second Letter*, 177 n. 199; cf. Furnish, *II Corinthians*, 366.

15. πλέον leads to tyranny and ἀδικία εὐδαίμων (Euripides, *Phoen.* 549); destroys relationship with neighbours (*T. 12 Patr.* A.2.6); along with δόλος and ἀδικία opposed to κοινωνία (*Corp. herm.* 13.7).

16. Dio Chrysostom, *Avar.* 10, my translation.

17. Plutarch, *Frat. amor.* 479A.

18. Seneca, *Lucil.* 90.36, cf. 36–46; Delling, "Πλεονέκτης, Πλεονεκτέω, Πλεονεξία," 269.

19. Walker, *Offer*, 138.

20. Héring, *Second Epistle*, 53; Martin, *2 Corinthians*, 218. Schmeller claims πλεονεκτέω and ἀδικέω refer to charges concerning the collection but is unsure about the background of φθείρω (*Zweite Brief*, 1:385).

21. Illegal acquisition of houses (P.Oxy 34.2708.11-14), theft by a spouse (P.Oxy. 65.4481.8), general reference to common property (P.Amh. 2.78.11-14) from Arzt-Grabner, *2 Korinther*, 248–9.

The gravity of the charge and protestation of innocence is perceived best from the immediate context. Paul's rejection of guilt follows a plea for reconciliation in 7:2a, "make room for us," which is linked to the broader appeal in 2 Cor. 6:11-13. Earlier, reconciliation was packaged as an affair primarily between God and Paul (5:18-19), who functions as an envoy of reconciliation to the Corinthians (5:20–6:2). It is likely that the God→Christ→Paul→Corinth relational dynamic rhetorically and theologically frames in the social import of the Paul–Corinthian relationship in 6:11-13 and 7:2-4 (see §1.1). In 6:11-13, 7:2-4, then, Paul establishes his comportment towards the community through references to παρρησία.[22] Paul's comments suggest that at present the overtures are not fully reciprocal: "you are not being restricted by us, but you are restricted in your affection" (6:12). Paul urges mutuality, "with the same recompense, Corinthians" (6:13), summoning the community twice to reciprocity, "be widened" (6:13) and "make room for us" (7:2a). While Paul's reference to παρρησία is viewed as a reference to "boldness" associated with true friendship[23] or personal and communal psychagogy,[24] Paul's use of the παρρησία in 2 Cor. 3:12; 4:3 (cf. 7:4; 1:12-14; 6:6, 7) likely counters a charge concerning alleged furtive conduct, not unlike the embezzlement accusation. Thus, παρρησία likely refers to honesty and transparency.[25]

The protestation of transparency and plea for reconciliation implies obstacles to that end. The context suggests that Paul has two obstacles in view. First, if 2 Cor. 6:14–7:1 is authentic, Paul implies that reconciliation with him involves a cessation of friendship with others.[26] The second obstacle to reconciliation involves the charge referred to three times through anaphora in 7:2b, a particular accusation of financial misdeed echoing Paul's general rejection of deceptive conduct.[27] Thus, Paul uses strong dissociative language regarding "unbelievers" and strong associative language regarding the apostle and the community.[28]

---

22. Bultmann, *Second Letter*, 175.
23. Edward N. O'Neil, "Plutarch on Friendship," in *Greco-Roman Perspectives on Friendship*, ed. John T. Fitzgerald, SBLRBS 34 (Atlanta: Scholars Press, 1997), 116.
24. Fredrickson, "Bold Speech," 108–62, 284–9, 299–307.
25. Duff, *Moses*, 77–8.
26. For the identification of the ἄπιστοι, see William J. Webb, *Returning Home: New Covenant and Second Exodus as the Context for 2 Corinthians 6.14–7.1*, JSNTSup 85 (Sheffield: Sheffield Academic, 1993), 184–99.
27. See Meyer, *Corinthians*, 2:230.
28. David A. deSilva, "Measuring Penultimate Reality: An Investigation of the Integrity and Argumentation of 2 Corinthians," *JSNT* 52 (1993): 53, 63–4.

At first glance, the issue of financial misdeeds cannot seem more unrelated from Paul's martial failures. How might Paul's apparent cowardice relate to accusations of aggressive grasping? Yet, Paul moves rather quickly, if not abruptly, from protesting his innocence (7:2b) and affirming his transparency (7:3-4) to narrating the positive effects of his disciplinary Severe Letter (7:5-16). Of course, the abrupt shift in topic and the restart of the narrative abruptly ended in 2:12-13 contributes to partition theories. Leaving those issues to the side, some ancient person (Paul or an editor) found intelligible the relationship between Paul's rejection of fraud, plea for reconciliation, and narration of effective discipline (7:5-16). This suggests that the narrative of Paul's use of his martial authority through the Severe Letter in 2:12-13, 7:5-16 in part provides (according to Paul or an editor) exculpatory evidence on the charge of fraud and furtive conduct—as καὶ γὰρ in 7:5 indicates—by giving account of his ability to punish a member of the community through a letter and also the community's obedience to Paul following the intermediate visit.

4.1.2. Second Corinthians 12:14-18

Second Corinthians 12:14-18 is generally considered the clearest evidence that Paul is accused of fraud in relation to the collection. In the previous unit, Paul has concluded his so-called Fool's Speech (11:21b–12:13), boasting in ignominious conduct before transitioning to a preview of his third visit (12:14–13:10).[29] However, continuity is evident in references to money matters (ἁμαρτία, 11:7; ἀδικία, 12:13), which may hint at the underlying charge of embezzlement. If so, the reality remains buried beneath Paul's stinging counter attack concerning his lack of maintenance.[30] As well, Paul's lack of communal discipline in the past (10:1-10) and the accusations of weakness and servility (10:1, 10; 11:7, 21; 11:30–12:10) take a view to future disciplinary issues (12:20–13:2) and the conversion of the apostle's weakness to power in his return (13:4; cf. 10:11).

A measure of uncertainty exists because scholars frequently understand that in 11:7-12 Paul responds to the accusation of ἁμαρτία (and ἀδικία in 12:13) concerning Paul's refusal of support as a sign of lack of affection, while 12:14-18 responds to the accusation of embezzlement.[31] The logical dissonance between rejecting support and ill-gotten gain leads a few

---

29. Windisch, *Zweite Korintherbrief*, 398.
30. Welborn, *Enmity*, 165.
31. Thrall, *Second Epistle*, 2:682–4; David Emilio Briones, "Paul's Financial Policy: A Socio-Theological Approach" (Ph.D. diss., Durham University, 2011), 290.

exegetes to consider that different groups stand behind each accusation.[32] Of course, an impressive coterie of interpreters asserts that Paul rejected support from the Corinthians, claiming that such a rejection precipitated challenges to Paul's apostolic legitimacy. Similarly, others follow Marshall's thesis that Paul's rejection attempted to prevent a patron–client relationship developing between the community and apostle, leading to many troubles.[33] These largely complementary approaches form something of a first principle in Corinthian research.

However, Schellenberg has supplied a paradigm-shifting hypothesis—that Paul was never offered support by Corinth (1 Cor. 9:1-18; 2 Cor. 11:5-15; 12:11-18) like he was by the Philippians (2 Cor. 11:8-9; 12:13), and is criticized for never authoritatively imposing the claim of support, as did his rivals (11:20-21).[34] This is a promising reading of 1 Corinthians 9, as Paul presents himself as the communal exemplar of not demanding a right (ἐξουσία, 9:12; 1 Cor. 11:1) in the context of questions concerning idol meat and dinner invitations (1 Cor. 8:1–11:1).[35] At the same time, Paul exerts significant effort attempting to defend himself (9:3) and to convince others that he does indeed possess such ἐξουσία like others (9:3-13), concluding his situation is superior and ideal for his mission, especially to Corinth (9:15-23).

In 2 Cor. 11:5-15 and 12:11-15, Paul moves from claims of inferiority (11:5; 12:11), to counterevidence of his superiority (11:6; 12:12) to his shaming of the community by claiming his lack of burden and support from the Macedonians as positive evidence of his love rather than a sin/an injustice (11:7-12; 12:13), and finally to his future conduct (11:12; 12:14-15).[36] Schellenberg questions whether Paul's rhetorical questions (11:7; 12:13) revolving around his support-free proclamation express or evade his interlocuters' discontent.[37]

Rather than presuppose a Corinthian offer rejected by Paul—a theory with surprisingly little evidence—Schellenberg argues that Paul presents his support-free apostleship as superior to those who receive support from Corinth.[38] In 2 Corinthians, the rivals receive such deference—a chief sign of authority and honor—while Paul does not. In this way, Paul

---

32. Bultmann, *Second Letter*, 235; Schmeller, *Zweite Brief*, 2:350.
33. Marshall, *Enmity*, 218–58; Chow, 107–10; Welborn, *Enmity*, 132–52.
34. Schellenberg, "Offer," 312–36.
35. Schellenberg, "Offer," 316–20; see Land, *Absence*, 222 passim.
36. Schellenberg, "Offer," 324–5.
37. Schellenberg, "Offer," 325.
38. Schellenberg, "Offer," 320–8.

refers in 11:7-12 and 12:11-15 not to hurt feelings, offence, or embarrassment among the community concerning a rejection of support, but, in part, to Paul's criticized impotence and servility in money matters (ἐμαυτὸν ταπεινῶν, 11:7), arguing for its virtue as evidence of sincerity in comparison with the rivals, who impose the claim of support which Paul argues is evidence of counterfeit, deceptive, and tyrannical leadership (11:1-3, 13-15, 20).

Among the advantages of Schellenberg's argument, it portrays a consistent image of Paul as weak (ταπεινόω, 2 Cor. 11:7; ἀβαρής, 11:9) in person (παρὼν πρὸς ὑμᾶς, 11:9). Of course, the difference between Paul's martial and pecuniary weakness is that his pecuniary weakness will remain consistent (11:9; 12:14), while his martial weakness may not (10:11; 13:4, 10). As well, it removes the need for two groups, one complaining about Paul's rejection of support, the other accusing him of embezzlement. Of course, this also challenges a fundamental narrative concerning how the community deduced Paul's fraudulent intent, to which we turn momentarily. Furthermore, Schellenberg's argument portrays elements in the community as chronically ambivalent towards Paul's claim to authority and his presence in Corinth, a consistent lack of support and deference bursting into outright affront during the intermediate visit. This fits with our argument of a growing animus between Paul and his detractors resulting in an affront and Paul's absence.

Yet, as in 2 Cor. 7:2, 12:14-18 evinces a lack of reciprocity between Paul and the community regarding the charge of financial misdeeds. In 2 Cor. 12:14-18, Paul emphatically announces his impending third visit (12:14a), further declaring again that he will not be a burden on the community, referring to his refusal to demand support (12:14b), unlike the replacement apostles (11:20-21).[39] His claim is substantiated by an appeal to his friendly disposition towards the community—he does not wish to obtain the community's possessions, he desires only them (12:14c). A secondary substantiation appeals to the parent–child metaphor, which Paul cites as a general principle (12:14b). In 12:15a, Paul thus pronounces that as a good parent, he is happy to spend and be spent on his children in Corinth. Although a gulf exists between him and the community, Paul cites his refusal to demand support as evidence of his friendly disposition. However, it is clear his detractors do not likely share such an assessment.[40] In this way, Paul has taken the community's lack of hospitality and transformed it into a mark of paternal love.

---

39. Schellenberg, "Offer," 326; cf. Land, *Absence*, 222.
40. Aejmelaeus, *Schwachheit*, 177–81.

The textual variant in v. 15b makes the verse uncertain, although here I side with the NA[28] on the principle of difficulty as ἀγαπῶ[ν] becomes a part of an implied paraphrastic construction.[41] It is likely that the adverbial conjunction εἰ participates as the first part of a rhetorical question in which Paul questions "If I love you exceedingly, am I being loved less?"[42] The correlative emphasis built around the comparative adverbs περισσοτέρως and ἧσσον highlights a clear contrast between Paul's affections and the community's reciprocation, which stands in the way of his amicable return.[43]

Paul construes the lack of reciprocity as tied not to Paul's lack of demand for support—as we might expect since it is evidence of Paul's unassertiveness—but to allusions of a charge of financial misconduct. As Welborn has catalogued, there is a strong consensus among scholars in this regard.[44] One senses that here we have arrived at the nerve of Paul's earlier language about sin and injustice (11:7; 12:11). It is unclear whether ἔστω functions retrospectively[45] or prospectively.[46] Since Paul has previously discussed his refusal to demand support (11:7-12) it is likely that 12:16a forms a concession of his detractors with the contrastive ἀλλά initiating the charge against him.[47] Paul states, "So it is [that] I did not overburden you, but being crafty by nature, I took you through trickery."

Importantly, the charge is not simply that Paul acted unscrupulously, but through the causal participle (ὑπάρχων πανοῦργος) he was in fact a deviant by nature (ὑπάρχων=ὢν φύσει).[48] Plummer aptly translates, "But being in character thoroughly unscrupulous."[49] The term πανοῦργος means "ready to do anything, wicked, knavish" and according to Welborn the word group is widely associated with financial conduct.[50]

---

41. Long, *II Corinthians*, 239.
42. Contra Meyer, *Corinthians*, 2:478, who reads it as a conditional sentence.
43. Long, *II Corinthians*, 239; cf. Bultmann, *Second Letter*, 234.
44. Welborn, *Enmity*, 168; Schmeller, *Zweite Brief*, 2:350-3; contra Aejmelaeus, *Salary*, 366–70; Land, *Absence*, 223 n. 66.
45. The idiom ἔστω δέ both points back to v. 15 and "is used to express a point on which the writer and readers are in at least provisional agreement" (Barnett, *Second Epistle*, 586; cf. Harris, *Second Epistle*, 888).
46. Windisch, *Zweite Korintherbrief*, 402; Furnish, *II Corinthians*, 558; Schmeller, *Zweite Brief*, 350.
47. Schmeller, *Zweite Brief*, 315; contra Aejmelaeus, *Schwachheit*, 167.
48. Harris, *Second Epistle*, 888.
49. Plummer, *Second Epistle*, 363; cf. Hughes, *Second Epistle*, 464 n. 150.
50. Welborn, *Enmity*, 169; cf. Sophocles, *Ant.* 300; P.Lond. 46.73.

Betz adds that πανοῦργος is opposite of ἁπλότης, as demonstrated in 11:3.[51] The observation is enlightening since Paul defends his conduct (ἀναστρέφω) as simple and sincere (ἁπλότης[52] and εἰλικρίνεια) in 1:12, rather than deceptive. The group of terms in 1:12 likely refers to "sly, calculating, degenerate behavior."[53] While there exist a number of areas where Paul is accused of unfit behavior, Hans Joseph Klauck points out, "ein konkreter Fall, wo seine Aufrichtigkeit in Zweifel gezogen wurde, war der Umgang mit den Kollektengeldern (12,16-18)."[54] Perhaps this is the case. In any event, it is of great importance that in the opening of the canonical letter body and in the context of a partial reconciliation (1:13-14),[55] Paul initially refers to a lack of reciprocity surrounding questions of Paul's probity, although it is unlikely that 1:13-14 refers only to financial accusations.

Returning to the charge, Paul's deviant character was manifested through δόλος, meaning "trick" or "stratagem."[56] In certain instances the term connotes financial misconduct.[57] Arzt-Grabner comments that in the papyri, δόλος functions as a "juristischer Terminus" associated with money matters.[58] However, in epic and dramatic Greek literature δόλος refers to devious actions (Homer, *Od.* 19.137; 494) or characters (Pindar, *Pyth.* 2.39). Arzt-Grabner concludes, "Die 'List' oder 'Arglist', deren Anwendung Paulus in seiner Funktion als Apostel von sich weist, hat in jedem Fall mit vorsätzlichem, betrügerischem Handeln zu tun, ob sie nun als für bestimmte Menschen charakteristische Wesensart oder als rechtlich gesehen zu ahnendes Delikt zu verstehen ist."[59] It is instructive that in 4:2, Paul renounces "underhand and disgraceful conduct" (τὰ κρυπτὰ

---

51. Betz, *Apologie*, 106 n. 450.

52. NA[28] reversed course from earlier editions, opting for ἁπλότητι over ἁγιότητι. The external evidence is evenly divided, but the decision in NA[28] is correct on internal grounds: Paul never uses ἁγιότητι elsewhere and the term ἁπλότης is central in Paul's defense by way of antonym (4:2; 12:16) and counterattack (11:3).

53. Schmeller, *Zweite Brief*, 1.83, my translation.

54. Klauck, *2 Korintherbrief*, 22; cf. Schmeller, *Zweite Brief*, 1.83; cf. Barnett, *Second Epistle*, 94.

55. Bieringer, "Plädoyer," 161; Vegge, *2 Corinthians*, 176.

56. LSJ s.v. δόλος.

57. Contra Harris, who claims by citing Lucian, *Hermotimus* 59 that the term δολόω "has no relation to monetary profit" (*Second Epistle*, 325). Yet in Lucian, it is the hucksters who sell wine, "adulterating (δολόω) and cheating and giving false measure." Here and in 2 Cor. 12:16 (cf. 4:2) the point is precisely that such behavior seeks financial gain.

58. Arzt-Grabner, *2 Korinther*, 523; cf. P.Oxy. 38.2857.5-7, 26-27.

59. Arzt-Grabner, *2 Korinther*, 523.

τῆς αἰσχύνης), further denying that he operates according to craftiness or financial trickery (περιπατοῦντες ἐν πανουργίᾳ μηδὲ δολοῦντες τὸν λόγον τοῦ θεοῦ κτλ.).

Since Paul did not receive support from Corinth (1 Cor. 9), the most likely, if not only, possibility is that Paul was charged with *plotting* to steal the collection. The series of rhetorical questions in 12:17-18 point in this direction. Paul questions, "Did I defraud [πλεονεκτέω] you through him—any of those that I have sent to you?" And in 12:18, "Did Titus defraud [πλεονεκτέω] you? Did we not conduct ourselves with the same spirit? In the same footsteps?" Against many interpreters who believe Paul is accused of embezzlement through his envoys,[60] it is more likely that Paul's attempts to establish his probity through Titus's positive reputation (cf. Phlm. 18).[61] Otherwise, Paul's argument would be ineffectively circular.[62]

Paul turns from a defense of his character in financial matters to the question of communal conduct (12:19-21) and his impending martial return (13:1-10). In 12:19 Paul pivots, claiming his apology is in fact for the edification of the community (12:19). With what appears to be seamless logic, he moves from pecuniary and character judgments to disciplinary issues in the community (12:20-21), notably referencing the immoral group, which he fears he will find in his return (12:21). To a degree, Paul shifts the argument to more advantageous terrain by questioning the community's moral fitness rather than defending his own (10:7; 13:5-9). Nonetheless, the charge of embezzlement and Paul's discipline of the community, or lack thereof, are once again strange discursive partners.

4.1.3. *Second Corinthians 2:11*

Second Corinthians 2:11 is the first reference to the term πλεονεκτέω. While its metaphorical usage results in only a brief comment, Paul's employment sheds some light. The term is employed yet again in reference to Paul's discipline and administration of the community as seen in the forgiveness to be granted to ὁ ἀδικήσας to prevent Satan's

---

60. Windisch, *Zweite Korintherbrief*, 404; Harris, *Second Epistle*, 889, and others.

61. Margaret M. Mitchell, "New Testament Envoys in the Context of Greco-Roman Diplomatic and Epistolary Conventions: The Example of Timothy and Titus," *JBL* 111.4 (1992): 650–1; Schmeller, *Zweite Brief*, 2:351–3; Welborn, *Enmity*, 117.

62. Windisch claimed the argument was a *"circulus vitiosus"* (*Zweite Korintherbrief*, 404).

fraud or theft of one (perhaps wealthy?)[63] member of the community[64] or a larger contingent of the community.[65] The two options are not mutually exclusive.[66]

All the same, Satan is represented as the true embezzler of the community. Yet, the metaphorical usage proffers aid in understanding the term πλεονεκτέω in the broader conflict. While πλεονεκτέω can have a wide range of meanings, including a basic desire for more, Paul describes Satan as an outsider who aims "to mislead or entrap God's people."[67] In the papyri, Arzt-Grabner concludes similarly that the charge of πλεονεκτέω implicitly portrays the offender "als Eindringlinge," and thus illegitimate members of a community.[68] In the context of financial deception, Paul states, "we know his thoughts [νοήματα]" or as Plummer suggests "his wiles," depicting Satan as a figure aiming to bilk the community of one of its members.[69] The term νοήματα belongs almost exclusively to 2 Corinthians and is employed negatively, twice in reference to nefarious figures (Σατᾶν, 2:11; ὁ θεὸς τοῦ αἰῶνος τούτου, 4:4), once in reference to the deception of the Corinthians by Paul's rivals (11:3).[70] Thus, Satan is an exposed con-artist scheming against the community.

This proves valuable as it is now clear that the πλεονεκ-language likely originates in the accusation against Paul and constrains its meaning within the broader conflict. The description of a fraud whose secret intentions have come to light sounds suspiciously like the judgments against Paul in 7:2 and 12:16-18 (cf. 2 Cor. 1:12-13; 4:2; 6:8c; 8:16-24; 9:4-5). And it is Paul's political legitimacy that is questioned (2 Cor. 2:16–3:4; 10:7; 11:3). Following Schmeller, it stands to reason that the charge of embezzlement originates with Paul's detractors and that in 2:11 Paul deflects the charge onto Satan.[71] Supporting this conclusion, Paul frequently deflects accusations against him onto other figures. Paul hasn't veiled his gospel, hiding his true motives (2 Cor. 4:2). Rather, the "god of this age" veils the truth

---

63. Welborn, *Enmity*, 41; cf. Ewald, *Sendschreiben*, 227.
64. Martin, *2 Corinthians*, 39; South, *Disciplinary Practices*, 94; Thrall, *Second Epistle*, 1:181.
65. Windisch, *Zweite Korintherbrief*, 91; Bruce, *I & II Corinthians*, 163; Furnish, *II Corinthians*, 163; Harris, *Second Epistle*, 233; Vegge, *2 Corinthians*, 79.
66. Schmeller, *Zweite Brief*, 1:140–1.
67. Frederick W. Danker, *II Corinthians*, ACNT (Minneapolis: Augsburg, 1989), 45.
68. Arzt-Grabner, *2 Korinther*, 249.
69. Plummer, *Second Epistle*, 63.
70. Plummer, *Second Epistle*, 63.
71. Schmeller, *Zweite Brief*, 1:141 n. 288.

from unbelievers (2 Cor. 4:3-4).[72] Just as the serpent (ὁ ὄφις) deceived (ἐξηπάτησεν) Eve by his trickery (πανουργία), so too Paul portrays his rivals as Satan's minions—deceptive agents (ἐργάται δόλιοι), cloaked to deceive (μετασχηματίζονται; cf. 2 Cor. 11:13-15). Johnson comments, "each reference to Satan in the Corinthian letters is situation-specific."[73] She concludes in 2:11, Satan "is ancillary to Paul's concern for the problem in the community."[74] The primary concern behind the description of πλεονεκτέω is in fact outstanding charges against Paul, which he skillfully appropriates to Satan. Yet, the passage in light of 2 Cor. 7:2, 12:16-18, and 1:12-14 suggests it is Paul who stands accused of being an exposed con-artist, an illegitimate outsider, perhaps who some are arguing should be denied access. It is an assertion that Paul can both at once parry and place onto another *in the context of his disciplinary administration of the community*.

On balance, the consensus is justified in contending that the verb πλεονεκτέω (2 Cor. 7:2; 12:16-18; 2:11) in 2 Corinthians refers to the charge that Paul was scheming to embezzle the collection. Judgments concerning Paul's furtive conduct (1:12-13; 4:2-3) and particularized accusations of embezzlement (7:2b; 12:15-18) run through the discourse. However, two added elements have emerged. First, Paul twice indicates the charge of embezzlement is linked to ongoing hostility between him and (an element of) the community (7:2; 12:15-16). Second, Paul's rejections and appropriation of the charge are always proximate to discourse about Paul's disciplinary and administrative efficacy, the issue at the nerve of Paul's recent visit, exit, and current absence. To the questions of the genesis of the accusation and its link to Paul's failure to discipline, we now turn.

4.2. *Embezzlement and Paul's Failure to Discipline*

Below we examine the weaknesses of the well-worn explanations concerning the genesis of the embezzlement charge, before offering a simpler explanation tied to the argument in Chapter 3.

---

72. Collange states regarding 4:2, "Nous pensons plutôt (avec Godet, Plummer, Leitzmann), qu'ici, Paul se défend et attaque à la fois" (*Enigmes*, 39). Rather than conceding the action in 4:2-4, Paul concedes a fact connected to the accusation and reverses it for his rhetorical goals, see Andrew Riggsby, "Appropriation and Reversal as a Basis for Oratorical Proof," *CP* 90.3 (1995): 245–56.

73. Lee A. Johnson, "Satan Talk in Corinth: The Rhetoric of Conflict," *BTB* 29.4 (1999): 153.

74. Johnson, "Satan Talk," 153.

4.2.1. Common Approaches

Despite the warrant for the claim that Paul is accused of embezzlement of the collection, no conclusive argument exists as to how the accusation emerges, although not for a lack of effort. Exegetes posit an array of hypotheses. Thrall, Betz, and Welborn posit variations of one popular conjecture—the charge of embezzlement is central to the ὁ ἀδικήσας conflict.[75] For one reason or another, the ὁ ἀδικήσας charged Paul with financial crimes during the intermediate visit. Another hypothesis as asserted by Wilfred L. Knox and sometimes put in the mouth of the ὁ ἀδικήσας deduces that Paul's *refusal of support* (1 Cor. 9) "was a mere pretext for exacting larger sums at a later date on the score of the alleged collection, which, it was hinted, might very well fail to find its way to those whom it was destined."[76] A third option brought forth by Marshall and Dale B. Martin involves a more complex hypothesis. The Corinthians arrived at such an accusation only by unearthing his acceptance of support from Philippi (2 Cor. 11:8) and comparing it to his rejection of the Corinthian offer (1 Cor. 9).[77] Long nuances this position, claiming that Paul indicates the acceptance of Macedonian support occurred only after their participation in the collection (2 Cor. 8:5).[78] Mitchell supplies a fourth and most recent option using a highly partitioned reconstruction, claiming that Paul's deviation in travel plans from 1 Cor. 16:2-7 to 2 Corinthians 8 (a distinct and subsequent missive) naturally explains the accusation. In 1 Cor. 16:2-7, Paul planned to send the collection with members of the community, but in 2 Cor. 8:16-24, the collection is to be handed over to Paul's emissaries, thus raising suspicions.[79]

The four hypotheses pose valuable possibilities, although room exists for critique. First, while it is possible to claim that the ὁ ἀδικήσας charged Paul with embezzlement, it is largely unfounded and, as so often is the case, in 2 Corinthians scholarship relies on an approach in which the hidden hands of the ὁ ἀδικήσας or the rivals are relied upon to explain so much mischief.[80] Second, that the Corinthians' view of Paul's support

---

75. Betz, *2 Corinthians 8 and 9*, 97, 143–4; Margaret E. Thrall, "The Offender and the Offence: A Problem of Detection in 2 Corinthians," in *Scripture: Method and Meaning—Essays Presented to Anthony Tyrrell Hanson*, ed. Barry P. Thompson (Pickering: Hull University Press, 1987), 65–78; Welborn, *Enmity*, 164–208, 425–6.

76. Wilfred L. Knox, *St Paul and the Church of Jerusalem* (Cambridge: Cambridge University Press, 1925), 328; see Barrett, *Second Epistle*, 324.

77. Martin, *Corinthian Body*, 95; Marshall, *Enmity*, 257.

78. Long, *Ancient Rhetoric*, 129.

79. Mitchell, "Letters," 330; see Schellenberg, "Offer," 327.

80. "Es liegt nahe, dass die Rivalen die Quelle dieser Verdächtigung waren" (Schmeller, *Zweite Brief*, 2:351).

policy—granting for the sake of argument that Paul rejected an offer—evolved from one of annoyance or offense to the charges of 7:2 and 12:16-18 requires a leap in logic. Offense or irritation is one thing; the accusation of criminal conduct is something else entirely. Third, that Paul hid the incoming support from Philippi or that a delegation arrived in Corinth under the cloak of secrecy is unlikely.[81] To a degree, these hypotheses rely too heavily upon claims like Marshall's, that support is a central issue in the cause of enmity in Corinth and that Paul's rejection of the offer aims to prevent the formation of an unequal friendship, or the similar claim that Paul's rejection of support undermined his claim to legitimacy.[82] Fourth, Mitchell's suggestion that Paul made an obvious and unforced error in immediately deviating from his plan in 1 Cor. 16:2-7 is possible but requires too much.[83] Beyond the heavy physical demand Mitchell's partition theory places upon manuscripts, Paul's reference to Titus and the brothers in 2 Corinthians 8 already indicates the existence of the accusation evidenced in Paul's careful use of envoys (8:16-24) and the Corinthians' cessation in the collection project (8:10-11).[84] Thus, despite the evidence that Paul responds to the serious accusation of embezzlement of collection funds, there is little solid ground from which to explain the charge.

4.2.2. *The Virtue Economy: Linking Passivity and Probity*

We wish to posit a simpler solution: the accusation of embezzlement arises predictably and naturally from Paul's behavior during the intermediate visit and absence. This, in turn, would help explain the logical links between issues of discipline and financial probity/collection, and suggest why Paul turns from one issue to the other frequently. Thrall rightly observes that the collection funds were never in Paul's possession.[85] It stands to reason that the charge is likely predictive in nature and relies upon Paul's past conduct. Thus, it is necessary to return to the intermediate visit in which Paul did not respond to affront with the vigor and force as threatened in 1 Cor. 4:18-21, but rather threatened and retreated.

---

81. Schellenberg, "Offer," 324.
82. Schellenberg, "Offer," 313.
83. "It is difficult to see how Paul could have blundered into such a counterproductive suggestion" (John S. Kloppenborg, "Fiscal Aspects of Paul's Collection for Jerusalem," *EC* 8 [2017]: 194 n. 134).
84. Kloppenborg, "Fiscal Aspects," 194.
85. Thrall, *Second Epistle*, 2:856.

In light of the evaluation of Paul's response to affront, it is important to observe the relationship between assertive action, surviving ordeals, and the trustworthiness of one's words.[86] In one sense, credibility of words could be substantiated by subsequent revelation of daring conduct. According to Plutarch, Porcia, desiring to know Brutus's secrets, covertly stabbed herself with scissors, approached Brutus and stated in part, "I know that woman's nature is thought too weak [ἀσθενὴς] to endure a secret…but now I know that I am superior even to pain." Subsequently, "she showed him her wound and explained her test [πεῖρα]." In response, Brutus breaks into adulation, praying "to show [φαίνω] himself a worthy [ἀξίωσις] husband."[87] Porcia's words gain credibility by revealing her rather masculine vigor.[88] Through her bold conduct, she is even able to push back against the notion that she is by nature (φύσις) too weak to be trusted.

Similarly, Sejanus's shielding of Tiberius as a grotto collapsed during a dinner led to the greater weight of his words, even if such esteem was not well placed. Tacitus comments, "As a result of this act he was held in still greater esteem, and though his counsels were ruinous, he was listened to with confidence, as a man who had no care for himself."[89] Barton comments as if a Corinthian scholar, "a person who had demonstrated his or her expendability had weighty words."[90] Thus, the words of those who had shown their mettle possessed a force more convincing than logic or wisdom.

Doubted reports gained credibility in similar fashion. In *Histories* 3.54, Tacitus goes to length to contrast the dubious Vitellius with the "notable courage" of Julius Agrestis, a centurion recently captured and sent to Rome by the Flavians following the rout at Cremona. Vitellius is represented as deceitful, one who through subterfuge (*dissimulatio*) suppresses the news of his force's defeat and who Agrestius attempts to rouse to "bold action," indicating his passivity in response to threat. Conversely, after Agrestis returned to Cremona to gather information for Vitellius, Tacitus comments that "[Agrestis] did not try to deceive" the Flavian general, Antonius. When Agrestis returned with the dire report, Vitellius "denied the truth of his report and even went so far as to charge him with having been bribed."

---

86. Barton, *Roman* Honor, 61–5.
87. Plutarch, *Brut.* 13.
88. For women displaying masculine virtues in trials, see 4 Macc. 15:28-30; *Martyrdom of Perpetua and Felicitas* 10; Moore and Anderson, "Masculinity," 265–72.
89. Tacitus, *Ann.* 4.59, trans. Barton, *Roman Honor*, 62.
90. Barton, *Roman Honor*, 62.

Agrestis responded, "since I must give you a convincing proof of my statements, and you can have no other advantage from my life or death, I will give you evidence that will make you believe." He committed suicide on the spot to substantiate the report. Tacitus opens *Histories* 3.55, claiming that Agrestis's action had its intended effect: "Vitellius was like a man wakened from a deep sleep." In both cases, passivity (effeminacy) was tied to suspicions or evidence of dubious character and untrustworthiness. Second, bold action substantiated an individual's credibility.

Failure to respond to an ordeal with daring action led to the collapse of one's credibility.[91] Of the public challenge, Barton comments, "[he] who failed the test of being seen was *improbus*, 'unsound,' not satisfying a standard, improper, incorrect, morally defective."[92] Sallust writes of Turpilius, who concluded because in flight "he preferred inglorious safety to an honorable name, he seems to have been a worthless and infamous character [*improbus intestabilisque*]."[93] In the case when one did not respond to a test with daring action, "the word of the *improbus* was worth nothing."[94] Here *improbus intestabilisque* is a technical phrase found in the Twelve Tables for a person disallowed to be a legal witness.[95] Similarly Tiberius Gracchus refers to the "lying lips" of the imperators whose words are of no value because they risk nothing themselves.[96] Cicero, quoting Ennius, refers to the "many who stayed at home for that reason remained unproved [*improbati*]."[97] Such was the untrustworthiness of other protean figures—the poor, actors, parasites—who remained by nature untested and unproven.[98] The evidence indicates that the Graeco-Roman virtue economy composed of the cardinal virtues, prudence (φρόνησις), temperance (σωφροσύνη), justice (δικαιοσύνη), and courage (ἀνδρεία) were often thoroughly interlocking, such that competency or failure in one area (courage) implied the same in other areas (truthfulness).[99]

---

91. Barton, *Roman Honor*, 61-4.
92. Barton, *Roman Honor*, 60; Moore and Anderson, "Masculinity" 269.
93. Sallust, *Bell. Jug.* 67.3.
94. Barton, *Roman Honor*, 60.
95. *Lex XII tabularum* 8.22 = Aulus Gellius, *Noct. att.* 15.13.11, in Barton, *Roman Honor*, 60 n. 134.
96. Plutarch, *Ti. C. Gracch.* 9.4-5.
97. Cicero, *Fam.* 7.6 = Ennius, *Trag.* 261, trans. Barton, *Roman Honor*, 60 n. 132.
98. Barton, *Roman Honor*, 62-3 cf. Juvenal, *Sat.* 3.144-46; 8.185-86; Cicero, *Quin.* 3.11; Plutarch, *Alc.* 23.3-5.
99. Plato, *Phaedr.* 69C; Philo, *Leg.* 1.63-72.

The collapse of Paul's credibility and the accusation that he intended to steal the collection are conditioned conclusions based on Paul's visit. Paul was bold (θαρρῶ) while away but abased (ταπεινὸς) when confronted (2 Cor. 10:1). It is no surprise that Paul's critics could conclude that since he exhibited martial weakness (ἡ παρουσία τοῦ σώματος ἀσθενὴς) in the moment of truth, his "words amount to nothing" (ὁ λόγος ἐξουθενημένος, 10:10). It is predictable that Paul's audience would suspect him of being ὑπάρχων πανοῦργος (12:16), a trickster by nature. Ancients considered a person's nature (ἔθος, φύσις) as largely fixed. And while commentators often comment on the pseudo-science of physiognomics, the reading of Paul's body to divine his character, it is quite evident that character was read also through responses to affront.[100] Paul's passivity suggested failure, which in turn implied deviant character.[101] As Porcia's comments suggest, weakness implied a mendacious, untrustworthy φύσις. For those not strong enough to impose their will, it would be natural to suspect acts of subterfuge.[102] Thus, the accusation of an act of δόλος against Paul in light of his martial passivity fits with Seneca's contrasts of Achilles's unmanly use of his mother's stratagem (*matris dolos*) with masculine courage and violence.[103] If Paul did not do what he said in the past, how could he be trusted to do so in the future regarding the collection? If Paul was too craven to respond to affront, how could he be trusted to manage so complex a project as an international relief fund? If he failed in one aspect of the virtue economy, could he be trusted in another, the just delivery of the collection? As demonstrated, impotence followed by absence implied judgment across Graeco-Roman antiquity. The accusations concerning Paul's financial probity are best understood as a culturally conditioned form of such a judgment against Paul.

This line of interpretation is preferable because it provides a culturally intelligible explanation of the origins of the accusation without appeal to the rivals or ὁ ἀδικήσας. Rather, it makes sense of the proximity of the accusations of embezzlement to discussions concerning (1) reciprocity between Paul and the community and (2) Paul's authority to discipline.

---

100. Harrill, "Invective," 211; Glancy, "Boasting," 129–30; for females and effeminates as cowardly, weak, and deceitful according to the canons of physiognomics, see Elizabeth Evans, "Physiognomics in the Ancient World," *TAPA* 59.5 (1965): 9, 36; Aristotle, [*Physiogn.*] 809a–810a.

101. See Watson, "Painful Letter," 345; Briones, "Paul's Financial Policy," 279; Savage, *Power*, 67.

102. For ἰσχυρός as opposite of δόλος, see Herodotus 4.201.

103. Seneca, *Tro.* 212–14.

Such concerns about Paul's financial probity organically arise from the culturally driven evaluation of Paul's martial inefficacy. It is thus entirely intelligible as to why Paul echoes and rejects suspicions of his capricious character in the opening to the canonical letter body (2 Cor. 1:13-14) and continues to reject charges of embezzlement (7:2b; 12:16-18), in part, substantiating such rejections through demonstrations of effective discipline (7:5-16) or threats of impending discipline (12:20–13:10).

4.2.3. *Other Approaches to the Link between Embezzlement and Inconstancy*

Scholars question the relationship between the accusation of embezzlement and the criticism of inconstancy in other texts (1:17; 10:1-11). Several interpreters claim that the accusations of inconstancy predate the charge of embezzlement.[104] However, Schmeller and others take the opposite track:

> Der Ausgangspunkt scheint eine finanzielle Angelegenheit gewesen zu sein, vermutlich der Unterhaltsverzicht, der mit der Kollekte in einen negativen Zusammenhang gebracht worden war (12,16-18). Die Scheinheiligkeit und Doppelzüngigkeit, die Paulus hier unterstellt wurden, dürften auch auf andere Aspekte seines Wirkens übertragen worden sein (bes. auf die Verlässlichkeit seiner Briefe und Besuche).[105]

None of the hypotheses supplies compelling rationale. However, Paul's failure to administer discipline provides explanatory power as to why Paul's credibility collapsed concerning financial probity and other matters of character.[106] Such suspicions in a host of areas are likely deductions tied to Paul's visit and subsequent absence.

Furthermore, our argument posits a more reasonable solution than Betz's and Marshall's influential theories that the stock images of the charlatan (γόης)[107] or flatterer (κόλαξ),[108] respectively, lay behind the criticisms of inconsistency (cf. 2 Cor. 1:12-14, 17; 4:2; 10:1, 10; 12:16-18). A lack of credibility existed as a common denominator between the

---

104. Influenced by the Hausrath–Kennedy hypothesis, Watson, "Painful Letter," 345; influenced by the Semler–Windisch hypothesis and viewed as a largely calumnious attack, Martin, *2 Corinthians*, 84.

105. Schmeller, *Zweite Brief*, 1:83; also Bultmann, *Second Letter*, 178; Klauck, *2 Korintherbrief*, 22.

106. Watson, "Painful Letter," 345; cf. Campbell, *Framing Paul*, 114.

107. Betz, *Apologie*, 52–3, 57–8, 132, 135, 139.

108. Marshall, *Enmity*, 281–340.

one who fails a challenge and the flatterer-parasite. The one who failed publicly lost credibility because they would not demonstrate masculine risk-taking; the flatterer-parasite lacked credibility because they had nothing to risk, pliantly adapting to surroundings. One was slavish because of their defeat; the other was slavish in order to climb.[109] Since Paul's relationship with the Corinthians can hardly be described as one of flattery in the sense of telling people what they wish to hear, and since we have evidence of a failure to respond to a challenge, it is most likely that doubts about his character stem from the events surrounding his hostile absence.[110]

4.3. Paul's Inconsistent Travel (2 Corinthians 1:15-17)

As discussed in the review of literature, there is good reason to conclude that 2 Corinthians aims to secure Paul's amicable return. As such, the early portion of the canonical letter addresses the other side of the coin, Paul's vexing absence (2 Cor. 1:15-22; 1:23–2:13; 7:5-16) following the intermediate visit. In the previous chapter, we presented evidence that the trouble concerning Paul's absence stems primarily from his failure to act decisively when challenged and suggest Paul's detractors desire not his return, but his continued absence. What then do we make of Paul's deliberations of his itinerary and the charge of ἐλαφρία and that Paul decides κατὰ σάρκα (1:17)?

4.3.1. Eschatological Confidence in Travel (2 Corinthians 1:13-14, 15-16)

Paul's presentation of his travel itinerary in 2 Cor. 1:15-16 is closely related to the preceding material (1:12-14) in which Paul rejects the suspicions surrounding his character, appeals for full recognition, and announces his hope of a mutual boast, "in the day of [our] Lord Jesus" (1:14). This is hope of dual survival of eschatological judgment, a significant shift from 1 Cor. 1:7-8, which refers only the community's eschatological verdict.[111] Paul then introduces in 2 Cor. 1:15 his travel plan, "Since I was sure of this, I wanted to come to you first so that you might have a second grace." Paul's confidence in 1:15 springs from the boast of his own conscience and his assurance of a mutual boast in the eschaton.[112] The link between

---

109. Cf. Athenaeus, *Deip.* 6.254c-d; Juvenal, *Sat.* 3.144-46, 8.185-86; Sallust. *Bell. Jug.* 24.2; Barton, *Roman Honor*, 62–3.
   110. See Guthrie, *2 Corinthians*, 108.
   111. Schmeller, *Zweite Brief*, 1:88.
   112. Similarly Vegge, *2 Corinthians*, 176; Land, *Absence*, 91–2.

the eschaton and a discussion concerning the potency and beneficence of Paul's arrival in Corinth is not all that unusual in light of the eschatological realism with which Paul colors his impending visit in 1 Cor. 4:18-21. The itineraries in the respective letters are dissimilar. Nonetheless, Paul bases his itinerary in 2 Cor. 1:15-16 upon his confidence and his desire to impart a second benefit (χάρις, 1:15) to the community, not to administer discipline. If Plan B (2 Cor. 1:15-16) superseded Plan A (1 Cor. 16:2-8), as is plausible, and if the discussion of arrivals here is connected to 1 Cor. 4:18-21, it suggests that Paul was initially confident his visits would be mutually edifying. The point then is that Plan B emerged, according to Paul, out of goodwill and a desire to impart a double benefit with no anticipation that he would be challenged.

With this in view, Paul poses two rhetorical questions in 2 Cor. 1:17, the first of which clearly expects a negative (μήτι) response: "Therefore, did I show levity [ἐλαφρία] desiring this?" Perhaps too quickly, scholars inquire as to the nature of the charge of ἐλαφρία and its relation to Paul's itinerary. However, with the rhetorical question Paul argues that his plan for a double visit resulting in a double benefit to the community cannot logically amount to ἐλαφρία, but its opposite, whatever that might be.[113] In 1:17b, Paul moves from the aorist (ἐχρησάμην) in 1:17a to the present tense (βουλεύομαι) in the second rhetorical question: "Or that which I decide, do I decide according to the flesh so that with me it is both yes and no?" Here the focus is not upon an act of ἐλαφρία but a larger concern of character, that Paul decides κατὰ σάρκα and thus seems to pan out to a larger frame of Paul's habituated character.[114]

4.3.2. *Levity and Character (2 Corinthians 1:17)*

An exegetical crux surrounds the meaning of the accusation of ἐλαφρία (1:17a) and the expressions κατὰ σάρκα, τὸ ναὶ ναὶ καὶ τὸ οὒ οὒ (1:17b). While interpreters find the meanings of the expressions elusive, there is general consensus that they are central to the meaning and function of 2 Corinthians and that they involve Paul's change in itinerary.[115] The biblical hapax ἐλαφρία may variously be defined as "behavior characterized by caprice and instability,"[116] "the lightness of character of a man who has no mind, who makes a promise without any real intention of

---

113. Land, *Absence*, 92–3.
114. Plummer, *Second Epistle*, 33; cf. Meyer, *Corinthians*, 1:153; contra Land, *Absence*, 94–5.
115. Thrall, *Second Epistle*, 1:140; Long, *Ancient Rhetoric*, 157.
116. L&N §88.99.

fulfilling it,"[117] and "to be both capricious in mind and of bad character."[118] The meaning of the expressions κατὰ σάρκα and ἵνα ᾖ παρ' ἐμοὶ τὸ Ναὶ ναὶ καὶ τὸ Οὒ οὔ are contested.[119] Yet the connection to the rhetorical question in 1:17a and the identical usage of κατὰ σάρκα in 10:2 and the similar expression in 1:12 (σοφίᾳ σαρκικῇ) grounds the expressions in the broader character accusations against Paul. While we have reasoned that 10:2 and 1:12-13a reflect criticisms emerging from Paul's failure to discipline and the culturally influenced conclusions regarding his character, scholars often view 1:17 entirely differently. Several interpreters view the accusation as a hatchet job against Paul, in which the detractors take the worst possible interpretation of Paul's historical happenstance.[120] Others take a more romantic line, claiming the accusation emerges from hurt feelings resulting from the community's unrealized desire for Paul's return.[121]

Neither line of interpretation adequately explains the narrow or broad context. For the reader, it is only clear in 2 Cor. 1:23 that what is primarily at stake is not Plan B itself but its incompletion.[122] Paul explains that his absence rather than his scheduled return aimed at sparing (φείδομαι) the community (1:23), a term that is linked to Paul's disciplinary warning during the visit and his threat of martial action upon his return (13:2). Paul proceeds through a circuitous and interrupted narrative (1:15-16; 2:1-13; 7:5-16) to supply exculpatory or at least mitigating evidence of the accusation in 1:17. Paul's plans for a double visit and the efficacious Severe Letter clears his name of ἐλαφρία and κατὰ σάρκα, not unlike the function of 7:5-16 in its canonical context, considering the accusation in 7:2b. Thus, Paul aimed to be efficacious in his plan for a double visit, but also spared the community (1:23) through an efficacious, disciplinary missive, rather than his planned arrival. This locates the accusations of ἐλαφρία and κατὰ σάρκα not in the world of calumny nor a disappointment with Paul's absence, but Paul's martial impotence on his second visit and subsequent character concerns which are linked to his ongoing absence.

117. Kennedy, *The Second and Third Epistles*, 36.

118. B. J. Oropeza, *Exploring Second Corinthians: Death and Life, Hardship and Rivalry*, RRA 3 (Atlanta: SBL, 2016), 108.

119. For recent summary of the interpretive options, see Guthrie, *2 Corinthians*, 108–9.

120. Viewed as a calumnious exaggeration by Marshall, *Enmity*, 318; Danker, *II Corinthians*, 17; Jerry L. Sumney, *Identifying Paul's Opponents: The Question of Method in 2 Corinthians*, JSNTSup 40 (Sheffield: Sheffield Academic, 1990), 131–9; Garland, *2 Corinthians*, 98.

121. Strachan, *Second Epistle*, 64; Garland, *2 Corinthians*, 173; Furnish, *II Corinthians*, 144.

122. Schmeller, *Zweite Brief*, 1:98.

The term ἐλαφρία glossed as "lightness" or "levity" is not an accusation of inconsistency in travel plans alone; it is inconsistency or variance in travel plans that have communal discipline in view, the very issue at the heart of 2 Cor. 10:1-11, 12:21, and 13:1-10 made more coherent in light of 1 Cor. 4:18-21.

Paul would not be unfamiliar with the cultural domain associated with fickleness. In Galatians, he martials the domain to establish his credentials. There, Paul is sturdy and reliable. His unique apostleship (Gal. 1:11-12) is substantiated by narratives of his constancy since his conversion, performing consistently whether in private or public (Gal. 1:18-24; 2:1-10, 11-14). In contrast, Peter and the Galatians appear as opposites. The community quickly change their tune because of the troublemakers (Gal. 1:6; 3:1) not unlike Peter in Antioch when visitors arrive from James (Gal. 2:12-13). The point is clear: Paul's voice is to be trusted, his apostleship is vindicated because of his trustworthy, consistent, and heroic conduct.

From this contextual view, Jennifer Larson's comments are instructive. The quality of "lightness" (ἐλαφρία, Lat. *levitas*) was the opposite of the masculine virtue of weightiness or dignity, *gravitas*. In terms of character, it described an individual who was fickle, unsteady, unreliable, or changeable. In traditional gender ideology, women's fickle character justified male oversight and control.[123] Plutarch contrasts, "a simple [ἐλαφρός], unassuming woman" as the ideal with its antithesis in a woman of "high estate" (βαρύς) who demonstrates "her determination to command and to dominate."[124] Again, at issue is passivity contrasted with action. While appropriate for a woman, when applied to a male leader like Paul, the charge of ἐλαφρία in 2 Cor. 1:17a (and to a degree the accusation in 1:17b) in the context of discipline points not to the figure of a flatterer,[125] but to a coward and weakling—although both share an overlapping cultural domain[126]—an unstable leader who does not demonstrate masculine risk-taking in person and whose absence is indicative of his passivity and impotence.[127] Thus, the echo of the charge of ἐλαφρία in failing to fulfil his disciplinary return is complementary to the accusation that Paul is βαρύς and ἰσχυρός through the letter but ταπεινός and ἀσθενὴς in person (2 Cor. 10:1, 10). The charge of ἐλαφρία adds a further layer of insight, indicating

123. Larson, "Paul's Masculinity," 92.
124. Plutarch, *Amat.* 7; "The ancients desired women to be in tutelage because of their lightness of mind" (Gaius, *Inst.* 1.144).
125. Contra Marshall, *Enmity*, 318–19, and others.
126. Larson, "Paul's Masculinity," 92–3.
127. Similarly Land, *Absence*, 92 n. 28.

that not only did some view his presence as evidence of cowardice, but also his ongoing absence.

Specifically, the accusation that Paul habitually decides κατὰ σάρκα (2 Cor. 1:17b), resulting in contradictory decisions, is best explained by the ancient virtue economy in which failure in one sphere implied slippage in other spheres. The language in 1:17b reflects not cowardice alone, but the inability to govern oneself with the result that Paul's yes can easily become no.[128] According to Cynic-Stoic logic, to control others, ideal leaders needed to control themselves.[129] Such moral language often centered upon appetites of food, drink, sleep, and sex. Plato (fl. ca. 428–ca. 347 BCE) claims that the agonistic struggle between rivals (at all levels of society) also involves an intrapersonal struggle. The good man is "stronger than himself" and the bad man is "weaker than himself."[130] Xenophon (fl. ca. 430–ca. 354 BCE) states, "[the] power to win willing obedience: it is manifestly a gift of the gods to the true votaries of self-control [σωφροσύνη]."[131] The virtue economy worked both ways. Just as risk-taking substantiated one's credibility and trustworthiness, so too one's inability to control external affairs suggested the opposite, that an individual was perhaps not in control of themselves. Similarly, Paul's inability to demonstrate martial courage and his current absence leads to the conclusion he has no control over his decisions, an issue he also engages in 2 Cor. 5:13.[132] There, Paul wishes for appropriate recognition in the community (5:11; cf. 1:13-14; 13:6) because of his work in preparing the community for judgment (5:10), supplying his supporters with a response to his detractors (5:12), who presumably think Paul is "out of [his] mind [ἐξίστημι]" (5:13).[133] As in our analysis of the intermediate visit and the accusations emanating from the aftermath, the accusations of ἐλαφρία and κατὰ σάρκα βουλεύομαι reflect a judgment against Paul, a judgment linked to Paul's passive presence and subsequent absence.

---

128. "The *duplication* of the ναὶ and οὔ strengthens the picture of the untrustworthy man who affirms just as fervently as he afterwards denies" (Meyer, *Corinthians*, 2:153).

129. Moore and Anderson, "Masculinity," 253; Dio Chrysostom, 3 *Regn.* 7, 10; Philo, *Mos.* 1.152-54.

130. Plato, *Laws* 626E as in Winkler, *Desire*, 49.

131. Xenophon, *Oec.* 21.12; see *Mem.* 1.5.1, 1.5.5; *Econ.* 12.13; *4 Macc.* 1:4; 7:20-23.

132. In 2 Cor. 5:13 Paul echoes the charge ἐξέστημεν (Weiss, *Primitive Christianity*, 1:343 n. 74; see Land, *Absence*, 133–4).

133. See Duff, *Moses*, 60–2, 65–9.

Thus, the accusation of ἐλαφρία is complementary to our interpretation of Paul's failure to affect discipline in person during the intermediate visit. Second Corinthians 1:17 echoes accusations of cowardice and passivity linked to Paul's absence, while in 2 Cor. 10:1, 9-10, 13:1-10, Paul addresses similar accusations regarding his failure in person and his use of disciplinary letters in his stead. While it is increasingly popular to see these texts as pointing to two different phases in the relationship, this is not necessarily so, as the echo of accusations of passivity in the context of Paul's visit and absence remain consistent. One is an accusation of a failure to act assertively in person and instead hide behind martial letters (10:1, 9-10); the other is a failure to return as promised to act punitively (1:17), defended in part by pointing to an efficacious martial letter (2:1-13; 7:5-16). While these could point to different phases in the social relationship, they just as easily may point to different vantage points on the same situation, strategically addressed by the author.[134] In both instances, Paul's manner during the intermediate visit and his ongoing subsequent absence imply and embody judgments against him. We have posited a culturally intelligible hypothesis as to how Paul's passive behavior during the intermediate visit could precipitate such an assertion in the realm of both financial probity and travel plans without appealing to the stock image of the flatterer-parasite or assertions that the accusation reflects either a calumnious invective or a longing for Paul's return.

4.4. *Communal and Political Consequences in Corinth*

In Chapter 3, we interpreted Paul's intermediate visit and absence by moving from broad socio-cultural matrices and theories to concrete political communities. Similarly, we have evaluated the accusations of embezzlement and levity from a socio-cultural framework. Now we wish to inquire as to what if anything these judgments would mean in Paul's political community in Corinth and the degree which it complements our conclusions in Chapter 3. What would these accusations suggest not in light of the ideal Mediterranean leader, but considering Paul's Corinthian ἐκκλησία?

4.4.1. *Communal Scrutiny*

First, in 2 Corinthians Paul responds to the kind of serious judgments from which he claimed immunity in 1 Cor. 4:3-5. In what context should we understand the evaluation of communal leaders perhaps like Paul? As discussed in the previous chapter, δοκιμασία scrutinies existed in

---

134. Cf. Schellenberg, *Education*, 67.

analogous social formations (§2.5.2; §3.3.6). Only after an officer's conduct was thoroughly vetted was s/he publicly recognized.[135] In contrast to Franz Poland's assertion that any semblance of δοκιμασία trials in associations involved focus only upon financial propriety, Last counters that in fact officials were regularly scrutinized in light of a host of deeds and qualities including their obedience to the association's *nomoi*.[136] The evidence presented by Last leads him to conclude that officials were routinely and thoroughly audited according to their propriety and total quality of service.[137]

4.4.2. Contractual Language in Corinth: Habituated Character

The *nomoi* of Paul's ἐκκλησία are unknown and plausibly never existed. However, Brian Rosner argues that the vice lists in 1 Cor. 5:10-11 are drawn primarily from Deuteronomy (LXX), suggesting the lists project a covenantal and thus contractual context.[138] This is supported by the Deuteronomic citation of the death penalty formula in 5:13. The provenance of this material, whether pre-baptismal catechesis, a now-lost summary of the limits of communal behavior, or Paul's unique formulation in response to an exigency remain unknown.[139] However, a general similarity exists between the vice-catalogue including the prescription for punitive sanctions in 5:9-10 (and to a lesser extent 6:9-10) and associational *nomoi*, further indicating a covenantal or constitutional context.[140]

This assertion is supported by 1 Cor. 6:1-11. Debate exists as to the form of the judicial apparatus prescribed, that is whether Paul recommends procedures similar to communal Jewish courts[141] or private arbitration.[142] Yet, as Kloppenborg points out, the process of intra-communal litigation

---

135. *IG* 1271.1-14; *IG* 1327.4-16; *IG* 1329.3-19; cf. Last, "Money, Meals, and Honour," 107–10.

136. Last, "Money, Meals, and Honour," 107–10; cf. Poland, *Geschichte*, 423.

137. Last, "Money, Meals, and Honour," 110; see *IG* 1271.1-14; *IG* 1327.4-16; *IG* 1329.3-19.

138. Rosner, *Paul, Scripture and Ethics*, 69–70.

139. Rosner, *Paul, Scripture and Ethics*, 70.

140. Ebel, *Die Attraktivität früher christlicher Gemeinden*, 182–3.

141. Ernst Bammel, "Rechtsfindung in Korinth," *ETL* 73 (1997): 112–13, and others.

142. Alan C. Mitchell, "I Corinthians 6:1-11: Group Boundaries and the Courts of Corinth" (Ph.D. diss., Yale University, 1986), 75–131; Bruce W. Winter, "Civil Litigation in Secular Corinth and the Church: The Forensic Background to 1 Corinthians 6.1-8," *NTS* 37 (1991): 568–9; Clarke, *Leadership*, 69.

is far more analogous to associational courts.¹⁴³ The prescription to avoid public courts neither reflect a sectarian impulse, nor was it unique. Rather, the fundamental point in 1 Cor. 5:1-13; 6:1-11—that the community must adjudicate certain offences (5:1-13) and that such cases must not go before outsiders (6:1-11)—was ubiquitous among voluntary associations.¹⁴⁴ Thus, there is good reason to suppose an emerging contractual framework and fledgling ambit of jurisdiction in Paul's ἐκκλησία.

Moreover, Paul clearly encourages the community to audit the conduct of its other leaders. Paul originally entrusts the delivery of the collection to those "you have approved [δοκιμάζω] through letter" (1 Cor. 16:3). Paul sends to Corinth the brother, whom "we have approved [δοκιμάζω] many times (2 Cor. 8:22)." Thus, leaders in Corinth other than Paul were subjected to a form of audit concerning their overall probity.

4.4.3. *Paul's Aim for Full Recognition (2 Corinthians 1:13-14)*

What relevance is this to the judgments faced by Paul in 2 Corinthians? Paul writes so that he might be recognized (ἐπιγινώσκω) completely by the community (2 Cor. 1:13-14). The same verb is used in reference to "recognizing" Paul's authority in 1 Cor. 14:37, where the legitimate prophet or spiritualist must first recognize Paul's legitimacy as one who writes "a command of the Lord." In 14:38, he states, "any who does not recognize [ἀγνοεῖ] [Paul's teaching as command], s/he will not be recognized [ἀγνοεῖται]." Conversely, Paul exhorts the community to recognize (ἐπιγινώσκετε) Stephanas, Fortunatus, and Achaicus due to their conduct in their trip to Ephesus (1 Cor. 16:17-18). And not only them, but τοὺς τοιούτους (16:18). This is likely the background to 2 Cor. 1:13b, rather than a cognitive/noetic interpretation.¹⁴⁵ There is remarkable parallelism between Paul's hope (ἐλπίζω) to be recognized (ἐπιγινώσκω, 2 Cor. 1:13-14), a hope to be revealed in the consciences of the community (2 Cor. 5:11b), and Paul's hope (ἐλπίζω) that the community knows (γινώσκω) that he is not unapproved (ἀδόκιμος, 2 Cor. 13:6). Some suspect that Paul faces an official scrutiny in 2 Corinthians.¹⁴⁶ Whether this is accurate or whether

---

143. Kloppenborg, "Egalitarianism," 256–8; cf. Ebel, *Gemeinden*, 195–6.
144. Gillihan, *Rule Scrolls*, 88; Kloppenborg, "Egalitarianism," 275; cf. Mathias Delcor, "The Courts of the Church of Corinth and the Courts of Qumran," in *Paul and Qumran*, ed. Jerome Murphy-O'Connor, SNTE (London: Chapman, 1968), 72; Benjamin Edsall, "When Cicero and St. Paul Agree: Intra-Group Litigation Among the Luperci and the Corinthian Believers," *JTS* 64.1 (2013): 25–36.
145. Similarly Long, *Ancient Rhetoric*, 155.
146. Long, *Ancient Rhetoric*, 118, 139–41; Welborn, *Enmity*, 198.

such language refers to an unofficial, scrutinizing gaze of the community, Paul responds to some form of evaluation concerning his leadership of the community, which has seemingly resulted in a loss of "recognition," not unlike the rejection of his political legitimacy (10:8; 13:3a).

What then can we infer about the scrutiny of Paul's conduct in his Corinthian ἐκκλησία? We have no conclusive evidence of a formal quasi-legal proceeding against Paul. However, a consistent argument against Paul is that he possesses deviant character. He is a trickster by nature (ὑπάρχων πανοῦργος, 2 Cor. 12:16), intending to bilk the community. He "decides according to the flesh" such that he gives contradictory answers (2 Cor. 1:17b). And of course, he is a coward in person, only able to summon courage from afar (2 Cor. 10:1, 10). These accusations suggest a rather pointed evaluation of Paul's habituated character.

While these evaluations are entirely expected according to the wider socio-cultural matrix following the intermediate visit, they may have particular political and penological consequences in Corinth's ἐκκλησία. As presented in Chapter 2, the criteria for expulsion from Corinth involved habituated, deviant character, rather than lone offences (1 Cor. 5:1, 10-11) (see §2.7.2). If there is a forming contractual awareness in Paul's ἐκκλησία as in other communities, then the accusations of deformed character likely meet the threshold found in 1 Cor. 5:11, to not associate with (συναναμείγνυμι) nor eat with (συνεσθίω) such a so-called member. There even exists shared cognates (πλεονεκτέω, 2 Cor. 7:2c; 12:18; πλεονέκτης, 1 Cor. 5:11; πλεονέκταις, 5:10; πλεονέκται, 6:10). In totality, then, Paul echoes a judgment that according to his own prescription he violated the communal contract and is operating outside the communal boundary of appropriate conduct. This suggests the possible goal of those who evaluated Paul. Perhaps this line of reasoning sounds implausible. However, one must then answer why more distant contextual fields (politics, cultural conventions, social institutions) would be more relevant than a more proximate context such as a community's *realia*. Thus, we tentatively conclude it is possible Paul is accused of violating the communal contract or ethos.

4.4.4. *Evidence of Withdrawal/Ostracism*

Ultimately, if this line of reasoning is plausible then we should expect evidence of social withdrawal like that prescribed in 1 Cor. 5:11 and consistent with analogous communal responses, whether concerning official acts of exile or informal ostracism. First, the collapse of the collection effort (2 Cor. 8:10-11) clearly signals a withdrawal of support from Paul's ministry. Consistently and across diverse partition hypotheses, commentators contend that the completion of the collection is a key indicator of complete reconciliation with Paul, a symbolic act that acknowledges Paul's authority (8:7-8).[147] Inasmuch as the completion of the collection forms an important liturgy for reconciliation through Titus's return, the collapse points to a strategic secession from Paul's ministry endeavors.

Second, the courting and support of replacement apostles indicates a further disengagement from Paul's leadership of the community (2 Cor. 10:12–11:29). Not to belabor the point, the consistent understanding of the rivals as the active ingredient in the crisis and the community as passive before the interlopers is historically unwarranted, as is the claim that 1 and 2 Corinthians refer to two radically different occasions, the former an intramural affair, the latter an issue with outsiders.[148] The uninvited presence of missionaries that possess the qualities lacked by Paul just as those deficiencies were under heavy critique is simply incredible. Nor is it likely that the rivals awoke these judgments against Paul with their presence. Some in the community already evaluated Paul along these lines in 1 Corinthians (4:3-4, 18; 9:3). It is far more likely that the presence of rival apostles indicates the desire of some in the community to break fellowship with Paul and find apostolic leadership elsewhere, thus an intensification of the problem in 1 Corinthians. That is, the rivals are evidence primarily of the desire to marginalize Paul in Corinth far more than a Mediterranean-wide strategy of Paul's rivals to subvert Paul's mission or a random and unfortunate arrival of interlopers. This hypothesis has historical precedent. In several στάσεις, disaffected portions of a community sought outsiders for sympathetic judgments when a breakdown in trust had occurred between the populace and local leaders.[149]

We have then a chronic lack of hospitality towards Paul by some in the community (1 Cor. 9; 2 Cor. 11:7-12), an affront to Paul's authority in the intermediate visit (1 Cor. 4:18-21; 2 Cor. 12:21–13:2), a subsequent cessation of support for the collection (2 Cor. 8:10; 9:2), echoes of serious judgments including a challenge to Paul's political legitimacy, and the presence of replacement apostles (2 Cor. 10:12–11:29). This evidence is compatible with other occurrences of judgment in which communities broke off support for prominent, displaced persons, save the unique office

---

147. Betz, *2 Corinthians*, 142; Dieter Georgi, *Remembering the Poor: The History of Paul's Collection for Jerusalem* (Nashville: Abingdon, 1992), 73; Vegge, *2 Corinthians*, 218–19.

148. See §1.3.

149. Börm, "Stasis," 64–5.

of apostle in the ἐκκλησία. We do not possess evidence of any outreach by the community towards Paul in 2 Corinthians as in 1 Corinthians (1:11; 7:1; 16:15). All the diplomatic envoys are sent by Paul to re-assert his place in the community and achieve Paul's amicable return (2 Cor. 2:1-4; 7:5-16; 8:16-21; 9:4-5). Such use of envoys and letters are attested in the campaigns of exiles aiming to secure a return.[150] This is not to say that by the time of 2 Corinthians Paul's campaign turned the tide in his favor through the Severe Letter and Titus's envoy. Rather, Paul's recent breakthrough indicates the degree to which the community had previously withdrawn from the relationship and continued to do so in part. While no conclusive evidence of a quasi-juridical proceeding exists, there is ample evidence that some in the community made deliberate moves to sideline Paul in his absence.

4.5. Conclusions

This chapter has demonstrated the explanatory power of our hypothesis that Paul failed to respond assertively to an affront by an immoral contingent during his intermediate visit and that due to his lack of masculine courage, his exit and absence reflected and embodied judgments against him widely intelligible across antiquity. While we argued that the criticisms of ταπεινός (10:1), ἀσθενής, and ὁ λόγος ἐξουθενημένος (10:10) in view of 1 Cor. 4:18-21 and alongside the challenges to Paul's apostolic legitimacy (10:7; 13:3a) place Paul firmly in the world of political displacement, in this chapter we have addressed seemingly unrelated charges concerning accusations of embezzlement (7:2; 12:16-18; 2:10, respectively) and variance in travel plans (1:15-17). Contrary to disparate and unwieldy theories concerning the inception of the charge of embezzlement, the implications behind the charge of ἐλαφρία, or the appeals to the stock image of the flatterer-parasite, I have demonstrated that it is probable these accusations stem from culturally driven assessments of Paul's character due to his failure to act decisively and courageously in the face of affront.

Beyond the judgments resonating with broad socio-cultural matrices, the evidence suggests that it is possible the accusations concerning Paul's intention to embezzle the collection and deviant character point to specific communal logic and *telos*. Communities often evaluated leaders intentionally in reference to communal norms and contracts, rather than according to the

---

150. See Appendix I.

socio-cultural ether. Particularly, in Corinth such accusations of diseased character would logically imply that the offender had violated the community's nascent contractual requirements (1 Cor. 5:10-11), resulting in the community's form of political displacement. While claims of a juridical proceeding against Paul remain incredible, we have ample evidence of the judgment of diseased character alongside the community's withdrawal of relations in favor of missionary rivals, features that resonate with MCE described in Chapter 2. From both the socio-cultural and communal vantage points, our initial interpretation of Paul's visit and subsequent absence from Corinth has been tested, resulting in further insights into the cascade of accusations and social behaviors echoed in 2 Corinthians. We posit, then, that it is highly plausible that 2 Corinthians is part of a larger campaign to respond to and conclude a frequent occasion in antiquity, a period of political displacement.

Conclusion to Part I

Informed by relevance theory, Part I aimed to (1) describe the phenomena that lay behind ancient discussions of and attempts to reconcile with and return to a community in order to outline the MCE (Chapter 2) and (2) explore the evidence in 2 Corinthians in order to perceive any resonance with such phenomena (Chapters 3 and 4). Our investigation yields the following findings:

1. Virtually Certain: Paul visited Corinth between the canonical letters. Yet, whereas scholars frequently reconstruct the visit with reference to ὁ ἀδικήσας or the rivals, the most determinative texts concerning the existence of the visit (2 Cor. 12:21; 13:1-2) point not to a conflict with a lone figure nor with outsiders, but with a sexually immoral and rebellious contingent within the community.
2. Virtually Certain: the intermediate visit appears, especially in light of 1 Cor. 4:18–21 and the test cases of apostolic authority in 1 Cor. 5:1-13; 6:1-11, 12-20, as a rejection of Pauline legitimacy and thus a contest over communal leadership and ethos.
3. Virtually Certain: the judgments that Paul is ταπεινός (10:1), ἀσθενής, and ὁ λόγος ἐξουθενημένος (10:10) function as communal commentary on Paul's visit and refer primarily to Paul's martial impotence and defeat during the intermediate ordeal and point to the wider evaluation both that Paul lost the contest with the immoral group and does not possess qualities of an ideal masculine leader necessary to order group life.

4. Highly Probable: Paul's martial threat, inaction, and subsequent exit (13:2) appear as an instance of defeat and displacement when viewed in light of both a protracted conflict witnessed in 1 Cor. 4:18-21, wherein Paul promises to come to Corinth to bring martial order to those who challenge his authority to order ἐκκλησία life and also the broader phenomena associated with political displacement.
5. Virtually Certain: the judgments that Paul is ταπεινός (10:1), ἀσθενής, and ὁ λόγος ἐξουθενημένος (10:10) are tied not simply to socio-cultural matrices, but a more specific, communal judgment that Paul is illegitimate (10:7; 13:3a). The revocation of communal status and rights are a fundamental feature of political displacement with clear analogies to Paul's passive response to affront. More particularly, the questioning of status relates to Paul's own discourse about the nature of ordeals in ἐκκλησία life and the role of absence as a sign of judgment (1 Cor. 3:4; 4:18-21; 5:1-13; 6:9-10; 11:28-30). That Paul behaved passively and left Corinth rather than his detractors drives the assessment that his communal status is illegitimate, without reference to an early Christian standard or the practices of the rivals.
6. Probable: the centrality of Paul's impotent response to a power-challenge and subsequent absence to the crisis in 2 Corinthians may be viewed in light of other judgments to which Paul responds, namely the claim that Paul intended to embezzle the collection (2 Cor. 7:2b; 12:16-18), that his absence evidenced levity (2 Cor. 1:17a), and that, in totality, he possessed diseased character (2 Cor. 1:17b; 12:16). In each instance, such moral reasoning is explainable through Paul's failure to administer discipline as promised and his ongoing return and underlies the contention that Paul is not made of ideal, leadership stock.
7. Possible: in Corinth's ἐκκλησία such judgments may suggest a communal scrutiny of Paul's leadership similar to those in analogous political communities and encouraged by Paul. Particular to the nascent contractual language employed in 1 Cor. 5:10-11 concerning habituated character as the standard of communal participation, the judgment that Paul is of poor character involves an argument in favor of total ostracism or displacement.
8. Virtually Certain: the outsider language against Paul is complemented by outsider conduct directed towards him: social withdrawal in the collapse of the collection effort, the support of the missionary rivals, and an absence of any evidence of communal outreach or support.

On balance, when the socio-cultural and political phenomena presented in Chapter 2 are placed alongside the evidence in 2 Corinthians, it is entirely reasonable to conclude that therein Paul attempts to secure an amicable return from a period of political displacement. Paul is, thus, not unlike a host of ancient figures, some known (Demosthenes, Cicero), most unknown, who voluntarily left a political community in the face of affront and hostility and subsequently employed a campaign to bring the period of displacement to a close. In this way, Paul's absence is not happenstance or simply a feature of his peripatetic ministry. Rather, it is connected to, if not the embodiment of a series of judgments against him, judgments that indicate a desire not for Paul's return but his continued absence.

An interpreter may insist on the interpretive priority of the ὁ ἀδικήσας or the rivals, hold to various partition theories, or still maintain the importance of rhetoric or Paul's support policy and still follow the basic argument. At minimum, an instance in which a prominent figure leaves a community following an affront, a challenge to his political power, followed by the community's judgment of illegitimacy, and the community's social withdrawal was a highly recognizable instance of political displacement. Yet, in 2 Corinthians scholarship this line of inquiry remains previously unpursued. This reconstruction stands in line with several efforts that attend to the social world, although with sustained focus upon the significance of exit and absence in conflict and tethered to the processes of political communities. Much more is at stake than simply an alternate socio-historical reconstruction. As a relevance-theoretic approach elucidates and scholarly instincts demonstrate, the evidence used for alternate reconstructions supplies potentially alternate, efficient contexts for interpretations of texts beyond those used for reconstruction.

Part II

Discourses of Displacement in 2 Corinthians

Paul faced a tall task in order to realize his epistolary and rhetorical aim of an amicable return. The success of the Letter of Tears (2 Cor. 2:5-11; 7:5-16) at some point in the crisis mitigated some of that undertaking, although Paul remained absent and under communal judgment. The results of Part I demonstrated that not only were the phenomena associated with political displacement manifest in the MCE, but such phenomena are also echoed in 2 Corinthians (absence after communal strife, defeat, loss of communal status/rank, evidence of judgment, withdrawal of support). Thus, any associated schemas or frames were likely more mutually manifest than previously realized by scholars. From a relevance-theoretic perspective, the more mutually manifest a representation of the world, the more relevant such representations will be as potential context for the interpretation of a text. Thus, we pose a perhaps overly simplistic question that can only be answered in part here, in light of our socio-historical study: what strategies did Paul employ to realize his aims?

One aid in this task arrives naturally, however, not without much risk, from those who experienced a similar fate as that of Paul and who, like him, employed literature to comment upon or reverse their situation as well as philosophical and epic writings that refer to displacement. Indeed, if Paul's socio-historical situation was not entirely as unique as often thought, as Part I demonstrates, then those who employed literature from such a social location may supply some measure of interpretive assistance. When considering Paul, foremost in this effort is Israel's prominent exilic tradition in the LXX. As well, a number of voluntary and involuntary exiles employed the stroke of the pen to mitigate the effects of displacement, to affect recall, to respond to accusations, and to keep one's memory alive in the community, employing and refashioning what a number of classicists have identified as multiple displacement tropes, which Gaertner refers to as a "discourse of displacement."[1] Heinz-Günther Nesselrath asserts

---

1. Gaertner, "Discourse of Displacement," 1–20.

the frequency of displacement lead to well-trodden displacement tropes.[2] However, Nesselrath is relatively unconcerned with non-elite life. We do not know how widely travelled such tropes were, or if the literary paradigms pervaded antiquity into non-elite strata. However, if our reconstruction holds water, then it is proper to consult judiciously with those who attempted to respond to or comment upon their displacement in order to perceive similar rhetorical strategies in 2 Corinthians.

Hazards abound, as indicated above. Samuel Sandmel warned over a half a century ago of "parallelomania," which he described as, "that extravagance among scholars which first overdoes the supposed similarity in passages and then proceeds to describe source and derivation as if implying literary connection flowing in an inevitable or predetermined direction."[3] Sandmel cautions, "the knowledge on our part of the parallels may assist us in understanding Paul; but if we make him mean only what the parallels mean, we are using the parallels in a way that can lead us to misunderstand Paul."[4] True enough. Yet, without parallels one runs the converse risk of *sui generis* interpretations such as those that reduce 2 Corinthians to a detached "theology of ministry." Thus, priority must be granted to Paul's discourse and the idiosyncrasies of an individual's communication and exigence with any insights coming from a broader discourse as perhaps evidence of the local appropriation of a "Traditionszusammenhang" or discourse of displacement.

Second and relatedly, literary traditions or parallels function as an interpretive tool, but just as everything can look like a nail to the person holding hammer, so too every passage can appear as a displacement text to the researcher familiar with the tradition. This problem is further elucidated by a relevance-theoretic approach, which emphasizes the nature of context as chosen (by the audience based upon principles of relevance) and protean not given and static. Thus, it would be a violation of the principles of relevance to impose the background material in Part I upon 2 Corinthians or even pre-selected texts. Thus, in view of the need to avoid a procrustean approach and the constraints of a thesis, there is need for some control to delimit our inquiry to appropriate, discreet textual units.

With an emphasis upon Paul's specific occasion and attempt to realize an amicable return, we turn to the results of Part I to identify the kind of impinging information that Paul's audience would likely perceive as clues and cues necessary in order to evoke as context the issues surrounding

---

2. Heinz-Günther Nesselrath, "Later Greek Voices on the Predicament of Exile: From Teles to Plutarch to Favorinus," in Gaertner, ed., *Writing Exile*, 97–108.

3. Samuel Sandmel, "Parallelomania," *JBL* 81.1 (1962): 1.

4. Sandmel, "Parallelomania," 5.

Paul's displacement from Corinth. Our specific reading has emphasized that Paul's displacement involves (1) a failure and defeat regarding a communal ordeal, (2) resulting in a range of judgments, (3) including judgments concerning Paul's character, and (4) a rejection (by at least some) of his political legitimacy. Thus, we posit that when these topics—ordeal accounts, judgments against Paul, discussion of his ethos, and communal legitimacy—are engaged in a discreet textual unit (allowing for some measure of implicitness), then it likely supplies enough contextual clues or triggers in the discourse to evoke the material in Part I.

Five textual units (2 Cor. 1:3-11; 2:12-13; 7:5-16; 11:30-33; 13:1-10) contain explicit references to at least three out of the four criteria listed above and thus, we contend, efficiently evoke the displacement context. These passages occur in structurally significant areas of the epistle (the opening and closing of the letter body, the plausible framing device for 2:14–7:4, and the so-called Fool's Speech). The passages occur after the intermediate visit according to the major partition theories. Four of the passages contain ordeal narrations containing accounts or scenes of apostolic dilemma (2 Cor. 1:3-11; 2:12-13; 7:5-16; 11:32-33) while in 2 Cor. 13:1-10, Paul refers to his impending return as an ordeal and further challenges the community "to test" and "to examine" themselves (13:5). Markedly, each passage centers upon the threat of punitive sanction or judgment, whether faced by Paul (2 Cor. 1:8-10; 11:32-33), the community (2 Cor. 2:12-13; 7:5-16; cf. 1:17), or both (2 Cor. 13:1-10). Finally, Paul's legitimacy is explicitly referenced thrice. The Asian and Macedonia/Troas ordeals bracket Paul's desire for full recognition by the community (2 Cor. 1:13-14). The Damascus scene participates in a larger discourse (2 Cor. 11:22–12:10) concerning Paul's legitimacy vis-à-vis the rivals as a servant of Christ (2 Cor. 11:23). And in 13:1-10, the passage centers upon proof of Paul's apostolic status (2 Cor. 13:3) and, conversely, the status of the community (2 Cor. 13:5-10).

Thus, in Part II we aim to demonstrate the relevance of Paul's political displacement for the interpretation of specific texts in 2 Corinthians and one route by which Paul aimed to achieve reconciliation and return. In Chapter 5 we interpret the ordeal narrations and demonstrate the way in which they offer a geographically particularized account of Christological reversal (Asia, Troas/Macedonia, Damascus) amidst Paul's frailty and impotence. In Chapter 6, we interpret 2 Cor. 13:1-10, arguing that Paul draws upon the Christo-logic of the ordeal narratives to reconcile and return to Corinth.

Chapter 5

PAUL'S ART OF THE ORDEAL: APOSTOLIC IMPOTENCE AND DIVINE AID IN OTHER PLACES

While I suggest that the reconstruction in Part I invites renewed interpretative efforts of several passages in 2 Corinthians, Paul's narrations of his apostolic ordeals supply a relevant starting point. Second Corinthians contains three accounts in four textual units of Pauline ordeals in vivid detail (2 Cor. 1:3-11; 2:12-13; 7:5-16; 11:30-33). We pose the following research questions for each passage: (1) In what way, if any, does the text relate to Paul's visit, exit, and the outstanding judgments against him *in absentia*? (2) How does Paul use the ordeal to negotiate the crisis in Corinth? (3) What is Paul attempting to achieve through the account?

To differing degrees, the ordeal narrations juxtapose Paul's passivity and impotence in the midst of trial and opposition in particular locations (Asia, Macedonia-Troas, Damascus) with God's action and power. Paul twice faces explicit threats of judgment in the narrations (2 Cor. 1:3-11; 11:30-33). In each case, God's intervention results in a *volte-face* for Paul. Furthermore, Paul negotiates the ordeal narrations with identifiable references to a broader discourse of displacement. We contend that the narratives in 2 Corinthians likely possess an apologetic and parenetic function which redefines the nature of the authentic Christian ordeal, affirms Paul's character and legitimacy, thus attempting to achieve the formation a unique communal ethos in their light and the social space necessary for Paul's amicable return. Below we briefly survey the significance of the ordeal accounts to ancient communities before turning to the exegesis of these passages.

5.1. Ordeal Narrations, Exemplarity, and Communal Formation

We recall that ancients frequently conducted therapy by ordeal, defining their social boundaries through a test. Extant literary sources evidence that such therapeutic effects were also intended for their audiences. Stories of daring, violent actions in the face of overwhelming odds were not only essential to many communal myths, but these accounts also inscribed civic virtues to be reproduced in next generation.[1] Spectacle was central to the cultural habit of prescriptive exemplarity, with scenes of daring acts or records of noble deeds reinforcing civic virtues. Exemplarity provides, writes Clive Skidmore, "the basic means of moral instruction from the earliest times."[2] While extant sources of ordeal narratives presume elite audiences, the wide dissemination of values through various media (e.g., visual culture: reliefs, coins, architecture, artwork, and funerary inscriptions and reliefs) suggests a generous cross-section of the Roman Empire and a broad circulation. Although the specific nature of those circulating values among non-elites remains uncertain, Maud Gleason comments that "the tremendous popularity of successful chariot-racing drivers and gladiators offers a clue."[3] Evidence suggests that subalterns could readily employ heroic masculine language to claim a space in Graeco-Roman society.[4]

In one representative, apocryphal, and elite account, Livy narrates the deeds of one of the most widely trafficked heroes, Horatius Cocles (2.10). In response to an attack by Etruscans and his comrades' fearful retreat behind the city walls "those who showed their backs as they withdrew from the conflict," Horatius fights the enemy single-handedly, hurling insults at his foes, and setting fire to a bridge to cut off the Etruscan advance (2.10.2-9). His heroism inspires the courage of others who rally to his aid. As the bridge is swallowed in flames, Horatius leaps into the Tiber and swims to safety fully armed under a hail of missiles (2.10.10-11). Livy is clear—it is upon such audacious, daring, and defiant figures that Rome's history hangs.[5] Polybius shares a similar account, though

---

1. N. M. Horsfall, "Virgil, History and the Roman Tradition," *Prudentia* 8 (1976): 84; Barton, *Roman Honor*, 87.
2. Clive Skidmore, *Practical Ethics for Roman Gentlemen: The Work of Valerius Maximus* (Exeter: University of Exeter Press, 1996), 3.
3. Maud Gleason, "Elite Male Identity in the Roman Empire," in *Life, Death and Entertainment in the Roman Empire*, ed. D. S. Potter and D. J. Mattingly (Ann Arbor: University of Michigan Press, 1999), 69–70.
4. See Bell, "Introduction."
5. Francesca Santoro L'hoir, "Heroic Epithets and Recurrent Themes in *Ab Urbe Condita*," *TAPA* 120 (1990): 230.

Horatius does not survive the ordeal. No matter, since the glory (εὐκλεία) he received was greater than his remaining years. Likewise, Horatius's story continues to engender in Roman youths an impulse for φιλοτιμία (55.4).

Francesca Santoro L'hoir has studied these heroic virtues as epithets in Livy's *Roman History*.[6] The epithets involved the noun *vir* (man) or *iuveni* (youth), modified by the adjectives *impiger* (energetic), *fortis ac strenuous* (strong and capable), *acer* (severe), and *unus* (one), which are used to describe persons upon whom Rome was established and defended against ferocious enemies.[7]

So widespread and accessible through diverse media was the story of Horatius Cocles and other similar accounts that Matthew Roller contends, "actors of every status took care to submit their actions to the scrutiny of the broad cross-section of the people… Exemplary discourse then encompasses all of Roman society, from the loftiest aristocrats to the humblest peasants, laborers, and slaves."[8] Values like those found among Livy and Polybius can also be found in epitaphs, such as that belonging to a particular soldier:

> Once I was most renowned on the Pannonian shore;
> amidst a thousand Batavians the strongest.
> With Hadrian watching I swam the huge waters
> of the Danube's deep in arms.
> While a bolt from my bow hung in the air—
> while it fell—I hit and shattered it with another arrow.
> Neither Roman nor Barbarian, no soldier with spear,
> no Parthian with his bow, could defeat me.
> Here I lie. My deeds I have entrusted to the memory of this stone.
> Whether another after me will emulate my deeds has yet to be seen.
> I am the first who did such things: my own exemplar.[9]

Thus, L'hoir's work supplies a heuristic against which to perceive the apologetic and moral formative implications contained in Paul's narrations, although we make no form-critical claims regarding Paul's accounts of affliction, but note only the common denominator of publicizing one's experiences of ordeal in view of the results of Part I.

---

6. L'hoir, "Heroic Epithets," passim.
7. L'hoir, "Heroic Epithets," 221.
8. Matthew B. Roller, "Exemplarity in Roman Culture: The Cases of Horatius Cocles and Cloelia," *CP* 99.1 (2004): 6.
9. Small. *Nerva* 336, as cited in Lendon, *Honour*, 245.

5.2. The God Who Raises the Dead (2 Corinthians 1:3-11)

With the proemium (2 Cor. 1:3-11), 2 Corinthians opens with Paul's treatment of afflictions or ordeals, which contains the theological struts of the epistle *in nuce*.[10] The main problem in deciding the structural limits involves whether the disclosure formula in 1:8 supplies a unit break.[11] The Pauline habit of offering thanksgiving *for* the audience is clearly amended in 1:3 with Paul's praise directed *towards* God, the Blessed One (εὐλογητός), which then comes full circle with the traditional expression of thanksgiving (εὐχαριστέω) in 1:11, albeit with the community thanking God for the χάρισμα granted to Paul, suggesting 1:3-11 forms a discreet unit.[12] Furthermore, the subunit (1:3-7) supplies the general theological claims that are particularized and explained in Paul's first ordeal narrative (1:8-11).

5.2.1. Suffering and Comfort in Pauline Ministry (2 Corinthians 1:3-7)

In 2 Cor. 1:3-7, Paul juxtaposes his experience of distress (θλῖψις) with divine comfort (παράκλησις). Paul opens in 1:3-7 with a thanksgiving to God and describes God's aid on Paul's behalf and Paul's exclusive role of mediating that aid to the community. The term θλῖψις frequently denotes the experience of trouble or trial.[13] In 2 Cor. 8:2, Paul uses θλῖψις as a modifier of δοκιμή (ordeal) referring to the Macedonians, "ordeal in regards to affliction." Thus, the letter-body begins with a deliberation upon the proper understanding of ordeals, both apostolic and communal—a highly relevant topic in light of Paul's intermediate visit.[14]

---

10. On the import of the proemium vis-à-vis epistolary and rhetorical aims, see Peter Arzt-Grabner, "Paul's Letter Thanksgiving," in *Paul and the Ancient Letter Form*, ed. Stanley E. Porter and Sean A. Adams, Pauline Studies 6 (Leiden: Brill, 2010), 156. For analysis and interpretation of the import of 2 Cor. 1:3-11 vis-à-vis the letter body, see Paul Schubert, *Form and Function of Pauline Thanksgivings*, BZNW 35 (Berlin: Töpelmann, 1939), 50; P. T. O'Brien, *Introductory Thanksgivings in the Letters of Paul*, NovTSup 49 (Leiden: Brill, 1977), 254–8.

11. For arguments for a new discursive unit starting in 1:8, see J. T. Sanders, "The Transition from Opening Epistolary Thanksgiving to Body in the Letters of the Pauline Corpus," *JBL* 81.4 (1962): 360–1; Long, *Ancient Rhetoric*, 152, and others.

12. Schubert, *Thanksgivings*, 50; Ivar Vegge, *2 Corinthians: A Letter about Reconciliation: A Psychological, Epistolographical and Rhetorical Analysis*, WUNT 2/239 (Tübingen: Mohr Siebeck, 2008), 151.

13. Mark A. Seifrid, *The Second Letter to the Corinthians*, ed. D. A. Carson, PNTC (Grand Rapids: Eerdmans, 2014), 60, 70, 136 n. 145.

14. Rather than perceive the importance of Paul's intermediate visit, interpreters assert that Paul's narration of his circumstances and his use of θλῖψις/παράκλησις is

In 2 Cor. 1:3, after Paul invokes "God, the Blessed One and Father of our Lord Jesus Christ," he continues to introduce God appositionally as the "the Father of compassions and the God of all encouragement." In 1:4, Paul, using an editorial "we," distinguishes himself as the recipient of comfort, for God is ὁ παρακαλῶν ἡμᾶς ἐπὶ πάσῃ τῇ θλίψει ἡμῶν. Paul, then, carefully represents himself as the mediator of divine comfort, "in order that [εἰς] we would be able to comfort those with any distress."[15] The reference then to the Corinthians' shared sufferings (τῶν αὐτῶν παθημάτων) in 1:6 is most likely didactic[16] and hortatory[17] rather than a reference to an actual hardship.[18]

5.2.2. A Death Sentence in Asia (2 Corinthians 1:8-9)

In 2 Cor. 1:8-11, Paul proffers an account of an unknown ordeal that occurred in Asia as a particularization of 1:3-7. He states, "For we do not want you to be ignorant, brothers, of our affliction which occurred in Asia, that beyond measure, beyond ability, we were burdened so that we despaired even of life. However, we indeed had the sentence of death in ourselves in order that we would depend not on ourselves but in the God who raises the dead" (1:8-9). The account is vivid in some regards, vague in others, and generally odd. Interpreters struggle to identify the historical referent behind the account and its function. Dominant theories of the former include an imprisonment, illness, or persecution,[19] while another line posits grief caused by Paul's soured relations with Corinth.[20] The opacity of the text renders all of these hypotheses speculative and notably, Paul narrates his turmoil in regards to the Corinthians in 2:12-13, 7:5, not 1:8-11.

---

prompted simply by his experience in Asia (cf. Arzt-Grabner, *2 Korinther*, 167) or by Titus's report (Reimund Bieringer, "The Comforted Comforter: The Meaning of Παρακαλέω or Παράκλησις Terminology in 2 Corinthians," *HvTSt* 67.1 [2011]: 6) or a combination of both events (Harris, *Second Epistle*, 137). The proemium is clearly transitional (Klauck, *Letters*, 21–3). For its inclusion in the letter body, see Arzt-Grabner, *2 Korinther*, 187.

15. O'Brien, *Thanksgivings*, 246.
16. O'Brien, *Thanksgivings*, 256; Vegge, *2 Corinthians*, 156.
17. Vegge, *2 Corinthians*, 158–61; also Olson, "Confidence Expressions", 111; Oropeza claims Paul's "associative language" is likely "rhetorical hyperbole" to build rapport (*Second Corinthians*, 69; Long, *Ancient Rhetoric*, 156).
18. But see Klauck, *2 Korintherbrief*, 19.
19. Harris, *Second Epistle*, 164–72.
20. David E. Fredrickson, "Paul's Sentence of Death (2 Corinthians 1:9)," *WW* 4 (2000): 99–107.

While the opacity of the narration warrants interpretive restraint, it is crucial to observe that the narration of the ordeal may point to the intermediate visit as a parallel than any historical referent "occurring in Asia." This is supported by Bachmann's and Martin's perception that the paradox of affliction/suffering and comfort touch the nerve of the conflict between Paul and his detractors.[21] Here the issue broadly involves the affliction and suffering of Paul, something coextensive with Paul's weakness. The account in 1:8-11 involves Paul under judgment, specifically the sentence of death (τὸ ἀπόκριμα τοῦ θανάτου, 1:9a).[22] Paul is capable of narrating events of his recent past in detail (Gal. 1:11–2:14; Phil. 2:25-30; 1 Thess. 3:1-10). Thus, it may be helpful to inquire not simply to what event does Paul refer but why does he refer to it in the manner he does?

5.2.3. *Death as Displacement Metaphor*

While the reference to the sentence of death is oblique, it has more than a tangential relationship to Paul's situation in Corinth. Paul's linguistically encoded description supports a link with the intermediate ordeal. The perfective ἐσχήκαμεν in 1:9a is a notoriously confusing.[23] The issue involves how a past "death sentence" from which Paul has been delivered (1:10a) could still have results continuing into the writer's present. As Christoph Heilig observes, "many reference grammars note that the perfect form seems to be used here either in place of the indicative aorist or the pluperfect." However, Heilig reports the insights of an anonymous linguist: "it seems to me that it's entirely possible that they are still living under a death sentence in 1.9. Perhaps there are cities that Paul cannot return to." For Helig, and rightly so, this "sets off whole fireworks of questions surrounding jurisprudence in Roman provinces and death penalties in antiquity."[24] As is now clear, displacement in its various forms, including official, Roman jurisprudence, functioned as a surrogate for the death sentence. An exiled figure could still be under a sentence,

---

21. Bachmann, *Zweite Brief*, 34–5; Martin, *2 Corinthians*, 10–11.

22. Thrall, *Second Epistle*, 1:118; Long, *Ancient Rhetoric*, 154; contra C. J. Hemer, "A Note on 2 Corinthians 1:9," *TynB* 23 (1972): 103–7, who never proffered an example of ἀπόκριμα with the modifier death.

23. See Harris, *Second Epistle*, 156–7.

24. Christoph Heilig, "Observations from a Linguistic Spectator: An Annual Report (Part 1: Introduction)," https://www.uzh.ch/blog/theologie-nt/2020/03/23/observations-from-a-linguistic-spectator/, *Zürich New Testament Blog*, 23 March 2020.

though the moment of crisis had passed and they had exited the region. If a writer wished to circuitously refer to a moment of displacement, the perfective verb with the direct object as τὸ ἀπόκριμα τοῦ θανάτου would be a way to do it.

Across antiquity, death functioned as a salient metaphor for displacement. Ernst Doblhofer states, "Die Vorstellung des Exultanten, daß er mit der Verbannung schon einen Tod gestorben und sein Exildasein dem Tode gleichzuhalten sei, ist von der Literaturwissenschaft als exiltypisch erkannt worden."[25] As our study suggests, since multiple forms of displacement functioned as a surrogate for the death penalty resulting in the loss of civic status, such a literary manifestation is hardly surprising. By the second century, the parallel was evident in contract law. The jurist Gaius writes, "loss of status is also said to determine partnership, because by the doctrine of civil law loss of status is regarded as equivalent to death."[26] Grasmück states an exile was effectively "bürgerlich tot."[27] Mary Claassen, explains, "the relationship between exile and death in Greek and Roman history is important for understanding the development of this literary subgenre; voluntary exile or suicide frequently pre-empted the imposition of the death penalty. It was no great step therefore when philosophy began to equate exile with death."[28]

Among Graeco-Roman authors, the literary representation of exile as death could take many forms. The trope is most easily observed from the Latin exilic writings of Cicero, Ovid, and Seneca. In his letters from exile, Cicero frequently referred to his departure and exile as death. To Quintus, he writes, "You would not have seen your brother, the man you left in Rome, the man you knew, the man who saw you off and said good-bye with mutual tears—you would not have seen any trace or shadow of him; only the likeness of a breathing corpse."[29] Similarly, Cicero writes of his state in exile as if he writes from beyond the grave. "For it is not only property or friends that I miss, but myself."[30] Even after his return, he recounts the

---

25. Ernst Doblhofer, *Exil und Emigration: Zum Erlebnis der Heimatferne in der römischen Literatur*, Impulse der Forschung 51 (Darmstadt: Wissenschaftliche Buchgesellschaft, 1987), 166.
26. Translated by Edward Post, *Gai Institutiones* (Oxford: Clarendon, 1904), 377.
27. Grasmück, *Exilium*, 65.
28. Jo-Marie Claassen, *Displaced Persons: The Literature of Exile from Cicero to Boethius* (Madison: University of Wisconsin, 1999), 20; cf. Sabine Grebe, "Why Did Ovid Associate His Exile with a Living Death?," *CW* 103.4 (2010): 500–508.
29. Cicero, *Quint. fratr.* fr. 1.3.1.
30. Cicero, *Att.* 3.15.2.

statecraft of Clodius and his supporters as "demanding the funeral dues even before the lamentations for death have arisen."[31]

Ovid further developed the trope of exile as a living death. Ovid writes of his liminal state,

> What dost thou trample on an empty shadow? Why attack with stones my ashes and my tomb? Hector was alive whilst he fought in war, but once bound to the Haemonian steeds he was not Hector. I too, whom thou knewest in former times, no longer exist, remember; of that man there remains but this wraith with bitter words? Cease, I beg, to harass my shade.[32]

From Pontus, Ovid describes himself as both barely alive and already dead: "I have lost all; life alone remains, to give me the consciousness and the substance of sorrow. What pleasure to thee to drive the steel into limbs already dead? There is no space in me now for a new wound."[33] Repeatedly, Ovid refers to his exile in Pontus as death[34] and his exit from Rome as his burial.[35] From exile, Ovid even writes his own funerary epigraph in the context of his desire to be obliterated rather than have his shade wander the earth.[36]

Seneca, writing from exile to his mother Helvia, describes himself as, "a man who was lifting his head from the very bier."[37] The point for Seneca in his consolation to his mother is that his grief in exile is comparable to his mother's grief over the death.[38] In the undependable *Athologia Latina*, a particular epigram is attributed to Seneca from Corsica, his place of exile.

> Go easy of the banished, that is, go easy of the finished ["the buried" in some mss.]
> May your earth rest lightly on the ashes of the living.[39]

---

31. Cicero, *Dom.* 98.
32. Ovid, *Trist.* 3.11.25-32; cf. Sophocles, *Oed.* 109–10; see also Doblhofer, *Exil*, 173.
33. Ovid, *Pont.* 4.16.47-52.
34. Ovid, *Trist.* 1.3.22-26; 1.3.89-102; 1.7.38; 3.14.20; 5.1.11-14; *Pont.* 1.9.17; 2.3.3.
35. Ovid, *Trist.* 1.1.118; 1.8.14.
36. Ovid, *Trist.*, 3.3.73-76.
37. Seneca, *Helv.* 1.3.
38. Elaine Fanthan, "Dialogues of Displacement: Seneca's Consolations to Helvia and Polybius," in Gaertner, ed., *Writing Exile*, 178.
39. Translated by James Ker, *The Deaths of Seneca* (Oxford: Oxford University Press, 2009), 104.

Appealing to popular wisdom, Publilius Syrus writes, "The exile with no home anywhere is a corpse without a grave."⁴⁰ A textual variant in Plautus reads, "there is no hope for the banished to destruction."⁴¹ The more reliable *Anthologia Graeca* attributes an epigraph to Leonidas of Tarentum he comments on exile, "This is more bitter than death to me/ Such is a wanderer, alive without remedy."⁴² The connection between death and exile led advocates of Roman exiles to dress in mourners' guise in order to sway sentiment and affect restoration.⁴³

In the Septuagint, death functioned as an apt metaphor for exile, although the emphasis was most often on the dual foci of exile and restoration, which will be discussed in Chapter 6. In Genesis 3, the penalty for Adam's disobedience is ultimately death (3:19), in which Adam's "departure" (ἀπέρχομαι) to the earth is preceded itself in expulsion (ἐκβάλλω) from the garden (Gen. 3:24). Exile looms so large in Israelite life that David M. Gunn and Danna Nolan Fewell aptly summarize, "loss of home, of native place, and in some cases, of family was such a traumatic experience in the life of Israel that it became, in Israel's literature, the critical characteristic of the human condition."⁴⁴ Inasmuch as Second Temple Judaism viewed Abraham and his family as the recapitulation of the human race, then we are warranted in assuming Israel's political disasters were likewise understood as metaphorical deaths.⁴⁵ Isaiah 5:13-15 makes the link clear by parallelism, "Therefore my people go into exile for lack of knowledge... Therefore Sheol has enlarged its appetite and opened its mouth beyond measure" (NRSV). Similarly, in Hosea 13, the prophet announces Israel's impending exile as a death (13:1, 8-9, 14). Moreover, as demonstrated previously, within Second Temple Judaism offences warranting the death penalty according to Scriptural mandate were often penalized by expulsion as a surrogate (§2.6). Evidence of such a practice in local, communal expulsions is evident in 1 Cor. 5:1-13 (§2.7.2). Although we have no evidence of such a proceeding against Paul, the evidence in Part I points to similar social

40. Publilius Syrus 118=e.9.
41. Plautus, *Capt.* 519.
42. Leonidas of Tarentum, *Anth. Pal.* 7.715.2-3, my translation; for the notion of exile as worse than death in Greek authors, see Euripides, *Hipp.* 895–1100, 1045–1050.
43. Kelly, *Exile*, 74–5; Appendix I.
44. David M. Gunn and Danna Nolan Fewell, *Narrative in the Hebrew Bible* (Oxford: Oxford University Press, 1993), 157.
45. Wright, *Faithfulness of God*, 783–95, passim.

behavior directed towards Paul, not least since much of antiquity did not distinguish significantly between voluntary and enforced absences. Thus, the notion of an ordeal in which Paul experiences the death penalty crosses the so-called Judaism–Hellenism divide and points efficiently by way of Asia to the circumstances in Corinth.

5.2.4. *An Echo of Corinthian Judgment with a Twist*

How then does Paul use his ordeal in Asia to negotiate the crisis in Corinth? The nature of the event is described as one of overwhelming difficulty, as seen in the redundant superlative expressions, "beyond measure, beyond ability, we were burdened" (1 Cor. 1:8a). The superlative objects of abundance (καθ' ὑπερβολὴν) and power (ὑπὲρ δύναμιν) both illustrate the "overflowing" nature of the sufferings of Christ (1:5a), and also exemplify Paul's weakness. While Paul supplies a highly subjective description of his affliction in 2 Cor. 1:8-11 (and 2:12-13; 7:5-6), here θλῖψις refers to concrete circumstances that completely penetrate the apostle rather than inward turmoil alone.[46] With the ὥστε clause, Paul reveals the result of affliction, ἐξαπορηθῆναι ἡμᾶς καὶ τοῦ ζῆν ("so that we despaired even of life"). The affliction was so great that there is no hint of deliverance from death.[47] In 1:9a, a related passage, Paul colors the ordeal with a punitive reference, stating, "but we indeed have had the sentence of death [τὸ ἀπόκριμα τοῦ θανάτου] in ourselves."[48] Paul portrays himself as powerless, passive, and overwhelmed, not unlike the exilic rhetoric above. Such a description echoes the very judgment against Paul emanating from the intermediate ordeal.

There is a catch, however. In contrast to Paul's inaction in the face of opposition, Paul emphasizes the saving intervention of God on his behalf. The "God who raises the dead" in fact delivered Paul. Paul writes, "[the God who raises the dead] rescued us from such a horrible death[49] and he will rescue[50] us in whom we have hope that indeed he will rescue us again" (1:10).[51] Paul's encounter with certain death ended with a divinely orchestrated reversal. Commentators observe the similarity

---

46. Schmeller, *Zweite Brief*, 1:59; Arzt-Grabner, *2 Korinther*, 167.
47. Bultmann, *The Second Letter to the Corinthians*, 27.
48. Thrall, *Second Epistle*, 1:118; Oropeza, *Second Corinthians*, 85 n. 24.
49. Following NA[28] ἐκ τηλικούτου θανάτου (ℵ A B C 33 1739*) over ἐκ τηλικούτων θανάτων (𝔓[46] 81 1739).
50. Likely ῥύσεται rather than ῥύεται or omitted; UBS[4] upgraded the variant from C to B.
51. The third occurrence of the verb is also future ῥύσεται as well, but with confusion around the particles ὅτι καὶ ἔτι. The variants that omit either ὅτι (𝔓[46] B D*

between Paul's phrase "the God who raises the dead," and the second benediction of the Amidah[52] and, less frequently, 4QRitPur.[53] In the Septuagint, similar phrases and concepts depict divinely orchestrated historical and political reversals for Israel.[54] This indicates that the meaning of terms παράκλησις and παρακαλέω is derived from the LXX in which comfort is experienced in God's historical intervention, not least in exile.[55] More particularly, Paul appeals to the God who raised Jesus and the early faith in that God, relating Jesus's divine reversal to his own circumstances.[56] Paul's reversal is not only divinely orchestrated, it is divinely predicated, with an allusion to the story of the Messiah Jesus, which Paul appropriates as "a stencil" for his epistolary and rhetorical ends.[57] While aspects of 2 Cor. 1:3-7 suggest Paul's experience of comfort is contemporaneous or concomitant with affliction (1:5), in the account of his ordeal, Paul presents the Christological sequence in which the apostle experiences two phases of existence, the first of which is reversed through God's power, although the perfective verb ἐσχήκαμεν in 1:9a indicates an ongoing aspect to the sentence. Thus, Paul takes on the criticism emerging from the intermediate event but places those criticisms in the context of another kind of ordeal, in which he is rescued and vindicated.

1739 1881 al) or ἔτι (D1 F G al) are best explained as stylistic omissions, thus 10b reads "in whom we have hope that (ὅτι) indeed he will rescue us again" (ℵ A C D2 Ψ 33 pm), cf. Long, *II Corinthians*, 31.

52. Barnett, *Second Epistle*, 87; Barrett, *Second Epistle*, 65; Thrall, *Second Epistle*, 1:119, and others.

53. "He who liberates the captives, restores sight to the blight, straightens the b[ent] (Ps 146:7-8). For He will heal the wounded, and revive the dead and bring good news to the poor (Isa 61:1)," translated by Geza Vermes, *The Complete Dead Sea Scrolls in English* (Harmondsworth: Penguin, 1997), 244.

54. Isa. 26:17-19; Hos. 6:1-2; Ezek. 37:1-14; Ps. 79:19; see Andrew Boakye, *Death and Life: Resurrection, Restoration, and Rectification in Paul's Letter to the Galatians* (Eugene, OR: Pickwick, 2017), 30–42.

55. Isa. 40:1; 51:3, 12, 19; see Thrall, *Second Epistle*, 1:104; Bieringer, "Παρακαλέω," 6–7; Pss. 70, 85, 93, see Otfried Hofius, "'Der Gott allen Trostes': παράκλησις und παρακαλέω in 2 Kor 1, 3-7," in *Paulusstudien*, WUNT 51 (Tübingen: Mohr Siebeck, 1989), 246.

56. Martin, *2 Corinthians*, 15; Windisch, *Zweite Korintherbrief*, 48.

57. Andrew Boakye, "Inhabiting the 'Resurrectiform' God: Death and Life as Theological Headline in Paul," *ExpTim* 128.2 (2016): 56; cf. Thomas Stegman, *The Character of Jesus: The Linchpin to Paul's Argument in 2 Corinthians*, AnBib 158 (Rome: Editrice Pontificio Istituto Biblico, 2005), 261–2; Scott wonders whether ἀπόκριμα is analogous to the verdict received by Christ when crucified (*2 Corinthians*, 33).

5.2.5. *Paul's Aims: Challenge the Detractors' Evaluation and Re-Establish Credibility*

What is Paul attempting to achieve through this ordeal narration? In general, interpreters assert the account aims to aid in Paul's reconciliation with the community. Since Chrysostom it has become commonplace to view the proemium as an excuse of sorts for Paul's absence.[58] This is unnecessary since Paul clearly mentions his reasons for absence in 2 Cor. 1:23 and 2:1, which has nothing to do with external circumstances. A secondary approach proposes that Paul imparts historical or emotional information to tap into the community's sympathy, not unlike the theatrics of supporters of Roman exiles.[59] Yet, Paul's description of powerlessness and despair would supply confirming evidence to the detractors, not pity.

That 2 Corinthians begins with a scene in which Paul faces affliction and judgment which echoes a widely travelled displacement discourse indicates Paul interacts intentionally with the communal evaluation of the intermediate visit. More likely, by narrating the Christological sequence in his ordeal in Asia, Paul skillfully redefines the nature of an ordeal for his community and thus the outstanding judgments against Paul. Just as Paul appeared impotent in Corinth, so too he appears overwhelmed and passive in Asia, perhaps compelled to leave. Long contends that 1:8-11 "begins to answer the charges and criticisms [Paul] faced. In response to the criticism that he is weak, Paul narrated that God delivered him and will do so again."[60] Thus, Paul recalibrates the nature of a genuine ordeal. Rather than being marked by competency, bravery, and aggression, a genuine ordeal possesses the marks of the Christological sequence—human passivity and powerlessness reversed by God's intervening action. As God reversed the judgment of the "sentence of death," so too Paul aims through the narration to overturn the evaluative structure by which Paul faces communal judgment.[61] This is made clear in 1:10-11 in which Paul looks proleptically to future divine rescues and summons the community to mutuality in prayer for his deliverance. Thus, while it is not clear whether Paul is narrating an event unknown to the community, the negated verb ἀγνοέω in 1:8 may refer to Paul's desire that the community "recognize" or "pay attention to" the significance of his rendering of the account in light of the intermediate ordeal.[62] This observation is

---

58. PG 61.420; Hughes, *Second Epistle*, 9; Marquis, *Transient Apostle*, 49, and others; see §1.2.4; §3.1.
59. Welborn, "Emotions," 39–47, and others; Appendix I.
60. Long, *Ancient Rhetoric*, 155.
61. See Long, *Ancient Rhetoric*, 192.
62. See BDAG, s.v. "ἀγνοέω" 2; Guthrie, *2 Corinthians*, 78.

complementary to George Lyons's thesis that Pauline autobiographical remarks often exist not to provide historical exactitude but perform crucial rhetorical functions.[63]

At the same time, the notion that God will rescue Paul in the future may also point to the reversal of ongoing judgments against him in Corinth. The idea of deliverance from exile was widely articulated through the metaphor of return as revivification (§6.1.4). Paul makes no reference to return regarding his ordeal in Asia. However, the paradigm of 2 Cor. 1:8-11 echoes Paul's ordeal in Troas/Macedonia (2:12-13; 7:5-16) that relates to Paul's absence (1:17) and clears the way for Titus's (chs. 8–9) and Paul's return (chs. 10–13), at least according to the canonical form of 2 Corinthians. Andrew Boakye claims that Paul's death to life account in 1:8-11 is a perfect compendium of Israel's death-to-life literary tradition.[64] In any case, through the description of the event, the παράκλησις received reflects Israel's exilic tradition of apocalyptic, historical reversal, although it is reoriented around the Messiah Jesus.[65] The recurrence of the future ῥύσεται in 1:10 prompts exegetes to consider what events Paul envisions ending in deliverance. With the future verb along with the future ἐπιγνώσεσθε in 1:13, some consider the second future occurrence to be a reference to the Parousia (1:14).[66] Yet, Paul has imbued his ordeal in Asia with eschatological significance, thus indicating that his future deliverance would likewise involve mundane events, not unlike his arrivals in Corinth. Paul even uses another future verb, γνώσεσθε (13:6), in relation to his return. Long claims ἔτι in 1:10 implies, "that Paul is still facing a deadly tribulation."[67] And while the apostolic career involves great difficulty, the letter—peristasis catalogues included (6:4-10; 11:23-28)—aims to reverse the principal trouble in Corinth. Again, the view to the future is tethered grammatically to Paul's certainty of the death sentence in Asia. Both enforced absences and hostile, voluntary absences were viewed as metaphoric deaths, which frequently functioned as a surrogate to the death

---

63. George Lyons, *Pauline Autobiography: Toward a New Understanding*, SBLDS 73 (Atlanta: Scholars Press, 1985), 123–76 passim.

64. Boakye, *Death and Life*, 30 n. 111.

65. Thrall and Bieringer both contend Paul draws upon the Hebrew verb נחם rendered by παρακαλέω in the LXX in Isa. 40:1; 51:3, 12, 19; cf. Isa. 57:18; 61:2 (Thrall, *Second Epistle*, 1:104; Bieringer, "The Comforted Comforter," 6–7). Otfried Hofius believes the sources to be Pss. 71 (70), 86 (85) and 94 (93), in part because the Psalms depict an individual who receives comfort from God as a demonstration of God's restoration, so that the community may be buoyed with hope ("2 Kor 1, 3-7," 246).

66. Klauck, *2 Korintherbrief*, 21; Barnett, *Second Epistle*, 88–9.

67. Long, *II Corinthians*, 23.

penalty. With this is mind, it is reasonable to assert that Paul opens the epistle with a reference to his deliverance from an opaque death sentence, which occurred in the shape of the Messiah Jesus with a proleptic view to his amicable return.

In any case, Paul employs the proemium, especially 2 Cor. 1:8-10, to contribute to the argument by providing warrant for Paul's renewed credibility. At its simplest, the apostle who has returned to life from the sentence of death argues for the return of his full political legitimacy in Corinth. In 1:12, Paul substantiates (γάρ) his request for mutuality in prayer (1:11) with his boast of "the testimony of his conscience," which involves "simplicity and sincerity [and] not in fleshly wisdom" regarding his "conduct (ἀναστρέφω) in the world," especially towards the Corinthians.[68] Paul's reference to his conscience (συνείδησις) and its testimony cannot refer simply to his private moral consciousness as if Paul abandons the account in 1:8–9 and retreats to his subjective introspection as evidence of his probity. Rather, Paul has experienced the sentence of death ἐν ἑαυτοῖς (1:9a) as well as divine deliverance resulting in internal persuasion regarding God's intervention (1:9b) and now in 1:12 uses that testimony of the conscience that has undergone the ordeal described in 1:8–9 to re-establish his proper conduct in order to appeal for complete recognition of his political legitimacy (1:13-14). The issues of character and action were linked in the ancient moral economy. Paul's narration of an ordeal in which God vindicated him based on the Christological sequence supplies his conscience with a boast of right conduct. The transformation of Paul's circumstance from powerlessness to divine empowerment is intended to lead to the transformation of the community's view of Paul's ethos and actions. The link between internal ethos or nature and external behavior in 1:12-14 is clear, but it is built upon a different kind of ordeal (1:8-10), an ordeal that makes room for passivity and powerlessness in light of God's Christological intervention.[69]

5.3. *The God Who Comforts the Abased* *(2 Corinthians 2:12-13; 7:5-16)*

Paul reemploys a second geographically particularized account concerning an ordeal in Troas and Macedonia (2 Cor. 2:12-13; 7:5-16). Like 2 Cor. 1:8-11, the account of divine reversal occurs during the interim since Paul's exit from Corinth. Unlike 1:8-11, the ordeal in Macedonia (and

---

68. Long, *II Corinthians*, 24; Plummer, *Second Epistle*, 23.
69. Cf. Lyons, *Pauline Autobiography*, 155–64.

Troas) relates directly to Paul's hostile absence (1:17, 23, 2:1) and the Severe Letter (2:1-11) the results of which (7:5-16), according to the canonical form of the letter, then relate directly to Titus's (chs. 8–9) and Paul's returns (chs. 10–13), rather than giving only a proleptic view to future rescues (1:10). Paul provides evidence of the comfort that he alone can supply the Corinthians, namely, "repentance to salvation" (7:10; 2:8, cf. 1:3-7). In this way, Paul claims that as God rescued him from death in Asia (1:9), so also, he has affected a similar reversal for his audience (1:3-7; cf. 2:5-6). A parallel between 2:12-13, 7:5-16 and 1:3-11 is evident.[70] Most importantly, both narratives depict a concrete, divine reversal of circumstance in Paul's life in two specific locations (Asia; Troas/Macedonia).[71] Indeed, Paul's narration of ordeals at this stage not only possesses geographic particularization, but geographic progression toward Corinth.[72] If 2 Corinthians is a compositional unity, Paul's framing of his apostolic defense (2:14–7:4) with the ordeal account indicates the heightened import of the affliction account.[73]

Contextually, the acute affliction narrative (2 Cor. 2:12-13; 7:5-7) participates in a broader discourse concerning Paul's effective punishment through the Severe Letter (1:23–2:13; 7:5-16) and logically links with Paul's aim of securing full recognition of his political legitimacy from the Corinthians (1:13-14). While this unit focuses upon judgment or the reversal of judgment upon a community member (2:5-11) and the community's passing of a test brought by Paul's disciplinary letter (2:8; 7:12), the text is a direct riposte to the accusation that Paul's absence (1:15-16) is evidence of his levity and diseased character (1:17). To the contrary, Paul contends his absence is not due to cowardice or effeminacy, but an effort to spare the community (1:23; 2:1). Thus, the unit displays circuitously that Paul's absence marked by the Severe Letter and Titus's envoy has been efficacious, resulting in "repentance to salvation" (7:10) and a summons to restore (παρακαλέω) the ὁ ἀδικήσας (2:8). The central point of the discourse, then, is to compel the audience to reverse its judgment that Paul's absence evidences cowardice and bad character through the account of reversals experienced during Paul's efficacious absence.

---

70. Bachmann, *Zweite Brief*, 128; Windisch, *Zweite Korintherbrief*, 227, and others.

71. Barnett, *Second Epistle*, 132–3; on Troas as distinct from ἐν τῇ Ἀσίᾳ (1:8), see Zahn, *Introduction*, 1:318 n. 4.

72. Georgi, *Remembering the Poor*, 193 n. 65.

73. Schmeller refers to technique as a "geschickte Verklammerung" that aims to increase the chances of the successful reception of 2:14–7:4 (*Zweite Brief*, 1:146).

5.3.1. *Aid to Corinth from Afar*

A fair amount of Paul's rhetoric in 2 Cor. 1:15–2:13, 7:5-16 resonates with a broader discourse of displacement: the patriotic exile. Interpreters following Ambrosiaster and Chrysostom have frequently looked the other way, interpreting the accusations against Paul (1:17) and his responses (1:23; 2:1) as indicating Paul's absence was unwelcome and hurtful.[74] We have rejected this reading for numerous reasons already discussed.

In its stead, we propose that Paul exploits the reality of displacement for his own ends. With the zero-sum calculus of ancient agonism, the geographic exit of a figure locked in social combat often symbolized defeat, ruin, and dishonor. However, such an exit functioned as a "safety-valve" to resolve civic discord saving communities from otherwise predictable violence. This positive communal effect and liminal status of displacement provided fodder for some exiles, especially those whose exits possessed a measure of volition, to argue that their absence was in fact a good deed that saved the community from destruction, rather than evidence of their guilt or cowardice.[75]

According to Cohen, the model of the person who flees to save the community was a favorite Latin trope among literary exiles.[76] Collatinus's displacement is represented as a choice to prevent tyranny in Rome while resolutely defending his innocence.[77] Q. Metellus Numidicus is said to have left Rome to prevent civil war.[78] Cicero strategically presented his *interdictio* as an act that saved Rome from civil war.[79] In *de Domo*, Cicero sublimates his exile, which he refers to as his "great humiliation" (*incredibilem dolorem*, 96), stating that his retreat was not due to wrongdoing, fear, or cowardice (95); rather it was the "noblest deed in the history of humanity" (95), for he fled "in order to save the lives of compatriots" (98). His exile "saved the state" (99). Yet, the trope is older than Cohen suggests, perhaps indicating a wider circulation. Andocides represents his flight as, "sorrow for myself, but immediate release for you," further claiming, "your deliverance meant my own ruin."[80]

The trope could include the beneficence of the exile from afar, further establishing one's patriotic ethos in exile. Andocides claims that during

---

74. See §3.1.
75. Similarly White, "Absence," 61–2.
76. Cohen, "Exile," 26 n. 52; cf. Claassen, *Displaced Persons*, 158–62.
77. Livy 2.2; 2.57-60; Dionysius of Hal. 4.64; Dio Cassius Frag. 24, ed. Reimar.
78. Cicero, *Planc.* 69; *Red. pop.* 6, 10, 11; *Pis.* 20; *Red. sen.* 25, 37, 38; *Sest.* 37; see Claassen, *Displaced Persons*, 290 n. 7.
79. Cicero, *Dom.* 98, cf. *Vat.* 8, [Cicero], Sallust 10; Dio Cassius 38.25.4.
80. Andocides 1.8, 9.

his absence, he continued to work for Athens by securing supplies for the Athenian navy, also securing grain for Athens.[81] Demosthenes, in arguing for his recall, testifies:

> You will not find me to have done wrong on the score of any of my measures, or a fit person to be deprived of my civic rights or destroyed, but a man who is as much devoted to your democracy as the best patriots—not to say anything invidious—who of all men now living has accomplished most in your behalf and of all men of my time has available the most signal tokens of devotion to you.[82]

Nor does his conduct evince "softness or effeminacy" (*Ep.* 2.25-26; cf. Aeschines, *Fals. Leg.* 150–51), which functioned as descriptors of passivity familiar to defeat and displacement. These claims are substantiated in part by Demosthenes's testimony of one of those "signal tokens of devotion," that in exile he defended Athens from censure for his own banishment.[83] Thus, the liminal state of exile paired with a pervasive tenet of political theory allowed some exiles to inflect their status, salvaging a representation of virtuous conduct on behalf of the community.

This is a fitting parallel to Paul's riposte to the accusations that he conducted himself in ἐλαφρία and makes decisions κατὰ σάρκα (2 Cor. 1:17). These, I have argued, are serious accusations of martial passivity and womanish character relating to his inability to administrate the community. There is a distinction with Paul's argument: the exiles listed above focused upon their exit as saving the state, Paul emphasizes his absence as an act that preserves the community. After attaching himself to God's stability as demonstrated in his mission to Corinth (1:18-22), Paul claims that his absence is not indicative of his cowardice, stating, "I call God as my witness against my life that in order to spare you I did not come to Corinth" (1:23), further claiming that he did not return in order to save the community from pain (2:1) and that through his absence "you might know the love that I have exceedingly towards you" (2:4). Paul, like other dissidents, defends his absence as evidence of his virtue and care for the community, rather than evidence of his passivity and poor character. It is a mistake, often made, to infer here (1:15–2:13) that Paul is aloof from the crisis, descending only to assuage his spoilt and jealous children.[84] Rather,

---

81. Andocides 1.11-12, 20-21.
82. Demosthenes, *Ep.* 2.24-25.
83. Demosthenes, *Ep.* 2.19.
84. For example, Hughes, *Second Epistle*, 34; Barrett, *Second Epistle*, 35–6; Furnish, *II Corinthians*, 144.

Paul exploits the logic of voluntarily leaving a community in a conflict and remaining absent to reclaim his social power by swearing that his absence following internecine strife actually benefited the community.

So too, Paul highlights his virtuous conduct on behalf of the community *in absentia* as a means of realizing his amicable return.[85] Paul narrates that the pain that would have befallen the community, fell instead to him, writing, "from great affliction and anguish of heart I wrote to you through many tears" (2 Cor. 2:4a). The proof of Paul's love of and service to the community is in the pudding. Paul demonstrates that his work has brought repentance and salvation to the community (7:10). Moreover, Paul continues to work for the benefit of the community in light of the efficacious Severe Letter, urging the forgiveness and return of the offender—another Christological reversal for a person likely facing another metaphorical death sentence (2:7; cf. 1:3-11)—attempting to protect the community from Satan's schemes (2:11). Indeed, Paul proffers a defense for his absence. Yet it is not in response to a desire for his return. It is a response to those who assert his absence is further evidence of his malignant character (1:17). Against those who assert his impotence, Paul demonstrates that his exit and absence were truly efficacious for the community. Like Demosthenes concerning Athens, Paul can claim to an extent that there is no evidence of cowardice or softness of character, only efficacy and love for Corinth.

5.3.2. *Dis-ease in Troas, Comfort in Macedonia*

Central to Paul's rebuttal to the charges in 2 Cor. 1:17 is the vivid ordeal narration found in 2:12-13 and 7:5-7 (8-15). As Windisch observed, 2:12-13 (and 7:5-16) logically belongs after 2:4.[86] This is not to insist that 2:12-13 is misplaced, only that 2:12-13 develops a major claim concerning the efficacy of Paul's absence and the degree to which he has born affliction on behalf of the community. The narration is often and predictably viewed as primarily an expression of pathos, a demonstration of Paul's love for Corinth.[87] This line rests upon two rather shaky premises: first, that the community pines for Paul's return and relatedly the way to assuage such hurt feelings is through demonstrating a sympathetic longing for the community. Second Corinthians, however, is far more focused upon questions concerning Paul's efficacy and credibility than his emotional commitment to the community. The subjective descriptions and emotional

---

85. Similarly White, "Absence," 59–60.
86. Windisch, *Zweite Korintherbrief*, 93.
87. Margaret E. Thrall, "A Second Thanksgiving Period in II Corinthians," *JSNT* 16 (1982): 112; Welborn, "Emotions," 45, and others.

language would more likely serve that end, defending against the accusation of cowardice. This is indicated in the language of 2:4 in which Paul desires the community "to know" (γινώσκω) his exceeding love for them, which resonates with cognates in 1:13-14 (13:6) that refer to recognition of Paul's political legitimacy (cf. 1:8). To that end, an account of another ordeal fits primarily as a demonstration of credibility.

The narrative begins with Paul's arrival in Troas, "for the gospel of Christ," only to neglect "a door having been opened by the Lord" (2 Cor. 2:12) because the turmoil he experienced due to Titus's absence, who was to deliver news of Paul's intervention through the Letter of Tears (2:1-13). So intense was Paul's οὐκ ἄνεσις "in spirit" that he left the mission field for Macedonia (2:13), where he experiences unrest "in body" (7:5). Paul's description of his subjective state in 2:13 (and 7:5) echoes the description in 1:8-9. While emotional content is evident, Paul narrates that the severity of the distress resulted in his failure to engage in a mission opportunity.[88] The narrative reemerges in 7:5 with an intensified account of Paul's unrest in Macedonia—"but we were afflicted in every way: fights without, fears within"—and shifts in 7:6 with the account of the Titus's arrival. The repetition of terms in 7:5 found in 2:13 likely alerts readers to a resumption of the ordeal narrative.[89] In his self-depiction, Paul appears riddled with dis-ease, paralyzed and penetrated by his affliction. This is something of a replay of Paul's description of utter despair in Asia (1:8-9), although now in some ways echoing the charge of levity in the context of Paul's martial conduct in Corinth. Thus, if ἐλαφρία (1:17) involves passivity and powerlessness, Paul certainly doesn't avoid such a characterization in 2:12-13 and 7:5. Rather, the self-representation indulges such an evaluation.

What is Paul's point? Like the Asian ordeal, Paul emphasizes God's potent aid on his behalf in the service of the community. The transition to God's intervention is sharp and initiated by a contrastive ἀλλά (7:6; cf. 1:9). With Titus's report Paul moves from paralyzing distress to rejoicing (7:7). Paul attributes the divine comfort to God, marked by the appositional phrase, ὁ παρακαλῶν τοὺς ταπεινούς ("the one who comforts the abased," 7:6). The expression is similar to descriptors in 1:3, 4, and 9 which mark God as the one who intervenes on Paul's behalf. Commentators perceive an intertextual allusion from Isa. 49:13 (LXX), a source text that refers to Judah's restoration from exile.[90] Some, who

---

88. Bachmann, *Zweite Brief*, 128; Klauck, *2 Korintherbrief*, 31.
89. Bieringer, "Plädoyer," 134.
90. Schmeller, *Zweite Brief*, 2:13, and others.

find the source text meaningful, claim the text refers to the Corinthians' restoration by accepting the Severe Letter.[91] While the community experiences its own divine reversal, this ignores the clear grammar that it is Paul who experienced God's comfort reserved for returning exiles, while clearing ground for Titus's and Paul's return. Many interpreters claim that ταπεινός in 2 Cor. 7:6 demands a psychological interpretation because of Paul's affective language in 7:5 (ἄνεσις, ἔσωθεν φόβοι).[92] Even if the audience could not efficiently access the source text, the terminology used and wider context in 2 Corinthians suggests something different. As demonstrated, the expression "[he] who is lowly [ταπεινός] when face to face" (10:1a) most likely originates with Paul's detractors, referring to Paul's supposed feckless response to an affront (12:21; 13:2) and lies at the nerve of Paul's absence. This fits the context in which Paul narrates his successful martial action in Corinth. Importantly, Titus delivers news of the punishment of the ὁ ἀδικήσας (7:7-12; 2:5-11) amounting to an idealized reversal of Paul's martial impotence.

Thus, at one level Paul narrates another ordeal of despair, failure, and concrete divine rescue, but now in relation to Corinth occurring in Troas/Macedonia. The God who rescued Paul from death in Asia did likewise in Troas/Macedonia, alleviating his distress and reversing the charge of ταπεινός in principle. The God who rescues Paul from the death sentence (2 Cor. 1:9) of which exile served as a surrogate is the God who comforts Paul in the same manner as the reversal of Judah's exile of which death was a central metaphor. Even in the context of Paul's effort to discipline the offender by letter—the place in 2 Corinthians in which Paul, historically and socially, is at his most effective—Paul portrays himself as overwhelmed by the ordeal and abased only to experience God's intervening reversal.

The apologetic and parenetic force of the account is linked back to 2 Cor. 1:17-22. Paul's riposte to the charge of levity and diseased character involves a staking of his own character upon the character of God, who is faithful, who establishes, anoints, and seals his ministry (1:18-22). The sturdiness of God's character and his affirmation of Paul are demonstrated through the ordeal narrative. Yet, while Paul's narration demonstrates that he possesses God's affirmation, Paul is again inflecting how such resolute and authenticating character manifests itself—through a rather

---

91. Beale, "Reconciliation," 576; Jonathan Kaplan, "Comfort, O Comfort, Corinth: Grief and Comfort in 2 Corinthians 7:5-13a," *HTR* 104.1 (2011): 442-3.

92. Bachmann, *Zweite Brief*, 298; Barnett, *Second Epistle*, 369 n. 16; Plummer, *Second Epistle*, 218; Hughes, *Second Epistle*, 266 n. 3; Harris, *Second Epistle*, 528; Bieringer, "Παρακαλέω," 4.

unimpressive autobiographical account, in which Paul at his most martial appears quite feckless and paralyzed only to be rescued through God's potent, affirming intervention. As Wright comments regarding Paul's self-deprecating vulnerability, "That, in a world where leaders were supposed to be socially respectable, exemplary characters, is exactly the point."[93]

Finally, the result of the event and Paul's course of action is reversal for the community. They have experienced "repentance to salvation" (2 Cor. 7:10; cf. 1:6), which is described as an ordeal (δοκιμή, 2:9; cf. 7:12). Paul and the community have thus experienced conjoint divine reversals and, if all goes well, the legitimacy of both should be affirmed. Thus, the ordeal supplies concrete evidence on which Paul's defense of his apostleship is built. In light of the intermediate visit, Paul strategically rehabilitates his political legitimacy while challenging the criteria upon which he was judged negatively, both in regards to the charge of levity (1:17) and also potentially in the case of embezzlement (7:2b) found nearby in the immediate context. However, Vegge argues that 7:5-16 records not a complete reconciliation but an idealized account of reconciliation as a hortative device.[94] Thus, 2:12-13, 7:5-16 may not be the full realization of Paul's comments in 1:3-11, but may point proleptically in the discourse to Titus's return to restart the collection (chs. 8–9) ahead of Paul's return (chs. 10–13).

5.4. *The God Who Delivers the Weak (2 Corinthians 11:30-33)*

In 2 Cor. 11:30-33, Paul offers a third narrative of a geographically particularized, Christological reversal in Damascus. Paul writes in 11:30-33, "If it is necessary to boast, I will boast about the things concerning my weakness. God, the Father of our Lord Jesus knows, who is blessed into the ages, that I am not lying. In Damascus, the ethnarch of King Aretas was guarding the city of Damascus to arrest me, and through a window I was let down in a basket through the wall and I fled his hands." Interpreters have found troublesome the asyndeton beginning with the phrase ἐν Δαμασκῷ along with the shift to narrative.[95] However, the emphatic locative phrase, along with the recurrence of εὐλογητός (11:31; cf. 1:3; 2:14), the shift to narrative, and the prospect of punitive sanction, supply adequate contextual clues linking the text to Paul's previous accounts of reversal, though which narratives are written first remain

---

93. N. T. Wright, *Paul: A Biography* (New York: HarperOne, 2018), 306.
94. Vegge, *2 Corinthians*, 95–140.
95. Plummer, *Second Epistle*, 332, and others.

debated.⁹⁶ The apostle who bypasses an open door for evangelization in Troas, escapes a client-king through another aperture in Damascus. Like the previous narratives, some form of potential sanction is in view. However, 2 Cor. 11:32-33 does not display the vivid subjective emphasis found in 1:8-11 and 2:12-13, 7:5-16. Nor does the text contain many of the lexical linkages found in the previous ordeal narratives. Rather, 11:32-33 possesses a brisk objective account of Paul's escape.

The Damascus ordeal occurs in the so-called Fool's Speech (11:21b–12:13). As such, the account negotiates Paul's claim to political legitimacy vis-à-vis the rivals (11:23). The account is connected to the preceding peristasis catalogue (11:23-29), providing an instance of danger, but also points forward (11:30–12:10), as the narrative is the first example of Paul's boast of "the things concerning weakness" (τὰ τῆς ἀσθενείας).⁹⁷ This suggests that the peristasis catalogue likewise depicts negatively Paul's weakness rather than his virtuous self-sufficiency or endurance.⁹⁸ Panning out to the larger unit (chs. 10–13), the cognate adjective ἀσθενής is used in the detractors' negative evaluation of Paul's intermediate visit (10:10). The verb ἀσθενέω appears in the context of Paul's inability to punish (11:21a) and in reference to his impending return (13:3, 4, 9). As well, the noun ταπεινός (10:1b; 7:6) and verb ταπεινόω (12:21) share semantic domain with ἀσθε- cognates referring to Paul's disciplinary impotence in person (10:1b; 12:21). Thus, Paul manages to weave together an account of impending judgment against him in Damascus with the more proximate judgment against him emerging from Corinth.

5.4.1. *Uncertainty Concerning the Purpose of the Damascus Ordeal*

The function of the Damascus ordeal has long troubled scholars who, questioning the logic of 2 Cor. 11:32-33, claim the text is an interpolation,⁹⁹ simply irrelevant,¹⁰⁰ or a riposte to his opponents' slanderous version of the story.¹⁰¹ Welborn comments, "the source of the critics' dissatisfaction lies in the obscurity of the narrative's intent."¹⁰² Plummer contends, "we

---

96. On the link with blessing period in 1:3, see Bachmann, *Zweite Brief*, 382.
97. Schmeller, *Zweite Brief*, 2:265.
98. Andrews, "Too Weak," 263–76 passim.
99. Windisch, *Zweite Korintherbrief*, 363-3; Eric F. F. Bishop, "Does Aretas Belong in 2 Corinthians or Galatians," *ExpTim* 64 (1953): 189; Betz, *Apologie*, 73 n. 201; Sundermann, *Schwache Apostel*, 155.
100. Lietzmann, *Korinther I–II*, 151; Bultmann, *Second Letter*, 218.
101. Plummer, *Second Epistle*, 332–3; Strachan, *Second Epistle*, 28; Harris, *Second Epistle*, 820.
102. L. L Welborn, "The Runaway Paul," *HTR* 92.2 (1999): 116–17.

must be content therefore to leave the reason for the sudden mention of this incident open."[103]

In the spirit of Plummer's assertion, greater optimism is found in interpretations appealing to the social world. These interpretations generally agree that Paul's flight from Damascus supplies a culturally intelligible example of weakness.[104] A majority follow Edwin Judge and explain Paul's weakness as an allusion to and parody of the *corona muralis*.[105] As the valiant soldier is first to scale the wall, Paul the coward is lowered in a basket. In general, Long's contention that Paul's boasts in 2 Cor. 11:16–12:10 correspond to the ancient apologetic practice of "self-adulation" remains instructive.[106] Accordingly, self-adulation could include military heroism, as well as genealogy, accomplishments, and prodigious religious experience. Conversely, Welborn claims Paul appeals to the stock image of the "runaway" associated with Dorian mime.[107] He argues that across the Fool's Speech Paul appeals to various stock fools, such as the "leading slave" (11:21b-23), "the braggart warrior" (11:24-27), "the anxious old man" (11:28-29), and "the learned imposter" (12:1b-4, 7-9).[108]

A number of commentators rightly find one or both interpretations unconvincing, yet contend that Paul's account remains humiliating.[109] These scholars rightly question whether an allusion to the *corona muralis* would resonate with the audience. There is no mention of Paul being "first" as in the honor, and complicating the interpretation, the rope and bucket find no parallel with siege warfare, which usually employed ladders or ramparts.[110] Welborn's thesis is impressive, with an array of citations; however, it hangs tenuously on the premise that the Fool's Discourse proper (2 Cor. 11:21b–12:10) is an intentional allusion not only to the theater but successive mimic figures. Both interpretive approaches depend upon an ironic interpretation in which Paul's self-adulation lampoons some dominant value, such as courage. Such a paradox as boasting in weakness may be counterintuitive, as Schellenberg claims, but it is not

---

103. Plummer, *Second Epistle*, 333.
104. Harris, *Second Epistle*, 820.
105. E. A. Judge, "Paul's Boasting in Relation to Contemporary Professional Practice," in Scholer, ed., *Social Distinctives of the Christians in the First Century*, 67–8; Furnish, *II Corinthians*, 542; Martin, *2 Corinthians*, 372; Barnett, *Second Epistle*, 553 n. 58; Peterson, *Eloquence*, 261–2; Vegge, *2 Corinthians*, 338.
106. Long, *Ancient Rhetoric*, 186–90.
107. Welborn, "Runaway Paul," 152–9.
108. Welborn, "Runaway Paul," 137.
109. Harris, *Second Epistle*, 820, 824; Schmeller, *Zweite Brief*, 2:346.
110. Harris, *Second Epistle*, 824; Oropeza, *Second Corinthians*, 655.

ironic.[111] So in what way is Paul's flight from Damascus an account of weakness and what function does the account possess? Plausibly, Paul's weakness is demonstrated both in his *flight* and *passivity*, and as such functions as a deliberate reference to and comment upon Paul's intermediate visit and exit.

5.4.2. *An Account of Flight*

Schmithals, we recall, rejected the notion that Paul left Corinth in shame in part because such conduct "[would] not even remotely correspond to the same Paul who wrote [2 Cor.] 11:23-33."[112] Scott B. Andrews responds that Paul's flight from Damascus exemplifies a lack of masculine courage (ἀνδρεία, *fortitudo*).[113] Yet, with a superior force guarding Damascus "to seize" Paul (2 Cor. 11:32), it is unclear what sufficiently masculine actions Paul might have taken. First, while parallel accounts are often neutral or positive, an account in which Paul responds to threat and opposition through passivity and flight resonates with a more proximate context—Paul's disciplinary inaction and exit from Corinth. Scott suggests, "perhaps the Corinthians would recall the apostle's ignoble retreat from Corinth during his second, painful visit to the congregation."[114] The analogy is promising, although almost entirely ignored. It is also incomplete at best since Paul escapes from an ethnarch of a powerful client-king in Damascus. Yet, Cicero reports that flight even in the face of overwhelming odds may be shameful and cowardly.[115] Concerning the outmanned slave-king Ennus, Diodorus (fl. ca. 80–ca. 20 BCE) comments, "[Ennus,] taking with him his bodyguards, a thousand strong, fled in unmanly fashion."[116] Plutarch following Polybius states that Perseus "suffered pitifully" (οἰκτρὰ ἔπασχε), escaping through a window.[117] Combined with his ensuing suppliant surrender the account is one of ignominy.[118] His eventual captor, Aemilius, states, "valour in the unfortunate obtains great reverence even among their enemies, but cowardice, in Roman eyes, even though it meets with success, is in every way a most dishonourable thing."[119]

---

111. Schellenberg, *Education*, 171.
112. Schmithals, *Gnosticism*, 104.
113. Andrews, "Too Weak," 272.
114. Scott, *2 Corinthians*, 220.
115. Cicero, *Fam.* 14.3.1-2.
116. Diodorus 34.2.22.
117. Plutarch, *Aem.* 26.2.
118. Plutarch, *Aem.* 26.7-12; contra Welborn, "Runaway," 119 n. 37.
119. Plutarch, *Aem.* 26.12.

Furthermore, putting aside the matter of an aperture, Paul depicts a test in which he responds by leaving. As demonstrated, leaving during moments of adversity could widely be characterized as dishonorable. With sufficient contextual clues as in 2 Cor. 11:30, escapes through apertures were viewed as shameful. The point of adversity according to so much ancient logic centers on the response to threat. Thus, Epictetus (fl. ca. 55–ca. 135 CE) comments that often when faced with death, exile, or hardship, "we show the spirit of running away," resulting in confidence (θαραλέος) of nature (φύσις) becoming cowardice and abjectness (ταπεινός) of nature.[120] Similarly, according to Dio Chrysostom, Diogenes states the noble man faces hardship, a form of contest (ἀγών), "disclosing no weakness," while most people respond by "always avoiding them by flight and never looking them in the face."[121] From such a perspective, Paul's account is a rather straightforward depiction of a weakness as demonstrated in leaving Damascus, similar to the characterization of his exit from Corinth.

The immediate context encourages this interpretation. In 2 Cor. 11:29, after listing twenty-five hardships, Paul offers an echo of an evaluation of his deeds: "Who is weak, and am I not weak? Who is tripped up [σκανδαλίζω] and am I not burned [πυρόω]?" There is no agreement on the meaning of the text. It is not uncommon to connect the passage primarily to 11:28 as a particular example of his pastoral care over his communities and his indignation over exploitative behavior.[122] Yet, this interpretation understands 11:29 as primarily a parenthetical comment upon 11:28. As Andrews demonstrates, all of the verbs involve status judgments against Paul converted into a self-proclaimed "inability to master his difficult circumstances."[123] The term ἀσθενέω is employed in 11:30–12:10 particularly in the sense of "events in which one is the object of hostility" and lacks the strength to respond affectively, a feature bound to the intermediate visit.[124] Beyond ἀσθενέω, the term σκανδαλίζω in 1 Cor. 8:13 is a feature limited to "the weak" concerning the issue of idol meat. The term πυρόω need not refer to Paul's emotional indignation, but as in 1 Cor. 3:15 it can point to failing an (eschatological) ordeal, a topic entirely salient to the circumstances behind 2 Corinthians. Thus, Paul in comparing himself with his rivals (cf. 2 Cor. 11:20-21) offers a compendium of the catalogue

---

120. Epictetus, *Diatr.* 2.1.10-12; see Andrews, "Too Weak," 268.
121. Dio Chrysostom, *Virt.* 11.15-18.
122. See Harris, *Second Epistle*, 813–15.
123. Andrews, "Too Weak," 271.
124. Michael L. Barré, "Paul as 'Eschatologic Person': A New Look at 2 Cor 11:29," *CBQ* 37.4 (1975): 513.

acknowledging his weakness and the way in which he is frequently "burned up" in ordeals.[125]

Significantly, Paul transitions to boasting of one such example of weakness. It just so happens to be an instance of a failure during an ordeal that involves leaving. Thus, when contextual clues are present, flight including flight through a window could be a dishonorable act, an instance in which a person failed to respond properly to a test. Such a clue is clear in 2 Cor. 11:30 (and 11:29) and combined with the evaluation of Paul's weak presence in Corinth (10:10a) and subsequent exit suggests that in boasting of his flight from Damascus, Paul is intentionally evoking the issues surrounding his exit from Corinth.

Likewise, the account of Paul's heavenly ascent (2 Cor. 12:1-10) compliments our reading of the Damascus ordeal as one of failure and weakness. While much has been written about the connection between the two ordeal narratives, clearly both aim at historical exactitude and chronological progression. Furthermore, one involves a flight from Damascus, the other a flight into Paradise.

Through close consideration of comparative ascents and contextual clues, Paula Gooder has furthered the linkage, arguing that Paul intentionally recounts a failed ascent to Heaven in which he only reaches the third heaven (perhaps in a seven-heaven framework).[126] Gooder observes that rather than fulfilling the expectation of the sojourner reaching God and receiving a revelation, Paul's account "in many aspects…appears incomplete: the terse description; scant detail; lack of a mention of God's throne; lack of any description of what is seen in heaven, all add to the feeling of incompleteness."[127] Gooder argues that there are two descriptions of the ascent, interrupted by a parenthetical comment. First, Paul recounts that he was snatched away into the third heaven and then into Paradise located within the third heaven (2 Cor. 12:2-4). Paul then restarts the account in in 7b-8. Rather than attach the dative phrase τῇ ὑπερβολῇ τῶν ἀποκαλύψεων in 12:7a to v. 7b-8, Gooder regards it as connected to the parenthesis in 12:5-6.[128] This results a parallelism in 12:7-8:[129]

---

125. Barré, "Eschatologic Person," 508–9.
126. Paula Gooder, *Only the Third Heaven? 2 Corinthians 12.1-10 and Heavenly Ascent*, LNTS 313 (London: T&T Clark, 2006), 191. My thanks to Jamie Davies for pointing me towards Gooder's convincing work.
127. Gooder, *Third Heaven*, 191.
128. Gooder, *Third Heaven*, 196.
129. Gooder, *Third Heaven*, 196.

5. Paul's Art of the Ordeal

For Gooder, this implies that the thorn and angel of Satan "are one in the same thing,"[130] implying that Paul's ascent ordeal describes opposition to Paul's heavenly ascent. To substantiate this, Gooder revisits the verb ὑπεραίρωμαι, claiming that the middle voice need not mean "I exalt myself" but may mean "to raise oneself up physically."[131] This indicates that the angel of Satan intercepts Paul, resulting in a interrupted, failed ascent, a true mark of weakness.

Gooder's research supplies a significant advance in understanding Paul's heavenly ascent. A few comments may further her insights. First, what Gooder regards as a parallel in 2 Cor. 12:7b-8 is in reality a chiasm, as Long demonstrates:[132]

A διὸ ἵνα μὴ ὑπεραίρωμαι,
  B ἐδόθη
    C μοι
      D σκόλοψ τῇ σαρκί
      D¹ ἄγγελος Σατανᾶ,
    C¹ ἵνα με
  B¹ κολαφίζῃ,
A¹ ἵνα μὴ ὑπεραίρωμαι

An accurate understanding of the form of the text strengthens Gooder's claim that the thorn and angel of Satan are identical. Indeed, ἄγγελος is in apposition to σκόλοψ, made more evident by the chiasm.[133] Second, Paul once again appears in an ordeal setting. The figure of Satan as one who applies a scrutinizing test clearly was in circulation (Job 1; Mk 1:12-13; Mt. 4:12-17; Lk. 3:1-13; 22:31-32). Paul, from this angle, fails the test according to conventional criteria: Satan interdicts his ascent, resulting in no vision of the throne. Third, the angel's forceful assault that stops

---

130. Gooder, *Third Heaven*, 197.
131. Gooder, *Third Heaven*, 200; LSJ, s.v. "ὑπεραίρω."
132. Long, *II Corinthians*, 232.
133. Long, *II Corinthians*, 228.

Paul in his tracks fits with the peristasis catalogue (2 Cor. 11:23-29), where Paul is the target of corporal punishment in earthly matters, and the picture emerging from the intermediate visit in which Paul is the recipient of the disciplinary rod rather than the one who wields it. Thus, Gooder's work highlights how Paul has moved from a shameful flight from an earthly ruler to a foiled ascent by a heavenly ruler.[134]

5.4.3. *An Account of Passivity*

Second, Paul's weakness is evidenced by his passivity in the Damascus ordeal. Facing a dire situation, Paul testifies in the passive voice, "I was lowered [ἐχαλάσθην] in a basket through a window in the wall" (2 Cor. 11:33; cf. Acts 9:23–25). Crucially, ἐχαλάσθην (11:33; cf. 12:3-4) describes Paul as a passive recipient of aid. Schmeller highlights that extrabiblical accounts of similar escapes highlight the fugitives' active role in evading capture.[135] Plutarch states that Perseus suffered "in letting himself down through a narrow window in the fortress, together with his wife and little children."[136] Similarly, Athenaeus (fl. second–third century CE) writes, "many Athenians…were lowering themselves from the walls with ropes and trying to escape."[137] Contrarily, Josh. 2:15 (LXX) records that "she [Rahab] lowered them [the spies] through the window." Yair Zakovitch writes of Josh. 2:15, "this manner of escape again emphasizes the passivity of the spies. Like marionettes they are dependent on Rahab's graces, their lives hanging in the balance every moment."[138] Josephus (fl. 37–ca.100 CE), however, redacts the story, making the spies the agents of their escape, writing, "they [the spies] departed, *letting themselves down* the wall by a rope."[139] There is little wonder as to the reason for the redaction or for the shocking aspect of Paul's boast. Passive verbs dominate Paul's failed heavenly ascent (ἁρπαγέντα, 12:2; ἐδόθη, κολαφίζῃ, 12:7). While these are often viewed as divine passives with theological insight, alternatively, a picture emerges of Paul as rag doll, tossed to and fro by circumstances

---

134. Gooder, *Third Heaven*, 205–6.
135. Schmeller, *Zweite Brief*, 2:267.
136. Plutarch, *Aem.* 26.2.
137. Athenaeus, *Deip.* 5.214a; cf. Livy 39.7.5; Josephus, *Ant.* 5.466-469.
138. Yair Zakovitch, "Humor and Theology or the Successful Failure of Israelite Intelligence: A Literary-Folkloric Approach to Joshua 2," in *Text and Tradition: The Hebrew Bible and Folklore*, ed. Susan Niditch (Atlanta: Scholars Press, 1990), 91.
139. Josephus, *Ant.* 5.15; C. Begg comments, Josephus's "[Rahab] seems to suffer both a quantitative and qualitative eclipse as compared with the biblical figure" ("The Rahab Story in Josephus," *LASBF* 55 [2005]: 128).

and forces beyond his control. Clement of Alexandria summarized the broader ethos, stating "it is given to man to act (τὸ δρᾶν), to woman to be acted upon (τὸ πάσχειν)."[140] Thus, the Damascus scene is one of weakness also, as seen in Paul's passivity, another feature echoing the judgments emerging from the intermediate ordeal and Paul's ongoing absence.

5.4.4. Divine Empowerment in Damascus

However, the ordeal in Damascus demonstrates Paul's deliverance from peril as in the previous accounts. Windisch rightly claims, "the emphasis lies solely on the contrast between the grave danger in which Paul hovered and the happy rescue."[141] Windisch's comment points to the emphasis shared in each of the previous ordeal narratives as well. The successful escape also emphasizes Paul's powerlessness. His rescue was not due to his own acumen or assertive action. The point resonates with Josh. 2:15, of which Zakovitch writes, "this story was selected to stand at the beginning of the account of God's saving acts towards Israel, in order to know that there is no wisdom and no heroism apart from God alone."[142]

Paul's account serves a similar purpose.[143] In refusing to be the hero in his own ordeal, Paul challenges the judgments against him and the typical qualities associated with masculine courage, claiming all such power comes from God. Moreover, Paul continues to redefine the attributes of a genuine ordeal, claiming the marks of the approved (δόκιμος, 2 Cor. 10:16) apostle, the legitimate "minister of Christ" (11:23), are found in the Christological sequence—human weakness superseded by divine strength.[144] As Jan Lambrecht states, "in vv. 32-33 Paul proceeds to illustrate by means of one particular event what it means for him to be 'weak' and yet to experience God's effective help."[145] The event in Damascus, like that in Asia and Macedonia, is another instance in which Paul has experienced both τὰ παθήματα τοῦ Χριστοῦ and, like Christ, God's intervening rescue.

---

140. Clement of Alexandria, *Paed.* 3.3.19.2, as quoted in Schellenberg, *Education*, 307.
141. Windisch, *Zweite Korintherbrief*, 363, my translation.
142. Zakovitch, "Humor," 96.
143. Schmeller, *Zweite Brief*, 2:257 n. 227.
144. Heinrici makes the point that Paul's escape is not simply a contrast of "natürlichen Ehren-Muthes" but Paul's assumption of the sufferings of Christ (*Zweite Brief*, 382–3).
145. Lambrecht, *Second Corinthians*, 195.

Yet, in the context of Paul's emphasis on his return (2 Cor. 10:1–13:10), Paul offers an account of flight from Damascus as a direct attempt to undermine the accusations against him emerging from his own passive presence and exit in Corinth. Beyond transparent autobiography, both the flight from Damascus and his account of a failed heavenly ascent (12:1-9a) supply his audience with historical evidence that rather than fail his ordeals as the community assumed, he is δόκιμος after all, if only according to different criteria. The climactic scene in Paul's discussion of legitimate apostleship is also the climax of Paul's failed heavenly ascent, involving not a vision of the throne but the words of the Lord (12:9). These words demonstrate that, though lacking according to the canons of effective leadership, Paul remains a recipient of divine χάρις (12:9a), which remains as incongruous and unmerited as ever in Pauline thought.[146] There Paul stands, having run from the ethnarch of Aretus in Damascus, stuck in the third heaven, encouraging the community to overturn its judgment and acknowledge Paul's legitimacy, allowing for an amicable return. Paul thus argues that his martial weakness is evidence for his legitimacy, not against it, because his person becomes the site for God's intervening power.

5.5. *Summary and Conclusions*

As part of his strategy to achieve an amicable return, in response to judgments of his outsider, deviant status, Paul employs a series of ordeal narratives concerning events occurring outside Corinth (2 Cor. 1:8-11; 2:12-13; 7:5-16; 11:30-33) that broadly evoke the issues surrounding Paul's intermediate visit. By his own account, Paul is no Horatius. In 2 Corinthians, Paul is overpowered in Asia. He flees from conflict in Damascus and is marooned in the third heaven. Even when imposing punitive sanction upon the community through a letter, Paul is paralyzed in Macedonia and Troas. By the measure of Livy's heroic epithets, Paul is an anti-hero. He is neither energetic (*impiger*), nor strong and capable (*fortis ac strenuous*), nor severe (*acer*), nor is he singlehandedly able to change his circumstances (*unus*). The epithets to the Pauline ordeal are "burdened beyond measure, beyond power," "despairing of life," "no relief," "abasement," and "weakness." All power and heroism belong to the God "who raises the dead," "comforts the lowly," and empowers the weak.

---

146. On the nature of grace in Paul and elsewhere, see Barclay, *Paul & the Gift*.

The ordeal narratives further evoke the fallout from the intermediate visit by appropriating a broader discourse of displacement. Like other exiles, Paul represents himself as facing death, even a death sentence *in absentia* (2 Cor. 1:8-11). Furthermore, Paul writes like others attempting to dispel the judgment of effeminate conduct (1:17) by demonstrating his salvific care for the community *in absentia* (1:23–2:13; 7:5-16) in which the ordeal in 2:12-13, 7:5-7 plays a significant role. Finally, Paul blatantly depicts a scene in which he flees from danger as an example of his weakness (11:30-33).

Paul's narratives challenge the definition of legitimacy in Corinth. Undoubtedly, Paul's ordeal narratives possess an apologetic element, defending him against the criticisms emerging from his intermediate ordeal. Rather than claim immunity from communal judgment as in 1 Cor. 4:3-5, in 2 Corinthians Paul responds to the reality of intensified judgments emanating, in part, from the intermediate visit by portraying himself as under judgment in other places and then strategically attaching such judgments to Christ and God. Through a Christological sequence, Paul demonstrates his consistent inactive or passive responses to difficulty and judgments alongside God's efficacious aid to overturn those verdicts (τὸ ἀπόκριμα τοῦ θανάτου, 2 Cor. 1:9; ταπεινός, 7:6; ἀσθένεια, 11:30). Thus, the divine overturning of those judgments in other locations encourages the audience in Corinth to do likewise.

At the same time, the accounts challenge the community to reject the criteria upon which they judge Paul as weak and impotent and rather embrace the ethos underlying his passive response. Importantly, the divine reversals imply God's vindication and approval of Paul and his mode of leadership, even if such incongruity and unmerited status fly in the face of the implied audience. In this way, the ordeal narratives contribute to the rehabilitation of Paul's status/rank, while simultaneously recalibrating the administrative norms and cultural criteria upon which the Corinthians evaluated Paul.

Chapter 6

Paul's Return to Corinth
(2 Corinthians 13:1-10)

The last sub-unit of the (canonical or partitioned) letter body (2 Cor. 13:1-10) is familiar territory. The text explicitly refers to an ordeal, proof, or test involving Paul (δοκιμή, 13:3a) which dialogically supplies a test for the community (13:5-7). The text references status accusations against both Paul, who is allegedly unapproved as Christ's spokesperson (13:3a), and also the community, which is to test whether they are "in the faith" (13:5). The threat of punitive sanction dominates the text as Paul quotes the Deuteronomic statute regarding legal witnesses (13:1; cf. Deut. 19:15) and cites the threat uttered during the intermediate visit (13:2). It is a threat that Paul obliquely implies he will carry out upon his arrival (13:4d). Similar to the previous ordeal narrations, Paul's logic argues positively for his character and legitimacy as manifested in the Christological sequence (13:4), which is to inform the character of the community (13:7). Thus, alongside the aggregation of phenomena related to political displacement as outlined in Chapter 2 and refined in Chapters 3 and 4, the reference to the intermediate visit and impending return in 13:1-10 make it highly probable that such phenomena are relevant for interpretation. Given that in 13:1-10 Paul blatantly attempts to achieve an amicable return, our interpretation continues to ask in what way does the passage relate to Paul's political displacement from Corinth and how does Paul use the discourse to negotiate the crisis in Corinth.

6.1. *Paul's Impending Test in Corinth (2 Corinthians 13:1-4)*

As a part of the larger unit (2 Cor. 12:14–13:10), the sub-unit 13:1-10 supplies Paul's final appeal for an amicable return. The sub-unit naturally divides into two smaller sections. The first (13:1-4) entails Paul's (foreboding) promise for the Christological sequence to conclude upon his return. The second (13:5-10) commands the community to evaluate its own legitimacy in order to experience restoration (13:9) ultimately to experience Paul's amicable rather than punitive return (13:10).

Following the asyndetic announcement of Paul's return, the use of Deut. 19:15 LXX in 13:1 supplies the segment with a punitive, judicial, and expulsionary context. This is true whether or not Paul refers to a judicial proceeding upon his return in which he presides or acts as prosecutor[1] or in which he appears in the dock,[2] or whether the usage is a metaphorical warning of impending judgment.[3] In light of 13:2, it is the Corinthians who are under punitive threat. Yet, in 13:3a Paul is on the defense, responding to accusations that he is illegitimate based upon the unrealized nature of that threat. As becomes clear, the unit demonstrates the two issues are fused. This is perfectly sensible since one source text (Deut. 19:15-21), under the principle of *lex talionis*, refers to reciprocal punishment to befall a false accuser (Deut. 19:20), who is not to be spared (οὐ φείσεται, Deut. 19:21; cf. 2 Cor. 13:2).[4] Furthermore, all of the source texts refer to protections in capital cases (Num. 35:30; Deut. 17:6; 19:11-13), which, as we have demonstrated, were punished through expulsions in the Second Temple Period (cf. Deut. 17:7; 1 Cor 5:13).

In 2 Cor. 13:2, Paul echoes his threat to the immoral group (τοῖς προημαρτηκόσιν, cf. 12:21) and "all the rest" (τοῖς λοιποῖς πᾶσιν), "when I come I will not spare [you] again" (13:2). The threat which Paul made in person (παρών) and now through the epistle (ἀπών) refers to the ordeal with his long-standing detractors in which his martial threats from 1 Cor. 4:18-21 went unfulfilled. Thus, the unit opens with a reference to *the ordeal* at the center of the crisis as found in 2 Corinthians, an ordeal possessing a spatial component in which Paul now absent and displaced once again threatens to force out his detractors in a martial return. This of course raises the question: How can Paul argue again for a martial arrival in light of the intermediate visit?

---

1. Filson, "Second Epistle," 417; Delcor, "Courts," 76; Barnett, *Second Epistle*, 598.
2. Long, *Rhetoric*, 139–41; Welborn, *Enmity*, 187–9, and others.
3. In which the witnesses correspond in some way to Paul's visits/warnings (Thrall, *Second Epistle*, 2:873; Harris, *Second Epistle*, 908; Schmeller, *Zweite Brief*, 367–8).
4. Welborn, *Enmity*, 188–9.

6.1.1. *Paul's Political Legitimacy and the Christological Sequence (2 Corinthians 13:3-4)*

The threat of impending discipline and the reference to Paul's intermediate visit transitions into a discourse about political legitimacy in the remainder of the segment (2 Cor. 13:3-4, 5-10). In 2 Cor. 13:3a, Paul supplies grounds (ἐπεί) for the threat of punitive action as evidence that Christ speaks in Paul. Paul's substantiation is not ironic, but speaks to the epicenter of the crisis of authority.[5] Rather, Paul threatens to succeed in the matter previously marked by failure according to his detractors. At a superficial level, such decisive action would supply proof by ordeal and thus reestablish Paul's claim to legitimacy in his return through the demonstration of aggressive, martial qualities that he lacked in the intermediate visit.

While 2 Cor. 13:2-3 is one sentence in Greek, the meaning of the relative clause in 13:3b is debated. The clause ὃς εἰς ὑμᾶς οὐκ ἀσθενεῖ ἀλλὰ δυνατεῖ ἐν ὑμῖν is sometimes viewed as a transparent affirmation of the Christ's powerful activity in the community, whether through Paul's missionary efforts[6] or as referencing Paul's impending visit.[7] However, the present tense use of the verbs (ἀσθενεῖ, δυνατεῖ) should be taken seriously, and thus not in reference to Paul's future arrival (cf. 13:4d). If so, it is not clear how Paul could refer positively to Christ's role as "powerful among you" at the time of composition. Previously, in 11:3 he writes that the community is possibly deceived and corrupted. That fear is paralleled by more fears of destructive behavior he expects to find upon his return (12:20-21), even questioning in 13:5 whether the community is "in the faith."

Moreover, in the previous ordeal narratives, Paul frequently characterizes God, through appositional phrases or similar constructions (2 Cor. 1:3, 4, 9; 7:6; 11:31). In these predicates, God is "comforting us in all our afflictions (1:4) and "the one who raises the dead" (1:9), "the one who comforts the abased" (7:6). In the relative clause in 1:10, God is described as ὃς ἐκ τηλικούτου θανάτου ἐρρύσατο ἡμᾶς καὶ ῥύσεται. Such expressions are completely at odds with 13:3b, which omits the reality of weakness.

---

5. Oostendorp, *Another Jesus*, 25; Thrall, *Second Epistle*, 2:879; Barnett, *Second Epistle*, 601–2; Vegge, *2 Corinthians*, 343; Schmeller, *Zweite Brief*, 2:369–70; contra Furnish, *II Corinthians*, 576.

6. Plummer, *Second Epistle*, 374; Barrett, *Second Epistle*, 335; Schmeller, *Zweite Brief*, 370–1.

7. Bachmann, *Zweite Brief*, 407–8; Hughes, *Second Epistle*, 478; Strachan, *Second Epistle*, 38; Héring, *Second Epistle*, 99.

Thus, 13:3b seems to function ironically,[8] functioning as a foil for Paul's redefinition of the relationship between weakness and power.[9]

In 2 Cor. 13:4 Paul presents his correction to the detractors' self-evaluation echoed in the relative clause and thus the proper grounds for Paul's claim that Christ speaks in him (13:3a).[10] The passage displays marked parallelism which offers the Christological justification for weakness:

4a: καὶ γὰρ   ἐσταυρώθη   ἐξ ἀσθενείας,

4b: ἀλλὰ   ζῇ   ἐκ δυνάμεως θεοῦ.

4c: καὶ γὰρ   ἡμεῖς ἀσθενοῦμεν ἐν αὐτῷ,

4d: ἀλλὰ   ζήσομεν   σὺν αὐτῷ   ἐκ δυνάμεως θεοῦ εἰς ὑμᾶς.[11]

There is much discussion as to whether the particles καὶ γάρ retain their traditional force as ascensive (καί) and explanatory-grounds (γάρ) or whether following Jan Lambrecht καὶ γάρ…ἀλλὰ possesses the concessive sense of "for although."[12] Lambrecht's argument suffers from relegating the importance of 13:4a and c as parenthetical concessions, when the emphasis seems to be on the successive aspects of Christ and Paul's existence.[13] Thus, καὶ γάρ in 13:4a substantiates and explains the notion of apostolic δοκιμή in 13:3a, while recalibrating the values present in 13:3b.

The striking parallelism links Christ with Paul's weakness and power. In 2 Cor. 13:4ab, Paul states, "he was crucified because of weakness [ἐξ ἀσθενείας] but he lives because of the power of God [ἐκ δυνάμεως θεοῦ]." The meaning of the dual use of ἐκ is debated, but it is best to understand both as prepositions of cause, "because of weakness."[14] It is generally accepted that ἀσθενείας refers to a human mode of existence.[15] This is a weak overgeneralization. The use of ἀσθε-cognates in 2 Corinthians 10–13 interacts with judgments against Paul's leadership qualities and often refer to Paul's inability to repel hostile actions. In the context of the

---

8. Windisch, *Zweite Korintherbrief*, 418; Bultmann, *Second Letter*, 242; Furnish, *II Corinthians*, 576; Aejmelaeus, *Schwachheit*, 357.

9. Harris, *Second Epistle*, 912.

10. Jan Lambrecht, "Philological and Exegetical Notes," in *Studies in 2 Corinthians* (Leuven: Leuven University Press/Peeters, 1994), 591.

11. Vegge, *2 Corinthians*, 345.

12. Lambrecht, "Notes," 594–5.

13. Barrett, *Second Epistle*, 327 n. 1.

14. Long, *II Corinthians*, 249–50.

15. Schmeller, *Zweite Brief*, 2:373.

accusation that Paul is feckless to implement discipline (10:1-11), and the narratival emphasis on Paul's passivity before potential punitive sanction (1:8-11; 11:32-33), Harris is correct to claim that ἐξ ἀσθενείας refers particularly to Christ's "non-retaliation or non-aggressiveness during his passion."[16] The claim is not ἀπέθανεν ἐξ ἀσθενείας but that Christ experienced the death sentence at the agency of others (ἐσταυρώθη) "because of weakness." It is Christ's passivity in weakness that leads to the reversal of 13:3b, in which Paul states, "but he lives because of God's power."

The shift in tenses highlights the contrast. Now, because of God's intervention, Christ lives. The point for Paul in the substantiation of his claim to δοκιμή (13:3a) is to correct the misconception in 2 Cor. 13:3b with the qualities associated with the respective phases of Christological existence. This is not the language of paradoxical simultaneity or concomitance of Christ who is both crucified and alive.[17] This is the language of the successive phases of the Christological sequence.[18]

In 2 Cor. 13:4cd the parallelism highlights the striking degree to which Paul's relationship with the Corinthians embodies the Christological sequence outlined in 13:4ab. The use of καὶ γάρ cannot supply the grounds for 13:4ab.[19] Rather, as a functional parataxis the parallel use of καὶ γάρ in 13:4cd ties Paul to his measuring rod. While Paul speaks of Christ's existence in the past (13:4a) and present (13:4b), he speaks in the present (13:4c) and future (13:4d) regarding himself.[20] Thus, I translate 13:4, "For indeed, he was crucified because of weakness but he lives because the power of God. For indeed, we are weak in him but we will live with him because of God's power with respect to you." While some consider the present tense phrase ἡμεῖς ἀσθενοῦμεν (13:4c) as a reference to the entirety of the apostolic existence, in the context of Paul's legitimacy (13:3a) the phrase functions as an affirmation of the accusation that he is weak, particularly as demonstrated during Paul's second visit to Corinth.[21] In the immediate context, as demonstrated in Chapter 5, Paul has generated historical accounts of administrative and masculine weakness within a broader strategy to defeat the assertion that the martial weakness evidence during the intermediate visit was disqualifying.

---

16. Harris, *Second Epistle*, 915; cf. Guthrie, *2 Corinthians*, 635.
17. Contra Bultmann, *Second Letter*, 243; Martin, *2 Corinthians*, 475; Klauck, *2 Korintherbrief*, 101.
18. Schmeller, *Zweite Brief*, 2:373.
19. Bachmann, *Zweite Brief*, 407; contra Plummer, *Second Epistle*, 375.
20. Lambrecht, "Notes," 589.
21. Aejmelaeus, *Schwachheit*, 368.

In 2 Cor. 13:4d, Paul claims that in the future he will experience a reversal parallel to that of Christ's resurrection (ζῇ ἐκ δυνάμεως θεοῦ). The reference to future life empowered by God seems to some to refer to future resurrection at the Parousia.[22] This would be the case without the modifier εἰς ὑμᾶς, omitted by Codex B likely because of the interpretive confusion it creates. Aejmaleaus states, "even though the words εἰς ὑμᾶς cause confusion in a context that seems to be purely eschatological, they, and just they unite the last clause with its wider context and with the subject of the actual dialogue between Paul and the Corinthians."[23] The preposition εἰς ὑμᾶς in 13:4b, "with regards to you," should be understood as a description of Paul's return to Corinth (13:1).[24] The majority who follow this line claim the impending empowered life displayed by Paul refers singularly to his promised punitive action.[25] In view of Paul's threat in 13:2 and the accusation that he is weak in martial discipline, 13:4d appears to function primarily as a threat to displace his detractors.

However, it would be an uncharacteristic use of the death and resurrection of Christ to substantiate Paul's return as *only* punitive. Paul consistently portrays the reversals he experiences in ordeals as occurring for the benefit (comfort, 2 Cor. 1:6; salvation, 2 Cor. 1:6; 7:10) of the Corinthians. As well, Paul refers elsewhere to his visits as efficacious in eschatological terms (1 Cor. 4:18-21; 2 Cor. 1:14, 15-16). Thus, while the immediate context (13:1-2) implies that 13:4d refers to punishment, Paul has supplied his audience with other connotations across the discourse also equipping them to anticipate positive communal outcomes or simple efficacy in Paul's arrival.

6.1.2. Theological Implications of Paul's Empowered Return

Unsurprisingly, several commentators attempt to interpret the relationship between Paul's present weakness and future empowerment as one of simultaneity,[26] or weakness as hidden strength,[27] with appeals to

---

22. As claimed by Käsemann, "Legitimität," 54; Georgi, *Opponents*, 279.

23. Aejmaleaus, "Christ Is Weak," 130.

24. Plummer, *Second Epistle*, 375; Héring, *Second Epistle*, 100; R. C. Tannehill, *Dying and Rising with Christ: A Study in Pauline Theology*, BZNW 32 (Berlin: Töpelmann, 1967), 99; Lietzmann, *Korinther I–II*, 161; Barrett, *Second Epistle*, 337; Martin, *2 Corinthians*, 476–7; Aejmelaeus, *Schwachheit*, 371; Schmeller, *Zweite Brief*, 2:375, and others.

25. Notably Munck, following Koch, *Paul*, 189–90.

26. Windisch, *Zweite Korintherbrief*, 418; Martin, *2 Corinthians*, 475; Guthrie, *2 Corinthians*, 635.

27. Merritt, *Word and Deed*, 148–9, and others.

2 Cor. 4:10-12 and/or 12:9-10 as determinative contexts. Vegge claims, "this is the form of apostolic power—a power that is manifested through weakness."[28] Similarly, Harris claims, "whereas Christ's states (death and resurrection) are successive...Paul's states (weakness and vitality) are at least potentially, simultaneous."[29] This however, like similar interpretations of 13:4ab, violates the differences in tenses in 13:4cd, the adversative (ἀλλά), and ultimately the parallel between Christ and Paul.

As is clear by now, 13:4 evidences Paul's habituated grammar of Christological reversal. Schmeller highlights that from the perspective of Luther's *theologia crucis*, 13:4 contains no hint of hidden power (Kraft als Schwachheit) or paradoxical simultaneity (Kraft neben/in Schwachheit) as in 2 Cor. 1:3-7; 4:7-18; 6:3-8; 12:1-10.[30] Rather, the movement from weakness to power, according to Plummer, involves a "surprising change."[31] I remain unconvinced that the concomitance of weakness in power in Paul's heavenly ascent (2 Cor. 12:9) is inconsistent with the successive phases of weakness and strength in Paul's return (13:4). The divine χάρις that establishes Paul's political legitimacy in Corinth may be unconditioned by and incongruous with normal qualifications of masculine leadership, but that χάρις possesses a generative *telos*. That Paul moves quickly to discussing his impending return (12:14) provides the text with a measure of drama as to the texture of that χάρις in his relationship with the Corinthians.

A full discussion of Paul's theology of weakness and strength in 2 Corinthians is beyond the scope of this project. Yet, from our study a central insight emerges: when describing ordeal accounts occurring in specific geographic locations, Paul refers consistently to weakness and strength as successive phases (2 Cor. 1:8-11; 2:12-13; 7:5-6; 11:32-33) based upon the Christological sequence. That sequence and Paul's embodiment of it is most obvious in 13:4, indicating 13:4cd refers to two successive phases in Paul's apostolic ministry to Corinth which is tethered to parallel phases in the life of Christ.[32] Unlike the intermediate visit characterized by weakness and passivity, his return will be characterized by divine empowerment.

28. Vegge, *2 Corinthians*, 347.
29. Harris, *Second Epistle*, 28.
30. Schmeller, *Zweite Brief*, 2:381.
31. Plummer, *Second Epistle*, 375.
32. Schmeller, *Zweite Brief*, 2:375.

6.1.3. *Christological Ordeal as Recalibrating Paul's Legitimacy*

In light of Paul's failed ordeal as construed by his detractors, 2 Cor. 13:3-4 contributes to Paul's ongoing recalibration of the characteristics of the authentic apostolic ordeal and by extension the social fabric of the community. In a canonical letter intent upon an amicable return, 13:3-4 indicates the ends to which the earlier accounts point; it presents the apostolic ordeal, *par excellence*. Paul references the supposed failed ordeal in 13:2-3a in which he repeats the threat given during the intermediate visit (13:2). The devastating evaluation of his failure to deliver the promised punishment is evident in 13:3a as he refers to the question of his legitimacy as Christ's spokesperson. Any claim to legitimacy in Corinth requires the passing of an ordeal (δοκιμή). Paul explicitly ties the nature of the δοκιμή to the Christological sequence. Paul argues that any apostolic δοκιμή must accurately reflect the character of the Messiah in whose name Paul speaks, therefore, challenging the logical and social foundations upon which the claims of illegitimacy rest. Thus, in 13:4ab, Paul demonstrates the two phases in Christ's passion, the crucifixion and resurrection. The former phase involves passivity and non-aggression, the latter, God's intervention resulting in vindication and empowerment. Unlike the previous ordeals, the two phases of the Christological δοκιμή correspond to two separate visits to Corinth.[33] From this vantage, his previous visit did not demonstrate his martial impotence, but simply the passivity and non-aggression of the Messiah (cf. 10:1) associated with the first phase in the Christological sequence. The second phase would commence upon his return as God acted to empower and vindicate Paul as δόκιμος (10:14), thus demonstrating his legitimacy.

Inasmuch as ordeals functioned in antiquity to reveal the truth about one's character and to establish one's place in the social hierarchy, Paul's redefinition likely possesses didactic and parenetic elements.[34] Ordeal accounts of leading figures not only depicted and reinforced the defining qualities of a communal ethos, but also did so by depicting the actions of a figure that saved the community. We recall that upon Paul's intermediate visit, he was challenged by the immoral group and that according to the

---

33. Helge K. Nielsen, "Paulus' Verwendung des Begriffs Δύναμις. Eine Replik zur Kreuztheologie," in *Die Paulinische Literature und Theologie. Anlässlich der 50. jährigen Gründungs-Feier der Universität von Aarhus*, hg.v. Sigfred Pederson, Teologiske Studier 7 (Arhus: Forlaget Aros, 1980), 146.

34. Similarly, Mario M. DiCicco, *Paul's Use of Ethos, Pathos, and Logos in 2 Corinthians 10–13*, MBPS 31 (Lewiston, NY: Mellen, 1995), 95.

canons of such an encounter, the public court of reputation evaluated Paul's inaction as evidence of impotence. There is good reason to suppose that the sexual profligacy counselled against in 1 Corinthians (6:12-20) and present during the second visit reflect the appropriation of elite values. As well, Paul's failure to affect discipline as threatened evidenced the failure to manifest martial discipline in accord with elite values. As demonstrated, analogous social formations often appropriated elite syntax and ethos, aiming to advertise imperial connections and to participate within the wider elite social apparatus. A similar impulse among some in Corinth likely lies at the root of the Corinthian crisis (§2.5.1). In 2 Corinthians, the issue has accelerated. The cultural compromise results in another Jesus, Spirit, and gospel (11:4) advanced by rivals who apparently exhibit many of the qualities that Paul rejected (11:1-16, 20).

The sequence in 2 Cor. 13:4 thus challenges the value system upon which Paul was deemed illegitimate and attempts to inscribe an alternative ethos. Martin summarizes 13:4 as the "grand (and noble) attempt by Paul to convince the Corinthians of their wrongdoing."[35] It is also Paul's attempt to set things to rights. Barton observes that the fluidity of a contest culture meant status was never fixed; individuals could retake lost social space.[36] Paul, in redefining the contours of the ordeal itself, however, does not simply threaten to win a future conflict, thus, proving himself. Rather, in the context of questions about character, Paul appeals to the once crucified, now risen Messiah as the ground of all deliberations concerning authentic apostleship or communal ethos.[37] As Jeffrey Crafton writes, "the Corinthians maintained a well-established system of social and religious standards against which leaders were judged. According to the Corinthians, Paul did not measure up. According to Paul, the Corinthians needed to change their measuring rod."[38] This is done in 13:4 along with the other ordeal narrations by highlighting both Christ's and Paul's weakness and passivity, which is reversed through God's potent intervention—all of which is paradigmatic of another evaluative and normative system, which Paul hopes supplants the criteria that led to so many problems in Corinth.[39] As the aggressive acts of heroes established and nourished many ancient communities' values,

---

35. Martin, *2 Corinthians*, 476.
36. Barton, *Roman Honor*, 35.
37. Raymond Pickett, *The Cross in Corinth: The Social Significance of the Death of Jesus*, JSNTSup 143 (Sheffield: Sheffield Academic, 1997), 202–3.
38. Crafton, *Agency*, 55.
39. Similarly DiCicco, *Paul's Use of Ethos*, 96.

Paul discursively rescues the communal definition of heroism in the face of an attempt to consign his apostleship and its ethos to oblivion in favor of a more culturally acceptable Jesus and apostleship. What appears initially (13:2-3) as a culturally recognizable therapy by ordeal in which Paul overpowers his adversaries in return, becomes a rather counter-cultural therapy for his auditors. Paul spares the community in his passive response to affront and exit (13:2), and he will return empowered not because of his own aggression and energetic response, but because of the vindicating power of God. The parenetic implications for communal ethos become clearer in 13:5-10.

6.1.4. *Return as Life: Paul and Other Dissidents*

Crucially, in 2 Cor. 13:3-4, Paul refers not simply to a redefined ordeal, but *an ordeal that includes and highlights a geographic return as life* (ζάω, 13:4d). While considering the immediate context (13:2, 10) ζήσομεν εἰς ὑμᾶς implies expulsionary discipline, as stated above, the expression possesses a broader valence. Interpreters highlight the eschatological significance attached to Paul's return. Following Koch and Munck, Aejmeleus claims, "he might have thought that the final eschatological judgment would be anticipated in a specific and odd way in Corinth simultaneously with his coming there."[40] However, Aejmaleaus observes, "the verb 'live' in this [punitive] connection is not the most natural verb," only to conclude, "but Paul probably uses it here for the purpose of formulating his own situation and rhetorical stance as symmetrically as possible with the two-phase situation of Christ described in 13.4a."[41] This risks suggesting that Paul dictated himself into a corner, using an unnatural term for a desirable rhetorical effect. Rather, ζήσομεν εἰς ὑμᾶς is a sublime expression for Paul when referring to his arrival in eschatological terms (1 Cor. 4:18-21) and in light of eschatological realities (2 Cor. 1:13-14, 15-16), not least now in light of his impotent prior presence. Paul also represents his deliverances from afflictions as resurrection-like rescues (2 Cor. 1:8-11). Thus, ζάω points to a divinely empowered efficacy in return.

Similarly, the lexical reference to life and the broader semantic domain is native to returning exiles. The *l'esprit de retour* consumed exiles such that those fortunate to return might logically conclude they had returned from a metaphoric death to life. The discourse of return as renewal/

---

40. Aejmeleus, "Christ Is Weak," 130.
41. Aejmeleus, "Christ Is Weak," 130; see also Nielson, "Δύναμις," 145–6.

revivification/resurrection is present in biblical and post-biblical texts as well as the broader Graeco-Roman contexts, although most of the evidence lies with the former.

Graeco-Roman authors can equate the spatial and social return with renewal and revivification. In a fragment, Alcaeus prays to Zeus, Hera, and Dionysius, "save (ῥύεσθε) us from these toils and vexatious exile."[42] For at least one Graeco-Roman writer whose prayers were answered, the link to revivification was clear. Upon his impending return, Cicero writes to Atticus using a Greek term to describe his return: "My friends' letters beckon me to a Triumph, something I feel I ought not to neglect in view of this second birth (παλιγγενεαίαν) of mine."[43] He sounds the same note in his speech before the Senate in which Cicero's return is to be marked as his new (eternal) birthday:

> Finally, what of the fact that upon the day which Lentulus made a day of new birth for myself, my brother, and my children, a day destined not to die with the present age, but to be held on record for all eternity,—the day, I mean, whereon he, in the assembly of the Centuries, which above all other assemblies our ancestors wished to be called and considered most authoritative, summoned me back to my country.[44]

Claassen comments on the passage, "if death is exile; then return is rebirth."[45]

Return as revivification is more attested in Old Testament and post-biblical texts, indicating an overlap in and expansion of displacement logic and discourse.[46] The post-biblical writing of Josephus demonstrates such an overlap. Josephus refers to Judah's return from exile as τὴν ἀνάκτησιν καὶ παλιγγενεσίαν τῆς πατρίδος, employing the same term used by Cicero to describe his return.[47]

While Josephus's reference is highly intelligible to a Graeco-Roman audience, the idea of Judah's return as a rebirth or resurrection is deeply rooted in the Old Testament. Isaiah 26:17-19 (LXX) involves a likely reference to the Assyrian crisis, which is reversed. The deathliness of 26:18 is reversed by Yahweh's promise in 26:19: ἀναστήσονται οἱ νεκροί,

---

42. Fr. 129.11-12 (Campbell): ἐκ δὲ τῶν[δ]ε μόχων / αργαλέας τε φύγας ῥ[ύεσθε], as in Ewen L. Bowie, "Early Expatriates: Displacement and Exile in Archaic Poetry," in Gaertner, ed., *Writing Exile*, 34.

43. Cicero, *Att.* 6.6.

44. Cicero, *Red. sen.* 27.

45. Claassen, *Displaced Persons*, 160.

46. Here I largely follow the argument of Boakye, *Death and Life*, 30–42.

47. Josephus, *Ant.* 11.66.

καὶ ἐγερθήσονται οἱ ἐν τοῖς μνημείοις. Similarly, Hos. 5:14 depicts exile for both Judah and Israel, contextually linked to failure to keep the covenant. Exile itself, poetically expressed as the devastating result of a lion (Yahweh) attacking its prey, is represented as a death. In Hos. 6:1-2, return from exile is represented as healing and revival. The language in 6:1 refers to divine reversals of Ephraim's fortunes in the form of return. In 6:2, the MT יְקִמֵנוּ וְנִחְיֶה is translated as ἀναστησόμεθα καὶ ζησόμεθα (LXX). While much debate surrounds the text, it is clear that 6:1-2 envisions a historical and political reversal of circumstances based on a return to the Lord (6:1). Boakye states, "Hosea 6:2-3 belongs with the tradition of freedom from captivity narratives in terms of resurrection."[48]

The most vivid depiction of return as revivification belongs to Ezek. 37:1-14. There the dramatic vision of disarticulated bones raised to life by the Spirit supplies a vivid metaphor for Israel's exile as death and return as resurrection. This is evident in 37:12 (LXX): ἐγὼ ἀνοίγω ὑμῶν τὰ μνήματα καὶ ἀνάξω ὑμᾶς ἐκ τῶν μνημάτων ὑμῶν καὶ εἰσάξω ὑμᾶς εἰς τὴν γῆν τοῦ Ισραηλ. Other examples reinforce the tradition of social and spatial return as revivification. Psalm 80 (79 LXX) is an Ephraimite lament in which prayers for restoration from national disaster, perhaps exile, appear as requests for return to life (ζωώσεις ἡμᾶς, Ps. 79:19).

The metaphorical link between displacement and death, return and renewal is evident in Lk. 15:32. The runaway son, who finds himself at the hands of pagan overlords only to come to his senses and return is perhaps Israel's story writ small.[49] In 15:32, Jesus states, "This brother of yours was dead [νεκρός] and he lived [ἔζησεν] and having been lost, he was found [εὑρέθη]." To describe the return of the son against the larger political backdrop with the phrase "was dead and he lived" fits within a logic shared across antiquity.[50] Thus, "to live" in the context of political displacement refers frequently to a reversal *volte-face* involving social restoration and spatial return.

Paul's description of his return (2 Cor. 13:1) with the verb ζάω (13:4d) likely employs a version of the return as revivification trope tailored to the situation. Like biblical and post-biblical usages, 13:4d possesses a similar eschatological coloring of a dramatic reversal in socio-spatial contexts. This is consonant with the more proximate discussion concerning Paul's presence in Corinth found initially in 1 Cor. 4:18-21. There, as we have already demonstrated, Paul's proleptic arrival is likewise presented with

---

48. Boakye, *Death and Life*, 37.
49. N. T. Wright, *Jesus and the Victory of God*, Christian Origins and the Question of God 2 (Minneapolis: Fortress, 1996), 126–30.
50. See Boakye, *Death and Life*, 41.

a measure of eschatological realism connected to Paul's martial strength and legitimacy. Looking back upon that visit in 2 Corinthians and its aftermath, it is entirely logical for Paul to continue to use eschatological expressions, although now drawing upon a broader displacement discourse in referring to his return as life and thus a reversal of the current judgment against him.

As scholars notice, Paul's usage suggests the possibility of or threat of force in return. On its face, a promise of force appears to call into question Paul's status as a political dissident. How can someone devoid of social power and legitimacy speak of his arrival as empowered? Does this not point to Paul's social power rather than away from it? And does this not suggest the community rather than Paul stands under sanction? For example, Walter Schmithals, in denying the possibility of a challenge to Paul's authority followed by his exit, indignantly claims of a parallel passage, "And what kind of unique light would it shed on the character of Paul if he should have written [2 Cor] 13:10 after he had left Corinth in flight."[51] First, there is a difference between rhetoric and reality and it seems clear that so much of 2 Cor. 13:3-4 aims at reconfiguring the debate concerning Paul's legitimacy, that is, an attempt to reclaim authority rather than simply acknowledge its existence. Second, sanctions and violence often accompanied return from displacement. According to Xenophon, after the democrats return to Athens, Thrasybulus warns the remaining oligarchs that they submit to the previous democratic laws.[52] Sulla, having been declared an exile by Marius, marched on Rome a second time and, assuming the dictatorship, launched a brutal series of proscriptions.[53] During his own exile, Dio speaks of reflection upon "wars waged by exiles seeking thus to be restored to their homes, wars waged beyond their strength against the popular governments and despotisms."[54] More representative of non-elite society, Robert Garland claims that returning exiles would often seek recriminations for abuse suffered.[55] Thus, the implication of punishment in return fits the broad features of a returning exile and is deployed by Paul in order to make a claim to social power. Since social and spatial expulsion stands at the center of the Corinthian crisis, Paul almost certainly refers to pushing out his detractors upon arrival. In conclusion, 13:10, like 13:4 and other passages, sheds a great deal of light upon Paul's character. It is precisely because of the Messiah's vindication

---

51. Schmithals, *Gnosticism*, 104.
52. Xenophon, *Hell*. 2.4.41-41.
53. Plutarch, *Sull*. 31.
54. Dio Chrysostom, *Exil*. 6.
55. Garland, *Wandering*, 182–3.

in the death–life sequence, that Paul can be confident that his return will be divinely empowered. Paul's logic of a vindicated return, including the possibility of punitive action, presumes, indeed relies upon, a past unsuccessful, impotent visit in particular, and a general mode of administration that cuts against the grain of the ideal Mediterranean male.

6.1.5. Conclusions

In 2 Cor. 13:1-4, Paul announces his impending return will bring to conclusion the ordeal in Corinth (13:2-3a) in a way consistent with the ordeals in Asia, Troas, and Damascus. Perhaps, in pursuing a harmonious return to Corinth, the tales of Paul's experiences of Christological reversal across the Mediterranean appeared as a triumphal procession (2:14).[56] In any event, if read canonically, Paul argues, appealing to his Christo-logic, that God would do for Paul in Corinth what he had done elsewhere.

Paul frames both his (past and present) weakness as one phase in the Christological sequence. Just as Christ was crucified and now lives because of God's power (13:4ab), so too Paul's supposed feckless response to an affront will be superseded in the second phase by God's intervention in Paul's return (13:4cd). The two phases correspond to the characteristics of Paul's two visits. The striking parallelism in 13:4 corrects the triumphalist notion in 13:3a that Christ "is not weak with respect to you but powerful among you." In doing so, Paul has explicitly redefined the contours of the apostolic test and so challenged the criteria upon which he is evaluated as illegitimate. Rather than the display of aggressive, violent masculinity in the response to an affront, the apostolic ordeal highlights passivity and non-aggression in the face of assault, entrusting one's vindication and empowerment to the God who raised Christ from the dead. While the phrase ζήσομεν εἰς ὑμᾶς implies a threat of expulsion, the expression reflects Paul's frequent eschatological inflection of his visits to Corinth, and in the context of Paul's hostile absence, it also reflects a widely travelled trope, which represented the restoration and return of an exile as

---

56. Early days of regimes were oft marked by the return of exiles ousted by the previous rule. For the democrats' triumphal return to Athens, see Xenophon, *Hell.* 2.4.39. "One of the most thrilling events in Athens's history was the return of the exiles following the overthrow of the Thirty. The democrats staffed a triumphal entry into Athens under arms that culminated in the sacrifice to Athena performed on the Acropolis" (Garland, *Wandering*, 183). For Sulla's triumph for the Mithridatic War, which included not simply the spoils of war, but recalled exiles marching into Rome to reclaim their civic status, see Plutarch, *Sull.* 34.1. For Cicero's representation of his return from exile as a triumph, see Cicero, *Att.* 4.1.4-5; *Sest.* 131; Plutarch, *Cic.* 33.5.

metaphorical revivification. Thus, in the face of sanction and challenge, Paul entrusts his social and spatial return to God even as it suggests the divinely empowered discipline and removal of his detractors.

6.2. *The Corinthian Test (2 Corinthians 13:5-10)*

Paul's final comments of the letter body involve a discussion of the community's legitimacy (13:5-6), an offer of prayer for the community's restoration (13:7-9), before a final appeal for his amicable return to Corinth (13:10).

6.2.1. *Questioning the Community's Legitimacy (2 Corinthians 13:5-6)*

For a text as rhetorically intense as 2 Cor. 13:1-4, Paul manages to supply his audience with a further jolt in 13:5, stating, ἑαυτοὺς πειράζετε εἰ ἐστὲ ἐν τῇ πίστει, ἑαυτοὺς δοκιμάζετε. What initially appears as a discussion of Paul's legitimacy transitions into a discussion of the political legitimacy of the community itself (13:5-10). The emphatic use of ἑαυτούς and the use of asyndeton suggests heightened emotion and urgency.[57] The imperative πειράζετε and δοκιμάζετε are likely synonymous, while the interrogative particle εἰ functions as a marker of an indirect question the content of which is ἐστὲ ἐν τῇ πίστει.[58] Paul commands, "Test yourselves whether you are in the faith; examine yourselves." Thus, in a segment in which Paul faces scrutiny as to his legitimacy because of his behavior and absence, Paul turns the tables on the community and commands their own self-examination as to whether it is legitimate.[59]

In 2 Cor. 13:5b, Paul supplies the rhetorical question, "Or don't you know yourselves Jesus Christ is among you [ἐν ὑμῖν]?" With the particle οὐκ, the question anticipates an affirmative answer. The positive answer is not likely the result of the self-examination.[60] Rather, Paul is confident the community would affirm that Christ is among them (ἐν ὑμῖν; cf. 13:3b). They would happily give "recognition" (ἐπιγινώσκω) to their own legitimacy while questioning Paul's (cf. 1:13-14). The pressing question is, as Furnish asserts, whether, "they really understand what this means: that Christ with them as their Lord, whose presence both graces them with new life and calls them to obedience."[61] It is a question of which iteration

---

57. Schmeller, *Zweite Brief*, 2:393; see Long, *II Corinthians*, 261–3.
58. Long, *II Corinthians*, 251.
59. Bachmann, *Zweite Brief*, 408.
60. Aejmelaeus, *Schwachheit*, 380.
61. Furnish, *II Corinthians*, 577.

of the Messiah they affirm, the culturally compromised, "different Jesus," or the Pauline Christ articulated in 13:4.

That the self-examination might not result in the same affirmation as the question in 2 Cor. 13:5b is evident from the exception, "unless you are unapproved [ἀδόκιμοί]" (13:5c). Most commentators consider 13:5c as an instance of irony, considering the affirmation in 13:5b as evidence that the community will ultimately pass the test.[62] Others suggest that the exception εἰ μήτι entertains the real possibility that the community will fail the test.[63] According to Guthrie, 13:5c is similar to other Pauline texts in which Paul "makes a statement of fact about the spiritual condition of those to whom he writes and then qualifies the statement" (cf. Rom. 8:9; 11:22; Col. 1:22-23).[64] If so, the qualification is not unlike the shift from 13:3b to 13:4. Without the possibility of the Corinthians' failure to pass the test, Paul's threats in 13:2 along with so much of 13:1-10 and the epistle become little more than rhetorical bluster. Perhaps, along with Gundry Volf and Vegge, it is best to perceive nuance in 13:5, in which the results of the examination may differ between those in the majority (2:6) and those still in defiance.[65]

The command for the Corinthians to examine themselves demonstrates the parenetic function of 2 Cor. 13:1-4. Barnett and Oropeza find the imperative for the Corinthians "to test themselves" as an echo of the well-known Delphic motto, "know yourself."[66] In this light, the summons is one of inward reflection in pursuit of wisdom, perhaps guided by Christ in prayer.[67] However, Cicero reinterpreted the motto, stating, "Accordingly the Pythian Apollo bids us 'learn to know ourselves'; but the sole road to self-knowledge is to know our powers of body and of mind [*nostri vim corporis animique*], and to follow the path of life that gives us their full employment."[68] This, of course, brings us full circle to the language of

---

62. Martin, *2 Corinthians*, 479; Volf, *Paul and Perseverance*, 219; Barnett, *Second Epistle*, 608; Perry C. Brown, "What Is the Meaning of 'Examine Yourselves' in 2 Corinthians 13:5?," *BSac* 154 (1997): 184; Harris, *Second Epistle*, 921.

63. Windisch, *Zweite Korintherbrief*, 421; Filson, "Second Epistle," 420; Aejmelaeus, *Schwachheit*, 380; Guthrie, *2 Corinthians*, 639–40.

64. Guthrie, *2 Corinthians*, 639.

65. Gundry Volf, *Perseverance*, 224–5; Vegge, *2 Corinthians*, 350; cf. Prümm, *Diakonia Pneumatos*, 1:719–22.

66. Barnett, *Second Epistle*, 608 n. 3; Oropeza, *Second Corinthians*, 719; Chrysostom, *4 Regn.* 57; *2 Glor.* 3; Plutarch, *Adul. amic.* 25 [65F]; Epictetus, *Diss.* 3.22.12.19-20.

67. Aejmelaeus, *Schwachheit*, 380.

68. Cicero, *Fin.* 5.16 [43].

the ordeal. Barton comments upon Cicero's interpretation, stating, "One learned through the contest the strength of one's body and spirit."[69] That Paul turns the tables on the community is no rhetorical sleight of hand. In light of the criticism of martial weakness against Paul as seen in his failure in an ordeal against his detractors, the summons to self-examination suggests that the community now must face its own eschatologically colored ordeal.

In 2 Cor. 13:6, the discourse develops in a surprising direction. The statement, "Now, I hope that you will know that we are not unapproved" is more likely an expression of desire for recognition of Paul's authority rather than a veiled threat.[70] Paul's hope in 13:6 is similar to that in 2 Cor. 1:13-14 (cf. 5:11) and thus indicates the centrality of the communal ordeal to the purpose of the epistle. Whereas the hope in 1:13-14 is that of the community's complete recognition of Paul resulting in a reciprocal boast in the "Day of [our] Lord Jesus," in 13:6 there exists a hope for the community's knowledge of Paul's approved status in the context of the community's eschatologically significant ordeal (13:4d).

The import of the examination is seen in the logic of 2 Cor. 13:6. Bultmann observes, "Surprisingly enough, Paul does not say ὅτι οὐκ ἀδόκιμοί ἐστε (or ὅτι δόκιμοί ἐστε). This indicates that both perceptions coincide."[71] Consistently commentators remark that 13:6 demonstrates that Paul and the Corinthians' fates are interwoven. To acknowledge Paul's legitimacy as articulated in 13:4 and demonstrated elsewhere is to pass their own ordeal as approved.[72] The logic is straightforward. For the community to pass the Pauline ordeal is to acknowledge, to know, Paul's approved status and to affirm the ethos therein. If they reject Paul's status, the community will itself become illegitimate.

6.2.2. *Questions of Communal Legitimacy: A Discourse of Displacement*

The discourse of a community's political legitimacy vis-à-vis the legitimacy of a leading person is native to the politics of displacement. The notion of the damage done to a community by the displacement of a leading citizen was known.[73] In Chapter 2, we demonstrated that one

---

69. Barton, *Roman Honor*, 35 n. 7.

70. Furnish, *II Corinthians*, 578; Thrall, *Second Epistle*, 2:892–3; Guthrie, *2 Corinthians*, 640–1, and others; contra Meyer, *Corinthians*, 2:508; Aejmelaeus, *Schwachheit*, 381–2, and others.

71. Bultmann, *Second Letter*, 246.

72. Similarly, Harris, *Second Epistle*, 922; Schmeller, *Zweite Brief*, 2:395, and others.

73. Sarah T. Cohen, "Cicero's Roman Exile," in Gaertner, ed., *Writing Exile*, 112.

of the aims associated with political displacement was delegitimizing a seminal figure often to reconstitute the community's memory space (§2.3.3). According to the same logic, when prominent figures went into exile, it was possible for dissenting voices to reverse the logic and argue that the community itself had become illegitimate.[74] To a degree, the rhetoric of political legitimacy appears to be bound to the practice of displacement.[75] The idea that the hostile absence of a leading figure results in the damage to the community's legitimacy likely finds it roots in the criticism of various tyrants' unjust rule evidenced by expulsions. For example, Alcaeus's prayer for his rescue from exile is paralleled with the desire for rescue of the people from its woes (δᾶμον ὑπὲξ ἀχεων ῥύεσθαι), caused by the tyrant Pittacus's, "devouring the city" (δάπτει τάν πόλιν).[76]

Thus, it was possible to claim the community rather than the dissident was actually exiled and illegitimate. Aulus Gellius records an excerpt of a letter from Quintus Metellus Numidicus (fl. ca. 160–ca. 91 BCE) written from *interdictio*: "They [Rome] indeed were cut off from every right and honour, I lack neither water nor fire and I enjoy the greatest glory."[77] In response to *interdictio*, Numidicus ironically comments the state has lost status and honor, not him. In his *Post reditum* speeches, Cicero goes to great lengths to argue that Clodius's lawlessness resulted in the exile of the *res publica*, rather than himself. In the face of violence he states, "with the republic banished, there could be no place for me in this city."[78] The violence against his estate evidenced the "extinction of the republic."[79] Indicating that his exit was a response to the absence of the *res publica* from Rome he states, "But realizing that my absence from this city would not outlast the absence from it of the republic itself, I did not think it my duty to remain there after its extinction."[80] Elsewhere he admits his exile but claims it occurred simultaneously with that of *res publica*: "it [the *res publica*] had shared my banishment."[81] The tradition is evident in Brutus's *De Virtute*. Seneca reports that after Brutus's failed attempt to retrieve Marcellus from exile, "he felt that he himself was going into exile instead of leaving him behind in exile."[82] Of Aristides

---

74. Cohen, "Exile," 70–84, and "Cicero," 109–28.
75. Cohen, "Cicero," 112.
76. Fr. 129.20, 23-24 as in Bowie, "Early Expatriates," 34.
77. Aulus Gellius, *Noct. att.* 17.2.7.
78. Cicero, *Red. pop.* 14.
79. Cicero, *Dom.* 137.
80. Cicero, *Red. sen.* 34.
81. Cicero, *Dom.* 141.
82. Seneca, *Helv.* 9.4.

banishment from Athens, Valerius Maximus (ca. 20 BCE–50 CE) writes, "Fortunate Athens, that after his exile could find a good man or a citizen to love her after banishing one in whose company Probity herself went abroad!"[83] The underlying logic seems to involve the conception of a political community, which opens itself to the charge of illegitimacy through unjust displacement.

Likewise, the restoration of dissidents could be portrayed as the restoration of a community's legitimacy. Cicero claims, "the whole human race testified by official and unofficial pronouncements that, unless I should be restored the republic could not be saved. But the reality of this restoration depends, gentlemen, upon your verdict."[84] Before the Senate, he states,

> My absence synchronized with the absence of laws, courts of justice, magisterial jurisdiction, the authority of the senate, freedom, a plentiful corn-supply, all reverence and all compunction in matters human or divine. Were these things to be lost to us for ever, I should rather bewail your misfortune than regret my own; but I recognized that, should a day come when they should be recalled, it would be my duty to return with them. I did not doubt that, if she were restored, she herself would bring me back with her.[85]

Similar logic is present in Seneca's comment on Marcellus: "The senate did indeed by public petitions obtain his recall, being so troubled and sad that on that day they all seemed to feel as Brutus did and to plead not for Marcellus but for themselves, lest they should be exiles if they should be without him."[86] If Marcellus returned, so the logic implies, the state itself would be restored. These sources suggest a possible underlying broader displacement logic in which the status of the community may be bound to the civic status of leading figures.

While it is unclear how much the trope of the exiled community pervaded non-elite society, Paul's logic of the illegitimate community vis-à-vis an illegitimate leader plausibly employs a version of it. The community's recognition of himself as approved or disapproved relates directly to the community's status as legitimate or illegitimate (2 Cor. 13:5-6). As our study has demonstrated, the intermediate visit involved a direct affront to Paul's governance of the community, to which Paul offered further threat and left Corinth. Such behavior could easily be construed as a defeat and displacement of the apostle. It is, thus, reasonable that in response to

---

83. Valerius Maximus, 5.3 ext. 3d.
84. Cicero, *Dom.* 99–100.
85. Cicero, *Red. sen.* 34.
86. Seneca, *Helv.* 9.6, trans. Cohen, "Exile," 76.

intermediate events and the ongoing campaign against him, Paul called into question the community's legitimacy because of its own lawless conduct and rejection of its apostle. In view of the lawless depiction in 12:20-21, and the ongoing campaign against him, Paul too can refer to the community as damaged and potentially unapproved.

This should not surprise the audience. Paul begins 2 Corinthians clearly hoping his letter will result in reciprocal recognition at the eschatological judgment (1:13-14). In Paul's discussion of his fitness (ἱκανός) as an apostle (2:16–3:6), he questions the fitness of the community by way of a sensory motif, describing those who mistakenly perceive his ministry as οἱ ἀπολλύμενοι (4:3) and οἱ ἄπιστοι (4:4).[87] According to Paul Duff, Paul portrays "his detractors as standing beyond the bounds of the ἐκκλησία."[88] Furthermore, in 2 Cor. 3:1–7:1, in response to judgments of illegitimacy, Paul carefully depicts his ministry of the καινή διαθήκη as energized by the Spirit (3:6), echoing Old Testament end-of-exile prophecy (Ezek. 36–37; Jer. 31). Paul portrays his work among the Corinthians as the herald of reconciliation (5:18-21), announcing to Corinth the eschatological day of salvation, the end of exile (6:2) from Isa. 49:8. According to David Starling, the intertextual quotation in 2 Cor. 6:17 of the imperative from Isa. 52:11, "[situates] the readers, typologically, in Babylon on the last day of exile, summoned homeward by divine 'promises' (7:1)."[89] Thus, Paul repeatedly depicts the rebellious community as outsiders, even exiles, in need of return.

In contrast to other dissidents, Paul does not await a communal verdict for his restoration and return. It is God who establishes Paul's fitness for apostolic office (2 Cor. 3:4) and who will reinstate his leadership of the community powerfully in return (2 Cor. 13:4). Thus, Paul has appropriated and reversed the topic of his failed ordeal and the question of his apostolic status, posing to the community the reconstrued Christological ordeal and status question implying that in rejecting Paul's leadership and casting judgment upon him according to the wrong canons, it is the community after all that is in danger of being illegitimate.

6.2.3. *Prayers for Communal Restoration (2 Corinthians 13:7-9)*

The increased emphasis upon the Corinthians' status and ordeal is demonstrated in 2 Cor. 13:7. Paul writes, "Now, we pray to God that you do

---

87. Duff, *Moses*, 136, 190, 213.
88. Duff, *Moses*, 390.
89. David I. Starling, *Not My People: Gentiles as Exiles in Pauline Hermeneutics*, BZNW 184 (Berlin: de Gruyter, 2011), 106.

nothing evil."⁹⁰ The subsequent ἵνα clauses mark the purpose of the prayer rather than its content.⁹¹ Thus, Paul continues, "not so that we might appear approved, but so that you might do what is good, though we might seem as if unapproved." What appear as aphorisms are in fact references to the parenetic and forensic aims of the epistle. To do nothing evil and to do good involves primarily the acceptance of Paul as Corinth's apostle, demonstrated by the completion of the collection, the behavior advocated by the immoral group (12:21; cf. 6:14–7:1), factionalism (2:5; 12:20), and support for the rivals.⁹² Thus Bultmann comments, "the prayer is thus equivalent in content with ὑμᾶς εἶναι δοκίμους, or with the prayer for the Corinthians' κατάρτισις (v.9)."⁹³ Thus, "the ὡς indicates that the ἀδόκιμος as uttered from the Corinthians' viewpoint is not a real ἀδόκιμος."⁹⁴ That Paul might appear ἀδόκιμος refers specifically to the possibility that Paul might not deliver punitive fireworks. As 13:6 makes clear, if the community "does good" then that is a result of their recognition of Paul's status.

In 2 Cor. 13:8, Paul clarifies the comment that he might appear ἀδόκιμος. The conjunction γάρ indicates 13:8 supplies the grounds for why Paul would appear as unapproved in 13:7.⁹⁵ Furnish comments, "there is widespread agreement that v.8 sounds like a general maxim affirming the sovereign power of *the truth*, but it is difficult to know exactly why Paul includes such a statement here."⁹⁶ For many commentators, the accent of study falls on the term ἀλήθεια.⁹⁷ However, in an epistle focused on the question of apostolic power, the verb δύναμαι is key.⁹⁸ The meaning of οὐ δυνάμεθά τι comes close to the very accusation against Paul.⁹⁹ However, Paul explains that his empowerment (δύναμαι) comes from God to act for the truth. Thus, the term ἀλήθεια likely is synonymous with τὸ καλὸν ποιεῖν, referring to Corinthians' successful examination.¹⁰⁰ While there may be an apologetic element, Paul is also offering paranesis on divine

---

90. For ὑμᾶς as the accusative subject of ποιῆσαι, see Long, *II Corinthians*, 253, and others; contra, Lietzmann, *Korinther I–II*, 160.
91. Windisch, *Zweite Korintherbrief*, 442; Harris, *Second Epistle*, 923; Long, *II Corinthians*, 253; Vegge, *2 Corinthians*, 351.
92. Harris, *Second Epistle*, 924.
93. Bultmann, *Second Letter*, 247.
94. Bultmann, *Second Letter*, 247.
95. Meyer, *Corinthians*, 2:510; Long, *II Corinthians*, 254.
96. Furnish, *II Corinthians*, 579.
97. Bultmann, *Second Letter*, 247–8; Barrett, *Second Epistle*, 339–40.
98. Barnett, *Second Epistle*, 611; Schmeller, *Zweite Brief*, 2.397.
99. Schmeller, *Zweite Brief*, 2:397.
100. Bultmann, *Second Letter*, 248; Harris, *Second Epistle*, 925.

empowerment. Paul has no power in and of himself. His ordeals aim to teach the Corinthians to rely on the God's transformative power, rather than human assertiveness.

Paul continues to offer clarification in 2 Cor. 13:9, which comprises two sentences: "For we rejoice whenever we are weak but you are strong. This, indeed, we are praying for—your restoration." In 13:9a, the conjunction γάρ continues to provide explanatory grounds and thus clarification, likely of Paul's claim in 13:8 that he can do nothing against the truth.[101] Here, strength and weakness are contrasted in a surprising way. Weakness refers to Paul's inability to enforce sanction because the community has deemed him approved.[102] Thus, any sense that Paul is weak is entirely ironic.[103] If there is a polemic implied here, as Martin and Barnett claim, it is a critique of the very ethos at the heart of the crisis of authority.[104] As Bultmann comments, if they repent, it is only because they admit Paul is δόκιμος and δυνατός in Christ.[105] Similarly, the community as οἱ δυνατοί is now significantly repurposed vis-à-vis the communal sentiment in 13:3b to reflect a repentant and enlivened community.[106] Lambrecht observes, "one is really strong when restored to good conduct."[107] Remarkably, the power that Paul hopes the community might experience is the power he claims that he will experience in the second phase of the Christological sequence in return to Corinth (13:4d).[108] Thus, 13:9a hopefully portrays a community that has passed its ordeal by submitting to Paul's example and authority, and thus, is experiencing empowerment through their own divine reversal.

The recurrence of εὐχόμεθα in 2 Cor. 13:9b indicates an *inclusio* with 13:7 and thus a close relationship between 13:7-9.[109] The likely prospective use of the direct object τοῦτο makes τὴν...κατάρτισιν appositional, indicating the content of Paul's prayer.[110] The term κατάρτισις, a biblical *hapax legomenon* and rare in Greek sources, may be translated

---

101. Meyer, *Corinthians*, 2:511; Harris, *Second Epistle*, 926; for the argument that 13:9 supports 13:7, see Bultmann, *Second Letter*, 248; Vegge, *2 Corinthians*, 352; Guthrie, *2 Corinthians*, 643.

102. Meyer, *Corinthians*, 2:511; Harris, *Second Epistle*, 926; Schmeller, *Zweite Brief*, 2:398; contra, Barnett, *Second Epistle*, 612.

103. Vegge, *2 Corinthians*, 353.

104. Martin, *2 Corinthians*, 483; Barnett, *Second Epistle*, 611.

105. Bultmann, *Second Letter*, 248; contra Bachmann, *Zweite Brief*, 412.

106. Similarly, Martin, *2 Corinthians*, 484.

107. Lambrecht, *Second Corinthians*, 222; cf. Guthrie, *2 Corinthians*, 644.

108. Similarly, Long, *II Corinthians*, 255.

109. Long, *II Corinthians*, 257.

110. Heinrici, *Zweite Brief*, 432.

"restoration," "training," and "the process of perfecting."[111] The cognates καταρτίζω and καταρτισμός supply evidence of meanings including "equip," "restoration," "reconciliation," "prepare," and "put in order."[112] The majority of interpreters supply the gloss "restoration."[113] The *inclusio* suggests that the meaning of κατάρτισις is indicated by the content in 13:7-9. If so, κατάρτισις would refer primarily to ceasing evil and doing good, referring primarily to the affirmation of Paul's political legitimacy and attendant ethos, completing the collection, rejecting the rivals, and welcoming Paul back to Corinth.[114] The sense is synonymous with Paul's appeal for reconciliation (5:20), although here the emphasis is on reconciliation and return.[115] With 13:5-6 in view, κατάρτισις would more specifically refer to the Corinthians passing their ordeal and demonstrating that they are indeed "in the faith" (13:5).

Panning out to the correspondence, Paul begins 1 Corinthians aiming at restoring concord (ἦτε κατηρτισμένοι ἐν τῷ αὐτῷ νοΐ καὶ ἐν τῇ αὐτῇ γνώμῃ, 1 Cor. 1:10) during a season of factionalism (σχίσματα, 1:10; ἔριδες, 1:11). As White reasons, chs. 1–4 aim at the restoration of concord, but Paul provides a final warning in 1 Cor. 4:18-21 if restoration does occur: "if restoration isn't achieved, 1 Cor. 4:21 offers and opposite measure: removal from the community."[116] While the translation, "restoration" is accurate, it is important to perceive its relation not only to restored relationships (God, Paul, factions), but a restoration of the community's status as approved and the avoidance of its opposite: removal from the community upon Paul's empowered arrival.[117]

What is remarkable about Paul's usage of κατάρτισις within 2 Cor. 13:1-10 is the degree to which the argument is the inverse of the audience's expectations according to the socio-historical situation. In a situation as we have described in which a leading figure exits a community in response to a challenge to his leadership, with subsequent judgments against him, and evidence of further social withdrawal, we might reasonably expect an ancient leader to appeal for the restoration of his status.

---

111. LSJ, s.v. "κατάρτισις"; BDAG, s.v. "κατάρτισις."

112. LSJ, svv. "καταρτίζω," "καταρτισμός"; BDAG, svv. "καταρτίζω," "καταρτισμός."

113. Furnish, *II Corinthians*, 573; Thrall, *Second Epistle*, 2:871; Harris, *Second Epistle*, 928.

114. Schmeller, *Zweite Brief*, 2:399.

115. Barnett, *Second Epistle*, 613.

116. White, *Discipline*, 179.

117. In this, Louw and Nida are justified in claiming κατάρτισις may be translated as "becoming fully qualified" (L&N, §75.5).

However, Paul through his rhetoric of political legitimacy questions the status of the community and so presents himself and the values associated with Christological sequence as the ordeal which the community must pass to be approved. Paul, thus, argues that through the intermediate visit and Paul's subsequent displacement, the community, rather than Paul, has suffered damage and elements within are in danger of expulsion. In likely drawing upon a wider discourse of displacement, Paul, who previously requested prayer for his future rescue (1:11), now prays not for his restoration, but the rehabilitation of the community to be realized in Paul's return. Such a moment would then be characterized as eschatological life for the community at Paul's return (13:4d).

6.2.4. *Final Plea for an Amicable Return (2 Corinthians 13:10)*

The final verse, 2 Cor. 13:10, demonstrates continuity with the segment and also stands somewhat detached as it reflects on the purpose of the epistle. Paul writes, "Because of this, I am writing these things while absent, in order that, when present, I may not act severely according to the authority that the Lord gave to me for building up and not tearing down." The demonstrative pronoun τοῦτο is most likely anaphoric, demonstrating a level of continuity with and development of 13:9. From this perspective, some interpreters argue 13:9b-10 offers the reason for writing chs. 10–13.[118] Yet, the aim of the epistle whether a unity or letter fragments, concerns Paul's amicable return, and, as such, may look back over the entire, unified letter.[119] As the letter ends, this aim is articulated in the sense of the Corinthians responding to their ordeal according to their exemplar Paul (and Christ). Thus, 13:10 stands parallel to 12:19.[120] As Long argues of 12:19, the text suggests the entire epistle appears as a defense of Paul's probity, which, however, aims for the community's edification.[121] If the community passes their test, Paul's return will indeed be characterized by "life" (13:4d) and return for the exiled community. The revivification will involve not only the reversal of Paul's communal status, but also the status of the repentant community.

---

118. Windisch, *Zweite Korintherbrief*, 424–5; Thrall, *Second Epistle*, 2:899–900.
119. Barnett, *Second Epistle*, 614; Garland, *2 Corinthians*, 551–2; Schmeller, *Zweite Brief*, 2:399.
120. Barnett, *Second Epistle*, 614.
121. Long, *Ancient Rhetoric*, 39–40, 118–19.

6.3. Conclusions

Paul concludes 2 Corinthians by arguing that the Corinthian ordeal will possess the marks of the Christological sequence just as in the other ordeal narratives. Yet, Paul engages and corrects the Corinthians' standard of proof by ordeal (13:3b) with the Christological sequence (13:4), which stands at the center of Paul's rhetoric of political legitimacy. The proof of apostolic status as demonstrated through the parallelism is thus redefined by the successive phases of the Christological sequence in which divine power reverses weakness. What the Corinthians misunderstood as defeat and displacement following the intermediate visit was, according to Paul, the first phase of the Christological sequence, of which the second phase would be realized in his return. In view of Paul's intermediate visit, the verb ζάω (13:4d) is a fitting description of Paul's often eschatologically colored arrivals now repackaged according to the Christological sequence, the language of other returning dissidents, and a *volte-face* reversal consistent with Paul's ordeal narrations.

The segment shifts from questions of Paul's political legitimacy to that of the community. The community is summoned to, "Test yourselves [to see] if you are in the faith. Examine yourselves" (2 Cor. 13:5). As some questioned Paul's legitimacy because of his inaction during the intermediate ordeal, Paul now places before the community its own ordeal. The nature of the Corinthian test involves, as indicated in 13:6, the affirmation of Paul and Christ as presented in 13:4 along with the ethos implied. The direct relationship between the legitimacy of a community and a leading figure is evident to interpreters. However, the background to the logic is not. In support of the thesis that Paul writes to end a period of political displacement from Corinth, exiles and those writing about exile frequently questioned the legitimacy of the community in response to unjust expulsions. Paul too, following the lawless affront of the immoral group (12:21; 13:2) and the ongoing campaign against him, questions whether the community is approved and in the faith, suggesting that it is the community, not him, that is in danger of illegitimacy and displacement. That the Corinthians' ordeal as posed by Paul involves the moral and social ethos of the community as mediated through Paul is evident from 13:7, in which Paul prays that they "might not do anything evil" and instead "do good." We contend that in contrast with the detractors' construal of the intermediate visit and its aftermath as well as the broader cultural intelligibility of a communal leader exiting in response to an affront, Paul employs the Christological sequence first to redefine the nature of an authentic ordeal and thus affirm his status as Christ's apostle to Corinth, and second, to present the community with its own ordeal, for which Paul hopes will result in a divine reversal, restoration, and return.

Summary of Findings

This attempt to interrogate the background of Paul's aim of reconciliation and return to conclude a period marked by strife and absence has produced a number of new findings previously unconsidered or underrepresented in Corinthian studies. Below we summarize the major contributions before considering implications for future investigation.

1. Attendant to the aim of reconciliation and return and consistent with the exigencies of strife and absence existed the phenomena for which we supplied the etic descriptor, political displacement, which was analyzed from the perspective of cultural conventions, political theory, penology, and non-elite society. To summarize, at each level of study, an individual's absence in the context of political displacement implied, involved, or embodied a judgment against the displaced person. With confidence, we can conclude that the broad contours of political displacement were present in the mutual cognitive environment shared by Paul and the Corinthians, and even instituted in Paul's ἐκκλησία in Corinth (1 Cor. 5:1-13; 6:9-10).
2. From the perspective of cultural conventions, political theory, and the general features of a non-elite political community, Paul's intermediate visit to Corinth and subsequent exit, a mainstay in Corinthian studies for the foreseeable future, should be understood as an intelligible occurrence of political displacement. This is largely complementary to scholars' ubiquitous narrations of the intermediate visit, although now grounded in the ancient social world and the Corinthian correspondence. On balance, the evidence (see below) indicates that Paul's absence from Corinth should be understood in a new light and of a different class than his absences from other communities. In 2 Corinthians, Paul's absence is in direct response to challenge, affront, internecine strife, and thus a recognizable instance of political displacement from which he writes to secure an amicable return.
3. While agreeing with the consensus concerning an intermediate visit by Paul to Corinth, this work rejects the copious reconstructions which foist responsibility for the negative nature of that visit upon the ὁ ἀδικήσας or the rivals. Rather, the most historically determinative texts (2 Cor. 12:21–13:2) indicate the event was characterized by a

negative interaction between Paul and a sexually immoral element in the community, although it is possible that the ὁ ἀδικήσας or the rivals are related to the event.

4. In the light of 2 Cor. 12:21–13:2 and 1 Cor. 4:18-21 as well as 1 Cor. 5:1-13; 6:1-11; 6:12-21, which form test cases for Paul's authority, the encounter during the intermediate visit is certain or virtually certain that the participants understood the encounter as an eschatologically colored ordeal, a deliberate challenge to Paul's leadership and thus a contest over the social ethos of the community, stemming from Paul's interventions in 1 Corinthians.

5. The judgments that Paul was ταπεινός (2 Cor. 10:1), ἀσθενής, and ὁ λόγος ἐξουθενημένος (10:10) during the visit implied that Paul behaved passively and left Corinth while his detractors remained (12:21). Such behavior, whether in the context of an affront or internecine strife, resonates with high probability with the phenomena of political displacement and indicates Paul's defeat and displacement from Corinth (cf. 1 Cor. 4:18-21).

6. It is virtually certain that the accusations in 2 Cor. 10:1, 10 relate to the specific judgment of Paul's political illegitimacy (10:7; 13:3a). While agreeing with the consensus that some in the community reject Paul's authoritative status, Paul's allegedly impotent behavior and exit predicates the judgment of illegitimacy in light of Paul's own discourses on the nature of ordeals and absence as judgment (1 Cor. 3:4; 4:18-21; 5:1-13; 6:9-10; 11:28-30) with clear analogies in other political communities and a common result for displaced persons.

7. It is probable that Paul's passive response to his challengers possesses sufficient explanatory power as to the origin of some of the other, seemingly unrelated accusations of embezzlement of collection funds (2 Cor. 7:2; 12:16-18), effeminate levity (1:17a), and deviant character (1:17b; 12:16; cf. 5:13). Failure in one area of the ancient moral economy often implied slippage in other areas.

8. In Corinth's ἐκκλησία, it is possible that the above accusations indicate the possibility of some form of a communal scrutiny of Paul's leadership. In particular, the accusations of diseased character may indicate an argument by some Corinthians believers to formally displace Paul in light of the contractual language in 1 Cor. 5:9-13, a supposition supported by evidence of social withdrawal and the courting of missionary rivals.

9. Our study in Part I indicates the presence of a potential contextual parameter for interpretation previously unconsidered. Guided by

relevance-theoretic principles, three narratives in four textual units (2 Cor. 1:3-11; 2:12-13; 7:5-16; 11:30-33) appear as ordeal narrations which evoke the judgments emanating from the intermediate visit, possessing apologetic and parenetic functions. In each case, Paul appeals to Christo-logic, arguing that God's intervening and vindicating power overturn judgments against Paul (τὸ ἀπόκριμα τοῦ θανάτου, 1:9; ταπεινός, 7:6; ἀσθένεια, 11:30). As well, Paul appropriates discourses of displacement (facing death, 1:8-11; patriotic care for the community in absentia, 1:23–2:13; 7:5-16; flight, 11:30-33), often drawing upon Israel's exilic tradition in the service of his aims.

10. The focus upon four discreet units (2 Cor. 1:3-11; 2:12-13; 7:5-16; 11:30-33) demonstrates that when discussing the relationship between apostolic suffering/weakness and divine empowerment in the context of specific, geographical locations, Paul depicts a relationship of successive states, rather than contemporaneity.

11. Thus, while Paul claims immunity from communal judgment in 1 Cor. 4:3-5, in 2 Corinthians Paul accepts the reality of communal judgment and responds by attaching his experiences of judgment to the Christological sequence. Thus, judgments against Paul are overturned by God's vindicating intervention.

12. In 2 Cor. 13:1-10, Paul appeals again to the Christological sequence to affirm his political legitimacy (13:3b-4), repeating the logic of Christological reversal in other places although now with his imminent return in view. Paul evokes a wider discourse of displacement by depicting his return as ζήσομεν εἰς ὑμᾶς (13:4d), reflecting a widely travelled trope in which revivification functioned as a metaphor for return and consistent with the eschatological realism connected to Paul's visit talk in the correspondence. As well, Paul summons the community to its own ordeal, suggesting like other displaced persons that the Corinthians rather than he might be truly illegitimate and thus displaced because of their rejection of their founding apostle (13:5-10; cf. 4:3-4; 6:14–7:1).

This work has remained intentionally uncommitted to a particular literary hypothesis, preferring to assess the strengths and weakness of various reconstructions in light of the insights generated. The literary and historical challenges in Paul's second canonical letter to Corinth render all literary reconstructions hypothetical. A tentative decision concerning literary integrity or the identity and sequence of letter fragments must be weighed by the principle of parsimony concerning "the criterion of physical possibility" according to Alistair Stewart-Sykes[122] and the criterion of analogy, following Philipp Vielhauser's dictum.[123] Stewart-Sykes demonstrates the immense physical demands upon copyists and editors as imagined in the redaction process, concluding that while complex redactional hypotheses of 2 Corinthians are "tenable" the physical demands created by more complex theories suggest "simpler constructions...are to be preferred."[124] Hans-Josef Klauck expounds upon Stewart-Sykes thesis and turns to the criterion of analogy by comparing the Corinthian correspondence to Cicero's letter collection.[125] Klauck notes that after Cicero's death, Tiro, his scribe, gathered, arranged, and edited Cicero's letters. Klauck's central contention is that modern critical editions of Cicero's correspondence detect "fifty to sixty cases—on 864 letters in all—where editors feel compelled to divide letters."[126] After analyzing this evidence as well as the time needed to compose a longer letter, Klauck concludes similarly to Stewart-Sykes, "partition theories are not *a priori* implausible, but they should be kept rather simple, serial addition being more probable than interpolation of fragments."[127] Schmeller made a similar conclusion a year after Klauck's publication, arguing that any partition in 2 Corinthians likely retains chronological accuracy.[128] He concludes, "Die Kompilationen, die wir in den Briefkorpora Ciceros finden, lassen allenfalls (!) eine addierende Vechmelzung chronologisch geordneter Paulusbriefe zu 2Kor plausibel erscheinen."[129] This conclusion is even further tempered by the late date of the manuscript tradition of Cicero's letter archive and the obvious question of to what degree Cicero's correspondence is a fitting analogy.

---

122. Alistair Stewart-Sykes, "Ancient Editors and Copyists and Modern Partition Theories: The Case of the Corinthian Correspondence," *JSNT* 61 (1996): 55.

123. "Analogien aus den Briefen und Briefsammlungen der Antike sind mir nicht bekannt" (Philipp Vielhauser, *Geschichte der urchristlichen Literatur* [Berlin: de Gruyter, 1975], 154).

124. Stewart-Sykes, "Ancient Editors," 64.

125. Hans-Joseph Klauck, "Compilation of Letter in Cicero's Correspondence," in *Early Christianity and Classical Culture, Comparative Studies in Honor of Abraham J. Malherbe*, ed. John T. Fitzgerald, Thomas H. Olbricht, and L. Michael White, SNT 110 (Leiden: Brill, 2003), 131–55.

126. Klauck, "Cicero's Correspondence," 139.

127. Klauck, "Cicero's Correspondence," 154.

128. Thomas Schmeller, "Die Cicerobriefe und die Frage nach der Einheitlichkeit des 2. Korintherbriefs," *ZNW* 95 (2004): 181–208.

129. Schmeller, "Die Cicerobriefe," 208.

The influential and brilliant works of Welborn and Mitchell, who employ aspects of Weiss–Bultmann and Schmithals–Bornkamm hypotheses, provide powerful social narratives of Paul and Corinthians' descent into enmity, displacement, and return, relying upon the existence of five asynchronous letters in 2 Corinthians. The hypothesis is attractive in light of the present study. Both scholars reject a caesura between 1 and 2 Corinthians and an extinct Letter of Tears, while emphasizing the role of the community and Paul's letters in the crisis that involves one central rupture. Yet, this study indicates that far too much weight is placed upon the role of 2 Corinthians 8 in generating the Corinthian conflict. Rather, the focus upon ordeal and displacement considering 1 Cor. 4:18-21 and 2 Cor. 10:1-11 and 13:1-10 supplies persuasive evidence regarding the nerve of the conflict and explanatory power concerning pecuniary suspicions echoes in 2 Corinthians. As well, the immense physical demand placed upon manuscripts and copyists and the asynchronous organization of the letters reduces the likelihood of the five-letter hypothesis. It may be tenable, but Welborn and Mitchell's reconstruction (as well as the Schmithals–Bornkamm and Weiss–Bultmann hypotheses) lack historical analogy and physical probability at present.

According to the criteria of possibility and analogy, it is plausible that 2 Corinthians is a composite letter of simple divisions, concealing two or three letters. In this way, the Hausrath–Kennedy hypothesis remains plausible, especially if the still-smoldering ὁ ἀδικήσας conflict (2 Cor. 2:5-11; 7:5-16) is intimately bound to the intermediate visit and crisis depicted in 2 Corinthians 10–13. There is some possibility that the impending ordeal Paul refers to in 13:1-10 is referenced retrospectively as a test that avoided punishment (2:9; 7:9) resulting in the repentance to salvation of the community (7:10) in response to the Tearful Letter. It is interesting to consider that Paul might employ a similar ordeal schema in 2:12-13 and 7:5-16 as he uses in 13:1-10 to merely narrate the reception of the letter in chs. 10–13. It too provides a coherent social narrative of ordeal → displacement → campaign for reconciliation and return, and its simplicity places fewer physical demands upon the manuscripts. Yet, the claim of asynchronous letters lacks historical analogy. As well, there is nothing in our study to suggest a shift in Paul's approach, "a sort of second conversion" between chs. 10–13 and chs. 1–9 as C. H. Dodd famously asserted.[130] Instead, Paul's language of ordeal remains consistent throughout, weaving together judgment and divine rescue

---

130. See C. H. Dodd, *New Testament Studies* (Manchester: Manchester University Press, 1953), 67–82.

according to the apostle's Christo-autobiography. When it comes to the administration of discipline, both halves of the letter depict martial action in apocalyptic terms. The issue is that in chs. 10–13 such discipline lies in the near future, while in 2:1-11, 7:5-16 discipline is in the past. However, it is not clear whether the past discipline of the ὁ ἀδικήσας is a preparatory and hortatory exemplar for Paul's future discipline in chs. 10–13 or whether the two instances are to be conflated. Again, both options remain tenable but the asynchronous nature of the Hausrath–Kennedy hypothesis makes it less preferable than synchronous arrangements of letter fragments.

The Semler–Windisch hypothesis places the least physical burden upon the manuscripts and has historical analogy. However, the present study finds the contention more improbable from the socio-historical background than the asynchronous hypotheses above. That an emergent situation reached Paul and resulted in the writing chs. 10–13 makes little sense when Paul spends these chapters focused upon his impending return and political legitimacy in light of the intermediate ordeal which, by nearly all accounts (of the Semler–Windisch hypothesis), occurred prior to the writing of 2 Corinthians 1–9. It may be historically analogous and physically possible, but it is socially implausible.

The compositional unity of 2 Corinthians remains a minority position, but the traditional structure (chs. 1–7, 8–9, 10–13) possesses sensible organization. Yet, the hypothesis has weaknesses. The Letter of Tears is relegated to extinction for almost all scholars. And the seemingly disjunctive transitions between units remain odd for some and unintelligible for others. Yet, while there are literary transitions everywhere in 2 Corinthians, they are not everywhere the same. The main issue remains the chasm between chs. 1–9 and 10–13. One plausible bridge would involve understanding different audiences for different sections of the letter. This would then indicate that chs. 1–7 focuses upon those responsive to the Letter of Tears and Titus's embassy, chs. 8–9 center upon the collection as symbol of reconciliation, and chs. 10–13 focus upon an unreconciled faction. In this case, the matter of the ὁ ἀδικήσας, the immoral group, and the rivals relate to one another in a manner unknown except through the constellation of Paul's martial administration of the community.

If Paul in 2 Cor. 10:1-11 (and 13:1-10) comments upon 1 Cor. 4:18-21 in light of Paul's intermediate visit, the supposed disjunction between chs. 8–9 and 10–13 may be overstated. It is both consistent with Paul's style to move from first person plural to singular when discussing his arrival to Corinth and also appropriate if 2 Cor. 10:1-11 intentionally comments upon 1 Cor. 4:18-21, a first person singular text. The logic present in the

Graeco-Roman virtue economy in which failure in one aspect (masculinity) might lead to accusations in another area (justice) also supplies, in part, some rationale for the move from the collection as a symbol of reconciliation (chs. 8–9) following Titus's successful disciplinary envoy (7:5-16) to addressing vociferously the judgments about his passivity and martial impotence, since the latter continue to stand logically in the way of the former, at least among some in the community.

The simplest hypothesis—the one requiring the least number of unproveable assumptions—would be to claim provisionally the compositional unity of the text and to attempt to explain "bumps" in the text according to complex exigencies.[131] However, this thesis does not depend upon the compositional unity nor any literary hypothesis to generate its key insights. Conversely, this study has not generated any major findings regarding partition hypotheses. Thus, central aspects of the present argument remain relevant to those who share differing literary reconstructions.

We have explored one route by which Paul achieved an amicable return (Part II). Future investigations may wish to explore further the way in which the phenomena of political displacement analyzed in Part I supply a salient contextual parameter to other texts in 2 Corinthians. What other strategies did Paul employ in light of his displacement? What if any insight is gained from reading 2 Cor. 5:1-10 in this light, not least Paul's contention that he is in exile (ἐκδημέω) from the Lord (5:6), especially considering the concerns that Paul's eschatology shifts from 1 Corinthians 15? As a text, 5:6-10 certainly interacts with a presence–absence motif through the home–exile antithesis. Importantly, while Paul references absence with judgment in some form or fashion in 1 Corinthians, in 2 Cor. 5:6 Paul's absence from the Lord does not indicate judgment. Rather, judgment not only exists in the future, Christ's βῆμα seat also exists spatially "out there." Might these supposed "shifts" in Pauline eschatology have more to do with Paul's rhetorical response to his displacement from Corinth? Does a similar Cynic-Stoic exile tradition shed any light on Paul's theologizing? Inasmuch as interpreters frequently refer to the collection (2 Cor. 8–9) as a sign of reconciliation in advance of Paul's return, what if any analogies existed in other political communities concerning liturgies or rituals attendant to an amicable return, and what if any light is shed through these analogies? Finally, is there any possibility that Paul's rhetoric concerning the rivals has persuaded modern scholarship to place the blame for the Corinthian crisis

---

131. Arzt-Grabner, *2 Korinther*, 147–8.

upon "outsiders," and to what accounts of ancient reconciliations and the rhetorical strategies therein shed any light on the use of insider–outsider dynamics?

This work may also participate in ongoing debates concerning gender roles in the American evangelical context. The evangelical movement's lionizing of masculine bravado in response to endless culture war klaxon alarms stretches from Billy Sunday to John Wayne to contemporary political allegiances and ecclesiological debates. Yet, within his cultural horizons, Paul pushes back against and recalibrates potentially analogous norms in view of the crucified and risen Messiah. Without presumption of an outcome of a modern appropriation nor without predetermining allegiance to an ideological camp, a deliberate study that holds together aspects of this inquiry with contemporary horizons may be of value.

Appendix I

CAMPAIGNING FOR RECONCILIATION AND RETURN

Exiles frequently sued for reconciliation through a coordinated campaign including the strategic choice of exile (if possible), a concerted effort by envoys to affect recall, and the dissidents' literary output. During the Republic, dissidents angled for return by choosing strategic locations near Rome to facilitate correspondence with friends who remained and allowed for a rapid return if the opportunity arose.[1] To C. Toranius, Cicero writes, "you could have found no more convenient place to stay in these distressing circumstances; for it is one you can leave and go wherever may be advisable with the maximum of ease and expedition. If he [Caesar] returns on time, you will be close at hand; whereas if something hampers or delays him (many things can happen), you will be where you can get all the news. This really does seem to me best."[2] Such correspondence indicates that exiles emphasized the choice of location, desiring ease of travel and efficiency of communication to aid in the prospect of return. While Roman exiles likely resided in every major city in the Roman Empire, the distance chosen from Rome indicated an exile's desire to return.[3] It may be that similar practices were employed in other eras among diverse types of political communities.

Envoys, family, and friends attempted to facilitate reconciliation and return through diplomatic maneuvers.[4] Isocrates's *To the Rulers Of the Mytilenaeans* supplies an apt example as he sues for the restoration and return of Agenor and his family. In Rome, using the guise of mourners—clothing traditionally worn by those charged with capital crimes—supporters of exiles including women and children often engaged

---

1. Kelly, *Exile*, Chapter 3; for clients, see Cicero, *Mur.* 89.
2. Cicero, *Fam.* 6.20.2; cf. 6.8.2.
3. Cohen, "Exile," 68 n. 163.
4. Keazirian, *Peacemaking in Paul*, 131.

in tearful histrionics before the populace and Senate to sway public opinion.[5] Beyond such public protests, friends also employed other tactics to affect restoration. Cicero's *interdictio* reveals a full-scale conspiracy on the part of his supporters to end his exile, even in the face of Clodius's intimidation.[6] P. Sestius journeyed to Gaul to court Caesar's support.[7] Friends attempted to pacify Cicero's opponents, like Metellus Nepos.[8] Discussions were held concerning the possible illegality of Clodius's bill.[9] After his defense of Milo failed to render an acquittal, Cicero redoubled his efforts and published an improved forensic display to advance his chances of restoration.[10]

As indicated, dissidents attempted to affect recall and reconciliation through their literary production. Notable Greek letters include Andocides's *On His Return* and Demosthenes's *Epistle* 2. The forensic archetype of Cicero's published *Pro Milone* was likely the published pamphlets and letters of Metellus Numidicus employed to sue for reconciliation.[11] Livy writes that the Tarquins delivered letters to Rome to arrange for their return.[12] Of such writings, Kelly claims, "the published letters could function as a sort of 'speech' by the banished man."[13] These often forensic publications were attempts often by letter—likely the most important form of exilic literature[14]—to preserve, and promote the presence of the political dissident before audiences powerful enough to enact reconciliation, a function consistent with the theoretical foundations of ancient epistolography, and consistent with the memory sanctions generally linked to political displacement. While we have no clear evidence of such use in association life, the use of letters to affect reconciliation and return is also clear at the non-elite level.[15]

---

5. Kelly, *Exile*, 74–5, see 73–7; theatrics for Popillius, Diodorus 34–35.26; for Marius, see Appian, *Bell. civ.* 1.63; for Ser. Sulpicius Galba, see Cicero, *de. Orat.* 1.288; for Cicero, *Red. sen.* 13, 37; for Metellus Numidicus, see Cicero, *Red. pop.* 6.

6. Kelly, *Exile*, 120–1.

7. Cicero, *Sest.* 63 (71).

8. Cicero, *Att.* 3.22.2-3; 3.24.2.

9. Cicero, *Att.* 3.15.5; see, Kelly, *Exile*, 120–1.

10. For Milo's unenthusiastic response to the published pamphlet, see Plutarch, *Cic.* 35; cf. Kelly, *Exile*, 126–7.

11. Kelly, *Exile*, 86–7.

12. Livy 2.3.6.

13. Kelly, *Exile*, 86.

14. Claassen, *Displaced Persons*, 12.

15. *BGU* 3.846; P.Giss. 17 (= P.Giss.Apoll. 13).

From within our historical reconstruction, Paul's employment of letters to Corinth and envoys (7:5-16; 8:16-24; 9:3) to affect reconciliation immediately prior to his return and even his geographical movement from Troas to Macedonia (2:12-13; 7:5-7), harkens these phenomena sometimes linked to political displacement.

Appendix II

THE ὁ ἀδικήσας CONFLICT

The ὁ ἀδικήσας conflict (2 Cor. 2:5-11; 7:5-16) supplies one of the most challenging tasks for the modern interpreter, for Paul never ostensibly indicates the identity of the offender (ὁ ἀδικήσας, 7:12), the offended (ὁ ἀδικηθείς, 7:12), or the nature of the offence.[1] Yet, the interpreter is expected to supply or assent to detailed reconstructions of the conflict. Beyond the obvious aspect that Paul writes to an audience well-versed in the dispute, Paul, to our frustration, focuses not upon the offence but on the positive developments brought about by the Letter of Tears, thus refracting the conflict through the lens of his aims. Remaining agnostic about some elements of the ὁ ἀδικήσας conflict, we aim to secure what can be known.

The clearest insight regarding the conflict emerges from attention to the ultimate aims of 2 Corinthians: complete reconciliation and return. Paul's circumspect style leaves open several interpretative possibilities. Yet, that style follows his very attempt to reconcile with the community. As Welborn demonstrates, "reconciliation was held to consist in an act of deliberate forgetfulness" and later as "ἀμνησία, an act of political forgiveness."[2] Because internecine strife and resultant displacement often involved serious charges and aggressive conduct, reintegration could often only occur if immunity was offered for behaviors committed during the breakdown.[3] Hesiod comments that λήθη (Oblivion) is the daughter of ἔρρις.[4] And Plutarch claims a reconciliation was sanctioned at the altar

---

1. Bieringer, "Plädoyer," 157.
2. Welborn, "Identification," 151, 152.
3. IPArk 24; Aristotle, *Ath. pol.* 39.6; crimes and debts P.Köln 7.313, here though in celebration of victory; C.Ord.Ptol. 53.
4. Hesiod, *Theog.* 226–27.

of λήθη.⁵ Amnesty was a part of the famous Athenian reconciliation and return of the democrats.⁶ Aelius Aristides comments that on the subject of στάσις people should remain silent lest in recounting the events the strife is renewed.⁷ According to Börm, political forgetfulness involved more than simply a fear of recalling civic trauma. Rather, "these inscriptions themselves are intended to document the restoration of concord within the polis and are products of negotiation; as such, they often avoid any explicit attribution of guilt."⁸

Welborn demonstrates that political forgetfulness manifested in literary forgetfulness in which writer's feigned ignorance and employed circuitous references concerning offenses and offenders.⁹ While Paul could be referencing any issue, it is plausible to assume Paul's central role in the conflict. From this perspective, Paul's forgetfulness is likely indebted to the partial resolution of the ὁ ἀδικήσας conflict, which he offers as an idealized exemplar in outstanding matters.¹⁰

Universally, scholars acknowledge that 2 Cor. 2:5-11 and 7:5-16 refer to the same situation.¹¹ With the exception of one scholar, all understand a single individual as the culprit, who is marked as τις λελύπηκεν (2:5) ὁ τοιοῦτος (2:6) ὁ ἀδικήσας (7:12).¹² Reconstructions include (a) the incestuous man from 1 Cor. 5:1-8,¹³ (b) an unknown Corinthian involved in a lawsuit with another believer,¹⁴ (c) a believer who insults one of Paul's

---

5. Plutarch, *Quaest. conv.* 9.6; cf. Aristotle, *Ath. Pol.* 39.6; Plutarch, *Cic.* 42.2; Valerius Maximus, 4.1, ext. 4.

6. Aristotle, *Ath. pol.* 39.6.

7. Aelius Aristides, 24.41.

8. Börm, "Stasis," 57.

9. Welborn, "Identification," 146–51 cf. Ps.-Libanius 15; Demosthenes, *Ep.* 2.2; Cicero, *Ad. Fam.* 5.8; Apollonius, *Ep.* 45.

10. Vegge, *2 Corinthians*, 91–2.

11. Welborn, *Enmity*, 23.

12. Thrall, "Offender," 72; Windisch, *Zweite Korintherbrief*, 237; Harris, *Second Epistle*, 222; Welborn, *Enmity*, 24. Cf. Land, *Absence*, 102–3, who understands the singular pronouns and participles to refer to a group.

13. Heinrici, *Zweite Brief*, 16, 93; Zahn, *Introduction*, 1:348–9; Hughes, *Second Epistle*, 54–8, 59–65; Lampe, "Church Discipline," 353–4; Hyldahl, "Frage," 299–302. South contends, "the identification of the 1 Cor as the 'sorrowful letter' is not essential to the identification of [the same offender in] 1 Cor 5/2 Cor 2" (*Disciplinary Practices*, 104). Similarly, Kruse, "Offender and the Offence," 129–39, and Garland, *2 Corinthians*, 121–3, who claim the offender from 1 Cor. 5 also challenged Paul's authority during the intermediate visit.

14. Krenkel, *Beiträge*, 305–7; Windisch, *Zweite Korintherbrief*, 238–9, and others.

envoys,[15] (d) a missionary rival who challenges Paul,[16] (e) a believer who steals the collection from Paul,[17] (f) a believer who insults Paul,[18] or (g) a believer who levels a legal charge against him.[19] In light of the punitive action and recommended restoration of the offender (2:5-11), and in concert with the aims of the epistle, it is virtually certain the ὁ ἀδικήσας was a member of the community.

It is reasonable to conclude with the majority position that Paul was the ὁ ἀδικηθείς.[20] Paul consciously mitigates his own role in the conflict (2 Cor. 2:5, 10; 7:12), a feature that in the context of reconciliation likely implies the opposite. In 2:5, Paul states, "if someone has caused pain [τις λελύπηκεν], he has not pained me, but in part—lest I be heavy handed—all of you."[21] Since Paul has previously stated he remained absent from Corinth in order to prevent a painful affair (λύπη, 2:1)—his return would be punitive (1:23)—it seems likely that τις λελύπηκεν is linked to negative conditions during the previous visit. The construction in 2:5 is likely conditional in form only, referring to a past event in a way to deflect its severity.[22] Moreover, Krenkel claims that in disjunctive propositions, when the first statement is negated followed by a strong adversative and positive statement, the negation is not total but places focus upon the second statement.[23]

Similarly, in 2:10 Paul initially claims ᾧ δέ τι χαρίζεσθε, κἀγώ, seemingly stating that he is in accord with the community's decision to forgive

---

15. Willibald Beyschlag, "Ueber die Christuspartei zu Korinth," *TSK* 38.2 (1865): 254, who understands Timothy as ὁ ἀδικηθείς, who found the community and a particular leader against Paul; cf. Findlay, "Paul," 3:711. This is entertained as a possibility by, Furnish, *II Corinthians*, 396; Frank Matera, *II Corinthians* (Louisville, KY: Westminster John Knox, 2003), 18.

16. Barrett, *Second Epistle*, 7, 86–90, 92–3.

17. Thrall, "Offender."

18. Weiss, *Primitive Christianity*, 1:342; Watson, "Painful Letter," 343–5, and others.

19. See especially Ewald, *Sendschreiben*, 225–7; Weizsäcker, *Zeitalter*, 296–8.

20. Kruse, "Offender and the Offence," 129–39; Vegge, *2 Corinthians*, 85–9, and others.

21. Cf. Long, *II Corinthians*, 42, 46.

22. Meyer, *Corinthians*, 2:169.

23. "Nicht das Eine ist die Haupt sache, der Punkt, auf den Alles ankommt, sondern das Andere" (*Beiträge*, 298); Krenkel cites Jn 6:32 as an example. M. Zerwick similarly claims, "In disjunctive propositions, it is a Semitic peculiarity to express one member negatively so as to lay more stress on the other, saying 'not A but B' where the sense is 'not so much A as B'" (*Biblical Greek*, trans. Joseph Smith, [Rome: Pontifical Biblical Institute, 1963], §445).

the offender. In the next statement, Paul claims, γὰρ ἐγὼ ὃ κεχάρισμαι, εἴ τι κεχάρισμαι, δι' ὑμᾶς ἐν προσώπῳ Χριστοῦ ("For whatever I have forgiven—if I have forgiven anything—it is for your sake in the presence of Christ"). Paul's use of the personal pronoun in 2:10 as in 2:5 along with 2:1 suggests that Paul himself was at the center of the conflict.[24] However, Paul aims to further reconcile with the community, notably demonstrating mutuality and reciprocity between Paul and the community in the act of forgiveness.[25]

With two previous examples of Paul deflecting his import to the conflict, in 2 Cor. 7:12 he states the purpose of the Letter of Tears, "it was not on account of the wrongdoer or the wronged, but so that your devotion to us might be revealed to you in the presence of God." Here, Krenkel and Zerwick's grammatical observation is apropos as in 2:5. Plummer comments, "here St. Paul does not mean that he had no thought of the offender or the offended person in writing; He means that they were not the main cause of his doing so."[26] Just as Paul excises himself as the focal point of the event in 2:5, 10, so too Paul highlights the ultimate purpose of the Letter of Tears—to save the community from afar, rather than relitigate the conflict.

Paul's habituated grammar, which constantly mitigates his own role in the conflict—a form of rhetoric associated with reconciliation—implies that Paul was likely the ὁ ἀδικηθείς. If so, Paul creates a parallelism between himself as the agent of divine reconciliation (δι' ἡμῶν, 2 Cor. 5:20) to the Corinthians (καταλλάγητε, 2 Cor. 5:20; ὑμᾶς, 2 Cor. 6:1) and God, the one who took the initiative of reconciliation with "us" (ἡμᾶς, ἡμῖν, 5:18). Both appear in the discourse as the offended party. Both stand ready to grant amnesty to offenders (2:6; 5:19b).[27] In the ὁ ἀδικήσας conflict proper, such amnesty takes the shape of Paul's own willingness to "forget" many of the details of the conflict, though as the offended

---

24. Martin, *2 Corinthians*, 37.
25. Barnett, *Second Epistle*, 130.
26. Plummer, *Second Epistle*, 224.
27. In regards to the meaning of μὴ λογιζόμενος, scholars often underscore the commercial context (Arzt-Grabner, *2 Korinther*, 338) or the theological context of imputation of sin (Martin, *2 Corinthians*, 141); however, in light of the topic of reconciliation, the political context must be highlighted and thus the likely reference to amnesty. For political reconciliation resulting in the cancelling of debts, see P.Köln 7.313.10-20; Harris connects the passage to Jer. 31:34 and comments, "when God forgives, he does not forget, but chooses not to 'remember'" (Harris, *Second Epistle*, 444).

party he continues to beckon the community to reconciliation with the ὁ ἀδικήσας (2:5-11) but centrally with himself (6:11-13; 7:2).[28]

The nature of the offence may be indicated both by the penal action against the ὁ ἀδικήσας and the legal valence of the terms attached to the conflict.[29] The rhetorical point for Paul is that community has faced an ordeal through the reception of letter and shown itself δοκιμή through its punitive response the letter (2:9; 7:12). Likewise, Paul has shown his absence to be efficacious in the administration of the community, rather than evidence of ἐλαφρία (1:17). Regarding the legal outcome of the Letter of Tears, Paul writes, "For this person, the punishment (ἐπιτιμία) imposed by the majority is sufficient" (2:6). The term ἐπιτιμία most likely refers, like ἐκδίκησις (7:11), to punitive action rather than a verbal censure,[30] not least since Paul writes to end the sanction (2:6-10), something that makes little sense in reference to a reprimand.[31] Though unknown, it is likely that the punishment involved an indefinite expulsion, not unlike what is found in 1 Cor. 5:1-13.[32] Recalling that analogous associations enforced temporary exclusions and expulsions, Paul's reversal of the communal decision (τοὐναντίον μᾶλλον, 2:7) and call for a new course of action (2:7-8) indicates the severity and indefiniteness of the initial punishment.[33] If so, the initial punishment would likely be the most severe form of discipline the community could enforce.

28. Welborn's argument for 2 Cor. 1:1–2:13; 7:5-16; 13:11-13 as "the letter of reconciliation" does not account for this parallelism and thus the plausible intelligibility between 5:18-21 with 2:1-11; 7:5-16 ("Identification," 152–3).

29. Zahn comments that several terms and expressions regarding the ἀδικήσας conflict—κυρόω (2:8), ἀπολογία (7:11), ἐκδίκησις (7:11), ὁ ἀδικήσας, ὁ ἀδικηθείς (7:12)—possess a "legal colouring," (*Introduction*, 1.347); Martin includes other forensic terms (ἐπιτιμία, 2:6; πρᾶγμα, 7:11; ἁγνός, 7:12) claiming they "are borrowed from criminal law" (*2 Corinthians*, 236).

30. Thrall, *Second Epistle*, 1:174; Harris, *Second Epistle*, 226; Vegge, *2 Corinthians*, 73; contra Bachmann, *Zweite Brief*, 118–19; Barrett, *Second Epistle*, 90.

31. Schmeller, *Zweite Brief*, 1:136.

32. Scholars understanding the punishment as a form of exclusion include, Meyer, *Corinthians*, 2:172; Harris, *Second Epistle*, 228; Barnett, *Second Epistle*, 126; Vegge, *2 Corinthians*, 76, and others.

33. Thrall and Furnish argue that the ἐπιτιμία was always a temporary exclusion, but across analogous social formations, the length of temporary exclusions was tightly defined. Not so here, implying an *ad hoc* shift in punishment. Further, the contrastive adverbs τοὐναντίον μᾶλλον resulting in forgiveness imply a change from the current course likely for the cause of further reconciliation. The more severe penalty would be expulsion (see Thrall, *Second Epistle*, 174; Furnish, *II Corinthians*, 161–2; White, *Discipline*, 217–21).

A group referred to as οἱ πλείονες rendered the punishment (2 Cor. 2:6), referring to a majority in distinction to a minority rather than an expression referring to the whole community.[34] The identity of the minority offers a notorious interpretive crux. Some scholars assert that the minority refers to holdouts that wish to see a stronger sanction.[35] Thus, it is argued that the contrastive adverbs τοὐναντίον μᾶλλον (2:7) indicate a minority who did not believe the punishment was severe enough.[36] However, ἱκανός (2:6) is likely temporal referring to the duration of the punishment, since the immediate context calls for an end to it.[37] Thus, τοὐναντίον μᾶλλον (2:7) is likely in contrast to the ongoing punishment rendered by οἱ πλείονες in accord with the Letter of Tears.[38] Furthermore, it makes little sense that a "pro-Pauline clique" would dissent from Paul's ruling during a crisis of authority.[39] Paul's presentation of the ὁ ἀδικήσας conflict is largely positive if not idealized and seems aimed at furthering reconciliation. Rather than continue to drive a wedge with the minority who disagrees with the punishment, it makes more sense that Paul recommends forgiveness as a part of a strategy to reconcile the majority with the minority and the community as a whole with himself.[40] Evidence exists elsewhere in 2 Corinthians of a renegade group, rather than a pro-Pauline faction, present during the intermediate visit and still in defiance of Paul (chs. 10–13 in general; 12:21; 13:2 in particular).[41] As stated above, both the ὁ ἀδικήσας conflict and the confrontation with the immoral group are referred to with the verb φείδομαι (1:23; 13:2) indicating a link between both issues.[42] Finally, since Paul seems to be supplying new information concerning the

---

34. Barnett, *Second Epistle*, 125; Furnish, *II Corinthians*, 155; Vegge, *2 Corinthians*, 73, and others; contra Barrett, *Second Epistle*, 91; Martin, *2 Corinthians*, 37.

35. Krenkel, *Beiträge*, 302; Bachmann, *Zweite Brief*, 111–12; Plummer, *Second Epistle*, 58; Zahn, *Introduction*, 333; Thrall, "Offender," 176; Harris, *Second Epistle*, 229; Welborn, *Enmity*, 36–7.

36. Kennedy, *Second and Third Epistles*, 100–109; Plummer, *Second Epistle*, 58; Harris, *Second Epistle*, 229.

37. Meyer, *Corinthians*, 2:172; Bultmann, *Second Letter*, 49; South, *Disciplinary Practices*, 92; Barnett, *Second Epistle*, 125 n. 16; Harris, *Second Epistle*, 228; Vegge, *2 Corinthians*, 74.

38. "τοὐναντίον μᾶλλον is in contrast to the ἐπιτιμία which was appropriate till now" (Bultmann, *Second Letter*, 49; also Lietzmann, *Korinther I–II*, 106; Vegge, *2 Corinthians*, 74).

39. Contra Plummer, *Second Epistle*, 58; Harris, *Second Epistle*, 229, and others.

40. Vegge, *2 Corinthians*, 76, 80.

41. Weizsäcker, *Zeitalter*, 298.

42. "To the minority there may have belonged partly the most lax in morals" (Meyer, *Corinthians*, 2:172).

forgiveness of the offender, it is difficult to imagine what harsher sentence a reticent minority might wish. Thus, in 2:5-11, 7:5-16, Paul likely has in view fostering internecine reconciliation and reconciliation between the dissenting minority and Paul. In this way, the reconciliation and return of a figure once hostile to Paul may promote reconciliation between Paul and a still-defiant contingent prior to his return. If so, it would not be the first time that internecine strife was overcome by political amnesia leading to return of various political dissidents and the rehabilitation of a previously strife-ridden political community.

Paul's political amnesia supplies interpreters with a weak branch upon which to make confident assertions. However, the ὁ ἀδικήσας conflict offers helpful hints. First, the ὁ ἀδικήσας conflict involved an expression of enmity towards Paul perhaps occurring during the intermediate visit (2 Cor. 2:1).

Second, if so, Paul responded to the affront initially by leaving Corinth. As demonstrated in Chapter 2, leaving in the face of a challenge was widely held as a sign of impotence, associated with defeat, and consistent with the features of a hostile absence (§2.2).

Third, after his exit, Paul sent the Letter of Tears, supplemented by the diplomatic work of Titus (2 Cor. 2:12-13; 7:6). Thus, by 2 Corinthians Paul had regained some momentum in Corinth. However, it is equally likely that no such support existed during the affront and exit. Overall, the flurry of writing, the use of envoys, and Paul's concern for a strategic location to discover Titus's report (2:12-13; 7:5-7) harkens the tactics employed by exiles to affect reconciliation and return.[43] This is evident whether through the canonical structure of the letter, as Paul presents the effective Letter of Tears (7:5-16) as clearing way for Titus's return (chs. 8–9) in advance of Paul's return (chs. 10–13), or through partition theories such as those advocated by Welborn Mitchell and others, which narrate a social progression from enmity and absence to reconciliation and return.

Fourth, a dissident minority remains, since only a portion of the community responded positively to the Letter of Tears (2 Cor. 2:6). This fits with the evidence in chs. 10–13 of a contingent of hostile detractors, present on Paul's visit, to whom Paul responds. Through the call to comfort and forgive the offender and in the depiction of a complete reconciliation, Paul aims to realize total reconciliation with the rebellious group and the majority and with the community as a whole. However, there is simply not enough evidence to warrant scholars' frequent, colorful reconstructions.

---

43. Appendix I.

Perhaps the ὁ ἀδικήσας refers to a particularly prominent and flagrant offender within the immoral group who was disciplined by some in the community following Paul's visit and in response to his efficacious Letter of Tears. In any event, Paul's employment of the ὁ ἀδικήσας conflict is multi-faceted, demonstrating in part his cruciform martial efficacy *in absentia* in the face of accusations, and laying the predicate for his return. What continues to be debated is whether the ὁ ἀδικήσας conflict prepares for Titus's (ch. 8) and Paul's return in chs. 10–13 or whether it is the final act the longstanding crisis of authority.

BIBLIOGRAPHY

Adeleye, Gabriel. "The Purpose of the 'Dokimasia.'" *GRBS* 24 (1983): 295–306.
Aejmelaeus, Lars. "Der 2. Korintherbrief als Drama von Streit und Versöhnung: Ein Plädoyer für die Briefteilung." *ZNT* 38 (2016): 49–54.
Aejmelaeus, Lars. "The Question of Salary in the Conflict Between Paul and the 'Super Apostles' in Corinth." *Fair Play: Diversity and Conflicts in Early Christianity: Essays in Honour of Heikki Räisänen*. Edited by Ismo Dunderberg, Christopher Tuckett, and Kari Syreeni. NovTSup 53. Leiden: Brill, 2002.
Aejmelaeus, Lars. *Schwachheit als Waffe. Die Argumentation des Paulus im "Tränenbrief" (2.Kor. 10–13)*. SFEG 78. Göttingen: Vandenhoeck & Ruprecht, 2000.
Allo, E. B. *Saint Paul: Seconde Epître aux Corinthiens*. ÉBib. Paris: Gabalda, 1937.
Alwine, Andrew T. *Enmity and Feuding in Classical Athens*. Austin: University of Texas Press, 2015.
Andrews, Scott B. "Too Weak Not to Lead: The Form and Function of 2 Cor 11.23b–33." *NTS* 41.2 (1996): 263–76.
Arnaoutoglou, Ilias. "Roman Law and Collegia in Asia Minor." *RIDA* 49 (2002): 27–44.
Arzt-Grabner, Peter. *2 Korinther*. PKNT 4. Göttingen: Vandenhoeck & Ruprecht, 2014.
Arzt-Grabner, Peter. "'I was intending to visit you, but…': Clauses Explaining Delayed Visits and Their Importance in Papyrus Letters and in Paul." Pages 220–31 in *Jewish and Christian Scripture as Artefact and Canon*. Edited by Craig A. Evans and H. Daniel Zacharias. London: T&T Clark, 2009.
Arzt-Grabner, Peter. "Paul's Letter Thanksgiving." Pages 129–58 in *Paul and the Ancient Letter Form*. Edited by Stanley E. Porter and Sean A. Adams. Pauline Studies 6. Leiden: Brill, 2010.
Ascough, Richard. *Paul's Macedonian Associations*. WUNT 2/161. Tübingen: Mohr Siebeck, 2003.
Ascough, Richard. "What Are They Now Saying about Christ Groups and Associations?" *CurBR* 13.2 (2015): 207–44.
Auer, Peter. "From Context to Contextualization." *LL* 3 (1995): 11–28.
Aune, David E. *The New Testament in Its Literary Environment*. Philadelphia: Westminster, 1987.
Bachmann, Philipp. *Der zweite Brief des Paulus an die Korinther*. KNT 8. Leipzig: Deichert, 1909.
Bammel, Ernst. "Rechtsfindung in Korinth." *ETL* 73 (1997): 107–13.
Barclay, John M. G. *Jews in the Mediterranean Diaspora: From Alexander to Trajan (323 BCE–117 CE)*. Berkeley: University of California Press, 1996.
Barclay, John M. G. "Mirror-Reading a Polemical Letter: Galatians as a Test Case." *JSNT* 31 (1987): 73–93.
Barclay, John M. G. *Paul & the Gift*. Grand Rapids, MI: Eerdmans, 2015.

Barclay, John M. G. "Thessalonica and Corinth: Social Contrasts in Pauline Christianity." Pages 181–203 in *Pauline Churches and Diaspora Jews*. Grand Rapids, MI: Eerdmans, 2011.
Barnett, Paul. *The Second Epistle to the Corinthians*. NICNT. Grand Rapids: Eerdmans, 1997.
Barré, Michael L. "Paul as 'Eschatologic Person': A New Look at 2 Cor 11:29." *CBQ* 37.4 (1975): 500–526.
Barrett, C. K. *A Commentary on the First Epistle to the Corinthians*. Black's New Testament Commentaries. Peabody, MA: Hendrickson, 1993.
Barrett, C. K. *A Commentary on the Second Epistle to the Corinthians*. New York: Harper, 1973.
Barrett, C. K. "Paul's Opponents in II Corinthians." *NTS* 17 (1971): 233–54.
Barton, Carlin A. *Roman Honor: The Fire in the Bones*. Berkeley: University of California Press, 2001.
Batten, Alicia. "The Moral World of Greco-Roman Associations." *SR* 36.1 (2007): 135–51.
Bauman, Richard A. *Crime and Punishment in Ancient Rome*. New York: Routledge, 1996.
Baur, Ferdinand C. *Paul, the Apostle of Jesus Christ*. Translated by Eduard Zeller. 2 vols. 2nd edn. London: Williams & Norgate, 1876.
Beale, G. K. "The Old Testament Background of Reconciliation in 2 Corinthians 5–7 and Its Bearing on the Literary Problem of 2 Corinthians 6.14–7.1." *NTS* 35.4 (1989): 550–81.
Begg, C. "The Rahab Story in Josephus." *LASBF* 55 (2005): 113–30.
Bell, Sinclair. "Introduction: Role Models in the Roman World." Pages 1–39 in *Role Models in the Roman World: Identity and Assimilation*. Edited by Sinclair Bell and Inge Lyse Hansen. Vol. 7 of *Supplements to the Memoirs of the American Academy in Rome*. Ann Arbor: University of Michigan Press, 2008.
Bergmann, Betinna. "The Roman House as Memory Theater: The House of the Tragic Poet in Pompeii." *ABull* 76.2 (1994): 225–56.
Betz, Hans Dieter. *2 Corinthians 8 and 9: A Commentary of Two Administrative Letters of the Apostle Paul*. Hermeneia. Philadelphia: Fortress, 1985.
Betz, Hans Dieter. *Der Apostel Paulus und die sokratische Tradition: Eine exegetische Untersuchung zu seiner "Apologie" 2 Kor 10–13*. Beiträge zur historischen Theologie 45. Tübingen: Mohr Siebeck, 1972.
Bieringer, Reimund. "Der 2. Korintherbrief als Ursprüngliche Einheit ein Forschungsüberblick." Pages 107–30 in *Studies on 2 Corinthians*. Leuven: Leuven University Press, 1994.
Bieringer, Reimund. "The Comforted Comforter: The Meaning of Παρακαλέω or Παράκλησις Terminology in 2 Corinthians." *HvTSt* 67.1 (2011): 1–7.
Bieringer, Reimund. "Plädoyer für die Einheitlichkeit des 2. Korintherbriefes. Literarkritische und inhaltliche Argumente." Pages 131–79 in *Studies on 2 Corinthians*. Edited by Reimund Bieringer and Jan Lambrecht. BETL 112. Leuven: Leuven University Press, 1994.
Bieringer, Reimund. "Zwischen Kontinuität und Diskontinuität: Die beiden Korintherbriefe in ihrer Beziehung zueinander nach der neueren Forschung." Pages 3–35 in *The Corinthian Correspondence*. BETL 125. Leuven: Leuven University Press/Peeters, 1996.
Bishop, Eric F. F. "Does Aretas Belong in 2 Corinthians or Galatians." *ExpTim* 64 (1953): 188–89.

Bleek, Friedrich. "Erörterungen in Beziehung auf die Briefe Pauli an die Korinther." *TSK* 3 (1830): 614–32.
Boakye, Andrew. *Death and Life: Resurrection, Restoration, and Rectification in Paul's Letter to the Galatians*. Eugene, OR: Pickwick, 2017.
Boakye, Andrew. "Inhabiting the 'Resurrectiform' God: Death and Life as Theological Headline in Paul." *ExpTim* 128.2 (2016): 53–62.
Börm, Henning. "Stasis in Post-Classical Greece: The Discourse of Civil Strife in the Hellenistic World." Pages 53–83 in *The Polis in the Hellenistic World*. Edited by Henning Börm and Nino Luraghi. Stuttgart: Franz Steiner, 2018.
Bornkamm, Güther. "The History of the Origin of the So-Called Second Letter to the Corinthians." *NTS* 8 (1962): 258–64.
Bosenius, Bärbel. *Die Abwesenheit des Apostels als theologisches Programm: der zweite Korintherbrief als Beispiel für die Brieflichkeit der paulinischen Theologie*. TANZ 11. Tübingen: Francke, 1994.
Boter, G. J. "Thrasymachus and ΠΛΕΟΝΕΞΙΑ." *Mnemosyne* 39.3 (1986): 261–81.
Bowie, Ewen L. "Early Expatriates: Displacement and Exile in Archaic Poetry." Pages 21–50 in *Writing Exile: The Discourse of Displacement in Greco-Roman Antiquity and Beyond*. Edited by Jan Felix Gaertner. Mnemosyne 83. Leiden: Brill, 2007.
Braginton, Mary V. "Exile under the Roman Emperors." *CJ* 39.7 (1944): 391–407.
Breytenbach, Ciliers. *Grace, Reconciliation, Concord: The Death of Christ in Graeco-Roman Metaphors*. SNTS 135. Boston: Brill, 2010.
Breytenbach, Ciliers. *Versöhnung: eine Studie zur paulinischen Soteriologi*. WUNT 60. Neukirchener: Verlag, 1989.
Briones, David Emilio. "Paul's Financial Policy: A Socio-Theological Approach." Ph.D. diss., Durham University, 2011.
Brock, Roger. *Greek Political Imagery from Homer to Aristotle*. London: Bloomsbury, 2013.
Brown, Perry C. "What Is the Meaning of 'Examine Yourselves' in 2 Corinthians 13:5?" *Bibliotheca sacra* 154 (1997): 175–88.
Browne, G. M. *The Papyri of the Sortes Astrampsychi*. Meisenheim am Glan: Verlag Anton Hain, 1974.
Bruce, F. F. *I & II Corinthians*. NCBC. Grand Rapids, MI: Eerdmans, 1971.
Bultmann, Rudolph. *The Second Letter to the Corinthians*. Translated by Roy A. Harrisville. Minneapolis: Augsburg, 1985.
Campbell, Douglas A. *Framing Paul: An Epistolary Biography*. Grand Rapids: Eerdmans, 2014.
Campenhausen, Hans von. *Ecclesiastical Authority and Spiritual Power in the Church of the First Three Centuries*. Translated by J. A. Baker. 2nd edn. Peabody, MA: Hendrickson, 1997.
Carlson, Stephen C. "On Paul's Second Visit to Corinth: Πάλιν, Parsing, and Presupposition in 2 Corinthians 2:1." *JBL* 135.3 (2016): 597–615.
Carston, Robyn. *Thoughts and Utterances: The Pragmatics of Explicit Communication*. Malden, MA: Blackwell, 2002.
Castor, Robert A. "The Shame of the Romans." *TAPS* 127 (1997): 1–19.
Chester, Stephen J. *Conversion at Corinth: Perspectives on Conversion in Paul's Theology and the Corinthian Church*. New York: T&T Clark, 2005.
Chow, John K. *Patronage and Power: A Study of Social Networks in Corinth*. JSNTSup 75. Sheffield: JSOT, 1992.

Claassen, Jo-Marie. *Displaced Persons: The Literature of Exile from Cicero to Boethius.* Madison: University of Wisconsin, 1999.
Clark, Billy. *Relevance Theory.* Cambridge Textbooks in Linguistics. New York: Cambridge University Press, 2013.
Clarke, Andrew D. *Secular and Christian Leadership in Corinth: A Socio-Historical and Exegetical Study of 1 Corinthians 1–6.* Leiden: Brill, 1993.
Cohen, Sarah T. "Cicero's Roman Exile." Pages 109–28 in *Writing Exile: The Discourse of Displacement in Greco-Roman Antiquity and Beyond.* Edited by Jan Felix Gaertner. Mnemosyne 83. Boston: Brill, 2007.
Cohen, Sarah T. "Exile in the Political Language of the Early Principate." Ph.D. diss., University of Chicago, 2002.
Collange, J.-F. *Enigmes de la Deuxième Epître de Paul aux Corinthiens: Etude Exégétique de 2 Cor. 2,14–7,4.* New York: Cambridge University Press, 1972.
Collins, Adela Yarbro. "The Function of 'Excommunication' in Paul." *HTR* 73 (1980): 251–63.
Conzelmann, Hans. *1 Corinthians: A Commentary on the First Epistle to the Corinthians.* Translated by James W. Leitch. Hermeneia. Philadelphia: Fortress, 1975.
Crafton, Jeffrey A. *The Agency of the Apostle: A Dramatistic Analysis of Paul's Response to Conflict in 2 Corinthians.* JSNTSup 51. Sheffield: JSOT Press, 1991.
Crook, Zeba A. "Honor, Shame, and Social Status Revisited." *JBL* 128.3 (2009): 591–611.
Dahl, Nils A. "Paul and the Church at Corinth According to 1 Corinthians 1:10–4:21." Pages 313–35 in *Christian History and Interpretation: Studies Presented to John Knox.* Edited by W. R Farmer, C. F. D. Moule, and R. R. Niebuhr. Cambridge: Cambridge University Press, 1967.
Danker, Frederick W. *II Corinthians.* Augsburg Commentaries on the New Testament. Minneapolis: Augsburg, 1989.
Danker, Frederick W. "On Stones and Benefactors." *CTM* 86 (1981): 351–56.
Delcor, Mathias. "The Courts of the Church of Corinth and the Courts of Qumran." Pages 69–84 in *Paul and Qumran.* Edited by Jerome Murphy-O'Connor. Studies in New Testament Exegesis. London: Chapman, 1968.
Delling, Gerhard. "Πλεονέκτης, Πλεονεκτέω, Πλεονεξία." *TDNT*, 266–74.
Derrett, J. D. M. "'Handing Over to Satan': An Explanation of 1 Cor 5:1–7." *RIDA* 21 (1979): 11–30.
deSilva, David A. "Measuring Penultimate Reality: An Investigation of the Integrity and Argumentation of 2 Corinthians." *JSNT* 52 (1993): 41–70.
DiCicco, Mario M. *Paul's Use of Ethos, Pathos, and Logos in 2 Corinthians 10–13.* Mellen Biblical Press Series 31. Lewiston, NY: Mellen, 1995.
Doblhofer, Ernst. *Exil und Emigration: Zum Erlebnis der Heimatferne in der römischen Literatur.* Impulse der Forschung 51. Darmstadt: Wissenschaftliche Buchgesellschaft, 1987.
Dodd, C. H. *New Testament Studies.* Manchester: Manchester University Press, 1953.
Duff, Paul B. *Moses in Corinth: The Apologetic Context of 2 Corinthians.* NovTSup 159. Leiden: Brill, 2015.
Duncan, G. S. *St. Paul's Ephesian Ministry.* London: Hodder, 1929.
Ebel, Eva. *Die Attraktivität früher christlicher Gemeinden: Die Gemeinde von Korinth im Spiegel griechisch-römischer Vereine.* WUNT 2.178. Tübingen: Mohr Siebeck, 2004.
Ebel, Eva. "Regeln von der Gemeinschaft für die Gemeinschaft? Das Aposteldekret und antike Vereinssatzungen im Vergleich." *Aposteldekret und antikes Vereinswesen: Gemeinschaft und ihre Ordnung.* Tübingen: Mohr Siebeck, 2011.

Edsall, Benjamin. "When Cicero and St. Paul Agree: Intra-Group Litigation Among the Luperci and the Corinthian Believers." *JTS* 64.1 (2013): 25–36.

Elliot, John H. *What Is Social Scientific Criticism?* Edited by Dan O. Via. Minneapolis: Fortress, 1993.

Engberg-Pedersen, Troels. "2 Korintherbrevs indledningsspørgsmål." Pages 69–88 in *Tro og historie: festskrift til Niels Hyldahl i anledning af 65 års fødselsdagen den 30 december 1995*. Edited by L. Fatum and M. Müller. FBE 7. Copenhagen: Museum Tusculanums Forlag, 1996.

Epstein, David F. *Personal Enmity in Roman Politics, 218–43 B.C.* New York: Croom Helm, 1987.

Evans, Elizabeth. "Physiognomics in the Ancient World." *TAPA* 59.5 (1965): 1–101.

Ewald, Heinrich. *Die Sendschreiben des Apostels Paulus*. Göttingen: Dietrich, 1857.

Fanthan, Elaine. "Dialogues of Displacement: Seneca's Consolations to Helvia and Polybius." *Writing Exile: The Discourse of Displacement in Greco-Roman Antiquity and Beyond*. Translated by Jan Felix Gaertner. Mnemosyne 83. Leiden: Brill, 2007.

Fee, Gordon. *The First Epistle to the Corinthians*. NICNT. Grand Rapids: Eerdmans, 1987.

Filson, Floyd V. "The Second Epistle to the Corinthians." Pages 263–425 in The *Interpreter's Bible*. Edited by George Arthur Buttrick, Walter Russell Bowie, Paul Scherer, John Knox, Samuel Terrien, and Nolan B. Harmon. Vol. 10 of 12. New York/Nashville: Abingdon, 1953.

Findlay, G. G. "Paul the Apostle." Pages 696–731 in *A Dictionary of the Bible*. Edited by James Hastings. Vol. 3 of 5. Edinburgh: T&T Clark, 1909.

Finley, M. I. *Politics in the Ancient World*. New York: Cambridge University Press, 1994.

Fitzgerald, John T. "Paul and Paradigm Shifts: Reconciliation and Its Linkage Group." Pages 241–62 in *Paul Beyond the Judaism/Hellenism Divide*. Edited by Troels Engberg-Pedersen. Louisville, KY: WJK, 2001.

Fitzmyer, Joseph A. *First Corinthians*. AYB 32. New Haven, CT: Yale University Press, 2008.

Flower, Harriet I. *The Art of Forgetting: Disgrace and Oblivion in Roman Political Culture*. Chapel Hill: University of North Carolina Press, 2006.

Forkman, Göran. *The Limits of the Religious Community: Expulsion from the Religious Community within the Qumran Sect, within Rabbinic Judaism, and within Primitive Christianity*. Coniectanea biblica: New Testament Series 5. Lund: Gleerup, 1972.

Forsdyke, Sara. *Exile, Ostracism, and Democracy: The Politics of Expulsion in Ancient Greece*. Princeton: Princeton University Press, 2005.

Fotopoulos, John. "Paul's Curse of the Corinthians: Restraining Rivals with Fear and Voces Mysticae (1 Cor 16:22)." *NT* 56 (2014): 275–309.

Fox, R. L. *Pagans and Christians*. Harmondsworth: Viking Penguin, 1986.

Fredrickson, David E. "Paul's Bold Speech in the Argument of 2 Corinthians 2:14–7:16." Ph.D. diss., Yale University, 1990.

Fredrickson, David E. "Paul's Sentence of Death (2 Corinthians 1:9)." *WW* 4 (2000): 99–107.

Friesen, Steven J. "Prospects for a Demography of the Pauline Mission: Corinth among the Churches." Pages 351–70 in *Urban Religion in Roman Corinth: Interdisciplinary Approaches*. Edited by Daniel N. Schowalter and Steven J. Friesen. HTS 53. Cambridge, MA: Harvard University Press, 2005.

Funk, Robert W. "The Apostolic Parousia: Form and Significance." Pages 249–68 in *Christian History and Interpretation: Studies Presented to John Knox*. New York: Cambridge University Press, 1967.

Furnish, Victor Paul. *II Corinthians*. AYB 32A. Garden City, NY: Doubleday, 1985.

Gaertner, Jan Felix. "The Discourse of Displacement in Greco-Roman Antiquity." Pages 1–20 in *Writing Exile: The Discourse of Displacement in Greco-Roman Antiquity and Beyond*. Edited by Jan Felix Gaertner. Mnemosyne 83. Leiden: Brill, 2007.

Gager, John G. ed. *Curse Tablets and Binding Spells from the Ancient World*. New York: Oxford University Press, 1992.

Garland, D. E. *2 Corinthians*. NAC 29. Nashville: Broadman, 1999.

Garland, Robert. *Wandering Greeks: The Ancient Greek Diaspora from the Age of Homer to the Death of Alexander the Great*. Princeton: Princeton University Press, 2014.

Geertz, Clifford. "Thick Description: Toward an Interpretive Theory of Culture." *The Interpretation of Cultures: Selected Essays*. New York: Basic Books, 1973.

Gehrke, Hans-Joachim. "Relevance Theory and Biblical Interpretation." Pages 217–40 in *The Linguist as Pedagogue: Trends in Teaching and Linguistic Analysis of the Greek New Testament*. Edited by Stanley E. Porter and Matthew Brook O'Donnell. Sheffield: Sheffield Phoenix, 2009.

Gehrke, Hans-Joachim. "Relevance Theory and Theological Interpretation: Thoughts on Metarepresentation." *Journal of Theological Interpretation* 4.1 (2010): 75–90.

Gehrke, Hans-Joachim. *Stasis: Untersuchungen zu den inneren Kriegen in den griechischen Staaten des 5. und 4. Jahrhunderts v. Chr.* Vestigia 35. München: Beck, 1985.

Georgi, Dieter. *The Opponents of Paul in Second Corinthians*. Philadelphia: Fortress, 1996.

Georgi, Dieter. *Remembering the Poor: The History of Paul's Collection for Jerusalem*. Nashville: Abingdon, 1992.

Gilchrist, J. M. "Paul and the Corinthians: The Sequence of Letters and Visits." *JSNT* 34 (1988): 47–69.

Gillihan, Yonder Moynihan. *Civic Ideology, Organization, and the Law in the Rule Scrolls: A Comparative Study of the Covenanters' Sect and Contemporary Voluntary Associations in Political Context*. Edited by Florentino García Martínez. Studies on the Texts of the Desert of Judah 97. Boston: Brill, 2012.

Glancy, Jennifer A. "Boasting of Beatings (2 Corinthians 11:23–25)." *JBL* 123.1 (2004): 99–135.

Gleason, Maud. "Elite Male Identity in the Roman Empire." Pages 67–84 in *Life, Death and Entertainment in the Roman Empire*. Edited by D. S. Potter and D. J. Mattingly. Ann Arbor: University of Michigan Press, 1999.

Gooder, Paula. *Only the Third Heaven? 2 Corinthians 12.1–10 and Heavenly Ascent*. LNTS 313. London: T&T Clark, 2006.

Gouldner, Alvin W. *Enter Plato: Classical Greece and the Origins of Social Theory*. New York: Basic Books, 1965.

Grasmück, Ernst Ludwig. *Exilium: Untersuchungen zur Verbannung in der Antike*. Edited by Alexander Hollerbach, Hans Maier, and Paul Mikat. Rechts- Und Staatswissenschaftliche Veröffentlichungen der Görres-Gesellschaft 30. Munich: Ferdinand Schöningh, 1978.

Gray, Benjamin D. "Exile and the Political Cultures of the Greek Polis, c. 404–146 BC." Ph.D. diss., Oxford University, 2011.

Grebe, Sabine. "Why Did Ovid Associate His Exile with a Living Death?" *CW* 103.4 (2010): 491–509.

Green, Gene L. "Lexical Pragmatics and Biblical Interpretation." *JETS* 50.4 (2007): 799–812.

Grosheide, F. W. *Commentary on the First Epistle to the Corinthians: The English Text with Introduction, Exposition and Notes.* NICNT. Grand Rapids: Eerdmans, 1953.

Gruen, Erich S. *Diaspora: Jews amidst Greeks and Romans.* Cambridge, MA: Harvard University Press, 2002.

Grundmann, Walter. "Ταπεινός." *TDNT* 8:1–27.

Gundry Volf, Judith. *Paul and Perseverance: Staying In and Falling Away.* WUNT 2.37. Tübingen: Mohr Siebeck, 1990.

Gunn, David, and Danna Nolan Fewell. *Narrative in the Hebrew Bible.* Oxford: Oxford University Press, 1993.

Guthrie, George H. *2 Corinthians.* BECNT. Grand Rapids: Baker, 2015.

Gutt, Ernst-August. *Relevance Theory: A Guide to Successful Communication in Translation.* Dallas and New York: SIL and UBS, 1992.

Gutt, Ernst-August. "Translation and Relevance." Ph.D. diss., University of London, 1989.

Hafemann, Scott J. *2 Corinthians: The NIV Application Commentary.* Grand Rapids: Zondervan, 2000.

Hafemann, Scott J. *Suffering & Ministry in the Spirit: Paul's Defense of His Ministry in II Corinthians 2:14–3:3.* Grand Rapids: Eerdmans, 1990.

Hall, David R. *The Unity of the Corinthian Correspondence.* JSNTSup 251. New York: T&T Clark, 2003.

Hamilton, Victor P. *Handbook on the Historical Books.* Grand Rapids, MI: Baker Academic, 2001.

Harland, Philip A. "Associations and the Economics of Group Life: A Preliminary Case Study of Asia Minor and the Aegean Islands." *SEÅ* 80 (2015): 1–37.

Harland, Philip A. *Associations, Synagogues, and Congregations: Claiming a Place in Ancient Mediterranean Society.* Minneapolis: Fortress, 2003.

Harland, Philip A. "Connections with Elites in the World of the Early Christians." Pages 385–408 in *Handbook of Early Christianity: Social Science Approaches.* Edited by Anthony J. Blasi, Paul-André Turcotte, and Jean Duhaime. Walnut Creek, CA: Alta Mira, 2002.

Harrill, J. A. "Invective Against Paul (2 Cor 10:10), the Physiognomics of the Ancient Slave Body, and the Greco-Roman Rhetoric of Manhood." Pages 189–213 in *Antiquity and Humanity: Presented to Hans Dieter Betz on His 70th Birthday.* Edited by Adela Yarbro Collins and Margaret M. Mitchell. Tübingen: Mohr Siebeck, 2001.

Harris, Gerald. "The Beginnings of Church Discipline: 1 Corinthians 5." *NTS* 37 (1991): 1–21.

Harris, Murray J. *The Second Epistle to the Corinthians: A Commentary on the Greek Text.* NIGTC. Grand Rapids, MI: Eerdmans, 2005.

Heilig, Christoph. "Observations from a Linguistic Spectator: An Annual Report (Part 1: Introduction)." Https://www.uzh.ch/blog/theologie-nt/2020/03/23/observations-from-a-linguistic-spectator/. *Zürich New Testament Blog*, 23 March 2020.

Heinrici, Carl Friedrich Georg. *Der erste Brief an die Korinther.* KEK 7. 8th edn. Göttingen: Vandenhoeck & Ruprecht, 1896.

Heinrici, Carl Friedrich Georg. *Der zweite Brief an die Korinther.* KEK 6. 8th edn. Göttingen: Vandenhoeck & Ruprecht, 1900.

Heinrici, Carl Friedrich Georg. "Die Christengemeinden Korinths und die religiösen Genossenschaften der Griechen." *ZWT* 19 (1876): 465–526.

Henderson, Ian. "The Second Sophistic and Non-Elite Speakers." Pages 23–35 in *Perception of the Second Sophistic and Its Times*. Edited by Thomas Schmidt and Pascal Fleury. Toronto: University of Toronto Press, 2011.

Héring, Jean. *The Second Epistle of Saint Paul to the Corinthians*. Translated by A. W. Heathcote and P. J. Allcock. 2nd edn. London: Epworth, 1967.

Hock, Ronald F. *The Social Context of Paul's Ministry: Tentmaking and Apostleship*. Philadelphia: Fortress, 1980.

Hofius, Otfried. "'Der Gott allen Trostes': παράκλησις und παρακαλέω in 2 Kor 1, 3–7." Pages 244–54 in *Paulusstudien*. WUNT 51. Tübingen: Mohr Siebeck, 1989.

Holmberg, Bengt. *Paul and Power: The Structure of Authority in the Primitive Church as Reflected in the Pauline Epistles*. Philadelphia: Fortress, 1980.

Horbury, William. "Extirpation and Excommunication." *Vetus Testamentum* 35.1 (1985): 13–38.

Horrell, David. *The Social Ethos of the Corinthian Correspondence: Interests and Ideology from 1 Corinthians to 1 Clement*. Studies of the New Testament and its World. Edinburgh: T&T Clark, 1996.

Horsfall, N. M. "Virgil, History and the Roman Tradition." *Prudentia* 8 (1976): 73–89.

Hughes, P. E. *The Second Epistle to the Corinthians*. New International Commentary of the New Testament. Grand Rapids: Eerdmans, 1962.

Hurd, John C. *The Origins of 1 Corinthians*. London: SPCK, 1965.

Hyldahl, Niels. "Die Frage nach der literarischen Einheit des Zweiten Korintherbriefes." *ZNW* 64 (1973): 289–306.

Jamir, Lanuwabang. *Exclusion and Judgment in Fellowship Meals: The Socio-Historical Background of 1 Corinthians 11:17–34*. Eugene, OR: Pickwick, 2016.

Jobes, Karen H. "Relevance Theory and the Translation of Scripture." *JETS* 50.4 (2007): 773–97.

Johnson, Lee A. "Paul's Epistolary Presence in Corinth: A New Look at Robert W. Funks' Apostolic Parousia." *CBQ* 68 (2006): 481–501.

Johnson, Lee A. "Satan Talk in Corinth: The Rhetoric of Conflict." *BTB* 29.4 (1999): 145–55.

Joshel, Sandra R. "Geographies of Slave Containment and Movement." Pages 99–128 in *Roman Slavery and Roman Material Culture*. Edited by Michelle George. Phoenix Supplementary 52. Toronto: University of Toronto Press, 2013.

Judge, E. A. "The Early Christians as a Scholastic Community." *JRH* 1 (1960): 4–15, 125–37.

Judge, E. A. "Paul's Boasting in Relation to Contemporary Professional Practice." *Social Distinctives of the Christians in the First Century: Pivotal Essays by E. A. Judge*. Edited by David M. Scholer. Peabody, MA: Hendrickson, 2008.

Judge, E. A. *Rank and Status in the World of the Caesars and St Paul*. Christchurch: University of Canterbury, 1982.

Judge, E. A. "The Social Identity of the First Christians: A Question of Method in Religious History." *Social Distinctives of the Christians in the First Century: Pivotal Essays by E. A. Judge*. Edited by David M. Scholer. Peabody, Mass.: Hendrickson, 2008.

Judge, E. A. *The Social Pattern of Christian Groups in the First Century*. London: Tyndale, 1960.

Kaplan, Jonathan. "Comfort, O Comfort, Corinth: Grief and Comfort in 2 Corinthians 7:5-13a." *HTR* 104.1 (2011): 433–45.

Käsemann, Ernst. "Die Legitimität des Apostles: Eine Untersuchung zu II Korinther 10–13." *ZNW* 41 (1942): 33–71.

Käsemann, Ernst. "Sentences of Holy Law in New Testament." *New Testament Questions of Today.* Translated by W. J. Montague. 2nd edn. London: SCM, 1969.

Keazirian, Edward M. *Peace and Peacemaking in Paul and the Greco-Roman World.* New York: Peter Lang, 2013.

Keener, Craig. *1–2 Corinthians.* NCBC. New York: Cambridge University Press, 2005.

Kelly, Gordon. *A History of Exile in the Roman Republic.* New York: Cambridge University Press, 2006.

Kennedy, James H. *The Second and Third Epistles of St. Paul to the Corinthians.* London: Methuen, 1900.

Ker, James. *The Deaths of Seneca.* Oxford: Oxford University Press, 2009.

Klauck, Hans-Joseph. *2 Korintherbrief.* NEchtB 8. Würzburg: Echter Verlag, 1986.

Klauck, Hans-Joseph. *Ancient Letters and the New Testament: A Guide to Context and Exegesis.* Translated by Dan P. Bailey. Waco, TX: Baylor University Press, 2006.

Klauck, Hans-Joseph. "Compilation of Letter in Cicero's Correspondence." Pages 131–55 in *Early Christianity and Classical Culture, Comparative Studies in Honor of Abraham J. Malherbe.* Edited by John T. Fitzgerald, Thomas H. Olbricht, and L. Michael White. NovTSup 110. Leiden: Brill, 2003.

Kloppenborg, John S. "Associations, Christ Groups, and Their Place in the Polis." *ZNW* 108.1 (2017): 1–56.

Kloppenborg, John S. "Fiscal Aspects of Paul's Collection for Jerusalem." *EC* 8 (2017): 158–93.

Kloppenborg, John S. "Greco-Roman Thiasoi, the Ekklēsia at Corinth, and Conflict Management." Pages 187–218 in *Redescribing Paul and the Corinthians.* Edited by Ron Cameron and Merrill P. Miller. Atlanta: Society of Biblical Literature, 2011.

Kloppenborg, John S. "The Moralizing of Discourse in Greco-Roman Associations." Pages 215–28 in *"The One Who Sows Bountifully": Essays in Honor of Stanley K. Stowers.* Edited by Caroline Johnson Hodge, Saul M. Olyan, Daniel Ullucci, and Emma Wasserman. Brown Judaic Studies 356. Providence, RI: Brown University, 2013.

Klöpper, Albert. *Kommentar über das zweite Sendschreiben des Apostels Paulus an die Gemeinde zu Corinth.* Berlin: Reimer, 1874.

Knox, Wilfred L. *St Paul and the Church of Jerusalem.* Cambridge: Cambridge University Press, 1925.

Konradt, Matthias. *Gericht und Gemeinde: Eine Studie zur Bedeutung und Funktion von Gerichtsaussagen im Rahmen der paulinischen Ekklesiologie und Ethik im 1 Thess und 1 Kor.* BZNW 117. New York: de Gruyter, 2003.

Koskenniemi, Heikki. *Studien zur Idee Und Phraseologie des griechischen Briefes bis 400 n. Chr.* Suomalaisen Tiedeakatemian Toimituksia B/102.2. Helsinki: Suomalaisen Kirjallisuuden Seura, 1956.

Kraftchick, Steven J. "Death in Us, Life in You: The Apostolic Medium." Pages 618–37 in *Society of Biblical Literature 1991 Seminar Papers.* Edited by E. H. Lovering. Atlanta: Scholars, 1991.

Kreinecker, Christina M. "Emotions in Documentary Papyri: Joys and Sorrow in Everyday Life." *DCLY* 2011.1 (2012): 451–72.

Kremer, Jacob. *Der erste Brief an die Korinther.* RNT. Regensburg: F. Pustet, 1997.

Kruse, Colin G. *2 Corinthians.* TNTC. Grand Rapids: Eerdmans, 1987.

Kruse, Colin G. "The Offender and the Offence in 2 Corinthians 2:5 and 7:12." *EvQ* 88.2 (1988): 129–39.

Kruse, Colin G. "The Relationship between the Opposition to Paul Reflected in 2 Corinthians 1–7 and 10–13." *EvQ* 61.3 (1989): 195–202.
Krenkel, Max. *Beiträge zur Aufhellung der Geschicht und der Briefe des Apostels Paulus*. Branschweig: Scuwetschke, 1895.
Kümmel, W. G. *Introduction to the New Testament*. 17th edn. Nashville: Abingdon, 1975.
Kwon, Oh-Young. "A Critical Review of Recent Scholarship on the Pauline Opposition and the Nature of Its Wisdom (Σοφία) in 1 Corinthians 1–4." *CBQ* 8.3 (2010): 386–427.
Lake, Kirsopp. *The Earlier Epistles of St. Paul: Their Motive and Origin*. London: Rivingtons, 1911.
Lambrecht, Jan. "Philological and Exegetical Notes." Pages 589–98 in *Studies in 2 Corinthians*. Leuven: Leuven University Press/Peeters, 1994.
Lambrecht, Jan. *Second Corinthians*. SP 8. Collegeville, MN: Liturgical, 1999.
Lampe, G. W. H. "Church Discipline and the Epistles to the Corinthians." Pages 337–61 in *Christian History and Interpretation: Studies Presented to John Knox*. London: Cambridge University Press, 1967.
Larson, Jennifer. "Paul's Masculinity." *JBL* 123.1 (2004): 85–97.
Lassen, Eva Maria. "The Use of the Father Image in Imperial Propaganda and 1 Corinthians 4:14–21." *TynBul* 42.1 (1991): 127–36.
Last, Richard. "Money, Meals, and Honour: The Economic and Honorific Organization of the Corinthian Ekklēsia." Ph.D. diss., University of Toronto, 2013.
Last, Richard. *The Pauline Church and the Corinthian Ekklēsia: Greco-Roman Associations in Comparative Context*. SNTSMS 164. New York: Cambridge University Press, 2016.
Lau, Te-Li. *Defending Shame: Its Formative Power in Paul's Letters*. Grand Rapids, MI: Baker Academic, 2020.
Lendon, J. E. *Empire of Honour: The Art of Government in the Roman World*. Oxford: Oxford University Press, 1997.
L'hoir, Francesca Santoro. "Heroic Epithets and Recurrent Themes In Ab Urbe Condita." *TAPA* 120 (1990): 221–41.
Lietzmann, D. Hans. *An die Korinther I–II*. HNT 9. Tübingen: Mohr Siebeck, 1949.
Lintott, Andrew. *Violence, Civil Strife, and Revolution in the Classical City*. Baltimore: Johns Hopkins Press, 1982.
Litfin, Duane. *St. Paul's Theology of Proclamation: 1 Corinthians 1–4 and Greco-Roman Rhetoric*. SNTSMS 79. Cambridge: Cambridge University Press, 1994.
Long, Fredrick J. *II Corinthians: A Handbook on the Greek Text*. BHGNT. Waco, TX: Baylor University Press, 2015.
Long, Fredrick J. *Ancient Rhetoric and Paul's Apology: The Compositional Unity of 2 Corinthians*. Edited by Richard Bauckham. SNTSMS 131. Cambridge: Cambridge University Press, 2004.
Longenecker, Bruce W. *Remember the Poor: Paul, Poverty, and the Greco-Roman World*. Grand Rapids, MI: Eerdmans, 2010.
Lütgert, Wilhelm. *Freiheitspredigt und Schwärmgeister in Korinth. Ein Beiträg zur Charakteristik der Christuspartie*. Gütersloh: Bertelsmann, 1908.
Lyons, George. *Pauline Autobiography: Toward a New Understanding*. SBLDS 73. Atlanta: Scholars, 1985.
Ma, John. "The City as Memory." Pages 248–59 in *The Oxford Handbook of Hellenic Studies*. Edited by George Boys-Stones, Barbara Graziosi, and Phiroze Vasunia. Oxford: Oxford University Press, 2009.
Mackintosh, R. "The Brief Visit to Corinth." *Expositor* 7th series, 6 (1908): 226–34.

MacMullen, Ramsay. *Changes in the Roman Empire: Essays in the Ordinary*. Princeton: Princeton University Press, 1990.

MacMullen, Ramsay. *Roman Social Relations: 50 B.C. to A.D. 284*. New Haven, CT: Yale University Press, 1974.

Malherbe, Abraham. "Antisthenes and Odysseus, and Paul at War." *HTR* 76.2 (1983): 143–73.

Malherbe, Abraham. *Social Aspects of Early Christianity*. Philadelphia: Fortress, 1983.

Malina, Bruce. *The New Testament World: Insights from Cultural Anthropology*. 3rd edn. Louisville, KY: Westminster John Knox, 2001.

Mann, Steven T. *Run, David, Run! An Investigation of the Theological Speech Acts of David's Departure and Return (2 Samuel 14–20)*. Siphrut 10. Winona Lake, IN: Eisenbrauns, 2013.

Marquis, Timothy Luckritz. *Transient Apostle: Paul, Travel, and the Rhetoric of Empire*. New Haven, CT: Yale University Press, 2013.

Marshall, I. Howard. "The Meaning of 'Reconciliation.'" Pages 117–32 in *Unity and Diversity in New Testament Theology*. Edited by Robert A. Guelich. Grand Rapids: Eerdmans, 1978.

Marshall, Peter. *Enmity at Corinth: Social Conventions in Paul's Relations with the Corinthians*. WUNT 2.23. Tübingen: Mohr Siebeck, 1987.

Martin, Dale B. *The Corinthian Body*. New Haven, CT: Yale University Press, 1995.

Martin, Dale B. *Slavery as Salvation: The Metaphor of Slavery in Pauline Christianity*. New Haven, CT: Yale University Press, 1990.

Martin, Ralph P. *2 Corinthians*. Word Biblical Commentary 40. Waco, TX: Word, 1986.

Martin, Ralph P. *Reconciliation: A Study of Paul's Theology*. Atlanta: John Knox, 1981.

Matera, Frank. *II Corinthians*. Louisville, KY: Westminster John Knox, 2003.

Mattern, Susan P. *Rome and the Enemy: Imperial Strategy in the Principate*. Berkeley: University of California Press, 1999.

Matthews, Victor Harold, Mark W. Chavalas, and John H. Walton. *The IVP Bible Background Commentary: Old Testament*. Electronic. Downers Grove, IL: InterVarsity, 2000.

Meadowcroft, Tim. "Relevance as A Mediating Category in the Reading of Biblical Texts: Venturing Beyond the Hermeneutical Circle." *JETS* 45.4 (2002): 611–27.

Merritt, H. Wayne. *In Word and Deed: Moral Integrity in Paul*. Emory Studies in Early Christianity. New York: Peter Lang, 1993.

Meyer, Ben F. *The Aims of Jesus*. Edited by Dikran Y. Hadidan. PTMS 48. Eugene, OR: Pickwick, 2002

Meyer, H. A. W. *Critical and Exegetical Handbook to the Epistles to the Corinthians*. Translated by D. D. Bannerman, David Hunter, and William Dickson. 2 vols. Edinburgh: T&T Clark, 1884.

Mitchell, Alan C. "I Corinthians 6:1-11: Group Boundaries and the Courts of Corinth." Ph.D. diss., Yale University, 1986.

Mitchell, Margaret M. "New Testament Envoys in the Context of Greco-Roman Diplomatic and Epistolary Conventions: The Example of Timothy and Titus." *JBL* 111.4 (1992): 641–62.

Mitchell, Margaret M. *Paul and the Rhetoric of Reconciliation: An Exegetical Investigation of the Language and Composition of 1 Corinthians*. Louisville, KY: Westminster John Knox, 1991.

Mitchell, Margaret M. "Paul's Letters to Corinth: The Interpretive Intertwining of Literary and Historical Reconstruction." Pages 307–38 in *Urban Religion in Roman Corinth: Interdisciplinary Approaches*. Edited by Daniel N. Schowalter and Steven J. Friesen. HTS 53. Cambridge, MA: Harvard University Press, 2005.

Momigliano, Arnaldo. "Camillus and Concord." *ClQ* 34.3/4 (1942): 111–20.

Moore, Stephen D., and Janice Capel Anderson. "Taking It Like a Man: Masculinity in 4 Maccabees." *JBL* 117 (1998): 249–73.

Moses, Robert. "Physical and/or Spiritual Exclusion? Ecclesial Discipline in 1 Corinthians 5." *NTS* 59 (2013): 172–91.

Mullins, Terrance Y. "Visit Talk in the New Testament Letters." *CBQ* 35 (1973): 350–58.

Munck, Johannes. *Paul and the Salvation of Mankind*. Translated by Frank Clark. Richmond, VA: John Knox, 1959.

Murphy-O'Connor, Jerome. "I Corinthians, V, 3–5." *RB* 84 (1977): 239–45.

Murphy-O'Connor, Jerome. *Paul: A Critical Life*. New York: Oxford University Press, 1997.

Nesselrath, Heinz-Günther. "Later Greek Voices on the Predicament of Exile: From Teles to Plutarch to Favorinus." Pages 97–108 in *Writing Exile: The Discourse of Displacement in Greco-Roman Antiquity and Beyond*. Edited by Jan Felix Gaertner. Leiden: Brill, 2007.

Niditch, Susan. *War in the Hebrew Bible: A Study in the Ethics of Violence*. Oxford: Oxford University Press, 1993.

Nielsen, Helge K. "Paulus' Verwendung des Begriffs Δύναμις. Eine Replik zur Kreuzetheologie." *Die Paulinische Literatur und Theologie. Anlässlich der 50. jährigen Gründungs-Feier der Universität von Aarhus, hg.v. Sigfred Pederson*. Teologiske Studier 7. Arhus: Forlaget Aros, 1980.

Nijf, Onno M. van. *The Civic World of Professional Associations in the Roman East*. DMAHA. Amsterdam: Gieben, 1997.

Oakes, Peter. *Reading Romans in Pompeii: Paul's Letter at Ground Level*. Minneapolis: Fortress, 2009.

O'Brien, P. T. *Introductory Thanksgivings in the Letters of Paul*. NovTSup 49. Leiden: Brill, 1977.

Olson, Stanley N. "Confidence Expressions in Paul: Epistolary Conventions and the Purpose of 2 Corinthians." Ph.D. diss., Yale University, 1976.

O'Neil, Edward N. "Plutarch on Friendship." Pages 105–22 in *Greco-Roman Perspectives on Friendship*. Edited by John T. Fitzgerald. SBLRBS 34. Atlanta: Scholars, 1997.

Oostendorp, D. W. *Another Jesus: A Gospel of Jewish-Christian Superiority in II Corinthians*. Kampen: J. H. Kok, 1967.

Oropeza, B. J. *Exploring Second Corinthians: Death and Life, Hardship and Rivalry*. RRA 3. Atlanta: Society of Biblical Literature, 2016.

Oropeza, B. J. "Situational Immorality? The Relevance of Paul's 'Vice Lists' for the Corinthian Congregation." *ExpTim* 110.1 (1988): 9–10.

Ousley, Arthur S. "Notes of Artemidorus' 'Oneirocritica.'" *Classical Journal* 592 (1963): 65–70.

Pattemore, Stephen. *The People of God in the Apocalypse: Discourse, Structure, and Exegesis*. SNTSMS 128. New York: Cambridge University Press, 2004.

Peppard, Michael. "Brother against Brother: Controversiae about Inheritance Disputes and 1 Corinthians 6:1–11." *JBL* 133.1 (2014): 179–92.

Peterson, Brian J. *Eloquence and the Proclamation of the Gospel in Corinth*. SBLDS 163. Atlanta: Scholars Press, 1998.

Pettinger, Andrew. *The Republic in Danger: Drusus Libo and the Succession of Tiberius*. Oxford: Oxford University Press, 2012.

Pickett, Raymond. *The Cross in Corinth: The Social Significance of the Death of Jesus*. JSNTSup 143. Sheffield: Sheffield Academic, 1997.

Plummer, Alfred. *A Critical and Exegetical Commentary on the Second Epistle of St. Paul to the Corinthians*. New York: Scribner's Sons, 1915.

Pogoloff, Stephen M. *Logos and Sophia: The Rhetorical Situation of First Corinthians*. SBLDS 134. Atlanta: Scholars, 1992.

Poland, Franz. *Geschichte des griechischen Vereinwesens*. Leipzig: Teubner, 1909.

Post, Edward, trans. *Gai Institutiones*. Oxford: Clarendon, 1904.

Prümm, Karl. *Diakonia Pneumatos: Der zweite Korintherbrief als Zugang zur apostolischen Botschaft. Auslegung und Theologie*. 2 vols. Rome: Herder, 1967.

Reitzenstein, Richard. *Hellenistic Mystery-Religions: Their Basic Ideas and Significance*. Edited by Dikran Y. Hadidian. PTMS. Pittsburgh: Pickwick, 1978.

Riggsby, Andrew. "Appropriation and Reversal as a Basis for Oratorical Proof." *CP* 90.3 (1995): 245–56.

Roetzel, Calvin. *2 Corinthians*. Abingdon New Testament Commentaries. Nashville: Abingdon, 2007.

Roetzel, Calvin. *Judgement in the Community: A Study of the Relationship Between Eschatology and Ecclesiology in Paul*. Leiden: Brill, 1972.

Roetzel, Calvin. "The Language of War (2 Cor. 10:1–6) and the Language of Weakness (2 Cor. 11:21b–13:10)." *BibInt* 17 (2009): 77–99.

Roller, Matthew B. "Exemplarity in Roman Culture: The Cases of Horatius Cocles and Cloelia." *CP* 99.1 (2004): 1–56.

Rosner, Brian. "'Drive out the Wicked Person': A Biblical Theology of Exclusion." *EvQ* 71.1 (1999): 25–36.

Rosner, Brian. *Paul, Scripture and Ethics: A Study of 1 Corinthians 5–7*. Leiden: Brill, 1994.

Sander, E. P. *Jesus and Judaism*. London: SCM, 1985.

Sanders, J. T. "The Transition from Opening Epistolary Thanksgiving to Body in the Letters of the Pauline Corpus." *JBL* 81.4 (1962): 348–62.

Sandmel, Samuel. "Parallelomania." *JBL* 81.1 (1962): 1–13.

Savage, Timothy B. *Power Through Weakness: Paul's Understanding of the Christian Ministry in 2 Corinthians*. SNTSMS 86. Cambridge: Cambridge University Press, 1996.

Schellenberg, Ryan S. "'Danger in the Wilderness, Danger at Sea': Paul and the Perils of Travel." Pages 141–61 in *Travel and Religion in Antiquity*. Studies in Christianity and Judaism/Etudes sur le christianisme et le judaisme 21. Waterloo, ON: Wilfrid Laurier University Press, 2011.

Schellenberg, Ryan S. "Did Paul Refuse an Offer of Support from the Corinthians?" *JSNT* 40.3 (2018): 312–36.

Schellenberg, Ryan S. *Rethinking Paul's Rhetorical Education: Comparative Rhetoric and 2 Corinthians 10–13*. Early Christianity and Its Literature 10. Atlanta: Society of Biblical Literature, 2013.

Schenk, Kenneth. *1 & 2 Corinthians: A Commentary for Bible Students*. Wesley Bible Commentary Series. Indianapolis, IN: Wesleyan Publishing House, 2006.

Schlueter, Carol J. *Filling Up the Measure: Polemical Hyperbole in 1 Thessalonians 2.14-16*. JSNTSup 98. Sheffield: JSOT Press, 1994.

Schmeller, Thomas. *Der zweite Brief an die Korinther*. 2 vols. EKKNT 8. Neukirchen-Vluyn: Neukirchener, 2010, 2015.
Schmeller, Thomas. "Die Cicerobriefe und die Frage nach der Einheitlichkeit des 2. Korintherbriefs." *ZNW* 95 (2004): 181–208.
Schmeller, Thomas. *Hierarchie und Egalität: Eine sozialgeschichtliche Untersuchung paulinischer Gemeinden und Griechisch-römischer Vereine*. Stuttgarter Bibelstudien 162. Stuttgart: Katholisches Bibelwerk, 1995.
Schmeller, Thomas. "No Bridge over Troubled Water? The Gap between 2 Corinthians 1–9 and 10–13 Revisited." *JSNT* 36.1 (2013): 73–84.
Schmithals, Walter. *Gnosticism in Corinth: An Investigation of the Letter to the Corinthians*. Translated by John E. Steely. Nashville: Abingdon, 1971.
Schmithals, Walter. "Die Korintherbriefe als Briefsammlung," *ZNW* 64.3–4 (1973): 287
Schnabel, Eckhard J. *Der erste Brief des Paulus an die Korinther*. HTA. Brunnen: Brockhaus, 2006.
Schrage, Wolfgang. *Der erste Brief an die Korinther*. 4 vols. EKKNT 7. Neukirchen-Vluyn: Neukirchener, 1991–2001.
Schröter, Jens. *Der versöhnte Versöhner: Paulus als unentbehrlicher Mittler im Heilsvorgang zwischen Gott und Gemeinde nach 2 Kor 2,14–7,4*. TANZ 10. Tübingen/Basel: Francke, 1993.
Schubert, Paul. *Form and Function of Pauline Thanksgivings*. BZNW 35. Berlin: Töpelmann, 1939.
Scott, James M. *2 Corinthians*. NIBCNT. Peabody, MA: Hendrickson, 1998.
Scroggs, Robin. "The Sociological Interpretation of the New Testament: The Present State of Research." *NTS* 26 (1980): 164–79.
Seifrid, Mark A. *The Second Letter to the Corinthians*. Edited by D. A. Carson. PNTC. Grand Rapids: Eerdmans, 2014.
Shemesh, Aharon. "Expulsion and Exclusion in the Community Rule and the Damascus Document." *DSD* 9.1 (2002): 44–74.
Singh-Masuda, Neil Raj. "Exilium Romanum: Exile, Politics and Personal Experience from 58 BC to AD 68." Ph.D. diss., University of Warwick, 1996.
Skidmore, Clive. *Practical Ethics for Roman Gentlemen: The Work of Valerius Maximus*. Exeter: University of Exeter Press, 1996.
Skinner, Marilyn B. "Ego Mulier: The Construction of Male Sexuality in Catullus." *Helios* 20 (1993): 107–30.
Smith, David Raymond. *"Hand This Man over to Satan": Curse, Exclusion, and Salvation in 1 Corinthians 5*. Edited by Mark Goodacre. LNTS 386. London: T&T Clark, 2008.
Smith, R. R. R. "Cultural Choice and Political Identity in Honorific Portrait Statues in the Greek East in the Second Century A.D." *JRS* 88 (1998): 56–93.
South, James T. *Disciplinary Practices in Pauline Texts*. Lewiston, NY: Mellen, 1992.
Sperber, Dan, and Deirdre Wilson. "Pragmatics, Modularity and Mind Reading." *ML* 17 (2002): 3–23.
Sperber, Dan, and Deirdre Wilson. "Précis of Relevance: Communication and Cognition." *BBS* 10 (1987): 697–754.
Sperber, Dan, and Deirdre Wilson. *Relevance: Communication and Cognition*. 2nd edn. Oxford: Blackwell, 1995.
Starling, David I. *Not My People: Gentiles as Exiles in Pauline Hermeneutics*. BZNW 184. Berlin: de Gruyter, 2011.
Stegman, Thomas. *The Character of Jesus: The Linchpin to Paul's Argument in 2 Corinthians*. AnBib 158. Rome: Editrice Pontifico Istituto Biblico, 2005.

Stewart-Sykes, Alistair. "Ancient Editors and Copyists and Modern Partition Theories: The Case of the Corinthian Correspondence." *JSNT* 61 (1996): 53–64.
Still, Todd D. *Conflict at Thessalonica: A Pauline Church and Its Neighbours*. JSNTSup 183. Sheffield: Sheffield Academic, 1999.
Strachan, R. H. *The Second Epistle of Paul to the Corinthians*. 7th edn. London: Hodder & Stoughton, 1964.
Strachan-Davidson, J. L. *Problems of the Roman Criminal Law*. 2 vols. Oxford: Oxford University Press, 1912.
Sumney, Jerry L. *Identifying Paul's Opponents: The Question of Method in 2 Corinthians*. JSNTSup 40. Sheffield: Sheffield Academic, 1990.
Sundermann, Hans-Georg. *Der schwache Apostel und die Kraft der Rede. Eine rhetorische Analyse von 2 Kor 10–13*. EHS 23.575. Frankfurt: Peter Lang, 1996.
Syme, Ronald. *The Augustan Aristocracy*. 2nd edn. Oxford: Clarendon, 1989.
Syme, Ronald. *The Roman Revolution*. New York: Oxford University Press, 1939.
Takács, Sarolta A. "Politics and Religion in the Bacchanalian Affair of 186 B.C.E." *HSCP* 100 (2000): 301–10.
Tannehill, R. C. *Dying and Rising with Christ: A Study in Pauline Theology*. BZNW 32. Berlin: Töpelmann, 1967.
Theissen, Gerd. *The Setting of Pauline Christianity: Essays on Corinth*. Translated by John H. Schütz. 2nd edn. Eugene, OR: Wipf & Stock, 2004.
Thiselton, Anthony C. *New Horizons in Hermeneutics*. Grand Rapids: Zondervan, 1992.
Thiselton, Anthony C. *Thiselton on Hermeneutics: Collected Works with New Essays*. Grand Rapids, MI: Eerdmans, 2006.
Thraede, Klaus. *Grundzüge griechisch-römischer Brieftopik*. Edited by Erik Burk and Hans Diller. Zetemata: Monographien zur klassischen Altertumswissenschaft 48. Munich: C. H. Beck, 1970.
Thrall, Margaret E. "The Offender and the Offence: A Problem of Detection in 2 Corinthians." Pages 65–78 in *Scripture: Method and Meaning—Essays Presented to Anthony Tyrrell Hanson*. Edited by Barry P. Thompson. Pickering: Hull University Press, 1987.
Thrall, Margaret E. *The Second Epistle to the Corinthians*. 2 vols. ICC. Edinburgh: T&T Clark, 1994.
Thrall, Margaret E. "A Second Thanksgiving Period in II Corinthians." *JSNT* 16 (1982): 101–24.
Thrall, Margaret E. "Super-Apostles, Servants of Christ, and Servants of Satan." *JSNT* 6 (1980): 42–57.
Todd, Stephen. *The Shape of Athenian Law*. Oxford: Oxford University Press, 1993.
Toner, Jerry. *Popular Culture in Ancient Rome*. Malden, MA: Polity, 2009.
Vandorpe, Kaitlijn. "'Protecting Sagalassos' Fortress of the Akra. Two Large Fragments of an Early Hellenistic Inscription (with an Appendix by Marc Waelkens)." *AncSoc* 37 (2007): 121–39.
Vanhoozer, Kevin. "From Speech Acts to Scripture Acts: The Covenant of Discourse and the Discourse of the Covenant." Pages 1–49 in *After Pentecost: Language and Biblical Interpretation*. Edited by Craig G. Bartholomew, Colin Green, and Karl Möller. Scripture and Hermeneutics 2. Grand Rapids, MI: Zondervan, 2001.
Vegge, Ivar. *2 Corinthians—A Letter about Reconciliation: A Psychological, Epistolographical and Rhetorical Analysis*. WUNT 2.239. Tübingen: Mohr Siebeck, 2008.
Venticinque, Philip F. "Family Affairs: Guild Regulations and Family Relationships in Roman Egypt." *GRBS* 50 (2010): 273–94.

Verboven, Koenraad. "The Associative Order: Status and Ethos of Roman Businessmen in [the] Late Republic and Early Empire." *Athenaeum* 95 (2007): 861–93.
Vermes, Geza. *The Complete Dead Sea Scrolls in English*. Harmondsworth: Penguin, 1997.
Voutiras, E., and K. Sismanides. "Δικαιοπολιτῶν Συναλλαγαί. Μια Νέα Επιγραφή Από Τη Δίκαια." *Ancient Macedonia: Seventh International Symposium*. Thessaloniki, 2007.
Walker, D. D. *Paul's Offer of Leniency (2 Cor 10:1)*. WUNT 2/152. Tübingen: Mohr Siebeck, 2002.
Waltzing, Jean Pierre. *Étude historique sur les corporations professionnelles chez les Romains depuis les origines jusqu'à la chute de l'Empire d'Occident*. 4 vols. Louvain: Charles Peeters, 1895–1900.
Watson, Alan, Theodor Mommsen, and Paul Krueger, eds. *The Digest of Justinian*. 4 vols. Philadelphia: University of Pennsylvania Press, 1985.
Watson, Francis. "2 Cor. X–XIII and Paul's Painful Letter to the Corinthians." *JTS* 35 (1984): 324–46.
Webb, William J. *Returning Home: New Covenant and Second Exodus as the Context for 2 Corinthians 6.14–7.1*. JSNTSup 85. Sheffield: Sheffield Academic, 1993.
Wees, Hans van. "Stasis, the Destroyer of Men." *Sécurité collective et ordre public dans les sociétés anciennes. Sept exposés suivis de discussions*. Entretiens sur l'Antiquité classique 54. Genève: Fondation Hardt, 2008.
Weiss, Johannes. *Der Erste Korintherbrief*. KEK 5. 9th edn. Göttingen: Vandenhoeck & Ruprecht, 1910.
Weiss, Johannes. *The History of Primitive Christianity*. Translated by Frederick C. Grant. New York: Wilson-Erickson, 1937.
Weizsäcker, Karl Heinrich von. *Das apostilische Zeitalter der christlichen Kirche*. Freiburg: Mohr, 1892.
Welborn, L. L. *An End to Enmity: Paul and the "Wrongdoer" of Second Corinthians*. BZNW 185. Berlin: de Gruyter, 2011.
Welborn, L. L. "On the Discord in Corinth: I Corinthians 1–4 and Ancient Politics." *JBL* 106 (1987): 85–111.
Welborn, L. L. "Paul's Appeal to the Emotions in 2 Corinthians 1.1–2.13; 7.5–16." *JSNT* 82 (2001): 31–60.
Welborn, L. L. "The Runaway Paul." *HTR* 92.2 (1999): 115–63.
White, Adam. *Paul, Community, and Disciple: Establishing Boundaries and Dealing with the Disorderly*. Paul in Critical Contexts. New York: Lexington Books/Fortress Academic, 2021.
White, Adam. "Paul's Absence from Corinth as Voluntary Exile: Reading 2 Corinthians 1:1–2:13 and 7:5-16 as a Letter from Exile." *JSNT* 43 (2020): 44–66.
White, Adam. "The Rod as Excommunication: A Possible Meaning for an Ambiguous Metaphor in 1 Corinthians 4.21." *JSNT* 39.4 (2017): 388–411.
Wilson, Deirdre, and Dan Sperber. *Meaning and Relevance*. New York: Cambridge University Press, 2012.
Wilson, Deirdre, and Dan Sperber. "Relevance Theory." Pages 607–32 in *Handbook of Pragmatics*. Edited by G. Horn and L. Ward. Oxford: Blackwell, 2004.
Windisch, Hans. *Der zweite Korintherbrief*. KEK 6. 9th edn. Göttingen: Vandenhoeck & Ruprecht, 1924.
Winkler, John J. *The Constraints of Desire: The Anthropology of Sex and Gender in Ancient Greece*. New York: Routledge, 1990.

Winter, Bruce W. *After Paul Left Corinth: The Influence of Secular Ethics and Social Change*. Grand Rapids: Eerdmans, 2001.
Winter, Bruce W. "Civil Litigation in Secular Corinth and the Church: The Forensic Background to 1 Corinthians 6.1–8." *NTS* 37 (1991): 559–72.
Winter, Bruce W. *Paul and Philo Among the Sophists: Alexandrian and Corinthian Responses to a Julio-Claudian Movement*. 2nd edn. Grand Rapids, MI: Eerdmans, 2002.
Witherington III, Ben. *Conflict & Community in Corinth: A Socio-Rhetorical Commentary on 1 and 2 Corinthians*. Grand Rapids: Eerdmans, 1995.
Wright, N. T. *Jesus and the Victory of God*, Christian Origins and the Question of God 2. Minneapolis: Fortress, 1996.
Wright, N. T. *Paul: A Biography*. New York: HarperOne, 2018.
Wright, N. T. *Paul and the Faithfulness of God*, Christian Origins and the Question of God 4. Minneapolis: Fortress, 2013.
Zaas, Peter S. "Catalogues and Context: 1 Corinthians 5 and 6." *NTS* 34 (1988): 622–29.
Zahn, Theodor. *Introduction to the New Testament*. Translated by John Moore Trout et al. 2nd edn. New York: Scribner's, 1917.
Zakovitch, Yair. "Humor and Theology or the Successful Failure of Israelite Intelligence: A Literary-Folkloric Approach to Joshua 2." Pages 75–98 in *Text and Tradition: The Hebrew Bible and Folklore*. Edited by Susan Niditch. Atlanta: Scholars Press, 1990.
Zanker, Paul. *The Power of Images in the Age of Augustus*. Translated by Alan Shapiro. Ann Arbor: University of Michigan Press, 1990.
Zeller, Dieter. *Der erste Brief an die Korinther*. KEK 5. Göttingen: Vandenhoeck & Ruprecht, 2010.
Ziebarth, Erich. *Das griechische Vereinswesen*. Leipzig: Hirzel, 1869.

Index of References

Hebrew Bible/ Old Testament		Deuteronomy		31 Samuel	
		12.1-5	80	16.17	47
Genesis		13.6	75, 80	17	47
2.25	45	13.16	79	17.1-10	47
3	179	17.2-7	80	17.12	47
3.10	45	17.6	203	17.24	47
3.19	179	17.7	80, 203	17.33	47
3.23	74	19.11-13	203	17.51	47
3.24	179	19.15-21	203		
		19.15	202, 203	2 Samuel	
Exodus		19.15	94	13.1-22	48
12.23	80	19.16-20	80	13.23-39	48
12.43	83	19.19	80	14.1–15.6	49
14.13	121	19.21	203	15.7-12	49
20.20	121	21.18-21	80	15.10	49
22.19	80	21.21	80	15.26	49
23.5	83	22.21-30	80	15.31	49
		24.7	80	16.13	49
Leviticus		28.10	75	16.22	49
1.2	83			19.3	49
20.6	75	Joshua		19.4	47
20.27	75	2.15	198, 199		
		3.10	80	2 Chronicles	
Numbers		7.25	80	36.16	121
12–20	128				
12	128	Judges		Job	
12.3	128	6.14	46	1	197
12.4-9	128	6.27	46		
12.10	128	6.36-40	46	Psalms	
12.14	128	8.6	47	70	181, 183
15.35	74	8.15	47	71	183
16.31-34	128	8.21	47	79 LXX	213
16.35	128	20.13	80	79.19	181, 213
20.1-13	128			80	213
35.30	203			85	181, 183

Psalms (cont.)		Zechariah		15.26	14
86	183	8.13	121	5.1624	78
93	181, 183				
94	183	**NEW TESTAMENT**		*1 Corinthians*	
146.7-8	181	*Matthew*		1–4	20, 23, 244
		4.12-17	197	1.7-8	153
Isaiah		6.10	94	1.8	180
5.13-15	179	7.51	94	1.10–4.21	111, 113
26.17-19	181, 212	10.8-10	21	1.10–4.16	111
26.18	212	10.14	39	1.10-11	107
26.19	212			1.10	111, 224
40.1	181, 183	*Mark*		1.11	163
49.8	221	1.12-13	197	1.17	23
49.13	189			2.1-5	101, 111, 113
51.3	181, 183	*Luke*			
51.12	181, 183	3.1-13	197	2.6–3.3	107
51.19	181, 183	1.52	116	3.1-4	111, 131
52.11	221	10.7	21	3.4	165, 228
57.18	183	10.10-12	39	3.12-15	127
61.1	181	15.32	213	3.13-15	100
61.2	183	22.31-32	197	3.13-14	125
				3.13	127
Jeremiah		*John*		3.14	129
2.30	80	6.32	240	3.15	129, 195
5.6	80	9.22	75	3.17	137
22.17	136	9.34	75	4.1-5	111
31	221	12.42	75	4.3-5	112, 125, 158, 201, 229
31.34	241	16.2	75		
				4.3-4	162
Ezekiel		*Acts*		4.4	118
6.14	80	7.51	94	4.5	112, 127, 128
22.27	136	8.1	47		
36–37	221	9.1-2	47	4.10-13	22
37.1-14	181, 213	9.23-25	198	4.14-21	16
37.12	213	13.51	39	4.14	113
		17.1-10	76	4.16-21	119
Hosea		18.1-18	101	4.16	108, 110, 112
5.14	213	22.4-5	47		
6.1-2	181, 213			4.17	113, 127
6.1	213	*Romans*		4.18-21	31, 77, 92, 106, 110, 111, 114, 115, 118, 121–3, 127, 129-31, 133,
6.2-3	213	1.13	18		
6.2	213	8.5-17	78		
13	179	8.9	217		
13.1	179	9.3	79		
13.8-9	179	11.22	217		
13.14	179	12.15	116		
		15.22	18		

	148, 154, 156, 162–5, 203, 207, 211, 213, 224, 228, 231, 232	5.10-11	82, 159, 161, 164, 165	11.18-34	129
				11.19	125
				11.27-34	84
		5.10	81, 161	11.28-30	129, 165, 228
		5.11	80–2, 161		
		5.12	84	11.29-32	84, 112
		5.13	80–2, 84, 159	12.3	133
4.18	96, 112, 113, 131, 162			12.13-18	22
		6.1-11	107, 112, 131, 159, 160, 164, 228	13.13	129
				14.1-33	107, 131
4.19-21	96			14.37	160
4.19	113, 131			14.38	160
4.20	113, 128	6.9-11	84	15	233
4.21	113, 128, 224	6.9-10	82, 84, 128, 129, 159, 165, 227, 228	15.9	47
				15.50	128
5	77, 88, 239			16	101
5.1–6.20	77, 106, 111			16.1-11	16
		6.9	84	16.1-4	6
5.1-13	74, 77, 80, 84, 85, 96, 104, 107, 112, 114, 129, 135, 136, 160, 164, 165, 179	6.10	161	16.2-8	154
		6.11	84	16.2-7	147, 148
		6.12-21	228	16.3	6, 125, 160
		6.12-20	104, 107, 108, 131, 133, 164, 210	16.5-7	6
				16.12	16, 111, 112
				16.15	163
		6.12-13	108	16.17-18	160
5.1-13	227, 228, 242	7.1	163	16.18	125, 160
		7.7	109, 110	16.22	79
5.1-8	77, 81, 82, 131, 239	7.32-35	109		
		8.1–11.1	131, 140	*2 Corinthians*	
5.1-5	77, 81	8.7-8	162	1–9	3, 5, 9, 231, 232
5.1	82, 161	8.13	195		
5.3-5	79, 81	9	21, 22, 137, 144, 147, 162	1–7	3, 4, 9, 12, 13, 232
5.3	95, 96, 110, 112, 114			1	6
		9.1-27	22	1.1–2.13	5-7, 13, 16, 242
5.5	78, 80–2	9.1-26	108, 112		
5.6-8	77, 78	9.1-18	140	1.1–2.11	26
5.7	82	9.3	162	1.1-11	13
5.9-13	31, 77, 80–2, 84, 228	9.24	45	1.3-11	31, 169, 171, 174, 185, 188, 191, 229
		10.7	133		
		10.23	108		
5.9-10	159	11.1	108, 110, 112, 140	1.3-7	174, 175, 181, 185, 208
5.9	96, 106, 133				
		11.7-11	22		
		11.12-15	22		
		11.17-33	107, 131		

2 Corinthians (cont.)

1.3	174, 175, 189, 191, 204		216, 218, 221	2.1	26, 96–8, 100, 101, 182, 185–7, 240, 241, 244
		1.13	160, 183		
		1.14	153, 183, 207		
1.4	175, 189, 204	1.15–2.13	15, 186, 187	2.4–7.4	8
1.5	181			2.4	5, 187, 188
1.6	191, 207	1.15-22	153	2.5-11	3, 8, 84, 98–100, 102, 103, 132, 136, 167, 185, 190, 231, 238–40, 242, 244
1.8-11	174, 175, 180, 182–4, 192, 200, 201, 206, 208, 211, 229	1.15-18	10, 11		
		1.15-17	17, 31, 153, 163		
		1.15-16	96, 101, 153–5, 185, 207, 211		
1.8-10	169, 184				
1.8-9	175, 184, 189	1.15	153	2.5-6	185
		1.16	12, 97	2.5	123, 222, 240, 241
1.8	174, 182, 189	1.17-22	190		
		1.17-18	24, 25, 31	2.6	103, 104, 115, 217, 241–4
1.9	176, 180, 181, 184, 185, 189, 190, 201, 204, 229	1.17	12, 103, 115, 133–5, 152-58, 161, 165, 169, 183, 185–9, 191, 201, 228, 242		
				2.7-8	242
				2.7	188, 242, 243
1.10-11	182			2.8	185, 242
1.10	180, 183, 185, 204			2.9	191, 231, 242
1.11	174, 184, 225	1.18-22	187, 190	2.10-11	172
		1.19	97, 101	2.10	163, 172, 240, 241
1.12–2.13	13	1.23–2.13	153, 185, 201, 229	2.11	134, 135, 144–6, 188
1.12–2.11	11				
1.12-14	138, 146, 152, 153, 184	1.23	11, 17, 18, 26, 89, 97, 100, 101, 111, 155, 182, 185–7, 240, 243	2.12-13	10, 31, 139, 169, 171, 175, 180, 183–5, 188, 189, 191, 192, 200, 201, 208, 229, 231, 237, 244
1.12-13	145, 146, 155				
1.12	23, 31, 135, 143, 155, 184				
		1.24	123		
1.13-14	2, 8, 133, 143, 152, 153, 157, 160, 169, 184, 185, 189, 211,	2.1-13	155, 158, 189		
		2.1-11	102, 105, 185, 232, 242		
				2.12	189
		2.1-4	10, 163	2.13	189
		2.1-3	11, 17	2.14–7.14	7

2.14–7.4	5–8, 13, 169, 185	6.4-10	183	7.5-6	180, 208
		6.4	128	7.5	139, 175, 189, 190
2.14–6.13	6, 13	6.6	138		
2.14	191, 215	6.7	138	7.6	189, 190, 192, 201, 204, 229, 244
2.16–3.6	221	6.8	145		
2.16–3.4	124, 145	6.9-10	128		
2.17	9, 23	6.11-13	2, 138, 242		
3.1–7.1	221	6.12	138	7.7-12	190
3.4	221	6.13	138	7.7	189
3.6	221	6.14–7.4	13	7.8-15	188
3.12	138	6.14–7.1	5, 138, 222, 229	7.9	231
4.2-4	146			7.10	185, 188, 191, 207, 231
4.2-3	146	6.17	221		
4.2	23, 143, 145, 152	7.1	221		
		7.2-4	2, 6, 138	7.11	103, 242
4.3-4	146, 229	7.2	4, 31, 134–6, 138, 139, 141, 145, 146, 148, 152, 155, 163, 165, 191, 228, 242	7.12	103, 185, 191, 238–42
4.3	138, 221				
4.4	145, 221				
4.7-18	208			7.16	12
4.7	23			8–9	3, 4, 9–13, 183, 185, 191, 232, 233
4.10-12	208				
5.1–6.2	39				
5.1-10	233				
5.3	128	7.3-4	139	8	5-7, 147, 148, 231, 245
5.5	128, 224	7.4-16	16		
5.6-10	233	7.4	12, 138		
5.6	233	7.5-16	3, 5–8, 10, 13, 16, 26, 31, 98–100, 102, 103, 105, 132, 139, 152, 153, 155, 158, 163, 167, 169, 171, 183–6, 188, 191, 192, 200, 201, 229, 231–3, 237–9, 242, 244	8.1–9.15	13
5.9-13	128			8.2	174
5.10	157			8.5	147
5.11	157, 160, 218			8.10-11	12, 148, 161
5.12	157			8.10	137, 162
5.13	31, 157, 228			8.16-24	145, 147, 148, 237
5.14–6.2	2, 3			8.16-23	16
5.18-21	221, 242			8.16-21	163
5.18-20	2			8.22	6, 160
5.18-19	138			9	6, 7
5.18	241			9.1-5	16
5.19	241			9.2	137, 162
5.20–7.3	11			9.3-13	140
5.20–6.2	2, 138			9.3	140, 237
5.20	224, 241			9.4-5	145, 163
6.1	241	7.5-7	185, 188, 201, 237, 244	9.12	140
6.2	221			9.15-23	140
6.3-8	208				

2 Corinthians (cont.)			124–6, 132, 144, 145, 163, 165, 228	11.8	147
10–13	3–10, 12, 13, 15, 99, 102, 103, 117, 125, 136, 183, 185, 191, 192, 205, 225, 231, 232, 243-45			11.9	141
				11.12	140
				11.13-15	141, 146
		10.8-10	115	11.16–12.10	193
		10.8-9	121	11.17-34	128
		10.8	100, 125, 161	11.17	128
				11.19	128
		10.9-10	158	11.20-21	99, 140, 141, 195
		10.10	5, 24, 31, 96, 99, 116, 118, 119, 121–3, 133, 139, 151, 152, 156, 161, 163–5, 192, 196, 228		
				11.20	141, 210
10.1–13.14	13			11.21–12.13	139, 192
10.1–13.13	13				
10.1–13.10	6, 7, 16, 115, 122, 200			11.21–12.10	193
				11.21-23	193
				11.21	139, 192
10.1–12.13	11			11.22–12.10	169
10.1-11	25, 94–6, 111, 115, 118, 123, 126, 134, 152, 156, 206, 231, 232			11.23-33	25, 88, 194
				11.23-29	192, 198
				11.23-28	183
		10.11	99, 115, 117, 126, 130, 139, 141	11.23-25	24
				11.23	169, 192, 199
				11.24-27	193
10.1-10	139	10.12–11.29	162	11.26	128
10.1-6	115, 126	10.12-18	125	11.27-30	128
10.1-2	115	10.12-16	131	11.28-29	193
10.1	24, 31, 96, 99, 116–19, 121, 123, 133, 139, 151, 152, 156, 158, 161, 163–5, 190, 192, 209, 228	10.18	124	11.28	195
		10.14	209	11.29	195, 196
		10.16	199	11.30–12.10	25, 139, 192, 195
		11.1-21	131		
		11.1-16	210	11.30-33	31, 169, 171, 191, 200, 201, 229
		11.1-3	141		
		11.3	143, 145, 204		
		11.4	210	11.30	195, 196, 201, 229
		11.5-15	140		
10.2	99, 116, 117, 121, 155	11.5	140	11.31-32	128
		11.6	24, 111, 140	11.31	191, 204
				11.32-33	169, 192, 199, 206, 208
10.3-6	115, 117, 121, 126	11.7-12	21, 125, 137, 139, 140, 142, 162		
10.3-4	23			11.32	194
10.7-11	115, 126			11.33	198
10.7-8	116	11.7	21, 23, 99, 139–42	12.1-10	196, 208
10.7	5, 31, 109, 115,			12.1-9	200
		11.8-9	140	12.1-4	193

12.2-4	196	12.20-21	8, 17, 98,			118, 132,
12.2	198		115, 117,			133, 155,
12.3-4	198		131, 144,			165, 190,
12.5-6	196		204, 221			202, 203,
12.7-9	193	12.20	98, 99, 222			207, 209,
12.7-8	196, 197	12.21–13.2	99, 101,			211, 217,
12.7	196, 198		103–5,			226, 243
12.9-10	208		109, 162,	13.3-4		100, 116,
12.9	200, 208		227, 228			117, 126,
12.11-18	140	12.21	8, 9, 26,			130, 204,
12.11-15	140		31, 96,			209, 211,
12.11	140, 142		98–101,			214, 229
12.12	140		103, 105,	13.3		31, 109,
12.13	21, 125,		106, 109,			111, 124,
	137, 139,		111, 117,			125, 130,
	140		131-33,			132, 161,
12.14–13.10	16, 104,		144, 156,			163, 165,
	139, 202		164, 190,			169, 192,
12.14-19	104		192, 203,			202–6,
12.14-18	11, 31,		222, 226,			209, 215,
	125, 139,		228, 243			217, 223,
	141	13.1-10	31, 95, 96,			226, 228
12.14-15	21, 140		104, 111,	13.4		100, 117,
12.14	12, 26,		115–18,			139, 141,
	90–2, 101,		124, 126,			192, 202,
	102, 104,		144, 156,			204–11,
	117, 141,		158, 169,			213–15,
	208		202, 217,			217, 218,
12.15-18	146		224, 229,			221, 223,
12.15-16	146		231, 232			225, 226,
12.15	141, 142	13.1-4	202, 215,			229
12.16-18	4, 134–6,		217	13.5-10		169, 203,
	143, 145,	13.1-2	26, 91, 94,			204, 211,
	146, 148,		96, 101–3,			216, 229
	152, 163,		164, 207	13.5-9		144
	165, 228	13.1	12, 90-92,	13.5-7		202
12.16	31, 142,		94, 101,	13.5-6		216, 220,
	143, 151,		132, 202,			224
	161, 165,		203, 207,	13.5		202, 204,
	228		213			216, 217,
12.17-18	144	13.2-3	204, 209,			226
12.18	144, 161		211, 215	13.6		125, 157,
12.19–13.1	11	13.2	8, 9, 31,			160, 183,
12.19-21	104, 144		92–101,			189, 218,
12.19	144, 225		105, 106,			222, 226
12.20–13.10	152		109, 111,	13.7-9		216, 221,
12.20–13.2	139		115, 117,			223, 224

2 Corinthians (cont.)		*Philippians*		15.23	119
13.7	202, 221–	1.20	94		
	3, 226	2.25-30	176	*4 Maccabees*	
13.8	222, 223	3.6	47	1.4	157
13.9-10	2,	3.8	47	7.20-23	157
	225			11.20-22	46
13.9	192, 203,	*1 Thessalonians*		15.28-30	149
	223, 225	2.1-20	76, 130	17.11-16	46
13.10	10, 94, 96,	2.2	76		
	100, 117,	2.16	75	**Dead Sea Scrolls**	
	126, 141,	2.18	18	*1QS*	
	203, 211,	3.1-10	176	2.19-22	75
	214, 216,			6.25–7.25	80
	225	*2 Thessalonians*			
13.11-13	6, 7, 242	1.5	128	*4Q270*	
13.11	12			7 i 12-13	81
16.3-7	12	*James*			
		1.9	116	*4QDa*	
Galatians		4.6	116	fr. 11.17-18	79
1.6	49, 156			fr. 11 5c-18	74
1.8-9	79	*1 Peter*		fr. 11.14c-16b	83
1.9	94	5.5	116	fr. 11.17-18	74
1.11–2.14	176				
1.11-12	156	*1 John*		*CD*	
1.13-14	47	2.19	75	12.4-6	74, 75, 80
1.18-24	156			19–20	75
2.1-10	156	*2 John*			
2.11-14	156	10	75	**Tosefta Talmud**	
2.11	130			*Baba Meṣ'iah*	
2.12-13	49, 156	*3 John*		2.33	83
2.12	45, 49, 130	10	75		
2.14	48			**Philo**	
3.1	156	Apocrypha		*In Flaccum*	
3.11	48	*Baruch*		18	55
3.14	48	4.5	121		
4.14	49			*De Iosepho*	
5.21	128	*1 Maccabees*		40–42	37
		3.14	121		
Colossians				*Legum allegoriae*	
1.22-23	217	*2 Maccabees*		1.63-72	150
		11.12	45		
Ephesians				*De praemiis et poenis*	
2.11-22	39	**Pseudepigrapha**		159	136
5.5	128	*3 Maccabees*			
		2.33	74	*De Somniis*	
		15.5	119	2.95	119

Index of References

De specialibus legibus
1.60   75

De vita Mosis
1.152-54   157
2.186   136
264   52

JOSEPHUS
Antiquitates judaicae
5.15   198
5.466-469 198
11.66   212

Vita
25   42

Bellum judaicum
5.335   119
6.362   44

APOSTOLIC FATHERS
1 Clement
30.2   116

CLASSICAL AND ANCIENT CHRISTIAN LITERATURE
Aelius Aristides
Orationes
23.31   52
23.54   52
24.21   52
24.37   52
24.41   239

Aeschines
De falsa legatione
150-51   187

In Timarchum
1.1   50
1.2   50

Suppliants
732   121

Andocides
1.8   186
1.9   186
1.11-12   187
1.20-21   187

Apollonius
Epistolae
45   239

Appian
Bella civilia
1.26   53
1.63   236

Apuleius
Metamorphoses
9.41   44

Archytas
fr.D25b   136

Aristotle
Athēnaīn politeia
39.1   37, 38
39.6   239

Ethica nicomachea
5.1.8-9   136
5.3.14   136
9.6.2   53

Physiognomonica
809a-810a 151

Politica
5.1.3-5.2.11 51
1284a3-b34   60
1284b21-22   52

Rhetorica
1.12.20   43
2.6.3   45

Artemidorus
Onirocritica
4.44   733

Athenaeus
Deipnosophistae
5.214a   198
6.254c-d   153

Aullus Gellius
Noctes atticae
7.13.3   109
7.14.3   120
15.13.11   150
17.2.7   219

Bacchylides
Lyricus
Fr. 24   52

Caelius
Fam.
8.8.2-3   61

Caesar
Bellum gallicum
8.24   120

Cicero
Epistulae ad Atticum
3.8.4   50
3.9.3   50
3.15.2   177
3.15.5   236
3.22.2-3   236
3.24.2   236
4.1.4-5   215
6.6   212
12.53   95
52.1   44

Pro Caecina
34.100   61

In Catalinam
4.20   120

Divinatio in Caecilium
63   126

De domo suo
95   186
96   186
98   54, 178
99-100   220
99   186
127-129   57
137   219
141   219

Epistulae ad familiares
2.9.2   95
5.4   50
5.8   239
6.8.2   235
6.20.2   235
7.6   123, 150
14.3.1-2   48, 194
14.4.2   83
15.16.1   95
16.16.2   95

De finibus
5.16   217

Pro Ligario
18   120

Pro Murena
89   235

De officiis
3.5.22   52

Orationes philippicae
1.9.21-23   61

In Pisonem
20   186

Pro Plancio
69   186
97   83

Pro Quinctio
3.11   150

Epistulae ad Quintum fratrem
fr. 1.3.1   177

Post reditum ad populum
6   186
10   186
11   186
14   219

Post reditum in senatu
25   186
27   212
34   219, 220
37   186
38   186

De republica
1.1.1   46
2.17.69   53
5.1.1   46

Pro Sestio
13.1   215
37   186
63   236
140   53

Pro Sulla
46   120
74   44
91   55

Tusculanae Disputationes
2.18.43   41

In Vatinium
8   186

Corpus hermeticum
13.7   137

Clement of Alexandria
Paedagogus
3.3.19.2   199

Demosthenes
Adversus Androtionem
56–57   136

Epistolae
2   236
2.2   239
2.16-17   37
2.19   187
2.24-25   187
2.25-26   187
2.26   54

In Midiam
43   60

Digesta
12.5.1   61
32.1.2   64
47.10.44   110
47.13.7   110
48.8.3.5   62
48.10.33   61
48.19.2   64
48.19.24   57
48.20.7   64
48.22.6   64
48.22.14   64

Dio
20–22   57

Dio Cassius
38.25.4   186
53.23.6   55
58.5.4   119
67.3.3   58
Frag. 24   186

Dio Chrysostom

Tarsica altera (Or. 34)
20	52
21	53
22–23	52

De regno i (Or. 1)
44	56

De gloria ii (Or. 67)
3	217

De regno iv (Or. 4)
57	217

De regno iii (Or. 3)
7	157
10	157

De avaritia (Or. 17)
10	136, 137

De exilio (Or. 13)
6	48, 214

Ad Nicaeenses (Or. 39)
8	53

De concordia cum Apamensibus (Or. 40)
16	37
24	119
24.22.10	110
40.55	61
79.20.1-3	120

De Virtute
11.15-18	195

Diodorus
3.3.2	126
19.1.1-4	60
34–35.26	236
34.2.22	194
34.2.33	123

Dionysius of Halicarnassus

Antiquitates romanae
2.76.3	52
4.64	186
6.69.4	37
6.86.5	52
7.30.2	52
7.42.1	52
8.29.3	37

Ennius

Tragedies
261	123, 150

Epictetus

Diatribai (Dissertationes)
2.1.10-12	195
3.22.12.19-20	217

Euripides

Hippolytus
1045-1050	179
895-1100	179

Phoenissae
509-10	42
510	120
549	136, 137

Gaius

Institutiones
1.144	156

Gran. Licin.
33.6-11C	126

Hesiod

Theogonis
226-27	238

Herodotus

Historiae
4.201	151

Homer

Iliad
1.85	121

Odyssey
19.137	143
19.494	143

Horace

Epistulae
1.7	18
2	19
8	19

Isocrates

Antidosis (Or. 15)
217	41

Epistulae
8, 1-4	37
8, 3-4	52

Juvenal

Satirae
3.144-46	150, 153
8.185-86	150, 153

Leonidas

Anth. pal.
7.715.2-3	179

Livy
1.41.3	41
2.2	186
2.3.6	236
2.32.9-12	52
2.57-60	186
6.42.9-12	52
9.6.9-10	44
22.61.10	44
24.4.9-10	61
25.6.7-9	44
39.7.5	198
40.8	52

Lysias		Pindar		*Amatorius*	
12.5	52	*Pythionikai*		7	156
		2.39	143		
		8.83-87	44	*An seni respublica*	
Maximus Valerius				*gerenda sit*	
5.4	45	Plato		787D	42
		Leges			
Minucius Felix		3.691a	136	*De auditu*	
Octavius		9.871B	79	44B	42
36.9	41	626E	157		
		881d-e	79, 83	*Brutus*	
Ovid		909c	79, 83	13	149
Fasti		955b	79, 83		
6.642	57			*Cato Major*	
		Phaedo		6.3	122
Ex ponto		69C	150		
4.16.47-52	178	228E	95	*Cicero*	
				19.7	119
Tristia		*Respublica*		30–31	55
1.1.118	178	359c	136	31.4-5	54
1.3.22-26	178			33.5	215
1.3.89-102	178	Plautus		42.2	239
1.8.14	178	*Casina*			
2.207	58	875-877	44	*Marcius Coriolanus*	
3.3.73-76	178			2.1	122
3.11.25-32	178	*Pseudolus*		15.5	119
3.14.20	178	35–36	95		
5.1.11-14	178	63–64	95	*De fraterno amore*	
5.1.79-80	95			2.13	52
		Pliny the Younger		479A	137
PG		*Epistulae*			
61.420-21	97	4.11.3	64	*Pericles*	
61.420	182			37.1	122
61.455	89, 97	Plutarch			
82.385	97	*Alcibiades*		*Quaestionum*	
		23.3-5	150	*convivialum libri IX*	
PL				9.6	239
17.173	89	*Quomodo adulator ab*			
			amico	*Sulla*	
Paulus		*internoscatur*		31	214
Sententiae		25	217	34.1	215
5.26.3	83				
		Aemilius Paullus		*Tiberius et Caius*	
Philostratus		26.2	194, 198	*Gracchus*	
Vit. Phil.		26.7-12	194	9.4-5	150
1.8	57	26.12	194	17	53

Polybius

1.16.4	122
6.10.14	46
6.14.6-8	61
15.21	51
22.6	62
23.11	52
55.4	173

Priscian
Inst. Gramm.

8.4.16	83

Ps.-Libanius

15	239

Quintilian
Institutio oratoria

12.5.3	43

Sallust
Bellum catalinae

51.22-23	61
51.40-42	61

Bellum jugurthinum

24.2	153
67.3	150

Seneca
Claud.

23.2	62

Dom.

8.3-4	58

Epistulae Morales

40.1	95

Ad Helvium

1.3	178
9.4	219
9.6	220

Ad Lucilium

36–46	137
90.36	137

Ad Polybium de consolatione

13.4	64

Troades

212-14	42, 151

Sophocles
Antigone

300	142

Oedipus coloneus

649	121

Suetonius
Divus Augustus

51	63
55.1	58
65.2	44
66	55

Gaius Caligula

28	64

Domitianus

10.2-3	64

Divus Julius

42	61

Nero

5.1	110

Tiberius

35.1-2	58
50	64
53	64
54	64

Tacitus
Agricola

32.1	52

Annales

1.6	64
1.53	64
3.17	57
3.24.2-3	58
3.24.5-7	55
4.13	64
4.59	149
6.7	44
6.29	64
6.5.1	44
12.21	55
14.17	52, 70
15.28	64
16.18-19	55

Historiae

1.68	123
3.54	149
3.55	150

Thucydides

3.82-83	51

Valerius Maximus

4.1	239
4.7.3	126
5.3	220
6.9.13	126

Valleius Paterculus

2.19.1	55

Xenophon
Hellenica

2.4.39-43	37
2.4.39	215
2.4.40-41	214

Hiero

7.1-10	41

Memorabilia

1.5.1	157
1.5.5	157
2.3.18	52

Oeconomicus

12.13	157
21.12	157

Index of References

OSTRACA, PAPYRI
AND TABLETS

C.Ord.Ptol
53	238

P.Amh.
2.78.11-14	136, 137

P.Dem.Berlin
3115 D 1.5-7	71

P.Dem Cairo
30606	71
30606.8, 20-21	71
30606.8, 24-25	71
31179.22	71, 72
31179.24-26	71

P.Dem.Lille
29.9-10, 25-26	71
29.13-14, 21-22	71

P.Fay.
123	18

P.Frieb.
4.56.2-9	17

P.Giss.
17	39, 236
17 lines 13-14	38
17 lines 9-10	38

P.Köln
7.313	238
7.313.10-20	241

P.Lond.
7.1979, 17-19	17
46.73	142
1926.16-18	95
2710.15-16	71

P.Mich.
3.203	17
5.243	69
5.243.3	71
5.234.8	137
8.482	95
15.751.26-30	18

P.Oxy.
12.1488.20-25	17
14.1773.5-16	18
34.2708.11-14	136, 137
38.2857.26-27	143
38.2857.5-7	143
42.3065, 16-17	18
46.3313.6-8	17
65.4481.8	136, 137

P.Oxy.Hels.
48	18
48.5-8	18

P.Panop.Beatty
2.97	136

P.Sorb.
3.103.9	137

P.Teb.
1.5.1-13	38

P.Turner
34.13	136
34.23	136

INSCRIPTIONS

AGRW
121	79
299	79

BGP
A 9.90	17

BGU
3.846	38, 39, 236
3.846 lines 5-9	38
3.846 line 10	38
3.846 line 11	38
3.846 line 16	38
3.846 lines 15-16	38
4.1080.1-10	95
4.1080.6-8	95
16.2636.10	96

CID
1.9B.40-45	71

CIL
14.2112	69, 71

GDI
5653C.10-12	79

GHI
85B, ll. 39-42	38

IDelos
1520.53-69	79

IDidyma
486	69

IEph
1386.3-5	72

IPark
24	238

IG
2.1275	71
2.1339.5-15	72
2.1339.57	72
2.1361.13-15	72
2.1368.A	71
2.1369	71
2.1369.40-44	72
12.3.330 C	125
1271.1-14	68, 159
1327.4-16	68, 159
1329.3-19	68, 159
1334	69
1368	69, 71

1368.27-28	68	*LSAM*		*SEG*	
1368.53-5	125	19	78	18.726.46-8	126
1368.84-95	127			31.122	71, 72
		OGI		33.1165	69
IGR		90.19-20	38	51.1105B.3-6	126
3.137	79				
4.1430	69	*SB*		*SIG*	
		8.989	38, 39	3.1109.72-91	71
ILS		8.989 line 2	38	985	78
7212.1.23-2.2	71	8.989 line 7	38	985.25-50	72
7212.1.26-2.2	71	8.989 line 8	38	987.35-36	79
7212.2.25-28	71	22.15779.10	96	1098	68
		24.1067.31-32	137		
IvP		24.16134.15-17	136		
I 249.26-30	126				

Index of Authors

Adeleye, G. 125
Aejmelaeus, L. 3, 5, 99, 104, 116–18, 122–4, 135, 141, 142, 205–7, 211, 216–18
Allo, E. B. 88, 90, 117
Alwine, A. T. 39–41, 51, 55
Anderson, J. C. 120, 149, 150, 157
Andrews, S. B. 25, 192, 194, 195
Arnaoutoglou, I. 70
Artzt-Grabner, P. 17, 18, 91, 95, 96, 136, 137, 143, 145, 174, 175, 180, 233, 241
Ascough, R. 65, 71
Auer, P. 29
Aune, D. E. 15

Bachmann, P. 104, 106, 117, 121, 176, 185, 189, 190, 192, 204, 206, 216, 223, 242, 243
Bammel, E. 159
Barclay, J. M. G. 48, 76, 87, 106–8, 200
Barnett, P. 13, 25, 92, 94, 100, 104, 105, 108, 116, 118, 122–4, 127, 130, 142, 143, 181, 183, 185, 193, 203, 204, 217, 222–5, 241–3
Barré, M. L. 195, 196
Barrett, C. K. 89, 90, 92, 94, 97-99, 101, 104, 105, 108, 116, 136, 147, 181, 187, 204, 205, 207, 222, 240, 242, 243
Barton, C. A. 41–4, 46, 109, 110, 149, 150, 153, 210, 218
Batten, A. 67, 79
Bauman, R. A. 58, 61-4
Baur, F. C. 91-93, 97, 102
Beale, G. K. 2, 190
Begg, C. 198
Bell, S. 56, 172
Bergmann, B. 57
Betz, H. D. 116, 117, 125, 135, 143, 147, 152, 162, 192

Beyschlag, W. 240
Bieringer, R. 3, 5, 8, 9, 26, 89, 91, 101–5, 143, 175, 181, 183, 189, 190, 238
Bishop, E. F. F. 192
Bleek, F. 90
Boakye, A. 181, 183, 212, 213
Boda, M. J. 36
Börm, H. 51, 162, 239
Bornkamm, G. 5
Bosenius, B. 11, 93
Boter, G. J. 136
Bowie, E. L. 212, 219
Braginton, M. V. 63, 64
Breytenbach, C. 2, 40
Briones, D. E. 139, 151
Brock, R. 52
Brown, P. C. 217
Browne, G. M. 66
Bruce, F. F. 4, 90, 101, 102, 145
Bultmann, R. 5, 92, 94, 97, 98, 100, 106, 116, 117, 124, 125, 137, 138, 140, 142, 152, 180, 192, 205, 206, 218, 222, 223, 243

Campbell, D. A. 12, 90, 96, 101, 105, 106, 116, 152
von Campenhausen, H. 77, 81
Carlson, S. C. 91, 94, 97, 98, 101, 111
Carston, R. 27
Castor, R. A. 43
Chavalas, M. V. 49
Chester, S. J. 107
Chow, J. K. 22, 82, 140
Claassen, J.-M. 177, 186, 212, 236
Clark, B. 27, 29
Clarke, A. D. 79, 159
Cohen, S. T. 59, 61–4, 186, 218–20
Collange, J.-F. 2, 146
Collins, A. Y. 77, 78

Conzelmann, H. J. 82
Crafton, J. A. 6, 210
Crook, Z. A. 109

Dahl, N. A. 112
Danker, F. W. 67, 145, 155
David, D. R. 77
Delcor, M. 160, 203
Delling, G. 136, 137
Derrett, J. D. M. 77
deSilva, D. A. 138
DiCicco, M. M. 209, 210
Doblhofer, E. 177
Dodd, C. H. 231
Duff, P. B. 108, 129, 138, 157, 221
Duncan, G. S. 89, 101

Ebel, E. 66, 71, 80, 82, 159, 160
Edsall, B. 160
Elliot, J. H. 20
Engberg-Pedersen, T. 91, 92, 97, 98
Epstein, D. F. 39, 41, 56
Evans, E. 151
Ewald, H. 88, 90, 100, 145, 240

Fanthan, E. 178
Fee, G. 77, 78, 80, 82, 83, 106, 114
Fewell, D. N. 179
Filson, F. V. 25, 118, 122, 136, 203, 217
Findlay, G. G. 88, 240
Finley, M. I. 40, 51, 53, 54, 56, 60
Fitzgerald, J. T. 3, 38
Fitzmyer, J. A. 107, 128
Flower, H. I. 57
Forkman, G. 77, 81
Forsdyke, S. 54, 59, 60, 79
Fotopoulos, J. 79
Fox, R. L. 69
Fredrickson, D. E. 117, 135, 136, 138, 175
Friesen, S. J. 30
Funk, R. W. 15, 16, 129
Furnish, V. P. 3, 4, 89, 90, 94, 97, 98, 100, 101, 104, 108, 116, 125, 137, 142, 145, 155, 187, 193, 204, 205, 216, 218, 222, 224, 240, 242, 243

Gaertner, J. F. 35, 167
Gager, J. G. 79
Garland, D. E. 10, 99, 102, 122, 155, 225, 239
Garland, R. 52, 53, 60, 66, 214, 215
Geertz, C. 30
Gehrke, H.-J. 51, 60, 110
Georgi, D. 5, 21, 125, 162, 185, 207
Gilchrist, J. M. 99
Gillihan, Y. M. 71, 74, 81, 83, 160
Glancy, J. A. 24, 25, 151
Gleason, M. 172
Gooder, P. 196-98
Gouldner, A. W. 42
Grasmück, E. L. 35, 36, 52–4, 59, 60, 62, 66, 67, 71, 177
Gray, B. D. 37, 38, 51, 53, 59, 60
Grebe, S. 177
Green, G. L. 27
Grosheide, F. W. 81
Gruen, E. S. 58
Grundmann, W. 99
Gundry Volf, J. 78, 80, 84, 217
Gunn, D. 179
Guthrie, G. H. 13, 91, 94, 99, 101, 153, 155, 182, 206, 207, 217, 218, 223
Gutt, E.-A. 27

Hafemann, S. J. 9, 112
Hall, D. R. 12, 90, 104
Hamilton, V. P. 49
Harland, P. A. 67, 70–2
Harrill, J. A. 24, 117, 143, 145, 151, 208
Harris, G. 77
Harris, M. J. 12, 88, 91, 94, 97-99, 101, 104, 105, 118, 122, 135, 136, 142, 144, 175, 190, 193, 195, 203, 205, 206, 217, 218, 222–4, 239, 241–3
Heilig, C. 176
Heinrici, C. F. G. 11, 65, 93, 97, 199, 223, 239
Hemer, C. J. 176
Henderson, I. 24
Héring, J. 89-91, 137, 204, 207
Hock, R. F. 21–3, 117
Hofius, O. 181, 183
Holmberg, B. 20–2
Horbury, W. 74, 75, 80, 81, 83
Horrell, D. 22, 108, 136
Horsfall, N. M. 172

Hughes, P. E. 11, 88, 90, 92, 105, 117, 125, 142, 182, 187, 190, 204, 239
Hurd, J. C. 106
Hyldahl, N. 11, 91-93, 97, 239

Jamir, L. 128
Jobes, K. H. 27
Johnson, L. A. 16, 146
Joshel, S. R. 66
Judge, E. A. 20, 23, 65, 193

Kaplan, J. 190
Käsemann, E. 21, 77, 80, 117, 124, 125, 207
Keazirian, E. M. 40, 235
Keener, C. 9
Kelly, G. 50, 52–4, 61–3, 83, 179, 235, 236
Kennedy, J. H. 4, 5, 93, 101, 155
Ker, J. 178
Klauck, H.-J. 95, 99, 124, 135, 143, 152, 175, 183, 189, 206, 230
Kloppenborg, J. S. 57, 67, 68, 70–2, 76, 79, 84, 148, 160
Klöpper, A. 90
Knox, W. L. 147
Konradt, M. 78
Koskenniemi, H. 15, 95
Kraftchick, S. J. 9
Kreinecker, C. M. 17
Kremer, J. 77, 83, 112–14, 128
Krenkel, M. 90-92, 94, 95, 239, 240, 243
Krueger, P. 57
Kruse, C. G. 3, 4, 102, 239, 240
Kümmel, W. G. 100
Kwon, O.-Y. 24

L'hoir, F. S. 172, 173
Lake, K. 90
Lambrecht, J. 136, 199, 205, 206, 223
Lampe, G. W. H. 78, 81, 83, 239
Land, C. D. 12, 25, 26, 93, 95, 97, 99, 111, 118, 140–2, 153, 154, 156, 157, 239
Larson, J. 24, 118, 156
Lassen, E. M. 113
Last, R. 30, 68, 99, 125, 129, 159
Lau, T.-L. 42, 45, 49
Lendon, J. E. 45, 67, 68, 109, 110, 120, 173

Lietzmann, D. H. 92, 98, 100, 117, 192, 207, 222, 243
Lintott, A. 52
Litfin, D. 23
Long, F. J. 11, 12, 19, 27, 92, 93, 142, 147, 154, 160, 174–6, 181–4, 193, 197, 203, 205, 216, 222, 223, 225, 240
Longenecker, B. W. 31
Lyons, G. 183, 184

Ma, J. 57
MacMullen, R. 66, 68, 110, 120
Mackintosh, R. 88
Malherbe, A. J. 20, 21, 23
Malina, B. 42, 43, 109
Mann, S. T. 49
Marquis, T. L. 17, 18, 182
Marshall, I. H. 2
Marshall, P. 22, 40, 41, 43, 98, 117, 140, 147, 152, 155, 156
Martin, D. B. 22, 107, 111
Martin, R. P. 2, 3, 21, 90, 94, 98, 100, 101, 116, 117, 135–7, 145, 147, 152, 176, 181, 193, 206, 207, 210, 217, 223, 241, 243
Matera, F. 240
Mattern, S. P. 109
Matthews, V. H. 49
Meadowcroft, T. 27
Merritt, H. W. 117, 207
Meyer, B. F. 1
Meyer, H. A. W. 11, 90, 98, 105, 108, 124, 136, 138, 142, 154, 157, 218, 222, 223, 240, 242, 243
Mitchell, A. C. 6, 7, 14, 108, 112, 159
Mitchell, M. M. 144, 147
Momigliano, A. 53
Mommsen, T. 57, 62, 64
Moore, S. D. 120, 149, 150, 157
Moses, R. 78
Mullins, T. Y. 16
Munck, J. 20, 98, 207
Murphy-O'Connor, J. 81, 108

Nesselrath, H.-G. 168
Niditch, S. 46, 47
Nielsen, H. K. 209, 211
van Nijf, O. M. 67, 69

O'Brien, P. T. 174, 175
O'Neil, E. N. 138
Oakes, P. 30, 31
Olson, S. N. 8, 175
Oostendorp, D. W. 25, 117, 118, 121, 124, 204
Oropeza, B. J. 82, 125, 155, 175, 180, 193, 217
Ousley, A. S. 70

Pattemore, S. 27, 28
Peppard, M. 84
Peterson, B. J. 100, 117, 193
Pettinger, A. 55
Pickett, R. 210
Plummer, A. 92, 98, 104, 105, 116, 122–4, 136, 142, 145, 154, 184, 190-93, 204, 206, 208, 241, 243
Pogoloff, S. M. 23, 117
Poland, F. 66, 71, 159
Post, E. 177
Prümm, K. 104, 217

Reitzenstein, R. 117
Riggsby, A. 146
Roetzel, C. 7, 25, 77, 123, 128, 129
Roller, M. B. 173
Rosner, B. 78, 80, 159

Sanders, E. P. 87
Sanders, J. T. 174
Sandmel, S. 168
Savage, T. B. 22, 118, 151
Schellenberg, R. S. 15, 17, 22, 24, 25, 118, 121, 122, 135, 140, 141, 147, 148, 158, 194, 199
Schenk, K. 4
Schlueter, C. J. 76
Schmeller, T.
Schmeller, T. 3, 13, 21, 25, 91, 92, 94, 97–101, 104, 116–18, 122, 124, 125, 135, 140, 142–5, 147, 152, 153, 155, 180, 185, 189, 192, 193, 198, 199, 203, 205–8, 216, 218, 222–5, 230, 242
Schmithals, W. 6, 88, 117, 194, 214
Schnabel, E. J. 113, 114
Schrage, W. 83, 106, 111, 112
Schröter, J. 2
Schubert, P. 174
Scott, J. M. 13, 181, 194

Scroggs, R. 20
Seifrid, M. A. 174
Shemesh, A. 75, 80, 81
Singh-Masuda, N. R. 55, 62–4
Sismanides, K. 37
Skidmore, C. 172
Skinner, M. B. 120
Smith, R. R. R. 56
South, J. T. 75, 77–81, 145, 243
Sperber, D. 27–9
Starling, D. I. 221
Stegman, T. 181
Stewart-Sykes, A. 230
Still, T. D. 76
Strachan, R. H. 89, 90, 136, 155, 192, 204
Strachan-Davidson, J. L. 61–4, 83
Sumney, J. L. 155
Sundermann, H.-G. 115, 117, 192
Syme, R. 39, 56, 63

Takács, S. A. 70
Tannehill, R. C. 207
Theissen, G. 21, 111, 125
Thiselton, A. C. 24, 27, 78, 82, 96, 113, 114, 127
Thraede, K. 15, 95
Thrall, M. E. 90, 91, 97, 100, 101, 125, 127, 136, 139, 145, 147, 148, 154, 176, 180, 181, 188, 203, 204, 218, 224, 225, 239, 240, 242
Todd, S. 59
Toner, J. 66

Vandorpe, K. 60
Vanhoozer, K. 27
Vegge, I. 3, 8, 9, 25, 91, 92, 95, 97, 98, 100, 103, 109–13, 116, 118, 119, 121, 122, 124, 127, 130, 135, 136, 143, 145, 153, 162, 174, 175, 191, 193, 204, 205, 208, 217, 222, 223, 239, 240, 242, 243
Venticinque, P. F. 68–70
Verboven, K. 66, 67, 71
Vermes, G. 181
Vielhauser, P. 230
Voutiras, E. 37

Walker, D. D. 25, 118, 137
Walton, J. H. 49
Waltzing, J. P. 66–8, 70

Watson, A. 57
Watson, F. 4, 5, 25, 104, 116, 118, 122, 151, 152, 240
Webb, W. J. 138
van Wees, H. 52
Weiss, J. 5, 14, 25, 102, 104, 106, 108, 118, 122, 124, 129, 131, 157, 240
Weizsäcker, K. H. von 90, 96, 102, 108, 111, 112, 116, 117, 240, 243
Welborn, L. L. 6, 7, 14, 22, 23, 71, 103, 105, 111, 116, 117, 123, 135, 139, 140, 142, 144, 145, 147, 160, 182, 188, 192-94, 203, 238, 239, 242
White, A. 26, 51, 52, 73, 75, 77, 113, 186, 188, 224, 242
Wilson, D. 27–9
Windisch, H. 4, 92, 94, 97, 98, 101, 104, 135, 139, 142, 144, 145, 181, 185, 188, 192, 199, 205, 207, 217, 222, 225, 239

Winkler, J. J. 40, 157
Winter, B. W. 24, 107, 111, 112, 117, 121, 159
Witherington III, B. 9, 13, 78, 108, 110, 113, 135
Wright, N. T. 84, 179, 191, 213

Zaas, P. S. 82
Zahn, T. 11, 12, 90, 94, 185, 239, 242, 243
Zakovitch, Y. 198, 199
Zanker, P. 56, 57
Zeller, D. 77, 81, 112, 113
Ziebarth, E. 66, 67, 71

www.ingramcontent.com/pod-product-compliance
Lightning Source LLC
Chambersburg PA
CBHW052153300426
44115CB00011B/1654